3 5/6

DATA PROTECTION IN THE UK

Peter Carey, LLB, LLM, Solicitor
Charles Russell

BLACKSTONE
PRESS LIMITED

Published by
Blackstone Press Limited
Aldine Place
London
W12 8AA
United Kingdom

Sales enquiries and orders
Telephone +44-(0)-20-8740-2277
Facsimile +44-(0)-20-8743-2292
e-mail: sales@blackstone.demon.co.uk
website: www.blackstonepress.com

ISBN 1 84174 127 2
© P. W. Carey, 2000

British Library Cataloguing in Publication Data
A catalogue record for this book is available from the British Library

Typeset in 10/11 Times by Montage Studios Limited, Tonbridge, Kent
Printed and bound in Great Britain by Antony Rowe Limited,
Chippenham and Reading

DATA PROTECTION IN THE UK

Contents

provisions — Regulatory activity — Journalism, literature and art — Research, history and statistics — Public inspection — Corporate finance — Examination marks — Other exemptions — *Disclosures required by law* — *Legal proceedings* — *Domestic purposes* — *Confidential references* — *Armed forces* — *Judicial appointments and honours* — *Crown or Ministerial appointments* — *Management forecasts* — *Negotiations* — *Examination scripts* — *Legal professional privilege* — *Self-incrimination* — *Human fertilisation and embryology* — *Adoption records and reports* — *Special education needs* — *Parental records and reports* — *Manual data held by public authorities* — *Parliamentary privilege*

Part 2: Transitional Exemptions — Introduction and definitions — *Eligible automated data* — *Eligible manual data* — Manual data — *Data forming part of an accessible record* — *Credit reference agency* — *Second transitional period* — Payrolls — Accounts — Unincorporated members' clubs — Mailing lists — Back-up data — Historical research — *Manual data* — *Automated data*

Introduction — Request for assessment — Information notice — *Time limit for compliance* — *Exemptions from compliance* — *Special purposes* — *Criminal offences* — Special information notice — *Time limit for compliance* — *Exemptions from compliance* — *Determination by the Commissioner* — *Criminal offences* — Enforcement notice — *Time limit for compliance* — *Special purposes* — *Criminal offence* — Appeals

Introduction — Unlawful obtaining or disclosure of personal data — Selling and offering to sell personal data — Enforced subject access — Disclosing the Commissioner's information — Obstructing or failing to assist in the execution of a warrant — Processing without a register entry — Failing to notify changes — Carrying on assessable processing — Failing to make certain particulars available — Failing to comply with a notice — Making a false statement in response to a notice — Liability of corporate officers — Immunity from prosecution

Introduction — Definitions — Limitations on processing of data — *Traffic data* — *Billing data* — *Marketing* — Calling and called line identification — *Outgoing calls* — *Incoming calls* — *999 or 112 calls* — *Malicious or nuisance calls* — Direct marketing using telecommunications systems — *Use of automated calling systems* — *Use of fax for unsolicited direct marketing* — *Unsolicited calls* — Telephone directories — Security — Non-itemised bills — Termination of unwanted call forwarding — Enforcement — Transitional provisions — The future

Introduction — Notification — Sensitive data — Employee data security — Outsourcing employer functions — Employee rights — *Manual data* — Automated decisions — Enforced subject access — Transferring employee data abroad — Employee surveillance

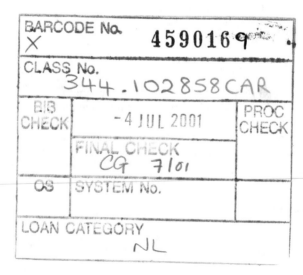

Foreword

Some time back, when asked to review some of the new publications that came out around the time of the Data Protection Act 1998 receiving Royal Assent, I remember commenting that it was essential to have one of those publications always to hand — as a constant reference tool.

The first version of this book, *Blackstone's Guide to the Data Protection Act 1998*, was one of those immensely successful early attempts to analyse the new Act. If I had a criticism, then, it was that some of the first guides written were, entirely understandably, focusing solely on the text of the new Act and how it had evolved from the Data Protection Act 1984.

In this new edition, Peter Carey has gone much further and must be commended for it, expanding his original work in the light of experience and discussion with the Data Protection Commissioner's Office. Peter has now extended the text quite considerably to address new areas such as the related EC Data Protection in Telecoms Directive, use of CCTV and (for many the most important) the Internet.

There is no doubt that the Internet and the use of websites in electronic commerce is focusing many minds on data protection issues. I particularly liked the way that, in his section on the Internet, Peter has attempted to give practical examples of what is, and is not, personal data in the context of websites. Is somebody's e-mail address personal data, for example?

One of the most important issues in relation to the Internet is how the restrictions imposed by the European Data Protection Directive on exporting data outside the EU are to be dealt with. Peter has writen a chapter on data exports, including some examples of great practical assistance. He looks at what happens if, for example, a businessperson travels overseas with a laptop, carrying personal data on it. What does he or she need to do to comply with the Eighth Data Protection Principle? Peter talks about self-regulatory mechanisms as a solution to the restrictions on transborder transfers and looks at codes of practice and the UK 'safe harbor' principles. Important work is currently being done in the field of the use of model contracts as a means to satisfy the test of adequacy under articles 26(2) or 26(4) of the Directive by both the International Chamber of Commerce and also the Confederation of British Industry.

By the time Peter produces the next edition of his book I feel sure that the data export regime will have changed so that the use of contracts within international groups of companies, for example, as a protective mechanism to enable data export, will have increased considerably and peraps Peter will be able to include a specimen agreement contract for his readers.

This is overall an excellent addition to any practitioner's bookshelf.

Heather Rowe
Chairwoman of the International Chamber of Commerce
International Working Party on Data Protection and Privacy

Preface

'Data protection' is essentially that area of the law that protects personal data. It is a set of rules which guides companies and organisations in their dealings with the information which identifies individual people, i.e. 'the data that distinguishes one person from another, such as name, address, date of birth, payroll number, and even DNA information and CCTV images. In the UK the law of data protection can be found mainly in the Data Protection Act 1998 (DPA), the world's most advanced and comprehensive data protection legislation.

The United Kingdom was required to pass the Data Protection Act 1998 as part of its European Union obligations under the European Data Protection Directive (95/46/EC). The motivation behind the Directive was a desire to promote personal data privacy rights and to harmonise the data protection laws of Member States. The Act was passed on 16 July 1998. However, most of the Act's provisions did not come into force until 1 March 2000.

The DPA replaced the Data Protection Act 1984 and cranks the impact of data protection legislation up a considerable notch. Those who are familiar with the old Act will find some common terminology in the new Act, but many of the definitions have changed. The new definition of 'processing', for example, now makes the law applicable to virtually anything that can be done with data, including merely reading it on a computer screen. Other new aspects of the 1998 Act include:

- enhanced data subject access rights;
- an individual's right to be informed of the logic behind automated decision taking;
- extension of the law to include certain manual records;
- a ban on sensitive data processing unless certain conditions apply; and
- a ban on the export of personal data to non-EEA countries.

A data subject is now entitled to know the data controller's source of personal data and may object to (and require the cessation of) certain kinds of processing, including automated processing and processing for the purposes of direct marketing.

I hope this Guide follows a logical sequence in terms of the material it covers. After a brief analysis of data protection laws from a historical perspective in Chapter 1, Chapter 2 considers the rights of data subjects under the new provisions. Chapter 3 looks at the Data Protection Principles, including case law under the old Act which is still expected to be relevant. Chapters 4, 5 and 6 take a closer look at those aspects of the Principles that are likely to cause most concern in practice, namely fair and lawful processing, sensitive personal data and data exports. Chapter 7 deals with manual data. Chapter 8 looks at the notification procedure in terms of the responsibilities of the data controller and the corresponding duties of the Data Protection Commissioner. Chapter 9 is divided into two parts: Part 1 looks at permanent exemptions from certain provisions of the Act for particular types of data; Part 2 considers transitional exemptions (which are available either until 23 October 2001 or, exceptionally, 23 October 2007). Chapter 10 looks at the enforcement regime and considers the purpose of information, special information and enforcement notices and Chapter 11 deals with the criminal offences created by the Act. The last part of the book considers data protection in the context of particular industry sectors or types of activity. The final four chapters cover data protection in relation to:

- telecommunications;
- employment;
- the Internet; and
- CCTV.

This book is designed to be a comprehensive guide to data protection in the UK. It is written from a standpoint which assumes no knowledge of data protection legislation. Those who have worked with the Data Protection Act 1984 will find much that is familiar, and I have tried to incorporate references to the old law where I have considered this to be useful. All references to section or schedule numbers are to the 1998 Act and all references to 'Regulations' are to statutory instruments made under powers conferred by the 1998 Act, unless otherwise stated. The Data Protection Act 1984 may be referred to as 'the old Act' or 'the 1984 Act'. I have attempted to use 'him' and 'her', and 'he' and 'she' interchangeably wherever possible; all references to one gender should be taken as including the other. The Data Protection Commissioner at the time of writing is female and so will be referred to by using the female gender.

The Human Rights Act 1998 (which incorporated the European Convention for the Protection of Human Rights and Fundamental Freedoms into UK law) is expected to have a significant impact on the interpretation of the DPA and is mentioned, where appropriate, throughout the text. The Freedom of Information Bill is expected to incorporate certain powers relating to information held by 'public authorities' within the 1998 Act and these are dealt with where relevant.

I am indebted to those readers of *Blackstone's Guide to the Data Protection Act 1998* who were kind enough to invite me to provide courses on data protection to their businesses and to provide me with invaluable insight into the practicalities of the topics covered in the previous book. I am also grateful for suggestions and advice on content from readers and I have been guided by those comments in this new edition. I continue to welcome any further opinions or requests for coverage in possible future editions.

Peter Carey
Charles Russell, London
pwcarey@hotmail.com

Acknowledgements

Thanks firstly to Dr Nigel Savage, for suggesting that I write *Blackstone's Guide to the Data Protection Act 1998* (the forerunner of this book) and thus stimulating my interest in data protection. His work (together with Chris Edwards) on the Data Protection Act 1984 will be familiar reading to most of those involved with data protection work in the last few years. Whilst very little of the Savage and Edwards *Guide to the Data Protection Act 1984* is used here, it proved to be essential background information. Many thanks therefore both to Nigel Savage and Chris Edwards for the background material.

Thanks to Rachel Tyack of the College of Law for help with original research, to Robert Wood of Osborne Clarke Solicitors for technical help with construction of diagrams and invaluable assistance with contents generally, and to Jo Sanders for proofreading and other assistance. Thanks also to Hayley Chisman for general assistance. Considerable help with recent research was kindly afforded by Emily James, Michelle Anderson, Lee-Ann Socha, Alison Owen and Catherine O'Connell. Special thanks to Rowan Chubb for many hours at the keyboard. Thanks to the following: Andrew Bravington of Cable and Wireless Communications plc for his expert guidance on telecommunications matters; Helena Simms of the office of the Data Protection Commissioner for her Internet expertise; Jason Saiban of Charles Russell for his guidance on IT law; and Jacqueline Reid of 11 South Square for her overall comments and guidance on the whole work.

Lastly, special thanks to the professional staff at Blackstone Press for their enthusiasm, support and encouragement.

For my Mother, Patricia Carey

Table of Cases

Table of Statutes

Table of Secondary Legislation

Chapter 1
Historical Background

THE NEED FOR DATA PROTECTION

The desirability of data protection legislation arose out of the growing use of computers in the 1970s and the threat to personal privacy that rapid manipulation of data potentially posed. The existing law at that time (which consisted of not much more than a possible action in breach of confidence) was insufficient to deal with concerns about the amount of information relating to individuals that was held by organisations in electronic form. In the early 1970s the Younger Committee on Privacy (Cmnd 5012, 1972) recommended ten guiding principles for the use of computers which manipulated personal data:

(a)   Information should be regarded as held for a specific purpose and should not be used, without appropriate authorisation, for other purposes.

(b)   Access to information should be confined to those authorised to have it for the purpose for which it was supplied.

(c)   The amount of information collected and held should be the minimum necessary for the achievement of a specified purpose.

(d)   In computerised systems handling information for statistical purposes, adequate provision should be made in their design and programs for separating identities from the rest of the data.

(e)   There should be arrangements whereby a subject can be told about the information held concerning him.

(f)   The level of security to be achieved by a system should be specified in advance by the user and should include precautions against the deliberate abuse or misuse of information.

(g)   A monitoring system should be provided to facilitate the detection of any violation of the security system.

(h)   In the design of information systems, periods should be specified beyond which the information should not be retained.

(i)   Data held should be accurate. There should be machinery for the correction of inaccuracy and the updating of information.

(j)   Care should be taken in coding value judgments.

The government's response to the Younger Report was to publish a White Paper (Cmnd 6353, 1975). In it the government stated that: 'the time has come when those who use computers to handle personal information, however responsible they are, can no longer remain the sole judges of whether their own systems, adequately safeguard privacy' (para. 30). The threat to privacy was identified by the White Paper as arising from five particular features or characteristics of computer operations:

(a)   They facilitate the maintenance of extensive record systems and retention of data in those systems.

(b)   They can make data easily and quickly accessible from many different points.

(c)   They make it possible for data to be transferred quickly from one information system to another.

(d)   They make it possible for data to be combined in ways which might not otherwise be practicable.

(e)   The data are stored, processed and often transmitted in a form which is not directly intelligible.

The remit of the Younger Committee had been to consider whether legislation was needed to 'give further protection to the individual citizen and to commercial and industrial interests against intrusion into privacy by private persons and organisations'. The Committee was therefore concerned more with privacy than with data protection as such. Although the proposals of the Younger Committee were never enacted, the government subsequently set up the Lindop Committee to obtain detailed advice on the setting up and composition of a Data Protection Authority. Paragraph 2.04 of the Lindop Committee's report (Cmnd 7341, 1978) stated:

The Younger Committee had to deal with the whole field of privacy. Our task has been to deal with that of data protection. In fact, the two fields overlap, and the area of overlap can be called 'information privacy' or, better, 'data privacy'. It is an important area, and we have a good deal to say about it in this report. But it is not by itself the whole field of data protection, and we have had to consider some matters which do not directly raise questions of privacy. However, we found it useful to examine the concept of data privacy, and its implications and consequences. For this purpose we have used the term data privacy to mean the individual's claim to control the circulation of data about himself.

The Lindop Report went on to recommend the establishment of a Data Protection Authority and Codes of Practice particular to different sectors of the business community. These proposals were not ultimately acted on.

It was the Council of Europe Convention of 1981 that provided the impetus for the passage of the Data Protection Act 1984, the provisions of which correspond more closely with the Convention than with the Lindop Report (in fact the Convention had, at least in part, been based on Sir Kenneth Younger's Report). The most compelling reason for this was the desire of Parliament to conform to an internationally agreed standard for data protection. Without such provision the UK was likely to be excluded from a new elite club of countries which provided for a basic level of protection for individuals and prohibited transborder data flows to non-members.

DATA PROTECTION ACT 1984

The UK's first Data Protection Bill was introduced into the House of Lords in December 1982 but its passage was halted by the 1983 General Election. A second Bill, introduced in July 1983, went on to become the Data Protection Act 1984.

General provisions

The 1984 Act introduced a new regime for the holding and processing of 'information recorded in a form in which it can be processed by equipment operating automatically in response to instructions given for that purpose' (data). For the first time, data users — those persons who hold data — were obliged to register with a supervisory authority: the office of the Data Protection Registrar (DPR). The Act introduced criminal offences for failing to comply with its provisions and a system of compensation for individuals who were caused damage by non-compliance.

The requirement to register with the DPR arose when a data user automatically processed 'personal data' (information which relates to a living individual who can be identified from the information, including any expression of opinion about the individual). The registration form requested the following details:

(a)   the name and address of the data user;
(b)   a description of the personal data held and a statement of the purposes for which the data are held;
(c)   a description of the sources from which the data are obtained, and persons to whom they may be disclosed;
(d)   a list of the countries to which any data may be transferred; and
(e)   an address for the receipt of requests from data subjects for access.

Once the Registrar was satisfied with the application, it was entered on the Register, which is open to public inspection (both at the premises of the DPR and also at their website: http://www.dataprotection.gov.uk). A person carrying on a computer bureau needed only to register his name and address. A data user who processed personal data without being registered committed a criminal offence.

A data subject had the right to request access to any personal data that a data user held on him or her (a small fee was chargeable) and the data user was obliged to supply the information within 40 days of the request. The request could be enforced by the DPR or in the courts.

A data subject who suffered damage which was directly attributable to the inaccuracy, loss or unauthorised disclosure of data, could claim compensation from the data user. This right was enforceable in the courts. A further enforceable right of the data subject was to have any erroneous information held by the data user rectified or erased.

Data protection principles

The regime under the 1984 Act was underpinned by certain fundamental principles, which formed a code for the proper processing of personal data. The legislation adopted the Continental model by expressing the eight principles in very general terms. For this reason they were not enforceable through the courts but only by the DPR and the Data Protection Tribunal. The principles, with one exception, were not dissimilar to those now contained in the 1998 Act, and were as follows:

1.   The information to be contained in personal data shall be obtained, and personal data shall be processed, fairly and lawfully.
2.   Personal data shall be held only for one or more specified and lawful purposes.
3.   Personal data held for any purpose or purposes shall not be used or disclosed in any manner incompatible with that purpose or those purposes.
4.   Personal data held for any purpose or purposes shall be adequate, relevant and not excessive in relation to that purpose or those purposes.
5.   Personal data shall be accurate and, where necessary, kept up to date.
6.   Personal data held for any purpose or purposes shall not be kept for longer than is necessary for that purpose or those purposes.
7.   An individual shall be entitled—
     (a)   at reasonable intervals and without undue delay or expense—
         (i)   to be informed by any data user whether he holds personal data of which that individual is the subject; and
         (ii)   to access to any such data held by a data user; and
     (b)   where appropriate, to have such data corrected or erased.
8.   Appropriate security measures shall be taken against unauthorised access to, or alteration, disclosure or destruction of, personal data and against accidental loss or destruction of personal data.

Although the principles formed the backbone of the 1984 data protection legislation, there was no requirement as such to comply with their provisions. There were, however, potential consequences for non-compliance, such as, for example, the service of an enforcement notice.

DATA PROTECTION DIRECTIVE

The European Data Protection Directive (95/46/EC) on the protection of individuals with regard to the processing of personal data and on the free movement of such data was adopted in October 1995. As with all EU Directives, Member States are obliged to pass national legislation which gives effect to the Directive by the implementation date prescribed. The Directive required implementation in Member States by 24 October 1998. The UK complied with its obligations by passing the Data Protection Act 1998.

The Directive can be seen as a general framework legislative provision which has as its aims:

(a)   the protection of an individual's privacy in relation to the processing of personal data; and
(b)   the harmonisation of data protection laws of the Member States.

It sets out the conditions under which the processing of personal data is lawful, the rights of data subjects and the standards of data quality. The Directive seeks to establish an equivalent level of protection for personal data in all Member States, so as to facilitate the transfer of personal data across national boundaries within the European Union.

The Directive applies to personal data processed wholly or partly by automatic means, and to manual data held in filing systems structured by reference to individuals, but it does not apply to activities which fall outside the scope of EU law. It excludes areas within Titles V and VI of the Treaty on European Union, public safety, defence, State security (including the economic well-being of the State when the processing relates to State security matters) and the activities of the State in areas of criminal law. It also specifically excludes domestic or household activities.

Article 6 establishes fundamental principles which have to be respected when personal data are processed. These principles are superficially similar to those in the 1984 Act. Detailed study, however, will reveal that they are of significantly wider application. Article 7 sets out a number of conditions which must be satisfied before data can be processed. Data processing must be under taken only with the data subject's consent except when processing is necessary:

(a) for the performance of a contract to which the data subject is party;

(b) for compliance with a legal obligation;

(c) to protect the vital interests of the data subject;

(d) to perform a task carried out in the public interest or in the exercise of official authority; or

(e) to meet the legitimate interests of the data controller, unless those interests are overridden by the interests or fundamental rights and freedoms of the data subject.

Certain special categories of data which reveal information about a person's racial or ethnic origin, political opinions, religious or philosophical beliefs, trade union membership, health or sex life, and data concerning offences and criminal convictions, may be processed only under certain strict conditions. One of these is the explicit consent of the data subject (except where the Member States' laws provide that the prohibition on sensitive processing cannot be waived by the data subject giving his or her consent).

The data subject has the right to be informed, where data are collected either from the data subject or from a third party, of the identity of the data controller, the purposes for which the data are used, and of any further information which is necessary to ensure fair processing.

Other rights include:

(a) the right of access to personal data without constraint, at reasonable intervals and without excessive delays or expense;

(b) the right to have incomplete or inaccurate data rectified, erased or blocked;

(c) the right to object to processing of personal data, and where there is a justified objection, to have the processing stopped;

(d) the right to object to personal data being used for purposes of direct marketing;

(e) the right not to be subject to a decision that has legal effects and which is based solely on automated processing of data (unless the decision is in connection with a contract where the results do not adversely affect the data subject, or is authorised by law and provided that the data subject's interests are safeguarded).

Data security must be such as to ensure that personal data are protected against accidental or unlawful destruction or accidental loss. Data must also be protected against unauthorised alteration, disclosure or access and all other forms of unlawful processing. The level of security must be appropriate to the risks represented by the processing and the nature of the data to be protected, having regard to the state of technology and cost.

The Directive sets out the conditions under which personal data which are being processed or which are intended for processing may be transferred to countries outside the European Union. In general, a transfer may only take place if the third country ensures an adequate level of protection for the rights and freedoms of data subjects. There are certain exceptions, for example, if the data subject gives consent or if the transfer is necessary or legally required on public interest grounds.

Each Member State is required to set up a supervisory authority to oversee the application in its country of the national provisions giving effect to the Directive. Computerised processing operations must be notified to and registered by the supervisory authority. It is for Member States to decide whether or not to apply these requirements to manual data. There is provision for exemption from, or simplification of, the notification requirements in certain cases.

Following successful representations from the UK, a provision was included in the Directive which allowed Member States to provide a derogation in relation to the processing of data already held in manual filing systems when the national provisions came into force. However, such filing systems must be made to comply with the provisions of the Directive before the expiry of 12 years from the date when the Directive was adopted, i.e., by 24 October 2007.

Member States are required to provide adequate legal redress (including compensation for damage) for breach of the provisions of the Directive.

DATA PROTECTION ACT 1998

The Data Protection Act 1998 implemented Directive 95/46/EC in the UK. It received the Royal Assent on 16 July 1998 and came fully into force on 1 March 2000.

Changes from the 1984 Act regime

The new Act, in implementing the Directive, takes data protection legislation to a new level of complexity. It provides a new definition of 'processing' (which includes virtually anything that can be done with data) and incorporates the following features which represent significant changes to the 1984 Act regime:

(a) *Manual processing* — Subject to the operation of transitonal provisions in the legislation, the 1998 Act applies to certain manual files as it does to automated data.

(b) *Legitimacy of processing* — New conditions for processing exist as minimum threshold requirements before processing may be lawfully undertaken.

(c) *Sensitive data* — A new category of personal data has been created. Sensitive personal data may not be processed unless one of a set of certain pre-conditions is satisfied.

(d) *Data exports* — Transfers of personal data to countries outside the European Economic Area are banned unless certain conditions are satisfied.

(e) *Data security* — Data may not be processed unless that processing complies with new security requirements.

(f) *Individual rights* — Significantly more and stronger rights for individuals exist under the new legislation including the right to compensation for damage or distress caused by unlawful processing.

SECONDARY LEGISLATION

At the time of writing no less than 19 separate sets of regulations have been produced by the Home Office. They add greater depth to, and in many cases, clarify, the provisions of the 1998 Act. The following legislation (which appears in Appendix 3) has been dealt with where relevant in the remaining chapters of this book:

1. The Data Protection Act 1998 (Commencement) Order 2000, No. 183
2. Data Protection (Corporate Finance Exemption) Order 2000, SI 2000/184
3. The Data Protection (Conditions under Paragraph 3 of Part II of Schedule 1) Order 200, No. 185
4. The Data Protection (Functions of Designated Authority) Order 2000, No. 186
5. The Data Protection (Fees under section 19(7)) Regulations 2000, No. 187
6. The Data Protection (Notification and Notification Fees) Regulations 2000, No. 188
7. The Data Protection Tribunal (Enforcement Appeals) Rules 2000, No. 189
8. The Data Protection (International Co-operation) Order 2000, No. 190
9. The Data Protection (Subject Access) (Fees and Miscellaneous Provisions) Regulations 2000, No. 191
10. The Data Protection Tribunal (National Security Appeals) Rules 2000, No. 206
11. The Consumer Credit (Credit Reference Agency) Regulations 2000, No. 2
12. The Data Protection (Subject Access Modifications) (Health) Order 2000, No. 413
13. The Data Protection (Subject Access Modifications) (Education) Order 2000, No. 414
14. The Data Protection (Subject Access Modifications) (Social Word) Order 2000, No. 415
15. The Data Protection (Crown Appointments) Order 2000, No. 416
16. The Data Protection (Processing of Sensitive Personal Data) Order 2000, No. 417
17. The Data Protection (Designated Codes of Practice) Order 2000, No. 418
18. The Data Protection (Miscellaneous Subject Access Exemptions) Order 2000, No. 419
19. The Data Protection Tribunal (National Security Appeals) (Telecommunications) Rules 2000, No. 731

OTHER LEGISLATION

Data protection is relevant to many areas of life and business which will be pertinent to other legislative provisions. However, of particular significance in the year 2000 was the coming into force of the Human Rights Act 1998. With its significant impact on the law of privacy generally, the European Convention on Human Rights is mentioned throughout this book where relevant.

The Freedom of Information Bill (which had not received the Royal Assent at the time of going to press) was due to amend the Data Protection Act 1998 in respect of data processed by public authorities. The Bill is dealt with where relevant throughout the text.

EU Directive 97/66/EC and its implementing legislation in the UK, the Telecommunications (Data Protection and Privacy) Regulations 1999, create new rights for subscribers to telecommunications services and are dealt with in Chapter 12.

Chapter 2
Rights of Individuals

INTRODUCTION

Chapter 1 shows how the historical development of data protection legislation is founded in a concern for the individual's right to privacy. The privacy rights contained in the 1984 Act are significantly enhanced in the 1998 Act. Not only is an individual entitled to more information from a data controller than before (such as details of the source of any data being processed) but he can now prevent certain types of processing from taking place.

All privacy rights in the Act will benefit from, and should now be interpreted in light of, Art. 8 of the European Convention for the Protection of Human Rights and Fundamental Freedoms, incorporated into English Law by the Human Rights Act 1998. Article 8 provides as follows:

(1)   Everyone has the right to respect for his private and family life, his home and his correspondence.

(2)   There shall be no interference by a public authority with the exercise of this right except such as is in accordance with the law and is necessary in a democratic society in the interests of national security, public safety or the economic well-being of the country, for the prevention of disorder or crime, for the protection of health or morals, or for the protection of the rights and freedoms of others.

The basic rights of the individual are contained in Part II of the 1998 Act, but in order to analyse them it will be necessary first to define some terminology, much of which is contained in Part I. The last section of this chapter discusses certain transitional rights which are available (for manual data processing only) until 23 October 2007.

The individual's rights are subject to certain exemptions enacted for the benefit of data controllers. The rights in this chapter should therefore be considered in conjunction with Chapter 9.

Rights

Access to personal data
Prevention of processing likely to cause damage or distress
Prevention of processing for direct marketing
Prevention of automated decision-taking
Rectification, blocking, erasure, destruction
Compensation
Request for assessment

INITIAL DEFINITIONS

For the purposes of the legislation the person who is protected is called the 'data subject'. The definition of data subject has not changed from the previous legislation and thus remains 'an individual who is the subject of personal data'.

Data

Section 1(1) of the 1998 Act defines 'data' as:

information which—
(a)   is being processed by means of equipment operating automatically in response to instructions given for that purpose,
(b)   is recorded with the intention that it should be processed by means of such equipment,
(c)   is recorded as part of a relevant filing system or with the intention that it should form part of a relevant filing system,
(d)   does not fall within paragraph (a), (b) or (c) but forms part of an accessible record, or
(e)   is recorded information held by a public authority and does not fall within any of paragraphs (a) to (d).

Paragraph (a) of this definition clearly refers to some form of computerised system; paragraph (b) deals with information intended to be automatically processed but which has not yet reached processing. Whilst the 1984 Act related only to automatically processed data (which includes computer printouts), paragraph (c) of the new definition of data extends data subjects' rights of access to material that forms part of a relevant filing system. The absence of any reference to equipment means that the Act covers manual paper-based records. This is likely, for UK businesses, to be one of the most costly and time-consuming aspects of the new regime. Material forming part of a relevant filing system and subject to processing which was already under way immediately before 24 October 1998 benefits from certain transitional provisions (see Chapter 7 for a detailed consideration of manual data). Paragraph (e) is due to be inserted into the 1998 Act by the Freedom of Information Bill extends data protection legislation to personal information held by public authorities. For these purposes public authorities include national and local government, the armed forces, the national health service, the police and certain others.

Relevant filing system

A 'relevant filing system' is defined (s. 1(1)) as:

> any set of information relating to individuals to the extent that, although the information is not processed by means of equipment operating automatically in response to instructions given for that purpose, the set is structured, either by reference to individuals or by reference to criteria relating to individuals, in such a way that specific information relating to a particular individual is readily accessible.

For further detail on relevant filing system and on manual data generally, see Chapter 7.

Accessible records

Paragraph (d) of the definition of 'data' includes accessible records within that definition. Section 68 defines an accessible record as a health record, an educational record or an accessible public record. Such material was included in the definition to ensure that rights of access to information under the Personal Files Act 1987, the Access to Health Records Act 1990 and the Education (School Records) Regulations 1989 fell within the 1998 Act.

Personal data

The provisions of the Act apply only to personal data. 'Personal data' is defined in s. 1(1) as:

> data which relate to a living individual who can be identified—
> (a)   from those data, or
> (b)   from those data and other information which is in the possession of, or is likely to come into the possession of, the data controller.

Personal data includes 'any *expression of opinion* about the individual and any *indication of the intentions* of the data controller or any other person in respect of the individual' (emphasis added). This clearly has personnel or human resources implications for employers — a manager's statement of intentions concerning an employee's promotion or demotion or the manager's opinion of an employee is within the definition (see Chapter 13). Certain statements of opinion by way of reference are exempt from certain provisions of the Act, as are records of intention in relation to negotiations and personal data processed for the purpose of management forecasting or planning — see Chapter 5, part 1.

It is interesting to note the definition of 'personal data' in the European Directive:

> personal data shall mean any information relating to an identified or indentifiable natural person . . .; an identifiable person is one who can be identified, directly or indirectly, in particular by reference to an identification number or to one or more factors specific to his physical, physiological, mental, economic, cultural or social identity.

This is somewhat wider than the definition in the Act and would extend to, for example, the processing of a CCTV image, even where a specific individual cannot be identified by name from that image (see Chapter 15). It will be remembered that, as a matter of law, the UK Act must be interpreted to give effect to the Directive.

Where a data controller possesses two databases then, provided an individual can be identified from the information in both together, the relevant content of each amounts to personal data. This is true even if the individual cannot be identified from one of the sources alone. If personal data are contained in an encrypted database and the data controller possesses (or is likely to possess at some time) the key for decryption then the encrypted data and the key together amount to personal data. The definition of personal data in the 1998 Act goes further than its predecessor by applying not only to information in the possession of the data controller, but also to information likely to come into the controller's possession. The Directive went even further by not including the words 'likely to come into the possession of', thus rendering an encrypted database personal data where the key existed anywhere in the world, however unlikely it was that the key would have come into the possession of the data controller. The Home Office chose to limit this aspect of the definition, but it remains unclear how the word 'likely' in s. 1(1)(b) will be construed. This may benefit controllers but such a restricted definition may not withstand challenge.

To be personal data the data must relate to a 'living individual'. There are two points to be made here which, whilst obvious, are nevertheless worth mentioning. The first is that the data must relate to a living person — once a person has died her rights under the legislation cease. The second is that the definition applies only to individuals. A database containing names and addresses of limited companies is therefore not caught. However, where such a database includes names of officers or employees within the company (e.g., contact names) it *will* fall within the definition of personal data.

Data controller

A 'data controller' is 'a person who (either alone or jointly or in common with other persons) determines the purposes for which and the manner in which any personal data are, or are to be, processed' (s. 1(1)). This is a wider definition than the corresponding 'data user' under the 1984 Act and means that there may be more than one data controller per piece of information. Where processing is undertaken solely due to an obligation imposed upon a person by legislation, such person is deemed to be the data controller.

The Act, by virtue of s. 5, applies to data controllers only if:

    (a)   the data controller is established in the United Kingdom and the data are processed in the context of that establishment, or

    (b)   the data controller is established neither in the United Kingdom nor any other EEA state but uses equipment in the United Kingdom for processing the data otherwise than for the purposes of transit through the United Kingdom.

Amendments to the Act by the Freedom of Information Bill are likely to provide that the data controller in relation to personal data processed by the House of Commons is the Corporate Officer of that House. The data controller for the House of Lords is the Corporate Officer of that House.

Data processor

A 'data processor' is any person (other than an employee of the data controller) who processes the data on behalf of the data controller. Data controllers often use third parties to process their data due to the time and cost savings involved. As long as the third party merely acts on the instructions of the data controller and does not itself determine the use of the data or the purposes of processing, it will be a data processor.

Data processors do not need to notify their data processing activities to the Commissioner, but they are required under the legislation to enter into a written contract with the data controller (see Chapter 3, Seventh Principle).

Where agents are employed by controllers to carry out activities which may include processing, controllers must take care not to rely on transitional exemptions which apply only to them and not to the agents.

Processing

'Processing', in relation to information or data, means:

obtaining, recording or holding the information or data or carrying out any operation or set of operations on the information or data, including—

(a) organisation, adaptation or alteration of the information or data,

(b) retrieval, consultation or use of the information or data,

(c) disclosure of the information or data by transmission, dissemination or otherwise making available, or

(d) alignment, combination, blocking, erasure or destruction of the information or data.

This definition of processing is very much wider than in the previous statute, and it is the belief of the first Data Protection Commissioner, Elizabeth France, that the concept of processing is probably without limit and could include *anything* that can be done with data. It certainly covers such things as opening and reading a manual file and even extends to merely calling up or reading a piece of information on a computer screen. The definition extends to the storage of information on a computer hard drive or any portable memory device as well as to the activities known as data matching, data mining and data warehousing. The recording of CCTV images of people's faces would also constitute processing (see Chapter 15).

Example 1

Postal Ordering Services Ltd advertises kitchen and bathroom products in a national newspaper. Fiona sees the advertisement and telephones the company for a brochure. She gives her name, address, telephone number and date of birth. The telephone operator enters this information into the company's computer database as Fiona is speaking. The terminology of the 1998 Act applies as follows:

Data controller	Postal Ordering Services Ltd.
Data subject	Fiona.
Personal data	information about Fiona's name, address, telephone number and date of birth.
Processing	this occurs where the personal data is: requested from Fiona; entered into the computer system; read on-screen; printed out; used to send a brochure.

Example 2

Caroline is employed by Safe Banking plc, a high-street bank. The personnel department holds payroll details on computer, and other records in written form. The written records are held in files sorted alphabetically by employee surname and contain details such as length of employment and staff and appraisal matters. They also contain line managers' recommendations for promotion. Safe Banking plc is the data controller. Caroline is the data subject. All the details concerning Caroline which are held on computer *and* in the personnel files are personal data. Any reading, alteration, copying, addition to, disclosure or transfer of that data will amount to processing for the purposes of the Act.

BASIC RIGHTS OF ACCESS

Section 7 of the 1998 Act provides that a data subject is entitled, upon written request to a data controller, to be promptly informed whether personal data of which the individual is the data subject are being processed by or on behalf of the data controller. A fee (usually subject to the statutory maximum — currently £10) may be charged by the data controller for this service and the data controller has 40 days (or such other period as may be prescribed) from the receipt by the data controller of such a request to comply with it. The 40-day time limit does not start to run until the data controller has received the fee and/or has been supplied with sufficient information to enable compliance with the request. A request for information need not be complied with if the data controller has received insufficient information to be satisfied as to the identity of the person making the request (and to locate the information which that person seeks) and has informed the person making the request of the need for such further information to be supplied. The Secretary of State may prescribe circumstances where a fee is not chargeable.

Where personal data are being processed by or on behalf of the data controller, the data subject is entitled to be given a description of:

    (a)   the personal data of which that individual is the data subject;
    (b)   the purposes for which they are being or are to be processed; and
    (c)   the recipients or classes of recipients to whom they are or may be disclosed.

In addition, the data subject is entitled to have communicated to him or her *in a form which is capable of being understood*:

    (a)   the information constituting any personal data of which that individual is the data subject; and
    (b)   any information available to the data controller as to the source of those data.

By virtue of the Data Protection (Subject Access) (Fees and Miscellaneous Provisions) Regulations 2000 a request for any of the above five pieces of information must be treated by a data controller as a request for *all* five.

Under the Freedom of Information Bill, a public authority (as defined in that Act) will not be obliged to comply with a request for access under s. 7 which relates to *unstructured personal data* unless the request contains a description of that data. 'Unstructured personal data' in this context means any personal data falling within para. (e) of the definition of 'data' (see above): 'other than information which is recorded as part of, or with the intention that it should form part of, any set of information relating to individuals to the extent that the set is structured by reference to individuals or by reference to criteria relating to individuals'.

In most cases the first of these rights of the data subject will be met by the data controller forwarding to the data subject a copy of the information (plus an intelligible explanation of its content where the meaning is obscure because, for example, codes or abbreviations have been used). Indeed, s. 8 contains an obligation to 'supply a copy in permanent form' unless:

(a)   the supply of such a copy is not possible or would involve disproportionate effort; or

(b)   the data subject waives this right.

The right to receive information as to the source of the data is a new right that did not appear in the 1984 legislation. Data controllers who are concerned about disclosing sources must be especially careful here. If information relating to a source is held by the data controller then it must be disclosed. If data has been obtained in a commercial setting, it will be extremely unlikely that the data controller will not be holding information on the source.

Example
(This example continues from example 1 earlier in the chapter.) Fiona receives the brochure from Postal Ordering Services Ltd but notices something odd about the address label on the packaging. Her name appears as 'Mrs Fiona E. Pain'. She feels sure that she did not tell the telephone operator her middle name, nor that she was married. She writes a letter to Postal Ordering Services asking for a copy of all the information it holds on her and details of the source of that information. Postal Ordering Services must supply Fiona with the information she has requested and must do so within 40 days of receiving her request plus the £10 maximum fee.

Automated decisions

Section 7(1)(d) provides that where the personal data are being processed automatically for the purpose of evaluating matters relating to the data subject and the processing has or is likely to be the sole basis of a decision significantly affecting the data subject, he or she is entitled to be informed by the data controller of the logic (save to the extent that it constitutes a trade secret — s. 8(5)) behind the decision-taking.

Regulations provide that a request under s. 7(1)(d) for such 'logic' is not to be treated as a request for other information under s. 7 unless expressly stated. Similarly a request for access under any other provision of s. 7 is not to be treated as a request for 'logic' unless expressly stated.

A common example of such an automated decision-making process is credit scoring. Where a computer program, as a result of information keyed in, decides whether to extend a loan to an individual then the individual concerned is entitled to a description of the decision-making process, i.e., the method by which the decision was reached. There is no requirement in the Act (contrast the right to receive information constituting the personal data and its source) that this information must be communicated in an intelligible form. It is possible that a data controller may be able to comply with the requirement in s. 7(1)(d) by supplying a general statement of the purpose and operation of the relevant software.

See 'Automated decision-taking' below for further discussion on the right to prevent such decisions being made.

Identifying other individuals

In certain cases the data controller will be unable to comply with a request for information without disclosing information relating to another individual who can be identified from the information requested, e.g., where data relates to two or more people and only one of them has made a subject access request. In determining whether another person can be identified from the information, a data controller is entitled to take into account not only the entirety of information that would otherwise be supplied to the data subject but also any information that the data controller reasonably believes is likely to be in the possession (or likely to come into the possession) of the data subject making the request. In the event that another person is likely to be identified, the data controller is entitled to refuse to comply with the data subject's request unless (s. 7(4)):

(a)   the other individual has consented to the disclosure of the information to the person making the request; or
(b)   it is reasonable in all the circumstances to comply with the request without the consent of the other individual.

Where the individual who can be identified from the information is in fact the source of the information the data controller is not excused from complying with the request altogether. Here the data controller must disclose so much of the information sought by the data subject as can be communicated without disclosing the identity of the source. This might be done by omitting any references to names or other identifying particulars.

In determining whether it is reasonable in all the circumstances to comply with the request without the consent of the other individual who may be identified, particularly relevant considerations are:

(a)   any duty of confidentiality owed to the individual;
(b)   any steps taken by the data controller with a view to seeking the consent of the individual;
(c)   whether the other individual is capable of giving consent; and
(d)   any express refusal of consent by the individual.

Multiple requests

The data subject is entitled to make as many requests for information from the data controller as he or she sees fit. However, the statute does save the data controller from excess paperwork by providing that a reasonable time must be allowed to elapse between requests. The data controller does not have to comply with a request that has been made too soon after compliance with a previous request. In determining what is a reasonable time for these purposes regard should be had to the following:

(a)   the nature of the data;
(b)   the purpose for which the data are processed; and
(c)   the frequency with which the data are altered.

Amendments to data

It may be, in the course of business or otherwise, that the data will be amended (whether, for example, by addition or deletion) between the time of the data subject's request being received by the data controller and the time of compliance with the request. The information forwarded to the data subject may be the post-amendment version of the data, but only where the 'amendment or deletion would have been made regardless of the receipt of the request' (s. 8(6)).

Credit reference agencies

There are slight modifications to the rights of access provisions in s. 7 where the data controller is a credit reference agency. Section 9 provides that any request for access by a data subject to a credit reference agency will be presumed to be a request for personal data relevant only to the data subject's financial standing. In this event the maximum fee is £2 and the prescribed period for compliance is seven working days. A data subject may rebut that presumption by expressly indicating that the request is not so limited.

A 'credit reference agency' is 'a person carrying on a business comprising the furnishing of persons with information relevant to the financial standing of individuals, being information collected by the agency for that purpose' (Consumer Credit Act 1974, s. 145(8)).

Where a credit reference agency receives a request for information under s. 7, the obligations of disclosure include a statement (in a form to be prescribed by the Secretary of State) of the individual's rights:

(a)   under the Consumer Credit Act 1974, s. 159 (removal or amendment provisions relating to incorrect information held by an agency (known colloquially as a 'notice of correction') — see Appendix 1); and
(b)   to the extent required by the prescribed form.

For specific transitional provisions concerning manual data held by a credit reference agency, see Chapter 9, part 2.

Court order

The right of access to data by data subjects may be enforced by the High Court or a county court (in Scotland by the Court of Session or the sheriff). Where a person has made a request for information (or logic behind decision-taking) and has not been supplied with that information, the court may grant an order requiring the data controller to comply with that request (s. 7(9)). In deciding whether the data subject is entitled to see the information (including the question whether such information is exempt from the provisions — see Chapter 9), the court may require access to the information on the basis that it is not shown (at that stage) to the data subject. Assistance from the Commissioner for either party to an application under s. 7(9) is available at the discretion of the Commissioner where a case involves processing for the 'special purposes' and concerns matters of substantial public importance.

Exemptions

By virtue of the Data Protection (Miscellaneous Subject Access Exemptions) Order 2000, the following types of personal data are exempt from the s. 7 subject access provisions:

(a)   human fertilisation and embryology information in the UK;
(b)   adoption records and reports in England and Wales, Scotland or Northern Ireland;
(c)   statements and records of a child's special educational needs in England and Wales, Scotland and Northern Ireland; and
(d)   in Scotland only, information provided by reporters for the purposes of children's hearing.

Certain other partial exemptions exist in relation to certain types of data, such as education, health and social work records — see Chapter 9.

Transitional provisions

During the first transitional period automated data which are subject to processing that was already under way immediately before 24 October 1998 are exempt from the requirements that the data subject be given:

(a)   a description of the data,
(b)   its purpose and likely recipients,
(c)   the source of the data,
(d)   the logic involved in automated decision-taking.

Eligible manual data are exempt from the subject access provisions in s. 7 during the first transitional period, except to the extent that they relate to financial standing or from part of an accessible record.
      For further discussion see Chapter 9, part 2.

FEES FOR SUBJECT ACCESS REQUESTS

To reflect the administrative inconvenience to a data controller and to deter frivolous applications by data subjects, the data controller is permitted to charge a fee for requests under s. 7. As stated above, the fee is, in most cases, subject to the statutory maximum of £10 (or £2 in the case of a credit reference agency). However, the maximum fee that may be charged is modified in relation to the following types of request.

Education records

Where the subject's access request relates to information concerning a current or ex-pupil at a school in England and Wales (modified provisions apply in the case of Scotland and Northern Ireland) which is processed by or on behalf of the governing body or a teacher at that school, no fee may be charged unless a permanent copy of the information is to be provided.

Where the information supplied is in permanent form which does not consist of paper (e.g., floppy disk) the maximum fee is £50. Where the information is to be supplied by virtue of a 'record in writing on paper' the maximum fee is subject to a sliding scale depending on the number of pages to be supplied, as set out in the following table:

Fees Table

Number of pages of information comprising the copy	Maximum fee
fewer than 20	£1
20–29	£2
30–39	£3
40–49	£4
50–59	£5
60–69	£6
70–79	£7
80–89	£8
90–99	£9
100–149	£10
150–199	£15
200–249	£20
250–299	£25
300–349	£30
350–399	£35
400–449	£40
450–499	£45
500 or more	£50

Health records

Any request by a data subject for access to information relating to his physical or mental health which has been made by a health professional (as defined in s. 69 of the Act) is subject to a maximum fee of £50 provided that the application:

(a) relates to material which is, at least partly, non-automated; and
(b) is made before 24 October 2001.

This transitional provision is designed to benefit data controllers who are requested to supply manual data in a permanent form during the Act's first transitional period. After 24 October 2001 the maximum fee that can be charged will revert to the normal £10.

It should be noted that when a data subject makes an access request in circumstances in which no permenant copy is to be provided, a fee must not be charged if the record has been at least partially created within the 40 days preceding the request.

PREVENTING PROCESSING LIKELY TO CAUSE DAMAGE OR DISTRESS

Section 10 provides that where the processing of personal data is causing or is likely to cause *unwarranted and substantial damage* or *unwarranted and substantial distress* to the data subject or another, the data subject is entitled to require the data controller (upon the expiry of a reasonable period) to cease, or not to begin, processing, unless one of the following apply:

(a) the data subject has given his or her consent to the processing;
(b) the processing is necessary—
    (i) for the performance of a contract to which the data subject is a party, or
    (ii) for the taking of steps at the request of the data subject with a view to entering into a contract;
(c) the processing is necessary for compliance with any legal obligation to which the data controller is subject, other than an obligation imposed by contract;
(d) the processing is necessary in order to protect the vital interests of the data subject;
(e) any other circumstance prescribed by the Secretary of State by order.

In order to take advantage of this power to prevent processing, the data subject must forward to the data controller a notice in writing (a 'data subject notice') and specify the reasons why the processing is or will cause damage or distress. The notice may specify the purpose or manner of processing that is objectionable. The data controller has 21 days from receipt of the notice to make a response. The response (which must be in writing) must consist of one of the following two options:

(a) a statement that the data controller has complied, or intends to comply, with the request in the data subject notice, or
(b) a statement that the data controller regards part or all of the data subject notice as unjustified and the extent to which the data controller has complied or intends to comply with it.

Court order

Where a data subject feels that the data controller has failed to comply (in full or in part) with the request in the data subject notice, he or she may apply to the court for an order for compliance. The court will make such an order where it is satisfied that the data subject notice was justified and that the data controller has failed to take such steps to comply with the notice as the court thinks fit. Assistance from the Commissioner for either party to such an application is available at the discretion of the Commissioner where a case involves processing for the 'special purposes' and concerns matters of substantial public importance.

Transitional exemption

Eligible automated data and eligible manual data are exempt from the rights in s. 10 during the first transitional period. For further discussion see Chapter 9, part 2.

PREVENTING PROCESSING FOR DIRECT MARKETING

The marketing strategy known as 'direct marketing' (defined as communication, by whatever means, of any advertising or marketing material which is directed to particular individuals — s. 11(3)) is subject to a right by the data subject to prevent processing for this purpose. Direct marketing includes the sending of letters to individuals which promote a certain product or service. Targeting an individual's e-mail account also constitutes direct marketing.

An individual may require, under s. 11(1), that the data controller (within a reasonable time) cease, or not begin, processing, for the purposes of direct marketing, personal data of which he or she is the data subject. The right does not apply to telecommunications billing data — see Chapter 12.

The request should be in writing. There is no provision which allows the data controller to specify the reasons that the data controller feels the data subject notice to be unjustified. There is no requirement of unwarranted damage or unwarranted distress. There are no exceptions to the right to prevent processing for the purposes of direct marketing. It is interesting to note that a provision in the Bill obliging the data controller to respond to the data subject's request within 21 days has been omitted from the Act. The paperwork that such a provision would have generated would have been prohibitive for data controllers, but the lack of such a provision deprives the data subject of any guaranteed feedback on his or her request for cessation.

The court can order compliance with the data subject notice where it is satisfied that the data controller has failed to comply with the notice. It has power to set out how the data controller should go about doing so.

Example

Janet is sent a letter through the post from Elham International plc inviting her to purchase a financial services product. Janet sends a letter to the company requesting it to delete her name, address and any other details from its database. Within a reasonable time of receiving the letter the company must cease processing Janet's personal data for the purposes of direct marketing. Elham International plc may continue to hold the information for other purposes.

Following an appropriate request from a data subject, data held for purposes other than direct marketing should be flagged in some way so that it is not used for direct marketing.

Transitional exemption

During the first transitional period, automated data which is subject to processing that was already under way immediately before 24 October 1998 are exempt from the right to prevent processing for direct marketing.

Eligible manual data are exempt from the right to prevent processing during the first transitional period.

For further discussion see Chapter 9, part 2.

AUTOMATED DECISION-TAKING

A data subject has the right to prevent the data controller from taking evaluation decisions concerning him or her by *automated means alone*. Should the individual wish to exercise this right he or she must send a notice in writing requiring the data controller to ensure that no decision taken by or on behalf of the data controller *which significantly affects that individual* is based solely on the processing of personal data by automatic means. Certain decisions are exempt (see below). One class of persons that the statute anticipates may be interested in this right is employees — s. 12(1) gives examples of matters which may be the subject of evaluation by automated processing:

(a)   performance at work;
(b)   creditworthiness;
(c)   reliability; and
(d)   conduct.

Where (in the absence of a notice having been sent by the data subject to the data controller) a decision significantly affecting that individual is taken wholly by automated means, the data controller must, as soon as reasonably practicable, inform the individual that such a decision has been taken. The individual then has the right to request the data controller to reconsider the decision or take a new decision on an alternative basis. This right must be exercised within 21 days of receipt by the data subject of the data controller's notification of the decision, and must be exercised in writing (a 'data subject notice'). It is interesting to note that although a data subject must be informed that an automated decision has been taken, there is no requirement to inform the data subject of his or her right to have the decision reassessed by human analysis.

Within 21 days of receipt of the data subject notice, the data controller must inform (in writing) the data subject of the steps the data controller intends to take to comply with the notice.

Example

A recruitment consultant offers jobs on its website. Applications are made on-line by individuals who fill in answers to certain questions about themselves. A computer program then determines whether the candidate will be invited for an interview. Donna applies for a job on-line but is rejected. In these circumstances Donna must be informed of the fact that the decision concerning her suitability for the job was taken by automated means.

Court order

A court may order the decision-taker (described in s. 12(8) as 'the responsible person') to reconsider the decision or take a new decision where the data subject can prove that the responsible person has failed:

(a)   to comply with the request from the data subject to ensure that no decision taken which significantly affects him or her is taken solely by automated means; or

(b)   (in the case of the data controller informing the individual of the decision and the data subject requesting reconsideration) to reconsider the, or take a new, decision.

Assistance from the Commissioner for either party to such an application is available at the discretion of the Commissioner if the case involves processing for the 'special purposes' and concerns matters of substantial public importance.

Exempt decisions

The requirement that the data subject must be informed of automated decision-taking and have such decisions retaken, and the right of the data subject to prevent such decision-taking, do not apply to 'exempt decisions'. An exempt decision is one where one of the conditions from *each* of the following two lists is present. The first list (s. 12(6)) is as follows:

(a)   the decision is taken in the course of steps taken for the purpose of considering whether to enter into a contract with the data subject; or

(b)   the decision is taken in the course of steps taken with a view to entering into such a contract; or

(c)   the decision is taken in the course of steps taken in the course of performing such a contract; or

(d)   the decision is authorised or required by or under any enactment.

The second list (s. 12(7)) contains two alternatives:

(a)   the effect of the decision is to grant a request of the data subject; or

(b)   steps have been taken to safeguard the legitimate interests of the data subject (for example, by allowing him or her to make appropriate comments).

One possible way for a data controller to comply with these requirements is to insert a clear statement in its documentation to the effect that the automated processing system is used to help it consider whether to enter into a contract with the data subject. Then, provided the data subject has asked for such a decision to be taken and either the decision is favourable or there is a right of appeal against an unfavourable decision, the processing will be exempt from the above provisions.

Example

A bank is considering an application by Michael for a loan. It has forwarded standard documentation to Michael which informs him that the decision whether to make the loan will be taken automatically by a computer. Michael reads the documentation and then applies for the loan. The loan is then extended by the bank. The processing of Michael's data is exempt from the right to prevent such processing.

The Secretary of State is empowered to create further exempt decisions by order but had not done so at the time of writing.

Transitional exemption

During the first transitional period automated data which is subject to processing which was already under way immediately before 24 October 1998 are exempt from the right to request that a decision affecting the data subject is not taken solely by automated means. For further discussion see Chapter 9, Part 2.

RECTIFICATION, BLOCKING, ERASURE AND DESTRUCTION

Under s. 14, where a court is satisfied that personal data processed by the data controller are inaccurate (i.e., 'incorrect or misleading as to any matter of fact' — s. 70(2)), it may make an order for the rectification, blocking, erasure or destruction of such data. In addition the court may order the rectification, blocking, erasure or destruction of any personal data which contain an expression of opinion that is based on the inaccurate data. Such rights do not differ markedly from those in the 1984 Act, save that that Act did not mention 'blocking'. There is no definition of this term in the Act and the Commissioner has yet to give an opinion on what it means. It is likely, however, to have its common meaning, namely the prevention of access.

Where the data, despite being inaccurate, accurately reflect information that was passed by the data subject (or a third party) to the data controller, the provisions are somewhat watered down. Here, as an alternative to making an order for rectification, blocking, erasure or destruction, the court may take one of two further courses of action open to it. The first is to make an order requiring the data to be supplemented by a court-approved statement of the true facts relating to the matters dealt with by the data. However, that option is only open to the court where:

(a)   having regard to the purpose or purposes for which the data were obtained and further processed, the data controller has taken reasonable steps to ensure the accuracy of the data, and

(b)   if the data subject has notified the data controller of the data subject's view that the data are inaccurate, the data indicate that fact.

The second (which is only available if either or both of the above two requirements have not been complied with) is to make an order which would have the effect of ensuring compliance with the requirements in (a) and (b) above. This second option may be accompanied by a further order requiring the data to be supplemented by a court-approved statement of the true facts relating to the matters dealt with by the data.

In many cases the inaccurate data held by the data controller will have been passed on to a third party (defined in s. 70(1) as 'any person other than (a) the data subject, (b) the data controller, or (c) any data processor or other person authorised to process data for the data controller or processor'). Where the court orders rectification, blocking, erasure or destruction, or is satisfied by the data subject's claim that personal data which have been rectified, blocked, erased or destroyed were inaccurate, it can, where it is reasonably practicable to do so, make an order that the data controller informs the third party of the rectification, blocking, erasure or destruction.

Additionally, an order for rectification, blocking, erasure or destruction may be made by the court where the data subject is entitled to compensation for damage as a result of the failure of a data controller to comply with any provision of the Act in respect of personal data and there is a substantial risk of further such failure (s. 14(4)). Where the court makes such an order it may order the data controller (unless it is not reasonably practicable to do so) to notify third parties to whom the data have been disclosed of the rectification, blocking, erasure or destruction. In determining whether it is reasonably practicable to make such an order in either of the above two cases the court will take into account the number of third parties to whom the inaccurate data have been disclosed. It is not clear whether this means that an order is less likely if the dessemination of inaccurate information is more widespread. If so, this would suggest that the larger the damage, the less effective will be the remedy.

Assistance from the Commissioner for either party to an application under s. 14 is available at the discretion of the Commissioner when a case involves matters of substantial public importance (s. 53).

For further discussion on the transitional right to rectification, blocking, erasure or destruction of 'exempt manual data', see below under 'Transitional rights'.

Transitional exemption

Eligible manual data are exempt from the right to rectification, blocking, erasure and destruction during the first transitional period. Certain eligible manual data are exempt from this right during the second transitional period. For further discussion see Chapter 9, Part 2.

COMPENSATION

An individual who suffers damage as a result of a contravention by a data controller of any provision of the Data Protection Act 1998 is entitled to compensation. Additionally, compensation for *distress* may be claimed in all cases where the individual has suffered damage. Compensation for distress without damage may be claimed only where the contravention relates to the processing of data for the 'special purposes', e.g., for the purposes of journalism or for artistic or literary purposes. (For further detail on the special purposes see Chapter 9, Part 1.)

When proceedings are brought against a data controller for compensation, it is a defence for the data controller to show that such care was taken as in all the circumstances was reasonably required to comply with the provision concerned.

Assistance from the Commissioner for either party to an application is available at the discretion of the Commissioner if a case involves processing for the 'special purposes' and concerns matters of substantial public importance.

Transitional exemption

During the first transitional period, automated data which are subject to processing that was already under way immediately before 24 October 1998 are exempt from the right to compensation in s. 13 except where such compensation relates to:

(a) a contravention of the fourth data protection principle,
(b) a disclosure without the consent of the data controller,
(c) loss or destruction of data without the consent of the data controller, or
(d) processing for the special purposes.

Eligible manual data are exempt from the right to compensation during the first transitional period. For further discussion see Chapter 9, Part 2.

REQUEST FOR ASSESSMENT

Any person who feels that he is directly affected by the processing of personal data may ask the Data Protection Commissioner to carry out an assessment of the processing to determine whether or not it is being undertaken in accordance with the provisions of the Act.

Two surprising features of this provision are the subjective nature of the request and the lack of any discretion on the part of the Commissioner — an assessment *must* be carried out by the Commissioner where she receives such a request from an individual who believes themselves to be the subject of processing, whether or not such belief is reasonable. The only circumstances where the Commissioner is not obliged to carry out an assessment are where appropriate information has not been supplied to enable the Commissioner to satisfy herself:

(a) as to the identity of the person making the request; and
(b) as to the identity of the processing in question.

Although the Commissioner cannot refuse to comply with any request, she does have some discretion in determining the manner in which it is appropriate to make the assessment. The factors which she can take into account are:

(a) the extent to which the request appears to raise a matter, of substance;
(b) any undue delay in making the request; and
(c) whether or not the person making the request is entitled to make an application under s. 7 (subject access request).

In the First Annual Report of the Data Protection Commissioner (published July 2000), Elizabeth France states that, due to anticipated lack of resources, assessments will be treated as falling within one of two categories. A 'summary' assessment will be undertaken on the documents presented to the Commissioner and without the need for investigation into the activities of the data controller. Such an assessment is likely to be utilised where the harm to the rights of the data subject is perceived to be small. An 'investigatory' assessment will be undertaken where there is reason to believe that the processing concerned could have a 'significant, unwarranted and adverse effect on individuals'. An investigatory assessment will involve an enquiry by the Commissioner into the processing activities of the data controller.

TRANSITIONAL RIGHTS

Further rights of data subjects in respect of exempt manual data only are available until 23 October 2007 under sch. 13 which adds a s. 12A to the Act until that time. 'Exempt manual data' for these purposes means:

(a)   from the commencement of the schedule to 23 October 2001, eligible manual data forming part of an accessible record (whether or not processing was already under way on 24 October 1998); and

(b)   from 24 October 2001 to 23 October 2007, eligible manual data (other than data which are processed only for the purpose of historical research) which were held immediately before 24 October 1998 and any other personal data forming part of an accessible record.

For the definition of 'eligible manual data' see Chapter 9, Part 2.

Under s. 12A(1) a data subject is entitled at any time, by notice in writing, to require the data controller:

(a)   to rectify, block, erase or destroy exempt manual data which are inaccurate or incomplete; or

(b)   to cease holding exempt manual data in a way incompatible with the legitimate purposes pursued by the data controller.

The notice must state the data subject's reasons for believing either of these matters (s. 12A(2)). If the data controller fails to comply with such a notice then the data subject may apply to the court for an order for compliance (s. 12A(3)). The court will grant such an order against the data controller if it feels that the notice was justified and that the data controller has failed to comply.

Assistance from the Commissioner for either party to an application under s. 12A is available at the discretion of the Commissioner if a case involves processing for the 'special purposes' and concerns matters of substantial public importance.

Chapter 3
Data Protection Principles

INTRODUCTION

Every data controller is, by virtue of s. 4(4) of the Data Protection Act 1988, under a duty to comply with the Data Protection Principles which are listed in sch. 1 to the Act. The Principles form the backbone of the legislation and their importance is underlined by the extent of the powers of the Data Protection Commissioner in relation to the issuing of information and enforcement notices (see Chapter 10).

The 1984 Act contained a similar set of Principles. However, this apparent familiarity can be misleading. Although they may appear substantially similar, the very wide meaning of processing and the lack of detail concerning registered purposes under the new provisions means that their effect is radically different. There are still eight in number, but the text of the first seven contains slightly more detail than before. The Eighth Principle in the new Act did not appear in the 1984 Act. It relates to the prohibition on transferring personal data to countries that do not have an adequate level of protection for the rights and freedoms of data subjects.

This chapter sets out each of the eight Principles and gives an overview of their application (the following three chapters consider the First and Eighth Principles in greater detail). Decisions of the Data Protection Tribunal and the courts are cited where they are a relevant extra-statutory aid to the interpretation of the Principles. Schedule 1 to the Act is divided into two parts — Part I lists the eight principles and Part II gives some guidance on the intended interpretation of the Principles.

FIRST PRINCIPLE

Personal data shall be processed fairly and lawfully and, in particular, shall not be processed unless—
  (a)   at least one of the conditions in Schedule 2 is met, and
  (b)   in the case of sensitive personal data, at least one of the conditions in Schedule 3 is also met.

The First Principle is more extensive than its counterpart in the 1984 Act. This is partly due to the fact that the definition of processing is considerably wider under the new provisions — see Chapter 2.

Processing will be unlawful unless one of the conditions in sch. 2 is met. The set of conditions in sch. 2 can therefore be seen as a 'threshold' or minimum standard for the processing of personal data. The sch. 2 conditions are discussed in detail in Chapter 4. In the case of sensitive personal data (see Chapter 5), processing will not be lawful unless one of the conditions in sch. 2 *and* one of the conditions in sch. 3 are met.

Compliance with sch. 2 and, where relevant, sch. 3 does not, however, *guarantee* that the processing will be fair and lawful. It may well be that the processing in question is unfair or unlawful (and thus not in compliance with the First Principle) for another reason (see for example, *British Gas Trading Limited* v *Data Protection Registrar* (1998) in Chapter 4). Furthermore, the processing may breach another of the principles or a provision in another statute or be in breach of the law of confidence and therefore unlawful.

There are a number of exemptions from the application of the First Principle (see Chapter 9).

Sensitive personal data

The Data Protection Act 1998 created a new category of data called 'sensitive personal data'.

A data controller who processes sensitive personal data must, in addition to satisfying one of the criteria in sch. 2, also comply with one of the conditions in sch. 3. It is thus vital for data controllers to check all sensitive processing to see that it complies with one of the provisions. The term 'sensitive personal data' is defined in s. 2 as meaning:

personal data consisting of information as to—
  (a)   the racial or ethnic origin of the data subject,
  (b)   his political opinions,
  (c)   his religious beliefs or other beliefs of a similar nature,
  (d)   whether he is a member of a trade union,
  (e)   his physical or mental health or condition,
  (f)   his sexual life,
  (g)   the commission or alleged commission by him of any offence, or
  (h)   any proceedings for any offence committed or alleged to have been committed by him, the disposal of such proceedings or the sentence of any court in such proceedings.

For further detail on sensitive personal data see Chapter 5.

General identifiers

Schedule 1, Part II, para. 4 of the Data Protection Act 1998 envisages secondary legislation in respect of 'general identifiers' by providing that personal data which contains a general identifier (falling within a description prescribed by the Secretary of State) will not comply with the First Principle unless there is compliance with any relevant provision laid down by the Secretary of State (at the time of writing there have been no such provisions). A 'general identifier' is:

any identifier (such as, for example, a number or code used for identification purposes) which:

    (a)   relates to an individual, and
    (b)   forms part of a set of similar identifiers which is of general application.

Examples of general identifiers are National Health Service numbers and National Insurance numbers.

If no regulations are made by the Secretary of State, there will be no restriction, as far as the First Principle is concerned, on the processing of a general identifier. However, it may be that the processing of a general identifier breaches another of the Principles.

SECOND PRINCIPLE

Personal data shall be obtained only for one or more specified and lawful purposes, and shall not be processed in any manner incompatible with that purpose or those purposes.

The First and Second Principles both concern the obtaining and other processing of information. The interpretation guidance in sch. 1 to the Act states that the purpose or purposes for which personal data are obtained may be specified:

    (a)   in a notice given by the data controller to the data subject, or
    (b)   in a notification given to the Commissioner.

Data are not to be processed in a manner inconsistent with the purpose for which they were obtained, in other words for a purpose that was not specified (either expressly or by obvious implication). In determining whether the manner of processing is compatible with that purpose, one of the factors to bear in mind is the purpose or purposes for which the personal data are intended to be processed by any person to whom they are disclosed.

In the *British Gas* case (see Chapter 4) the Registrar claimed that British Gas had contravened the Second and Third Principles in the 1984 Act (which taken together, had substantially similar wording to the Second Principle in the 1998 Act) by holding, using and disclosing customer details for the purpose of debt collection and tracing. This was not challenged by British Gas, who took steps to discontinue the practice.

Practically speaking the Second Data Protection Principle probably imposes a requirement on data controllers who disclose personal data to third parties to impose contractual obligations on the third party to process the data only for purposes compatible with the data controller's original specified purpose. The alternative would be to revert to the data subjects to obtain permission for a new purpose.

THIRD PRINCIPLE

Personal data shall be adequate, relevant and not excessive in relation to the purpose or purposes for which they are processed.

There are no interpretation provisions for the Third Principle in the Act. However, this Principle does not differ in any significant way from the equivalent Principle (the

Fourth) in the 1984 Act (save that the 1998 Act applies to certain manual records and purposes that are no longer clearly defined, registered purposes).

Tribunal litigation on this principle arose out of the community charge (or 'poll tax') regime. Various data subjects complained that information held about them for the purposes of administering the community charge was more than was required for the purpose. The Data Protection Registrar refused the applications to register (under the 1984 Act) of several local authorities on this basis. In *Community Charge Registration Officers of Runnymede Borough Council, South Northamptonshire District Council and Harrow Borough Council* v *Data Protection Registrar* (DA/90 24/49/3) the Tribunal found that, whilst the holding of 'some additional information' was permissible in certain circumstances, the holding on a database of a substantial quantity of property information obtained from voluntary answers on the canvass forms was far more than was necessary for the purpose.

In a similar case (*Community Charge Registration Officer of Rhondda Borough Council* v *Data Protection Registrar* (DA/90 25/49/2)) the CCRO for Rhondda continued to request dates of birth from individuals on community charge forms after the Registrar suggested that such information should be excluded from the forms, save in exceptional circumstances. The CCRO contended that the dates of birth were necessary for distinguishing between people in an area in which many had both last and first names in common. Despite a lack of statistics, the Tribunal accepted that there could be more persons with names in common in Rhondda than in other parts of the country. However, the appellant did not seek to limit the database to only hold dates of birth of persons who were living at the same address with identical names. The Tribunal held that:

the information the appellant wishes to hold on database concerning individuals exceeds substantially the minimum amount of information which is required in order for him to fulfil the purposes for which he has sought registration namely to fulfil his duty to compile and maintain the Community Charges Register.... We are satisfied by the evidence before us that the wide and general extent of the information about dates of birth is irrelevant and excessive.

In similar circumstances today a data controller could comply with the Third Principle by inserting an instruction as follows:

'Please provide your date of birth only if there is another person living in your house with both the same last and first name as you so that we are able to differentiate between you and that other person.'

FOURTH PRINCIPLE

Personal data shall be accurate and, where necessary, kept up to date.

The Fourth Principle will not be breached where inaccurate information in personal data accurately records information obtained from the data subject or a third party if the data controller has taken reasonable steps to ensure the accuracy of the data. Where the data subject has informed the data controller of the inaccuracy of the data, the data must indicate that fact. Thus the data controller is under an obligation to take reasonable steps to verify the accuracy of the data obtained. What is reasonable will depend on the circumstances and particularly on the purpose for which the data were obtained.

There is no definition of 'accurate' in the Act, but s. 70(2) gives the meaning of 'inaccurate':

> For the purposes of this Act data are inaccurate if they are incorrect or misleading as to any matter of fact.

FIFTH PRINCIPLE

Personal data processed for any purpose or purposes shall not be kept for longer than is necessary for that purpose or those purposes.

As with the Third Principle there is very little difference between this Principle and its counterpart (the Sixth) in the 1984 Act and the wording is self-explanatory. Keeping data beyond the length of time necessary for the purpose for which the data were processed will breach the Fifth Principle. There are no interpretative provisions in the Act that relate to this Principle.

Data cotrollers are advised to keep personal data they hold under constant review and to delete all information which is no longer required for the purpose or purposes for which it was obtained.

SIXTH PRINCIPLE

Personal data shall be processed in accordance with the rights of data subjects under this Act.

The interpretation provisions in sch. 1 state that a person will breach this Principle only if he:

(a)   contravenes the rights of access provisions in s. 7,

(b)   fails to comply with a justified request to cease processing under s. 10 or fails to respond to such a request within 21 days of its receipt,

(c)   fails to comply with a request under s. 11 to cease direct marketing processing,

(d)   contravenes s. 13 by failing to comply with a request in relation to automated decision-taking (either to prevent such a decision being taken or to have it reconsidered) or failing to notify the data subject that a decision was taken on such a basis or failing to reply to the data subject within 21 days of the receipt of such a request, or

(e)   contravenes s. 12A (see Chapter 2, 'Transitional rights') by failing to comply with a notice given under subsection (1) of that section to the extent that the notice is justified.

SEVENTH PRINCIPLE

Appropriate technical and organisational measures shall be taken against unauthorised or unlawful processing of personal data and against accidental loss or destruction of, or damage to, personal data.

The Seventh Principle provides, in essence, that appropriate care must be taken of personal data. The interpretation provisions in sch. 1 suggest that account must be taken of the state of technology (and its cost) available to the data controller at the relevant time. The protective measures must ensure a level of security which is appropriate to the harm which might result from the events mentioned in the Seventh Principle and the nature of the data to be protected. Data controllers should monitor changes in technology so that they do not inadvertantly breach the Seventh Principle by failing to upgrade existing systems.

The Seventh Principle imposes an obligation on the data controller to ensure the reliability of all employees who have access to personal data. This obligation applies so far as is reasonable in the circumstances. The familiar balancing test should be employed, with a greater degree of training being needed where there is a greater importance that the data be secure.

One way that data controllers could be relatively certain of compliance with the Seventh Principle is to ensure that all data security accords with BS7799 (for further detail see Chapter 8).

Data processors

A 'data processor' is defined in s. 1(1) as 'any person (other than an employee of the data controller) who processes the data on behalf of the data controller'. Where processing is to be carried out by a data processor the data controller must choose the data processor with care and, in particular, should ensure the provision of sufficient guarantees by the data processor in relation to appropriate security measures. Additionally the data controller must take reasonable steps to ensure that the data processor complies with such security measures. The arrangement for processing between the data controller and the data processor must be contractual and evidenced in writing. The contract must be exclusive in respect of the data processor's instructions concerning the data, and must oblige the data processor to comply with the obligations contained in the Seventh Principle.

If data are processed by one company on behalf of another (even when the companies are part of the same group) there must be a written contract between them — informal arrangements are insufficient — and it must require the processor to comply with the provisions of the Seventh Principle. The data controller's obligation to check the processor's security measures could be undertaken by the submission of a detailed questionnaire to prospective data processors before an appointment is made.

EIGHTH PRINCIPLE

Personal data shall not be transferred to a country or territory outside the European Economic Area unless that country or territory ensures an adequate level of protection for the rights and freedoms of data subjects in relation to the processing of personal data.

The European Economic Area consists of the 15 Member States of the European Union plus Norway, Iceland and Liechtenstein. There is no restriction on the transfer of information *between* those countries.

A transfer of personal data to any *other* country is unlawful unless that country has an adequate level of protection for such data. See Chapter 6 for a full discussion of 'adequacy' and of the application of the Eighth Principle.

Chapter 4
Fair and Lawful Processing

INTRODUCTION

The First Data Protection Principle requires that data be both fairly and lawfully processed and is perhaps the most complex of all the Principles. The wide definition of processing leads to a correspondingly broad application of this Principle. This chapter considers the implications for data controllers of the requirement that the processing of personal data be both fair and lawful.

In all cases personal data will need to be both obtained and used fairly and lawfully. Certain information will need to be supplied (or made available) to the data subject at the time of data capture. Further, all processing of personal data will be unlawful unless it complies with one of the conditions contained in sch. 2 to the Data Protection Act 1998 — these conditions are discussed later in this chapter.

OBTAINING DATA

The 1984 Act required data to be both 'obtained' and 'processed' fairly. The new provision relates only to processing, but the definition of processing (see Chapter 2) now includes 'obtaining'. Case law relating to the definition of 'obtaining' personal data therefore remains relevant to processing under the new regime. It is essential that data controllers obtain information correctly, i.e., in accordance with the First Principle. Failure to do so puts all subsequent processing in jeopardy. Not only must data be obtained fairly within the guidelines in sch. 1, Part II of the Act, but the obtaining itself must meet the relevant sch. 2 and, where relevant, sch. 3 conditions (see below).

The interpretation provisions in sch. 1 to the Act state that in determining whether the processing is fair regard must be had to the method of obtaining the data. It is clear that processing will be unfair when any person from whom data has been obtained is deceived or misled as to its intended purpose.

In *Innovations (Mail Order) Ltd* v *Data Protection Registrar* (DA9231/49/1), a mail-order company obtained business in two principal ways: by receiving orders from its catalogues and by receiving orders in response to its advertisements in the media. Customers were informed of the possibility of their details being used for other purposes only after their details had been obtained. The company engaged in the practice known as 'list rental' (trading in lists of customers' names and addresses) and many of the customers from both categories were used for this purpose. It was the Registrar's contention that all customers had to be informed of all intended uses for their personal details at the time the order was made, i.e., at the time the customers supplied their details to the company. The company argued that the practical constraints this would cause for its general media advertising made such a practice unacceptable. The Data Protection Tribunal found that the absence of a warning in the general media advertising might lead to an assumption on the part of individual members of the public that their details would not be traded. This meant that some members of the public would be misled and therefore that the obtaining of the information was indeed unfair.

INFORMATION TO BE SUPPLIED TO THE DATA SUBJECT

The information that must be supplied to the data subject at the time the data is obtained depends upon whether the personal data was obtained from the data subject herself or from some other person.

Data obtained from the data subject

Data obtained from the data subject will (according to sch. 1, Part II, para. 2(1)(a) and (3) of the 1998 Act) not be treated as processed fairly, and hence will breach the First Principle, where the data controller does not ensure (so far as is practicable) that the data subject has, or has ready access to, certain information. This information is listed in the box below and may be called the 'information requirements'. There is no indication in the Act as to what set of circumstances would need to exist for it not to be 'practicable' to provide the data subject with the information requirements.

Information Requirements

(a) The identity of the data controller.
(b) The identity of any representative of the data controller.
(c) The purpose or purposes for which the data are intended to be processed.
(d) Any other information which is necessary to enable the particular processing to be fair.

The giving of such information to the data subject is dealt with in art. 10 of the European Data Protection Directive and may be referred to as an 'Article 10 Notice'.

Example

A website provides tailor-made news items which it sends by e-mail to its registered members. To become a member an individual must provide name, address, e-mail address and the type of news items in which he or she is interested. Here the website must provide the details in (a)–(d) in the box above. This should ideally be on the same 'page' as is used for data capture, but could also be in an appropriate Privacy Policy.

It is interesting to note that as far as paragraph (d) is concerned, the information needed to be transmitted to the data subject to enable the processing to be fair could extend to informing her of the right to object to direct marketing (see Chapter 2). The views of the Commissioner on this point are unknown at the time of writing. However the prevailing attitude that may be detected from the administration of enforcement notices by the Commissioner is that a restrictive interpretation is likely.

Data obtained from a third-party

Where data have *not* been obtained from the data subject but from someone else, processing will be unfair unless the data controller ensures (so far as is practicable) that, 'before the relevant time or as soon as practicable after that time', the data subject has or has ready access to the information contained in the box above ('an Article 11 Notice'). Data may be obtained from someone other than the data subject where, for example, it is comprised in a list of information transferred from one data controller to another (e.g., list rental) or where the data are supplied by a friend or relative of the data subject to the data controller (e.g., member-get-member schemes). For these purposes, by virtue of para. 2(2) 'the relevant time' means:

(a)   the time when the data controller first processes the data, or
(b)   in a case where, at the time of first processing, there is likely to be disclosure of the data to a third person within a reasonable period:

(i)   where the data are so disclosed, the time when that occurs,
(ii)   the time when the data controller becomes, or ought to become, aware that the data are unlikely to be disclosed within that reasonable period, or
(iii) the end of that reasonable period.

There is no definition of 'reasonable period' in the Act. The Data Protection Commissioner is expected to issue advice about what may constitute a reasonable period, which may vary according to circumstances. It is likely to depend on the type of processing in question, the effect on the data subject and the ease of providing such information.

Example
A market researcher telephones Susie and asks her for information about her shopping habits. Susie tells the researcher which supermarket she uses and gives a list of some basic products that she and her husband, Mark, commonly purchase. Here Mark must be informed, as soon as practicable after the telephone conversation takes place, of the identity of the researcher or the researcher's employer and the purpose of requiring the information that Susie has given. Where the market researcher is acting as agent for another, Mark must be informed of those matters within a reasonable period of time.

Where the data controller did not obtain the information from the data subject there is an exception to the obligation to notify the data subject of the matters listed in the box above. This applies where one of the following two primary conditions is true:

(a)   the provision of that information would involve a 'disproportionate effort', or
(b)   the recording of the information to be contained in the data by, or the disclosure of the data by, the data controller is necessary for compliance with any legal obligation to which the data controller is subject, other than an obligation imposed by contract.

Where information is obtained from a third-party and one of the above primary conditions applies, the obligation to inform the data subject of the information requirements is nullified.

Disproportionate effort

The first of the 'primary conditions' (which allow a data controller to escape from his or her obligation to notify the data subject of the information requirements) requires any effort on the part of the data controller in contacting the data subject to be 'disproportionate'. There is no definition of 'disproportionate' in the Act or in the Directive, nor a precise description of what it relates to. However, it can be reasonably inferred that in order for this primary condition to operate the effort involved in contacting the data subject must be disproportionate to the prejudice caused to the data subject's rights by the lack of any such contact. Thus, where the effort needed to contact the data subject is considerable, such effort is likely to be disproportionate unless it is outweighed by severe consequences for the data subject, e.g., because it involves significant, or otherwise important, processing (for example, of sensitive personal data). Basically, it is a question of balance and relevant factors will be the time and expense involved in the data controller providing the relevant information to the data subject and the prejudicial effect on the data subject caused by the withholding of such information.

Example
Jamie's grandmother is soon to be 80. For her birthday Jamie arranges for a bouquet of flowers to be sent to her by the local florist. If the florist records the name and address of Jamie's grandmother, the provisions of the First Principle require the florist to give the grandmother the relevant information, thus ruining the surprise. The telephone conversation to the grandmother from the florist might be along the following lines: 'We have information about you concerning the delivery of flowers. Please try to act surprised when they arrive.' (This comical scenario was foreseen by the Home Office and much discussed at the Committee stage of the Bill.)

It could be argued that, in the example above, the grandmother must be informed of the processing, and hence the surprise ruined, because the effort by the data controller in contacting the single data subject is minimal. On the other hand, the prejudice caused to the grandmother in withholding the information is also minimal and, it could be argued, cannot outweigh any effort involved. It has been suggested that the first primary condition will only apply where the data controller has obtained a massive database of personal data so as to obviate the need to contact every data subject immediately, but this is not supported by a literal construction of the legislation.

In order to be able to benefit from the 'disproportionate effort' primary condition, the data controller must keep a record of the reasons why he believes the disapplication of the information requirements to be necessary (Data Protection (Conditions Under Paragraph 3 of Part II of Schedule I) Order 2000). Further, data controllers must provide the information contained in the information requirements to any data subject who requests it unless it is not possible to determine if he is processing data about the individual, in which case a notice to that effect must be given.

Legal obligation

The second of the two primary conditions provides that the information requirements will be disapplied where data are obtained from someone other than the data subject where the processing by the data controller is necessary to comply with a legal obligation other than a breach of contract. Examples include statutory duties upon certain organisations to compile lists of individuals who belong to certain groups or professional bodies. A prerequisite to the operation of the second primary condition is that a data subject must always be provided with the information requirements by the data controller where he requests it.

PRESUMPTION OF FAIRNESS

There is a presumption in para. 1(2) of sch. 1, Part II to the 1998 Act that data will have been obtained fairly where they are obtained from a person who:

(a)   is authorised by or under any enactment to supply it, or
(b)   is required to supply it by or under any enactment or by any convention or other instrument imposing an international obligation on the UK.

However, the presumption will only apply where the data subject has been supplied with the information requirements as described above.

CRITERIA FOR LAWFUL PROCESSING

Processing will be unlawful, and hence will breach the First Data Protection Principle, where the data controller has failed to comply with any legal obligation. For the sake of clarity, such legal obligations may be divided into two categories:

(a)   those contained in the Data Protection Act 1998 itself; and
(b)   any other relevant legal provision.

1998 Act unlawfulness

For processing to be lawful within the 1998 Act, at least one of the conditions in sch. 2 to the Act must be met. There are no exceptions to this rule. The first condition relates to the data subject giving his or her consent to the processing, and is probably the most important. In many cases, such as list rental, the first condition is the only one that could possibly apply.

The six conditions in sch. 2 are set out in the following box and described further below.

Criteria for lawful processing
1.   Consent of the data subject
2.   Contractual necessity
3.   Non-contractual legal obligation of the data controller
4.   Vital interests of the data subject
5.   Functions of a public nature
6.   Legitimate interests of the data controller

1. The data subject has given consent to the processing

There is no definition of consent in the 1998 Act. At the time of drafting the Bill, it was the view of the Home Office that the courts 'know what consent means', thus rendering a definition unnecessary. Article 7(a) of the European Data Protection Directive speaks of 'unambiguous' consent. Again the Home Office felt this distinction unnecessary when drafting the Bill and preferred the view that ambiguous consent is not consent. It will, of course, be for the data controller to decide, in the first instance, what is meant by consent. The data controller's view will be subject to that of the Commissioner and ultimately the courts.

What amounts to consent may depend on the identity of the person consenting as well as on the form that such consent takes. In the *British Gas Trading* case (below) the Data Protection Tribunal drew a distinction between new and existing customers for the purpose of determining when the requirement of consent would be satisfied. New customers could indicate their acquiescence (to the processing of their details for the purposes of marketing) at the time of entering into the agreement for the supply of gas, or in a document returned by the customer to confirm the arrangements for the supply of gas (such as either an opt-in box ticked or an opt-out box left blank). With existing customers it would not be enough simply to send them a leaflet giving them an opportunity to object to the processing of information beyond gas-related purposes. Consent would only be made out, said the Tribunal, where such customers were informed of the likely use for the data and were given a choice to agree or not, and either consented then and there or did not object to such use. Alternatively, a form could be used which indicated consent or, by not filling in an opt-out box, indicated no objection to the proposed processing. The Tribunal made it clear that there had to be some *response* to British Gas, i.e., that a failure to respond should not be taken as consent. The case was decided of course under the 1984 legislation and concerned a monopoly service provider to evidence consent.

'Consent' as required by sch. 2 to the 1998 Act should be contrasted with 'explicit consent' as required for the processing of sensitive personal data in sch. 3 (see Chapter 5). The implications of omitting the word 'explicit' in sch. 2 is that implied consent is acceptable. Further, there is no requirement that consent be in writing, although for the protection of the data controller it is suggested that some form of permanent record is advisable.

A data subject will not be taken to have consented to processing of which he was not informed or could not reasonably be taken to expect. Thus, a data controller who gathers personal data for one purpose will be acting without the consent of the data subject if it is processed for another non-obvious purpose.

Example
A website provides basic information on plumbing contractors in every town of the UK. In order to gain access to such information users of the site are requested to register by providing their name and e-mail address. The company which runs the website then sends its registered users' e-mail addresses to local plumbers. Here the data subject has not consented to the disclosure of her personal data to third parties. The data controllers' processing will therefore be unlawful (unless it complies with one of the other criteria for lawful processing).

2.   The processing is necessary—

> *(a)   for the performance of a contract to which the data subject is a party, or*
> *(b)   for the taking of steps at the request of the data subject with a view to entering into a contract.*

Where the data controller has entered into contractual relations with the data subject it is easy to envisage types of processing which will be necessary for contractual performance. Examples include passing a purchaser's details to the issuer of his credit card for payment purposes and sending a data subject's name and address to a courier for the delivery of items bought by the data subject.

The word 'necessary' should not be overlooked. It is not defined in the Act and should therefore be given its usual meaning. Processing by a data controller will not be necessary for contractual performance where the contract could be performed in some other way without the need for such processing.

3.   The processing is necessary for compliance with any legal obligation to which the data controller is subject, other than an obligation imposed by contract

Any statutory or other legal obligations imposed on the data controller will ensure compliance with sch. 2 to the Act where the processing is necessary to comply with that obligation. Contractual obligations covered by condition 2 are excluded from condition 3.

This condition would be fulfilled, for example, where a statute required an organisation to make public a list of its members. The processing involved in making this public disclosure would be legitimate under this condition.

4.   The processing is necessary in order to protect the vital interests of the data subject

The word 'vital' is key to this condition and is likely to be construed narrowly. The European Data Protection Directive speaks of protecting an interest which is 'essential for the data subject's life'. An emergency situation would therefore be covered. It is likely that 'vital interests' extends only to life-and-death circumstances.

Example
Jo travels to France for a skiing holiday. Unfortunately she is caught in an avalanche while skiing off-piste and requires emergency hospital treatment. The French hospital requires Jo's medical records to be transferred from the UK, but Jo is unable to consent to such transfer as she is unconscious. In this case, the processing by Jo's UK doctor (sending the records to France) is legitimised for sch. 2 purposes by virtue of the fact that it is necessary to save Jo's life.

5.   The processing is necessary—

> *(a)   for the administration of justice,*
> *(b)   for the exercise of any functions of either House of Parliament,*
> *(c)   for the exercise of any functions conferred on any person by or under any enactment,*
> *(d)   for the exercise of any functions of the Crown, a Minister of the Crown or a government department, or*

(e)   for the exercise of any other functions of a public nature exercised in the public interest by any person.

This condition will cover many public-sector data controllers. The last of the four alternatives is drafted somewhat more widely than the first three and there is no definition of 'public interest'. It is this alternative that is therefore likely to attract most controversy and litigation. It may, for example, extend to the processing of closed-circuit television images. It is likely that this provision was intended to cover privately constituted bodies that perform public functions in regulation or discipline, e.g., BMA.

Article 8 of the European Convention for the Protection of Human Rights and Fundamental Freedoms (made part of UK law by the Human Rights Act 1998) will inevitably have an impact on the operation of this condition. Article 8 provides as follows:

1.   Everyone has the right to respect for his private and family life, his home and his correspondence.
2.   There shall be no interference by a public authority with the exercise of this right except such as in accordance with the law and is necessary in a democratic society in the interests of national security, public safety or the economic well-being of the country, for the prevention of disorder or crime, for the protection of health or morals, or for the protection of the rights and freedoms of others.

It remains to be seen how the courts will interpret this provision, but it is clear that all UK legislation (including the Data Protection Act) must be construed in such a way as to comply with the Convention.

6.   The processing is necessary for the purposes of legitimate interests pursued by the data controller or by the third party or parties to whom the data are disclosed, except where the processing is unwarranted in any particular case by reason of prejudice to the rights and freedoms or legitimate interests of the data subject

The starting point here is the existence of a legitimate interest of the data controller. The processing must be necessary for that legitimate interest and must not be unwarranted. The processing will be unwarranted where it is prejudicial to the rights, freedoms or legitimate interests of the data subject.

It can be seen then that there is a need for a balancing act to be undertaken between the legitimate interests of the data subject and those of the data controller. The lack of any definition of 'legitimate interests' in the Act makes this condition unclear and the most needful of all the conditions of litigation for clarification. What can be gathered with a reasonable degree of certainty is that legitimate interests of a data controller will include the ability to carry out usual commercial activities, and those of a data subject the rights and freedoms guaranteed by the European Convention for the Protection of Human Rights and Fundamental Freedoms. Of perhaps most significance are arts. 8 and 10 of the Convention. Article 8 is set out above. Article 10 provides that:

1.   Everyone has the right to freedom of expression. This right shall include freedom to hold opinions and to receive and impart information and ideas without

interference by public authority and regardless of frontiers. This Article shall not prevent States from requiring the licensing of broadcasting, television or cinema enterprises.

2.   The exercise of these freedoms, since it carries with it duties and responsibilities, may be subject to such formalities, conditions, restrictions, or penalties as are prescribed by law and are necessary in a democratic society, in the interests of national security, territorial integrity or public safety, for the prevention of disorder or crime, for the protection of health or morals, for the protection of the reputation or rights of others, for preventing the disclosure of information received in confidence, or for maintaining the authority and impartiality of the judiciary.

In light of the intended supremacy of human rights legislation over other legal provisions it seems clear that where the interests of the data controller and those of the data subject are perceived to be equal, the Commissioner and the tribunal will determine the interests of the data subject to be the most important. Even in the absence of the Human Rights Convention it should be remembered that data protection legislation is, after all, aimed principally at protecting the privacy of the individual.

The Secretary of State may, by order, specify circumstances in which the legitimate interests condition will or will not be satisfied. Such a widely drawn power could, in theory, legitimise any processing by a data controller by deeming it to outweigh the interests of the data subject. The Secretary of State had made no such orders at the time of writing.

Other unlawfulness

The main restriction on processing data outside the provisions of data protection legislation is the law of confidentiality. Confidence will be breached (and thus an action for breach of confidence will lie) where, as Megarry J. stated in *Coco v A N Clarke (Engineers) Ltd* [1968] FSR 415:

(a)   the information has the necessary quality of confidence;
(b)   the information has been imparted in circumstances importing an obligation of confidence; and
(c)   there is an unauthorised use of the information to the detriment of the original communicator of the information.

Information will have the necessary quality of confidence when it is of a confidential character. The courts apply an objective test in determining whether information has a confidential character: would the reasonable man, in the position of the defendant, have realised that the information in his possession is confidential? Information will not have the necessary quality of confidence if it is in the public domain.

The information will be imparted in circumstances imposing an obligation of confidence where there is a relationship between the parties that would lead the reasonable man to conclude that the information should be kept secret. Thus, a clearly audible exchange between A and C in a crowded market place will not lead to an obligation of confidence no matter how confidential the information. Others present in the market place who hear the conversation will not be under an obligation of confidence either, as there is no existing relationship between them and the speaker.

There are, however, several types of relationship that the courts have held to be sufficient for this purpose, for example, the relationship which exists between an employee and employer, between two commercial concerns undertaking a business negotiation with each other and between one family member and another.

A further type of relationship that may give rise to an obligation of confidence, and one that is of particular significance to the media, is that of a journalist and the person who provides him with information. The obligation will most commonly arise when the journalist is aware that the information is being provided covertly and the person providing the information is the original source of it. It is less clear whether an obligation of confidence arises if the information is sent to the journalist anonymously or where it is provided overtly by a person who has received the information from another.

Not every use of the information by the recipient will be sufficient to found an action for breach of confidence; it must be an unauthorised use. This rarely presents much difficulty for claimants in practice and in many cases the unauthorised use will involve some form of data processing. Once it has been established that the information was of confidential character and was imparted in circumstances imposing confidentiality then it will rarely be difficult to show that the dissemination of that information is an unauthorised use.

Aside from the law of confidence, information will be processed unlawfully (and therefore in breach of the First Data Protection Principle) where it is processed in one of the following ways:

(a)   in breach of contract;
(b)   by a body acting outside of its allotted powers (*ultra vires*);
(c)   in breach of copyright; or
(d)   in contravention of the provisions of the Computer Misuse Act 1990.

TRIBUNAL PRECEDENT

There is a dearth of actual precedent on what may and may not amount to fair processing. One example arose in the case of *British Gas Trading Limited* v *Data Protection Registrar* (1998), which was an appeal against an enforcement notice that had been issued in July 1997 under the old data protection legislation. The enforcement notice claimed that British Gas was contravening the First Data Protection Principle by unfairly and unlawfully processing personal data relating to individual customers for the supply of gas.

As far as lawfulness was concerned, the Registrar claimed that British Gas had acted *ultra vires*, in breach of:

(a)   s. 42 of the Gas Act 1986;
(b)   an implied contractual term; and
(c)   confidence.

The Data Protection Tribunal dismissed all of these claims. However, the Registrar was more successful in its claim that British Gas had acted unfairly. Essentially, the relevant facts were that British Gas had two main databases, a tariff gas bill database and a marketing database. In early 1997 the company enclosed a leaflet entitled 'Your Data Protection Rights' with each gas bill that it sent out. The leaflet stated that British Gas wished to:

(a)   write to its customers about its products and services;

(b)   send to its customers information about products and services offered by other reputable organisations; and

(c)   pass on information about customers to other companies in the British Gas Group so that customers could receive information about those companies' products and services directly from them.

If customers did not wish to receive such information they could decline by returning a form to British Gas. The registrar felt this to be unfair in that customers should be required to opt in rather than opt out, particularly since statistically it was likely that a very small proportion of the recipients would be aware of having received the notice or the effect of failing to respond.

In determining the issue of fairness the Tribunal took into account the monopoly (as it then was) of British Gas and found the processing of personal data for disclosure to third parties for marketing purposes was unfair unless done with the consent of the data user. (It is interesting to note that under the new legislation the First Principle would be breached (by virtue of sch. 2) on the same set of facts where a customer did not give consent.)

In a similar case the following year — *Midlands Electricity Plc v Data Protection Registrar* (1999) — the Registrar had issued an Enforcement Notice following a complaint from an individual that he had received advertising materials from Midlands Electricity that he had not consented to receive. Midlands Electricity had engaged in a direct-marketing campaign which involved enclosing an advertising leaflet (the Homebright magazine) with their customers' quarterly bills. The leaflet not only promoted the services of Midlands Electricity but also those of third parties such as Boots and Midlands Gas. The Tribunal found that this type of processing of the customers' personal data was unfair and therefore in breach of the First Data Protection Principle. Customers were sent the Homebright magazine as a matter of general policy and had not been given an opportunity to consent or otherwise to the use of their personal data for this purpose.

On the issue of consent it is interesting to note the thinking of the Tribunal which is apparent from the following extract from the judgment:

With existing customers, as with new customers ... we do not consider that it is sufficient merely to send to the customer a leaflet providing them with an opportunity to object to their personal data being processed for purposes beyond those electricity related purposes or other purposes, such as energy conservation, which we have identified as being available for processing without consent and without unfairness to which we have referred. It would we consider be sufficient to prevent processing for other purposes being unfair, if individual customers are informed that MEB wishes to continue to send them Homebright magazines containing third-party offers selected by them or such other type of marketing or promotions that MEB would wish to carry out, provided that they are given the choice to agree or not and either consent then and there or do not object to their personal data being processed so as to enable such use to take place. Alternatively thereafter, and before such processing takes place, the customer returns a document to MEB or by other means of communication received by MEB indicates consent to, or by not filling in an opt-out box, or other means indicates no objection to, processing for such type or types of marketing or promotion.

AM I PROCESSING DATA FAIRLY?

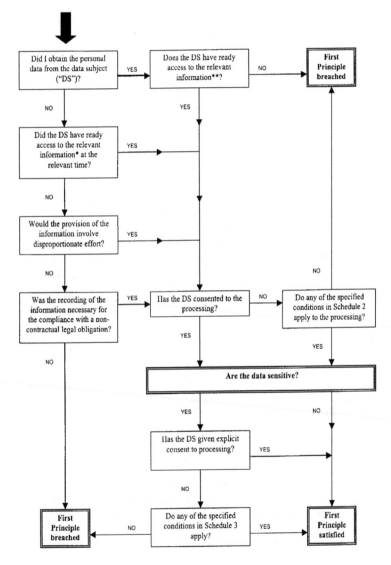

* The information specified in Schedule 1 Part II, paragraph 2.3   ** The time defined in Schedule 1 Part II, paragraph 2(2)

Chapter 5
Sensitive Personal Data

INTRODUCTION

The Data Protection Act 1998 created a new category of personal data known as sensitive personal data (defined below). Under the 1998 Act, special rules apply to the processing of sensitive personal data and these are discussed in this chapter. Interestingly, the Data Protection Act 1984 envisaged the concept of sensitive data by giving the Secretary of State the power to make regulations in relation to such data, but no regulations were ever made.

Data controllers are forbidden from processing sensitive personal data unless one or more of 19 criteria, or conditions, are established. Nine of those 19 conditions can be found in the statute itself, whilst a further ten appear in the Data Protection (Processing of Sensitive Personal Data) Order 2000. It is thus vital for data controllers to check all sensitive processing to ensure that it falls within at least one of the provisions.

Sensitive personal data is defined in s. 2 as personal data consisting of information relating to the data subject as to one or more of the matters listed in the box below.

Sensitive Personal Data

(a) Racial or ethnic origin.
(b) Political opinions.
(c) Religious beliefs or other beliefs of a similar nature.
(d) Trade union membership.
(e) Physical or mental health or condition.
(f) Sexual life.
(g) The commission or alleged commission by the data subject of any offence.
(h) Any proceedings for any offence committed or alleged to have been committed by the data subject, the disposal of such proceedings or the sentence of any court in such proceedings.

Certain types of data processing will clearly fall within one of the definitions of 'sensitive' in the box above. Examples include an employer's record of the trade union membership of its employees, airline information showing that wheelchair access is required for a particular passenger and hotel booking data disclosing that a guest requires kosher food.

Arguments over aspects of the definitions that are less clear are ongoing, and are set to continue for some years. Disputes over, for example, whether the racial or ethic origin of a data subject could be gleaned from a surname or family name (e.g., Jones, Patel, McGregor, Abdullah) have been debated since the legislation was proposed. A similar concern arises where, for example, an individual undertakes an Internet search for her local Baptist church — could the data controller be processing sensitive personal data on the data subject in this scenario? The answer depends upon what the Commissioner's (and ultimately the courts') interpretation of the legislation will be. Is a mere indication of one of the aspects of the definition of sensitive personal data enough for the relevant processing to be sensitive? Or is it necessary for the processing to be conclusive as to its sensitive nature? Most likely it is something in between these two positions, which has yet to be defined.

THE CONDITIONS FOR PROCESSING

The 19 conditions for the lawful processing of sensitive personal data appear in the following box and are discussed below.

Conditions for Processing
1. Explicit consent
2. Employment law obligations
3. Vital interests of the data subject
4. Not-for-profit organisation existing for political, philosophical, religious or trade union purposes
5. Information made public by the data subject
6. Legal rights
7. Public functions (administration of justice, etc.)
8. Medical purposes
9. Records on racial equality
10. Unlawful activity detection
11. Protection of the public
12. Public interest disclosure
13. Confidential counselling
14. Insurance and pensions — family data
15. Insurance and pensions — processing
16. Religion and health — equality or opportunity
17. Political opinions
18. Research
19. Police processing

The first nine conditions are contained in sch. 3 to the 1998 Act, the remainder being found in Regulations (see Appendix 3). It should be remembered that *all* processing, whether or not it is sensitive, requires compliance with a sch. 2 condition (see chapter 4) and that therefore the following criteria are *additional* requirements for sensitive data.

1. The data subject has given his or her explicit consent to the processing of the personal data

This condition is likely to be the most commonly used in practice. The distinction between 'explicit consent' as required by sch. 3 to the Act and 'consent' in sch. 2 is unclear, but it is likely that explicit consent will not be made out if the data subject is not fully informed of all relevant information about the proposed processing. Explicit consent will, therefore, require a rewording of the pre-1998 Act data protection notices. Instead of a box being provided for a data subject to opt out of further processing, a box should ideally be provided requiring a data subject to fill in a tick, or better still, provide a signature (an opt-in provision), to indicate consent. A possible alternative is that a data protection notice could be worded in such a way that it amounts to consent. Whether the latter is possible is a matter for speculation and it should be noted that the Commissioner does not favour this approach. The effectiveness of such a notice will doubtless depend on the wording it contains, its permanence, the nature of the sensitivity of the data, and the extent to which appropriate efforts were made to bring it to the attention of the data subject.

Where explicit consent is given by a data subject, such consent will also operate to legitimise the processing for sch. 2 purposes (one of the sch. 2 conditions relates to obtaining the 'consent' of the data subject). In order to be certain of compliance with the explicit consent condition, data controllers should ensure that they are in possession of proof of such consent. Controllers should therefore obtain consent in writing or some other recordable form wherever possible.

2. The processing is necessary for the purposes of exercising or performing any right or obligation which is conferred or imposed by law on the data controller in connection with employment

Sensitive personal data may be processed to comply with employment law obligations. The Secretary of State is empowered to produce regulations which exclude the operation of this condition or specify further conditions that are to be complied with in certain circumstances. No such regulations had been produced at the time of writing.

The most common type of sensitive personal data processing in this context is the monitoring by employers of their workforce. Employers must not, for example, discriminate against employees on the grounds of race or disability. It should be remembered, however, that the processing concerned must be necessary for the relevant purpose. This requirement of 'necessity' will not always be easy to make out.

3. The processing is necessary to protect the vital interests of the data subject or another person

This condition can only be invoked where:

(a) consent cannot be given by, or on behalf of, the data subject;
(b) the data controller cannot reasonably be expected to obtain the consent of the data subject; or
(c) in a case concerning the protection of the vital interests of another person, consent by or on behalf of the data subject has been unreasonably withheld.

There is no definition of vital interests in the Act, but the view of the Commissioner is that reliance on this condition may only be claimed where the processing is necessary for matters of 'life and death'. Health data will thus benefit from this condition, such as where a data subject has a communicable disease and 'another person' is in danger of infection. The data subject could not give consent if he or she is unconscious or cannot be found — this condition would allow the disclosure of the relevant data. If the data subject simply refuses permission, a data controller which is a health authority would be able to utilise the third alternative above. Emergency situations will be covered by this condition, such as where medical records are needed urgently by the A&E Department of a hospital — a doctor or some other health official could transfer the sensitive medical data to the hospital in reliance on this condition.

It is not clear how this condition interrelates with condition 8, medical purposes. The fact that there are two similar conditions may lend weight to the argument that 'vital interests' covers matters other than life-and-death scenarios. Condition 8 requires the processing to be carried out by a health professional. The vital interests condition is not limited in this way but would extend to processing by any person.

4.   The processing is carried out as part of the legitimate activities of a not-for-profit body or association

In order to take advantage of this condition, the body or association must exist for political, philosophical, religious or trade-union purposes and the processing must:

(a)   be carried out with appropriate safeguards for the rights and freedoms of data subjects,
(b)   relate only to individuals who either are members of the body or association or have regular contact with it in connection with its purposes, and
(c)   not involve disclosure of the personal data to a third party without the consent of the data subject.

5.   The information contained in the personal data has been made public as a result of steps deliberately taken by the data subject

Where the data subject has introduced sensitive personal data into the public domain it will not be a breach of the First Data Protection Principle to process such information. It may prove difficult to determine what the words 'deliberately' and 'made public' actually mean. Although a data subject who has broadcast information in a television interview can be said to be deliberately making such information public, the same may not be true of a data subject who makes a personal announcement to a gathering of friends under implied conditions of confidence.

6.   The processing is necessary in relation to legal rights

Here the processing must be necessary for one of the following three purposes:

(a)   obtaining legal advice;
(b)   establishing, exercising or defending legal rights; or

(c)   the conduct of any legal proceedings (including prospective legal proceedings).

Most activities of solicitors in carrying out the instructions of their clients will be covered by this condition. So too will be the processing by data controller clients in communicating with their lawyers and in preparing for such communications.

7.   *The processing is necessary—*

   (a)   for the administration of justice,
   (b)   for the exercise of any functions of either House of Parliament,
   (c)   for the exercise of any functions conferred on any person by or under an enactment, or
   (d)   for the exercise of any functions of the Crown, a Minister of the Crown or a government department.

This condition does not appear in the European Data Protection Directive. However, Member States are permitted to make additional conditions where they incorporate 'suitable safeguards' and are in the public interest. It is interesting to note that no such safeguards appear in this condition.

The Secretary of State may exclude the operation of, or attach additional requirements to, this condition as he sees fit. At the date of writing the Secretary of State had not done so.

8.   *The processing is necessary for medical purposes*

For this condition to apply the processing must be undertaken by a 'health professional' or someone who owes a similar duty of confidentiality. Medical purposes is defined fairly widely to include:

   (a)   preventative medicine,
   (b)   medical diagnosis,
   (c)   medical research,
   (d)   the provision of care and treatment,
   (e)   management of healthcare services.

This is not an exhaustive list and therefore other medical purposes could fall within the definition. The Directive's definition of medical purposes did not include 'medical research'. This has been a controversial addition to the Act by the UK government. A health professional is defined as meaning any of the following:

   (a)   a registered medical practitioner;
   (b)   a registered dentist as defined by s. 53(1) of the Dentists Act 1984;
   (c)   a registered optician as defined by s. 36(1) of the Opticians Act 1989;
   (d)   a registered pharmaceutical chemist as defined by s. 24(1) of the Pharmacy Act 1954 or a registered person as defined by art. 2(2) of the Pharmacy (Northern Ireland) Order 1976;
   (e)   a registered nurse, midwife or health visitor;

(f) a registered osteopath as defined by s. 41 of the Osteopaths Act 1993;
(g) a registered chiropractor as defined by s. 43 of the Chiropractors Act 1994;
(h) any person who is registered as a member of a profession to which the Professions Supplementary to Medicine Act 1960 for the time being extends;
(i) a clinical psychologist, child psychotherapist or speech therapist;
(j) a music therapist employed by a health service body; and
(k) a scientist employed by such a body as head of a department.

9. The processing is necessary to trace equality of opportunity between peoples of different racial or ethnic backgrounds

This condition was added by the Commons at the committee stage and relates to the need to do research on, and keep records in relation to, equality of opportunity. It relates only to the first category of sensitive data, i.e., information relating to racial or ethnic origin. The processing must be with a view to the promotion or maintenance of equality of opportunity and there must be appropriate safeguards for the rights and freedoms of data subjects.

The Secretary of State may specify circumstances in which it will be deemed that processing has, or has not, been carried out with appropriate safeguards.

10. Processing in relation to unlawful activities

The processing must be:

(a) in the substantial public interest;
(b) necessary for the purposes of the prevention or detection of any unlawful act or failure to act; and
(c) necessarily carried out without the explicit consent of the data subject being sought so as not to prejudice those purposes.

This condition would cover many types of police processing as well as processing by data controllers who wish to detect or report on criminal activity.

11. Processing necessary for the protection of the public

The processing must be:

(a) in the substantial public interest;
(b) necessary for the discharge of any function which is designed for protecting members of the public against—

(i) dishonesty, malpractice, or other seriously improper conduct by, or in the unfitness or incompetence of, any person, or
(ii) mismanagement in the administration of, or failure in services provided by, any body or association; and

(c) necessarily carried out without the explicit consent of the data subject being sought so as not to prejudice the discharge of that function.

12. *Publications in the public interest*

The disclosure of personal data must be:

(a)   in the substantial public interest;
(b)   in connection with—

(i)   the commission by any person of any unlawful act or failure to act (whether alleged or established),
(ii)   dishonesty, malpractice, or other seriously improper conduct by, or the unfitness or incompetence of, any person (whether alleged or established), or
(iii)   mismanagement in the administration of, or failure in services provided by, any body or association (whether alleged or established), or

(c)   for the purposes of journalism, literature or art; and
(d)   made with a view to the publication of those data by any person, and the data controller reasonably believes that such publication would be in the public interest.

13. *Processing which is necessary for confidential counselling*

The processing must be in the substantial public interest and:

(a)   necessary for the discharge of any function which is designed for the provision of confidential counselling, advice, support or any other service; and
(b)   carried out without the explicit consent of the data subject because the processing—

(i)   is necessary in a case where consent cannot be given by the data subject,
(ii)   is necessary in a case where the data controller cannot reasonably be expected to obtain the explicit consent of the data subject, or
(iii)   must necessarily be carried out without the explicit consent of the data subject being sought so as not to prejudice the provision of that counselling, advice, support or other service.

14. *Insurance and pensions — processing of family data*

The processing must be:

(a)   necessary for the purpose of—

(i)   carrying on insurance business, or
(ii)   making determinations in connection with eligibility for, and benefits payable under, an occupational pension scheme as defined in s. 1 of the Pension Schemes Act 1993,

(b)   of sensitive personal data consisting of information falling within s. 2(e) of the Act relating to a data subject who is the parent, grandparent, great grandparent or sibling of—

(i)   in the case of paragraph (a)(i), the insured person, or

(ii)   in the case of paragraph (a)(ii), the member of the scheme;

(c) necessary in a case where the data controller cannot reasonably be expected to obtain the explicit consent of that data subject and the data controller is not aware of the data subject withholding his consent; and

(d) of a type which does not support measures or decisions with respect to that data subject.

15. *Insurance and pensions — old processing*

The processing must be:

(a) of a sensitive personal data in relation to any particular data subject that was subject to processing already under way immediately before 1 March 2000;

(b) necessary for the purpose of—

(i)   carrying on insurance business, as defined in s. 95 of the Insurance Companies Act 1982, falling within Classes I, III or IV of sch. 1 to that Act; or

(ii)   establishing or administering an occupational pension scheme as defined in s. 1 of the Pension Schemes Act 1993; and

(c) either—

(i)   necessary in a case where the data controller cannot reasonably be expected to obtain the explicit consent of the data subject and that data subject has not informed the data controller that he does not so consent, or

(ii)   necessarily carried out even without the explicit consent of the data subject so as not to prejudice those purposes.

16. *Processing relating to religion and health*

The processing of sensitive personal data consisting of information as to religious beliefs or physical or mental health of the data subject is permissible so long as it is:

(a) necessary for the purpose of identifying or keeping under review the existence or absence of equality or opportunity or treatment between persons—

(i)   holding different religious beliefs, or

(ii)   of different states of physical or mental health or different physical or mental conditions,
with a view to enabling such equality to be promoted or maintained;

(b) of a type which does not support measures or decisions with respect to any particular data subject otherwise than with the explicit consent of that data subject; and

(c) of a type which does not cause, nor is likely to cause, substantial damage or substantial distress to the data subject or any other person.

Where any individual has given notice in writing to any data controller who is processing personal data for the above purposes requiring that data controller to cease processing personal data in respect of which that individual is the data subject at the end of such period as is reasonable in the circumstances, that data controller must have ceased processing those personal data at the end of that period.

17. Processing of political opinions

Sensitive personal data processing consisting of the political opinions of the data subject is permissible if it is:

(a)   carried out by any person or organisation included in the register maintained pursuant to s. 1 of the Registration of Political Parties Act 1998 in the course of his or its legitimate political activities; and

(b)   of a type which does not cause, nor is likely to cause, substantial damage or substantial distress to the data subject or any other person.

Where any individual has given notice in writing to any data controller who is processing such personal data for these purposes requiring that data controller to cease processing personal data in respect of which that individual is the data subject at the end of such period as is reasonable in the circumstances, that data controller must have ceased processing those personal data at the end of that period.

18. Research data

This condition relates to processing which is in the substantial public interest and is necessary for the research purposes (see s. 53) so long as it is:

(a)   of a type which does not support measures or decisions with respect to any particular data subject otherwise than with the explicit consent of that data subject; and

(b)   of a type which does not cause, nor is likely to cause, substantial damage or substantial distress to the data subject or any other person.

19. Police processing

The processing must be necessary for the exercise of any functions conferred on a constable by any rule of law. This condition allows the police to carry out their normal functions in connection with the detection of crime. The most obvious type of sensitive data that will be used in this context is previous criminal convictions and suspected criminal activity. However, the condition is not limited to processing which appears in the final category of sensitive data. The police are therefore able to process data relating to other aspects of the definition, such as the physical or mental condition of data subjects and their religious beliefs — useful in the cases of drug addicts or suicide risks.

ADVICE TO DATA CONTROLLERS

Data controllers should undertake a thorough audit of their data processing activities to determine whether any sensitive data processing is carried on. Where such processing has been carried on by a data controller before 24 October 1998, the transitional provisions may operate to allow its continuation until 23 October 2001 — procedures should be adopted which ensure compliance from that date. In all other cases the processing must immediately cease unless it complies with one of the 19 conditions above.

Care should be taken to ensure that all processing or potential processing of sensitive personal data is fully investigated. Although, for example, an application or registration form used by a data controller in his business for gathering customer details does not expressly request sensitive data, such data may nevertheless be supplied by the customer when completing the form. Appropriate procedures should be adopted to ensure that sensitive data are not processed by the data controller, i.e., that such information is ignored by the keyboard operators when inputting the data into the system.

Where the processing of sensitive personal data is an essential part of the data controller's activities, the 19 conditions should be checked to see if any will legitimise the processing. If none currently apply, consideration should be given to whether the processing can be brought within the remit of any of the conditions. If not, the data subject should be requested to give explicit consent to the processing. It should be remembered that explicit consent could never exist where the data subject is merely informed of the processing — some positive activity on the part of the data subject is required. Ideally the data controller should obtain the signature of the data subject. Use of a tick-box arrangement will be a suitable alternative in most cases. Data controllers should remember that they might be expected to provide proof of explicit consent (where this condition is relied on) at some future stage.

Chapter 6
Data Exports

INTRODUCTION

The globalisation of electronic communications and the rapid growth of the Internet has made the transfer of personal data abroad both extremely easy and of great potential value. Data may be exported in a variety of ways and for a number of purposes, the following of which are merely examples:

(a)   A multinational organisation based in the United States with offices in the UK and other European Union (EU) countries maintains a computer network which connects all its sites. Considerable quantities of data (including personal data) are regularly transferred across various points on the network.

(b)   A UK company engages in cross-border list rental. Lists of customers or marketing data are transferred to organisations abroad.

(c)   A UK company's entire personal data stock is transferred to Switzerland as a result of the purchase of the company by a Swiss organisation.

(d)   The forwarding of an e-mail by a person in the UK to a person in Hong Kong (the e-mail will contain, at the very least, personal data in the form of the e-mail addresses of the sender and the person from whom the sender received the e-mail).

(e)   The transfer to India of manual (paper-based) personal data for the purpose of such data being entered into a computer database before being returned to the UK.

In none of these cases is it entirely clear that the activity concerned can be carried out lawfully under the legislation. The Data Protection Act 1984 regime did not restrict the export of personal data from the UK. It merely required the transferee to register an intention to make such transfers. The position under the Data Protection Act 1998 is radically different: *all* exports of personal data to non-European Economic Area countries (referred to in this chapter as 'third countries') are prima facie *illegal* unless the country of the transferee ensures an adequate level of protection for the rights and freedoms of data subjects.

There are a number of exemptions from this restriction whereby personal data may be transferred without breaching the Eighth Principle, as set out in sch. 4 to the 1998 Act. The most significant involves obtaining the consent of the data subject for the relevant export, but each of the exemptions will be considered in detail below.

This chapter considers the Eighth Principle, its implications and the methods and practices that might be employed to satisfy its provisions. It also considers the transitional provisions of the Act which bestow immunity from the effects of the Eighth Principle for certain data exports until 23 October 2001. Consideration is given to certain arrangements that exist between the EU and third countries to allow the international flow of personal data to remain within the law — the best-known being the 'safe harbor' principles developed jointly by the United States and the EU.

THE BAN ON DATA EXPORTS

In an attempt to ensure the security of personal data and the privacy of the individual citizen of the EU in a global context, the European Data Protection Directive on which the 1998 Act is based introduced a measure which effectively encourages third countries to adopt data protection measures similar to those of the EU. The Eighth Data Protection Principle provides:

> Personal data shall not be transferred to a country or territory outside the European Economic Area unless that country or territory ensures an adequate level of protection for the rights and freedoms of data subjects in relation to the processing of personal data.

One of the first considerations is whether or not any given transmission of data abroad amounts to a 'transfer' within the meaning of the Act. There are two factors which are particularly relevant in determining whether such a transmission constitutes a transfer for those purposes:

(a)   whether the country of the transferee of personal data is outside the European Economic Area (EEA); and
(b)   whether the transmission in question actually amounts to a transfer.

The first factor is considerably more capable of precise definition than the second. The list of countries forming part of the EEA is continually expanding. At the time of writing the current members of the EEA are those shown in the box below.

Members of the European Economic Area		
Austria	Belgium	Denmark
Finland	France	Germany
Greece	Iceland*	Ireland
Italy	Liechtenstein*	Luxembourg
Netherlands	Norway*	Portugal
Spain	Sweden	UK
* Non-EU Members		

Data transfer

Determining precisely what will and will not amount to a data transfer is crucial for the purposes of determining whether any particular transmission of personal data is prohibited by the Eighth Principle. Although the Data Protection Bill, upon which the 1998 Act is based, included a (very wide) definition of what would amount to a transfer, no definition of the term appears in either the Directive or the 1998 Act. The Commissioner has stated, as an interim definition, that in the absence of a legislative definition, 'transfer' should have its ordinary meaning, i.e. 'to convey from one place, person, ownership, object, group, etc., to another'. It is fairly clear, on the basis of this definition, that in each of the five numbered examples at the beginning of this chapter there is a transfer of personal data. But there are circumstances where it may be less easy to make such a determination. Consider the following scenario.

Example

A businessperson proposes to take his laptop computer on business abroad with him. The computer has personal data on its hard disk. During his trip he intends to visit three third countries where he will process personal data both in his hotel bedrooms and at meetings, hooking-up to his company's computer network in the UK at various times to obtain up-to-date personal information (including personal data) and generally to communicate with the office.

This example was considered by the Commissioner in a paper which looked at the adequacy of a third country's data protection measures. But it is useful to take a step back and look at it from the point of view of data transfer. At what point, if at all, can the transfer be said to take place? Is it when the businessperson lands at the airport of the third country? Or when he first uses the laptop? Or is it only when he receives personal data from the UK down the telephone line? It could be argued that the data on the laptop are not being transferred to a third country at all, as they remain in the possession and control of the businessperson at all times — there is no transmission from one person to another. However, this latter argument seems to fly in the face of the intention of the Act, which is to ensure, by legislative means, the safety and security of personal data. At the time of writing there is no clear answer to these questions. Data controllers are therefore advised to take a cautious approach until the matter is adequately resolved.

Transfer or transit?

A distinction must be drawn between 'transfer' and 'transit'. Personal data are not transferred to a country merely by virtue of being sent there *'en route'* to another country. The fact that an electronic transfer of data to an EEA country may be routed through a third country does not bring the transfer within the provisions of the Eighth Principle. Any substantive processing of the personal data in a third country will, however, make such a country a country of transfer and the Eighth Principle will be applicable.

Example

In the electronic transfer of employee data from Company A in the UK to Company B in Germany, the data is sent via a routing which includes a telecommunications network in Switzerland (a non-EEA state). Here the transfer has been made between two countries of the EEA and thus the Eighth Principle is irrelevant — the data was merely in transit when present in Switzerland.

It seems that data controllers would be best advised to adopt a cautious approach on the question of what constitutes a transfer until a definitive statement has been made by the Commissioner or the court has made a relevant ruling.

ADEQUATE LEVEL OF PROTECTION

Once it has been determined that the data controller is transferring personal data abroad, the next question to consider is whether there is an 'adequate level of protection for the rights and freedoms of data subjects'. A transfer of personal data to any non-EEA country is unlawful unless that country has an 'adequate level of protection' for the rights and freedoms of data subjects. Essentially the question that should be asked is: 'Does the country of the transferee have in place a system of data protection that is equivalent to the protection afforded to individuals by the EU Directive?'

It is important to bear in mind that the duty to make the determination of adequacy is on the data controller who is exporting the data (the 'exporting controller'). There should, therefore, be evidence of a rational decision-making process undertaken by the exporting controller in relation to each transfer or set of transfers.

Guiding factors

Schedule 1 to the 1998 Act contains some guiding factors that should be considered when determining adequacy.

- *The nature of the personal data*

  If the data to be exported are sensitive personal data, the requirement of adequacy to protect the rights and freedoms of data subjects in relation to such data is less likely to be satisfied. On the other hand, where the data are not sensitive it will be easier to show that the, albeit possibly limited, data protection regime in the third country is adequate. Where the data are widely available in the public domain, e.g., names of famous actors, the transfer to the third country is unlikely to hinder any relevant rights.

- *The country or territory of origin of the information contained in the data*

  Where the origin of the data, as opposed to the origin of the transfer of the data, is a country of poor data protection standards, the corresponding transfer to a similar country is more likely to be acceptable, as it will not be necessary to put the data subject in a better position than he would have been in if there had never been a transfer abroad of his personal data.

- *The country or territory of final destination of the data*

  The final destination of the data may be a different location than the place of initial transfer. It is the data protection regime of the country of the initial transferee that is centrally relevant to the adequacy test. But it may be known that the data will be likely to be transferred to a new country from the third country. Such a country may have a poor data protection regime.

- *The purposes for which, and period during which, the data are intended to be processed*

  The purposes of transfer and the duration of the intended processing are factors that should be considered by the data controller in assessing adequacy. The longer the processing period the more likely that deficiencies in the system will expose the data to risks.

- *The law in force in the country or territory in question*

  A determination must be made as to the adequacy of the data protection laws in the country where the transferee resides.

- *The international obligations of that country or territory*

  The question to be considered here is whether the country where the transferee resides is bound by any relevant treaties or other similar obligations in respect of the processing of personal data. If so, an analysis of the relevant provisions should be undertaken.

- *Any relevant codes of conduct or other rules which are enforceable in that country or territory (whether generally or by arrangement in particular cases)*

  What codes of conduct on data protection are in force in the country where the transferee resides? Are those codes of general application, or are they industry- or sector-specific? For further detail on the relevance of self-regulatory regimes, see below.

- *Any security measures taken in respect of the data in that country or territory*

  Encryption techniques and appropriate information security practices should be employed to ensure that data are unlikely to be subject to third-party access. It has been suggested that compliance with British Standard BS 7799 will give a presumption of such protection.

It should be remembered that the above list of factors is not exhaustive. A data controller should consider other factors that may be relevant as well as any specific advice or guidance issued by the Data Protection Commissioner (whether general or sector-specific) from time to time. One further factor that may be relevant is the type of transfer. If data are being transferred merely for the purpose of processing by a data processor then there may be less concern for the rights and freedoms of the relevant data subjects.

'Safe' countries

On the basis of the above tests, the Commissioner has made a preliminary determination that in all likelihood, and at the date of going to press, the following countries or territories will be regarded as 'safe' for data exports:

- (a) Hong Kong;
- (b) New Zealand;
- (c) Quebec;
- (d) Switzerland; and
- (e) Hungary.

ADEQUACY

EU guidance

There has been much speculation that the EU Commission will produce a list of countries that provide an adequate level of protection for the rights and freedoms of data subjects. Such a list (likely to be known as a 'white list') would free data controllers from the need to make a determination as to adequacy in respect of each transfer undertaken. At the time of writing, such a list was imminent. Exporting controllers should check the Commissioner's website (see Appendix 6) for updates on the white list.

However, even after a white list has been produced, exporting controllers may still be under a duty to make some determination in respect of data exports. The EU Data Protection Working Party, set up under the Directive to consider data protection issues (see art. 29 of Directive 95/46/EC), has indicated that the inclusion of a country on a white list may not justify *all types* of data processing in that country. Those categories of processing that would give rise to further compliance issues were expressed to be the following.

(a) *Sensitive data* — the processing of sensitive personal data (see definition in Chapter 2) may require additional safeguards. In particular, the data subject's consent to the processing of sensitive personal data abroad may be required.

(b) *Direct marketing* — a data subject should be able to prevent personal data being transferred abroad for this purpose.

(c) *Automated decision-taking* — where one of the purposes of data export is the taking of evaluation decisions concerning the data subject by automated means, the individual should have the right to know the logic involved in such a decision-making process.

It will be noted that these three categories form the rights conferred on data subjects generally by the 1998 Act — see Chapter 2 for further detail.

The third country's legal regime

It may be that the data protection laws of a third country do provide an adequate level of protection for the rights and freedoms of data subjects in relation to the particular type of data export that is contemplated. It is recognised that it may be difficult for many exporting controllers, particularly those with limited resources, to make a detailed determination of a third party's legal regime. The Commission has stated that an exporting controller should at least be aware of the degree to which an analysis of the third party's legal structure is appropriate. In many cases the extent of examination required will depend upon the type of export contemplated. It is suggested that the extent of a data controller's resources should also be relevant. Where a UK company proposes to set up a subsidiary or branch in a third country for the purposes of transferring to it all its data processing operations, it may be necessary for that company to undertake a detailed analysis of the data protection regime in place in that country.

The EU's Data Protection Working Party has suggested the following approach to assess adequacy of third countries' legal regimes based on certain 'Content Principles' and 'Procedural/Enforcement Requirements'.

Content principles

The basic principles to be included are the following.

1.   The purpose limitation principle

Data should be processed for a specific purpose and subsequently used or further communicated only insofar as this is not incompatible with the purpose of the transfer. The only exemptions to this rule would be those necessary in a democratic society on one of the grounds listed in art. 13 of the Directive (broadly comparable with a number of the primary exemptions and miscellaneous exemptions in the Act — see Chapter 9).

2.   The data quality and proportionality principle

Data should be accurate and, where necessary, kept up to date. The data should be adequate, relevant and not excessive in relation to the purposes for which they are transferred or further processed.

3.   The transparency principle

Individuals should be provided with information as to the purpose of the processing and the identity of the data controller in the third country, and other information insofar as this is necessary to ensure fairness. The only exemptions permitted should be in line with art. 11(2) of the Directive (comparable with the exceptions from the provision of the 'fair processing information' in accordance with the 'fair processing code' in the Act).

4.   The security principle

Technical and organisational security measures should be taken by the data controller which are appropriate to the risks presented by the processing. Any person acting under the authority of the data controller, including a processor, must not process data except on instructions from the controller.

5.   The rights of access, rectification and opposition

Data subjects should have the right to obtain a copy of all data relating to them that are processed, and a right to rectification of those data where they are shown to be inaccurate. In certain situations they should also be able to object to the processing of the data relating to them. The only exemptions to these rights should be in line with art. 13 of the Directive (which deals with matters such as national security, defence and public security).

6.   Restrictions on onward transfers

Further transfers of personal data by the recipient of the original data transfer should be permitted only where the second recipient (i.e. the recipient of the onward transfer) is also subject to rules affording an adequate level of protection. The only exceptions permitted should be in line with art. 26(1) of the Directive.

Examples of additional principles to be applied to specific types of processing are:

(a) *Sensitive data* — Where 'sensitive' categories of data are involved (those listed in art. 8 of the Directive) additional safeguards should be in place, such as a requirement that the data subject give explicit consent to the processing.

(b) *Direct marketing* — Where data are transferred for the purposes of direct marketing, the data subject should be able to 'opt out' from having the data used for such purposes at any stage.

(c) *Automated individual decision* — Where the purposes of the transfer is the taking of an automated decision in the sense of art. 15 of the Directive (which has its equivalent in s. 12 of the Act), the individual should have the right to know the logic involved in this decision, and other measures should be taken to safeguard the individual's legitimate interest.

Procedural and enforcement requirements

Essentially a data protection regime should:

(a) *Ensure a good level of compliance with its rules.* A good system is generally characterised by a high degree of awareness among data controllers of their obligations, and among data subjects of their rights and means of exercising them. The existence of effectiveness and dissuasive sanctions can play an important part in ensuring respect for rules, as of course can systems of direct verification by authorities, or independent data protection officials.

(b) *Provide support and help to individual data subjects in the exercise of their rights.* The individual must be able to enforce his rights rapidly and effectively without prohibitive cost. To do so there must be some sort of institutional mechanism allowing independent investigation of complaints.

(c) *Provide appropriate redress to the injured party where rules are not complied with.* This is a key element which must involve a system of independent adjudication or arbitration which allows compensation to be paid and sanctions imposed where appropriate.

Self-regulatory regimes

As indicated above, one of the interpretation provisions contained in sch. 1 to the Act states that, in determining the adequacy of a third country for data transfers, regard is to be had to 'any relevant codes of conduct or other rules which are enforceable in that country or territory'. In other words the possibility of a third country providing an adequate level of protection is not destroyed merely by virtue of its lack of data protection legislation: non-legal rules may be sufficient to satisfy the Eighth Principle, as set out in sch. 1 to the Act.

Codes of practice are becoming increasingly common in specific industry sectors. It is one way that commerce has chosen to show that it is responsible generally for ensuring compliance with minimum standards (cynics would add that it has the added benefit of warding off legislation in the field in question). The UK, for example, has many such codes of conduct, some of which enjoy virtually quasi-legal status. Examples include the Programme Code, issued by the Independent Television Commission, and the various codes of practice issued by the Securities and Futures Authority.

The mere existence of a self-regulatory set of rules in a third country, whether of general application or sector-specific, will not however be enough to satisfy the adequacy hurdle *per se*. What is of central importance is the issues of compliance with, and enforceability of, such a code. The EU Working Party has suggested asking the following questions when evaluating self-regulatory codes for adequacy purposes.

(a)   Does the code contain rules which ensure compliance with the following key factors that are central to the EU data protection regime?

       (i)   The data should be processed for a specific purpose and not subsequently used in a way incompatible with that purpose (*the purpose limitation principle*).
       (ii)   The data should be adequate, relevant and not excessive for its purpose (*the proportionality principle*).
       (iii)   The data should be accurate and kept up to date (*the data quality principle*).
       (iv)   Insofar as it is necessary to ensure fairness, individuals should be provided with information as to the purpose of the processing and the identity of the data controller (*the transparency principle*).
       (v)   Appropriate measures are taken to ensure the security of the data (*the security principle*).
       (vi)   The data subject should be able to obtain a copy of personal data relating to him and insist on rectification where it is inaccurate.

(b)   Is the code in plain language?
(c)   Does it prevent disclosure of data to persons who are not governed by the code?
(d)   Does the code apply to a whole industry as opposed to small groupings of companies within a sector (the latter could be confusing to individuals in terms of application)?
(e)   Is the code effective in ensuring compliance with its rules? Further factors to determine here include:

       (i)   the method of publication of the code;
       (ii)   whether the code is voluntary or compulsory;
       (iii)   whether there are any auditing arrangements; and
       (iv)   the ramifications of non-compliance (merely remedial, as opposed to punitive sanctions, are unlikely to be enough).

(f)   Is there an effective method for dealing with data subject complaints?
(g)   Will the data subject be entitled to redress/compensation?

THE 'SAFE HARBOR' PRINCIPLES

By the very nature of its constitution and the absence of data protection laws, the legal system of the United States cannot be said to provide an adequate level of protection for the rights and freedoms of data subjects. The Eighth Data Protection Principle effectively brings certain aspects of international trade and e-commerce between the EU and the US to a standstill. This potentially disastrous scenario led to the commencement of high-level discussions and negotiations between the US

Department of Commerce and the Directorate General XV of the European Commission in early 1998.

The 'Safe Harbor' Principles, a self-imposed regime in the US to satisfy the requirements of EU law, were approved by all EU Member States and by the Commission in June 2000. However, the Principles were blocked by the Parliament in July 2000. Under art. 25(6) of the Directive, the EU Commission is empowered to make a finding that a third-party country ensure an adequate level of protection by virtue solely of an international commitment that it has entered into. It was hoped, and it is anticipated (following the objections of the Parliament being resolved), that the Safe Harbor Principles willo be the first such finding.

It should be noted that the Safe Harbor Principles will apply solely to US–EU data transfers and that compliance with the principles by US companies is entirely voluntary. By undertaking to comply with the Principles a US company may receive imports of personal data from the EU. There are currently seven such principles under discussion.

1. Notice

An organisation must inform individuals what types of personal information it collects about them and how it collects that information. The organisation must also disclose the purposes for which it collects such information, the types of organisations to which it discloses the information, and the choices and means by which the organisation offers individuals for limiting its use and disclosure. The notice must be provided in clear and conspicuous language that is readily understood and made available when individuals are first asked to provide personal information to the organisation.

2. Choice

An organisation must give individuals the opportunity to choose (by opting out) whether and how personal information they provide is used (where such use is unrelated to the use(s) for which they originally disclosed it). Individuals must be provided with clear and conspicuous, readily available, and affordable mechanisms to exercise this option. For certain kinds of sensitive information, such as medical information, they must be given affirmative or explicit (opt-in) choice.

3. Onward transfer

Individuals must be given the opportunity to choose whether and the manner in which a third party uses the personal information they provide (when such use is unrelated to the use(s) for which the individual originally disclosed it). When transferring personal information to third parties, an organisation must require that third parties provide at least the same level of privacy protection as originally chosen by the individual. For certain kinds of sensitive information, such as medical information, individuals must be given an opt-in choice.

4. Security

Organisations creating, maintaining, using or disseminating records of personal information must take reasonable measures to assure its reliability for its intended use and must take reasonable precautions to protect the data from loss, misuse, unauthorised access or disclosure, alteration, or destruction.

5. Data integrity

An organisation must only keep personal data that are relevant for the purposes for which it has been gathered, consistent with the principles of notice and choice. To the extent necessary for those purposes, the data should be accurate, complete, and current.

6. Access

Individuals must have reasonable access to information about them derived from non-public records that an organisation holds and be able to correct or amend that information where it is inaccurate. Reasonableness of access depends on the nature and sensitivity of the information collected and its intended uses. For instance, access must be provided to an individual where the information in question is sensitive or used for substantive decision-making purposes that affect that individual.

7. Enforcement

Effective privacy protection must include mechanisms for assuring compliance with the principles, recourse for individuals, and consequences for the organisation when the principles are not followed. At a minimum, such mechanisms must include (a) readily available and affordable independent recourse mechanisms by which individuals' complaints and disputes can be resolved; (b) systems for verifying that the attestations and assertions businesses make about their privacy practices are true and privacy practices have been implemented as presented; and (c) obligations to remedy problems arising out of and consequences for organisations announcing adoption of these principles. Sanctions must be sufficient to ensure compliance by organisations and must provide individuals the means for enforcement.

THE GOOD PRACTICE APPROACH

The Commissioner has issued a summary of the steps to be taken by 'exporting controllers' (data controllers proposing to transfer personal data to a third country) so as to achieve a consistency of approach to any assessment of adequacy — see the following box.

The 'Good Practice Approach'

1. Consider whether (or the extent to which) the third country in question is the subject of a Community finding or a presumption of adequacy.
2. Consider the type of transfer involved and whether this enables any presumption of adequacy (for example, in the case of controllers, to processor transfers to be made).
3. Consider and apply the 'adequacy test', including consideration of the application and use of contracts and/or codes of conduct to create adequacy.
4. Where there is no adequacy, or where there is doubt in this respect, look to the derogations contained in sch. 4 to the Act, pursuant to which the transfer may proceed if they are satisfied.

The first step of the Commissioner's suggested approach involves consideration of any available 'white list'. The second and third steps could be regarded as different aspects of the same question and, in any event, the use of contractual provisions to achieve adequacy is something that is of greater relevance to the so-called derogations in the fourth step. The fourth step itself is not necessarily concerned with the 'adequacy' of anything because the exemptions contained in sch. 4 to the Act apply whether or not any data export achieves an adequate level of protection for the rights and freedoms of the data subjects.

THE EXEMPTIONS

Schedule 4 to the Act contains a list of nine circumstances (see box below) whereby the Eighth Data Protection Principle will be excluded from application. In other words, compliance with one of the conditions effectively legitimises the transfer to a third country.

Schedule 4 Exemptions

1. The data subject has given consent to the transfer.
2. The transfer is necessary:
(a) for the performance of a contract between the data subject and the data controller, or
(b) for the taking of steps at the request of the data subject with a view to his entering into a contract with the data controller.
3. The transfer is necessary:
(a) for the conclusion of a contract between the data controller and a person other than the data subject which:
    (i)   is entered into at the request of the data subject, or
    (ii) is in the interests of the data subject, or
(b) for the performance of such a contract.
4. The transfer is necessary for reasons of substantial public interest.
5. The transfer:
(a) is necessary for the purpose of, or in connection with, any legal proceedings (including prospective legal proceedings),
(b) is necessary for the purpose of obtaining legal advice, or
(c) is otherwise necessary for the purposes of establishing, exercising or defending legal rights.
6. The transfer is necessary in order to protect the vital interests of the data subject.
7. The transfer of part of the personal data on a public register and any conditions subject to which the register is open to inspection are complied with by any person to whom the data are or may be disclosed after the transfer.
8. The transfer is made on terms which are of a kind approved by the Commissioner as ensuring adequate safeguards for the rights and freedoms of data subjects.
9. The transfer has been authorised by the Commissioner as being made in such a manner as to ensure adequate safeguards for the rights and freedoms of data subjects.

Some of these exemptions, save the last two (which are discussed below), have been dealt with elsewhere in this book. Conditions one, two and six are discussed in Chapter 4. Condition five has been looked at in Chapter 5. Although those chapters dealt with exemptions for different purposes, the wording of the exemptions is identical and there is no reason to believe that there would be any variation in terms of application.

The third condition refers to it being necessary to transfer the data abroad due to a contract which exists with the data subject or in the interest of the data subject. Use of the word 'necessary' restricts what might otherwise be regarded as a wide exception. The words 'necessary' and 'substantial' appear in the fourth condition — transfers which are necessary for reasons of substantial public interest are likely to extend beyond transfers of data concerning international tax dodgers. The seventh condition relates to public registers and legitimises transfers of personal data to third countries where the personal data concerned are available within a Member State in a public register. Such a provision prevents the need for the enquirer to travel to the UK to obtain information which is publicly available here.

Contractual provisions

The eighth condition refers to transfers of a kind which have been approved by the Data Protection Commissioner for the purposes of the Eighth Data Protection Principle. It is widely expected that the Commissioner will authorise draft contract terms, but at the time of writing none were in existence. The Commissioner's website should be monitored for any such publication in the future (see Appendix 6).

Both the International Chamber of Commerce and the Confederation of British Industry are currently working on drafts of model contract terms which are widely expected to legitimise transfers of personal data for the purposes of the Eighth Data Protection Principle.

Approval by the Commissioner

The final condition provides that the data may be transferred to a third country where such transfer is specifically approved by the Commissioner. Use of this condition would necessitate the data controller applying for permission to send data abroad. The Commissioner has stated that she wishes to discourage such applications.

CAN I SEND PERSONAL DATA ABROAD?

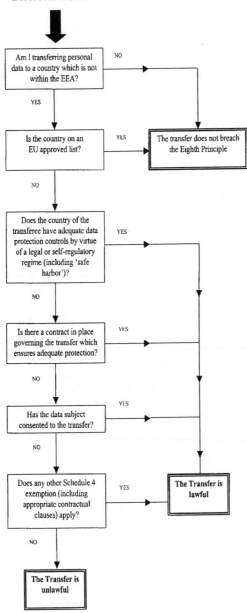

Chapter 7
Manual Data

INTRODUCTION

For the first time in English law, the Data Protection Act 1998 applied the data protection legal regime to paper-based records. Prior to this it was common to advise persons who did not want others to gain access to their records (e.g., journalists making notes about the sleeping habits of politicians) to write them down on paper instead of typing them into a computer. The 1998 Act applies only to certain types of paper-based records (those recorded as part of a relevant filing system or forming part of an accessible record). However, the definition of 'relevant filing system' covers any records that are 'structured' for ease of reference and it is therefore likely that any manual data falling outside of these provisions are virtually useless to their owner in any event.

The transitional provisions of the legislation give exemption for manual data processing from significant requirements of the Act (for example, compliance with the Data Protection Principles and subject's access rights) until 23 October 2001, and from a smaller set of requirements until 23 October 2007. Whilst this constitutes a limited reprieve for those who keep paper-based records, data controllers should be advised to urgently put in place procedures for dealing with manual data so as to be ready for October 2001. It should be remembered that there is no exemption for manual data forming part of a relevant filing system that was not in place prior to 24 October 1998.

WHAT IS MANUAL DATA?

The 1998 Act's definition of 'data' includes information which 'is recorded as part of a relevant filing system or with the intention that it should form part of a relevant filing system'. There is no requirement that such data be processed automatically and hence it is this part of the definition of data that extends to manual processing. Relevant filing system is defined as meaning:

> any set of information relating to individuals to the extent that, although the information is not processed by means of equipment operating automatically in response to instructions given for that purpose, the set is structured either by reference to individuals or by reference to criteria relating to individuals, in such

a way that specific information relating to a particular individual is readily accessible.

Thus, not only will information in a filing system itself amount to data (and hence personal data when it relates to an individual), but so too will any written or manually typed document that is intended to be included in such a system from the moment it is created.

There is considerable controversy over precisely what is included within this definition. It seems that the key characteristics of a relevant filing system are the structuring by reference to individuals and/or the ready accessibility of specific information. Recital (27) of the European Data Protection Directive states that 'files or sets of files as well as their cover pages, which are not structured according to specific criteria, shall under no circumstances fall within the scope of this Directive'.

Concern about the impact of extending data protection legislation to manual data has been expressed most vociferously in the field of employment. A set of manual personnel files, each relating individually to a specific employee, could well fall within the definition. So too could a card-index filing system. However, the Government has expressed some concern over the impact of the new legislation on small- to medium-sized enterprises, particularly in light of the fact that the most likely manual files that such enterprises hold are personnel files. It could be argued that a personnel file in which everything is inserted merely in date order will not be structured in such a way that the internal contents of the files will be readily accessible and hence will not fall within the definition of manual data. Such files would therefore not be caught by the Act. On the other hand, where personnel files contain pro formas or internal structuring so that there is, for example, a section for attendance at work, a section for training courses taken and a section for professional qualifications gained, this will be a file which contains an internal structure that renders the information readily accessible.

A single ring binder containing an individual's personal data may not be a structured file, and therefore would not form part of a relevant filing system. It is unlikely that an unstructured collection of papers which only incidentally contain personal data would be caught by the provisions. If manually recorded data do not form part of a relevant filing system then there is no need to comply with any of the provisions in the Act so far as those data are concerned.

RECOMMENDED ACTION

Data controllers should immediately put in place a procedure to locate and identify all manual data to which the Act applies. An audit should be undertaken of all paper-based folders, card index systems, 'rolladex' systems, ring binders and notebooks. Where such storage media potentially fall within the definition of a relevant filing system, they should be catalogued by reference to the date that each database came into existence and the type of personal data they contain. It would be helpful, for the purposes of the second transitional period (see below), to identify also the date that each new piece of information was inserted in the record.

By taking the above action, data controllers will be in a better position to comply with subject access requests after 24 October 2001. It should be remembered that any 'new' manual data processing after 24 October 1998 may need to be disclosed to the data subjects making access requests even before the end of the first transitional period. Further, data controllers will be obliged to make appropriate data disclosure to data subjects whether or not their manual data processing has been notified to the Commissioner (see below).

NOTIFICATION REQUIREMENTS

There is no compulsory requirement to notify manual data processing to the Data Protection Commissioner.

Voluntary notification

By virtue of s. 18(1) of the Act, it is possible for a data controller who processes manual data to choose to make a notification where he is exempt from such a requirement. This is true whether or not the data controller additionally processes automated data. Voluntary notification is likely to be attractive to those data controllers who do not wish to comply with the disclosure requirements imposed upon non-registered data controllers by virtue of s. 24 (see below).

SUBJECT ACCESS REQUESTS

A data controller is under the same duty to make information available to data subjects in respect of notified manual processing as he is in relation to automated processing (for further detail see Chapter 7). Non-notified manual processing is, however, subject to a different regime.

Section 24 of the Act makes it a criminal offence, following written application by a data subject, to fail to make certain information available to a data subject about non-notified manual processing. Further, such information must be made available free of charge and within 21 days of the request. The information that must be made available is:

(a)   the data controller's name and address,

(b)   if the data controller has nominated a representative for the purposes of this act, the name and address of the representative,

(c)   a description of the personal data being or to be processed by or on behalf of the data controller and of the category or categories of data subject to which they relate,

(d)   a description of the purpose or purposes for which the data are being or are to be processed,

(e)   a description of any recipient or recipients to whom the data controller intends or may wish to disclose the data, and

(f)   the names, or a description of, any countries or territories outside the European Economic Area to which the data controller directly or indirectly transfers, or intends or may wish directly or indirectly to transfer, the data.

For further details on the meaning of these provisions, see Chapter 8.

Example

Rock and Roll Dance Clubs plc keep a record of their membership in a paper-based filing system. Each new member of the dance club fills in a form and these forms are stored in alphabetical order by surname of members. Rock and Roll have not yet notified their manual processing to the Data Protection Commissioner. James Alexander, one of the members, sends an e-mail to Rock and Roll requesting data protection disclosure. Rock and Roll must send James a list of the information they hold on him and must do so within 21 days and without charge.

Data controllers do not have to comply with a s. 24 request in respect of *eligible* manual data until 24 October 2001. Eligible manual data are those manual data which were subject to processing that was already under way immediately before 24 October 1998 (see below).

TRANSITIONAL PROVISIONS

Eligible manual data

Manual data processing which was already under way immediately before 24 October 1998 (eligible manual data) benefits from certain exemptions in both the first and second transitional periods (to benefit during the latter period the relevant data must additionally have been 'held' immediately before 24 October 1998). The table below sets out the exemptions for eligible manual data other than those forming part of an accessible record or where the data controller is a credit reference agency.

Eligible Manual Data	
First Transitional Period	**Second Transitional Period**
(1 March 2000 – 23 October 2001)	(24 October 2001 – 23 October 2007)
	NB: the relevant data must have been *held* immediately before 24 October 1998.
• The Data Protection Principles • Subject access rights • Right to prevent processing • Right to rectification, blocking, erasure and destruction • Notification requirements	• The First Data Protection Principle (except to the extent that it requires the data subject to have access to the information requirements) • Second Data Protection Principle • Third Data Protection Principle • Fourth Data Protection Principle • Fifth Data Protection Principle • Rights to rectification, blocking, erasure and destruction

Accessible records

Eligible manual data forming part of an accessible record whether or not processing was already under way on 24 October 1998 are exempt from the following provisions during the first transitional period:

    (a)   the Data Protection Principles, except the Sixth Principle so far as relating to ss. 7 and 12A,
    (b)   Part II of the Act, except ss. 7, 12A and 15,
    (c)   Part III of the Act.

Accessible records are defined in s. 68 of the Act as meaning 'health records', 'educational records' and 'accessible public records' (the latter being defined in sch. 12 as including certain records relating to social work and local authority housing).

Credit reference agencies

Eligible manual data which consists of information relevant to the financial standing of the data subject and in respect of which the data controller is a credit reference agency (see definition in Chapter 2) are exempt from the following provisions during the first transitional period:

    (a)   the Data Protection Principles, except for the Sixth Principle so far as relating to ss. 7 and 12A;
    (b)   Part II of the Act, except ss. 7, 12A and 15;
    (c)   Part III of the Act.

Chapter 8
Notification

INTRODUCTION

One notable feature of the UK's data protection regime is that data controllers must inform the national data protection authority of their data processing. The registration procedure for controllers of personal data under the Data Protection Act 1998, is however, slightly less formal and complex than that under the 1984 Act. The new regime requires a data controller to provide certain information to the Commissioner together with a fee (£35 at time of writing). The information may be supplied by telephone or via the Internet. The Commissioner will then 'enter' that information on a register. The purpose of notification is to ensure easy access by individuals to information about the data controllers who process personal data (data processors do not need to notify).

'Notification' replaces the 1984 Act 'Application for Registration' to reflect the fact that the data controller is no longer applying for permission to be included on the register but is simply informing the Commissioner of his processing. This is because entry on the register can no longer be refused.

Subject to certain exceptions, the processing of personal data without notification is a criminal offence. Article 18(1) of the European Data Protection Directive provides that:

> Member States shall provide that the [data] controller or his representative, if any, notify the supervisory authority before carrying out any wholly or partly automatic processing operation or set of such operations intended to serve a single purpose or several related purposes.

Individuals who process personal data for personal, family or household affairs are exempt from notification (and all other provisions of the 1998 Act). Other types of processing may benefit from one of the exemptions from notification (discussed below) but data controllers undertaking such processing must remember that they are obliged to comply with the remaining provisions of the Act.

A data controller who has registered its processing with the Data Protection Registrar under the provisions of the 1984 Act need not notify under the new Act until the expiry of the existing registration (for further detail see below under 'Effect of 1984 Act Registration').

The detailed requirements of notification and the exemptions therefrom can be found in the Data Protection (Notification and Notification Fees) Regulations 2000 — see Appendix 3.

PROHIBITION ON PROCESSING WITHOUT NOTIFICATION

Generally speaking, data controllers must not process personal data unless such processing has been notified to the Commissioner. To be more precise, s. 17(1) of the Act provides that the processing of personal data will be unlawful (and under s. 21(1), a criminal offence) if all of the following apply:

(a)   an entry in the register maintained by the Commissioner has not been made,

(b)   the notification regulations (if any) relating to deemed registration do not apply,

(c)   notification regulations giving exemption from the need for notification do not apply, and

(d)   it is not the case that the sole purpose of the processing is the maintenance of a public register.

However, the prohibition in s. 17 applies only to personal data which consist of information falling within the first two paragraphs of the definition of 'data' (i.e., being or intended to be automatically processed). Processing of personal data without notification is therefore lawful (unless it is 'assessable processing' — see below) where it consists of information which:

(a)   is recorded as part of a relevant filing system (manual data); or

(b)   forms part of an accessible record (see definition in Chapter 2).

Therefore, the processing of manual records (or accessible records), even if they fall within the definition of data in the new Act, is not subject to notification to the Commissioner. Voluntary notification under s. 18 is possible for processors of manual data (see below).

Where voluntary notification does not take place, the data controller is subject to the disclosure provisions in s. 24 — see 'Duty of disclosure' below.

A data controller who both manually and automatically processes personal data will need to notify in respect of the automatically processed data and may do so in respect of the manual (or accessible record) processing. If such a data controller chooses not to notify in respect of the manual processing then he must, under paragraph (g) of the registrable particulars (discussed below), state that notification does not extend to the manual records.

Transitional provisions exempt a data controller who is registered under the 1984 Act from the prohibition in s. 17(1) — see below, 'Effect of 1984 Act registration'.

Criminal offence

A data controller who processes personal data in contravention of the above provisions will be guilty of a criminal offence unless he can show that he exercised all due diligence to comply with the duty of notification. The maximum punishment is a fine of £5,000 in magistrates' court or an unlimited fine in the Crown Court.

REQUIRED INFORMATION

A data controller who wishes to be included in the register of data controllers maintained by the Commissioner must 'give a notification' under s. 18 of the Act. The notification must specify:

(a)   the registrable particulars, and
(b)   a general description of the measures to be taken to ensure compliance with the Seventh Data Protection Principle.

Registrable particulars

Section 16(1) provides that the registrable particulars of a data controller are those shown in the following box:

Registrable Particulars of a Data Controller

(a)   The data controller's name and address.
(b)   The name and address of any representative of the data controller.
(c)   A description of the personal data being or to be processed and the category of data subjects to which they relate.
(d)   A description of the purpose of processing.
(e)   A description of any intended recipients of the data.
(f)   A list of the countries outside the European Economic Area (EEA) that will or might be in receipt of the data from the data controller.
(g)   A statement (if relevant) of the fact that certain data processed by the data controller is of a type that is excluded from notification.

The address of the data controller should be his or her principal place of business in the UK. Where the data controller is a company this should be the company's registered office. Partners may submit a notification in the name of the partnership, with the address being the firm's principal place of business. Notification in respect of the governing body and a head teacher at any school may be made in the name of the school.

Where the data controller is established outside the EEA and uses data processing equipment in the UK other than merely for the purpose of transit through the UK, the data controller may choose to include the name of his representative (see s. 5(1)(b) and 5(2)). The nomination of a representative is no substitute for providing details of the data controller's own name and address and is therefore an additional requirement.

Help with descriptions of data, categories of data subjects and purposes can be obtained from the Commissioner's Office, which will provide standard templates for descriptions for different types of businesses. Alterations can be made to the details in the standard templates if they do not precisely fit the actual processing carried on by the data controller.

As far as 'intended recipients' are concerned the data controller should include information as to all persons likely to receive the data. This can be done in general terms and, where appropriate, should include employees and agents of the data controller as well as third parties. If data are to be transferred to a data processor (see definition in Chapter 2) this information should be included.

The data controller must inform the Commissioner of those countries outside the EEA to which he intends (or might intend) to transmit personal data. In this way an individual data subject will be able to discover whether such a transfer of his personal details is possible. It should be noted that data controllers who post personal data to a website will be taken to be making a worldwide transfer because the website will be accessible from any country. Such data controllers should indicate 'worldwide' on the notification form.

The registrable particulars do not include information as to the source of the data. Contrast the regime under the 1984 Act where the data user had to inform the Registrar of the data source.

Technical and organisational measures

The Seventh Data Protection Principle requires appropriate technical and organisational measures to be in place to ensure that personal data are not subject to:

(a)   unlawful or unauthorised processing; or
(b)   accidental loss, destruction or damage.

It should be noted that only a 'general description' of the technical and organisational measures is required for the purposes of notification, and such descriptions do not appear on the public register. Detailed specifications of computer systems are therefore unnecessary — a statement of compliance with the British Standard on Information Security Management BS7799 (see below) should, however, be made wherever possible.

The data controller should state that the organisation of its data processing operations includes appropriate training of employees who will be processing personal data, as well as suitable checks to ensure the reliability of such employees. As far as physical security of the data is concerned, the data controller should be in a position to state that it has appropriate procedures in place to restrict access to sites, buildings, computer rooms, desks, storage areas, equipment and other facilities where unauthorised access could compromise security. Controls on access to information include procedures for authority and authenticating users (such as password protection for website access) as well as use of encryption techniques. Data controllers should have a 'business continuity plan', i.e., a contingency plan which identifies the business functions and assets which would need to be maintained in the event of a disaster and the procedures for restoring them.

Where the data controller uses data processors for data operations, he should include a statement in his notification to the effect that he has entered into a contractual arrangement with all such data processors which includes a provision obliging them to comply with the requirements of the Seventh Data Protection Principle.

Part of the notification procedure requires data controllers to state whether measures are being taken to protect the security of personal data and to provide 'yes' or 'no' answers to the questions which appear in the box below. It should be noted that notification cannot be refused by the Commissioner in any circumstances and hence a 'no' answer to any or all of the questions has no immediate negative effect on a data controller. It is, of course, possible that the Commissioner's compliance department could subsequently make a determination that the data controller is not taking appropriate security measures.

Security Statement Questions

- Are the measures based on an assessment of the risks involved in the processing?

- Do such measures include:
  — Adopting an information security policy?
  — Taking steps to control physical security?
  — Putting in place controls on access to information?
  — Establishing a business continuity plan?
  — Training your staff on security systems and procedures?
  — Detecting and investigating breaches of security when they occur?

- Have you adopted the British Standard on Information Security Management BS7799?

BS7799

Compliance with British Standard 7799 on Information Security Management — Specification for Information Security Management Systems constitutes 'best practice' for organisations that electronically process personal data. BS7799:1999 is divided into two sections. The first is a standard code of practice which lists tasks and procedures to undertake for greater data security. It covers all forms of communication, including voice and graphics and media such as mobile phones and fax machines. Part 2 is a standard specification for Information Security Management Systems (ISMS) and describes the recommended process for setting up an ISMS. Compliance with BS7799 can be undertaken in-house or by using a consultant. Certification of compliance can be obtained after a visit from an 'assessor' to the premises of the data controller. As there is no control mechanism for assessors and certification bodies, data controllers should ensure that the body used to undertake their certification has been accredited by the Department of Trade and Industry under the c:cure scheme (see http://www.c-cure.org).

EXEMPTION FROM NOTIFICATION

Certain processing is exempt from the requirement of notification. It must be remembered, however, that exemption from notification does not remove the processing from the sphere of regulation generally, i.e., such processing must comply with the remaining requirements under the Act (including the Data Protection Principles) unless it benefits from some other relevant exemption — see Chapter 9. The exemptions available are shown in the following box and discussed in more detail below.

Exemptions from Notification

- National security
- Domestic purposes
- Public registers
- Staff administration
- Advertising, marketing and public relations
- Accounts and records
- Non-profit making organisations
- Certain disclosures

It should be noted, however, that all processing for one of the following purposes must be notified, irrespective of any potentially applicable exemption:

- private investigation
- health administration and services
- policing
- crime prevention and prosecution of offenders
- legal services
- debt administering and factoring
- trading/sharing in personal information
- constituency casework
- education
- research
- administration of justice
- consultancy and advisory services
- canvassing political support
- pastoral care
- financial services and advice
- credit referencing
- accounts and records (where a credit reference agency is involved)

National security

There is no requirement to notify the processing of data for the purpose of national security. A certificate signed by a Minister of the Crown to the effect that certain processing is required for the purpose of national security is conclusive evidence of that fact. Such a certificate is subject to a right of appeal by any person who is the subject of such processing (for further detail see Chapter 9, 'National Security').

Domestic purposes

The processing of personal data by an individual only for the purposes of that individual's personal, family or household affairs (including recreational purposes) is exempt from the requirements of notification, as well as from all other provisions of the Act.

Public register

Data controllers who are engaged in processing for the sole purpose of the maintenance of a public register ('any register which is open to public inspection or open to inspection by any person having a legitimate interest either by or under an enactment or in pursuance of any international agreement') are exempt from the requirement of notification.

Staff administration

In contrast to the regime under the 1984 Act, there is no need to notify processing undertaken by employers for the purpose of staff administration. The Data Protection (Notification and Notification Fees) Regulations 2000 refer specifically to the following purposes as being those that are exempt: appointments or removals, pay, discipline, superannuation, work management or other personnel matters in relation to the staff of the data controller.

The staff administration exemption will be relevant only where all the following apply to the processing:

(a) it is of personal data in respect of which the data subject is—

(i) a past, existing or prospective member of staff; or
(ii) any person the processing of whose data is necessary for the above purposes;

(b) it is of personal data consisting of the name, address and other identifiers of the data subject or information as to—

(i) qualifications, work experience and pay; or
(ii) other matters the processing of which is necessary for the above purposes;

(c) it does not involve disclosure of the personal data to any third party other than—

(i) with the consent of the data subject; or
(ii) where it is necessary to make such disclosure for one of the above purposes;

(d) it does not involve keeping the personal data after the relationship between the data controller and staff member ends, unless and for so long as it is necessary to do so for one of the above purposes.

For the purposes of the staff administration exemption, the term 'staff' includes independent contractors and unpaid workers. For further detail see Chapter 13.

Advertising, marketing and public relations

Notification is not required in respect of processing (unless it is assessable processing — see below) for the purposes of advertising or marketing the data controller's business, activity, goods or services and promoting public relations in connection with that business or activity, or those goods or services. As might be expected, the exemption does not cover processing by data controllers where the data controller's business is the *provision* of advertising, marketing and public relations services. In fact the exemption will be lost by any marketing activity relating to a third-party business which is undertaken by the data controller.

The exemption from notification will not apply unless all of the following are applicable to the processing:

(a)   it is of personal data in respect of which the data subject is—

    (i)   a past, existing or prospective customer or supplier; or
    (ii)   any person the processing of whose data is necessary for one of the above purposes;

(b)   it is of personal data consisting of the name, address or other identifiers of the data subject or information as to other matters the processing of which is necessary for the above purposes;

(c)   it does not involve disclosure of the personal data to any third party other than—

    (i)   with the consent of the data subject; or
    (ii)   where it is necessary to make such disclosure for one of the above purposes;

(d)   it does not involve keeping the personal data after the relationship between the data controller and customer or supplier ends, unless and for so long as it is necessary to do so for the above purposes.

Accounts and records

Mainstream business record-keeping, such as the administration of customer and supplier records, is exempt from the need to notify. This exemption, which at first sight appears quite wide, will be lost where the data controller uses the services of a credit reference agency in respect of the personal data or where it provides accounting or accountancy services for its customers. Specifically, notification is not required in respect of processing which is undertaken for one or more of the following purposes:

(a)   keeping accounts relating to any business or other activity of the data controller;
(b)   deciding whether to accept any person as a customer or supplier;
(c)   keeping records of purchases, sales or other transactions for the purpose of ensuring that the requisite payments and deliveries are made or services provided by or to the data controller in respect of those transactions; or

(d)   for making financial or management forecasts to assist the data controller in the conduct of any such business.

To qualify for the exemption, the above processing must:

(a)   be of personal data in respect of which the data subject is—

(i)   a past, existing or prospective customer or supplier; or
(ii)   any person the processing of whose personal data is necessary for one of the above mentioned purposes;

(b)   be of personal data consisting of the name, address and other identifiers of the data subject or information as to—

(i)   financial standing; or
(ii)   other matters the processing of which is necessary for one of the above mentioned purposes;

(c)   not involve disclosure of the personal data to any third party other than—

(i)   with the consent of the data subject; or
(ii)   where it is necessary to make such disclosure for one of the above mentioned purposes; and

(d)   not involve keeping the personal data after the relationship between the data controller and customer and supplier ends, unless and for so long as it is necessary to do so for one of the above mentioned purposes.

The accounts and records exemption does not apply to personal data processed by or obtained from a credit reference agency.

Non-profit-making organisations

Notification is not required in respect of processing carried out by a data controller which is a non-profit-making body or association, provided that the processing is for the purposes of establishing or maintaining membership of or support for the body or association or providing or administering activities for individuals who are either members of the body or association or have regular contact with it. This exemption is designed to catch small clubs, voluntary organisations, church administration and some charities.
The processing concerned must comply with all of the following requirements:

(a)   it is of personal data in respect of which the data subject is—

(i)   a past, existing or prospective member of the body or organisation;
(ii)   any person who has regular contact with the body or organisation for one of the above purposes; or
(iii)   any person the processing of whose personal data is necessary for one of the above purposes;

(b)   it is of personal data consisting of the name, address and other identifiers of the data subject or information as to—

(i)   eligibility for membership of the body or association; or
(ii)   other matters the processing of which is necessary for one of the above purposes;

(c)   it does not involve disclosure of the personal data to any third party other than—

(i)   with the consent of the data subject; or
(ii)   where it is necessary to make such disclosure for one of the above purposes;

(d)   it does not involve keeping the personal data after the relationship between the data controller and the data subject ends, unless and for so long as it is necessary to do so for the exempt purposes.

Certain disclosures of personal data

Notification is not required of processing which consists only of the disclosure of personal data to any person which:

(a)   is required by or under any enactment, by any rule of law or by order of the Court; or
(b)   may be made by virtue of an exemption from the 'non disclosure provisions' (see definition in Chapter 9).

TRANSITIONAL EXEMPTIONS

The first and most significant transitional exemption relates to those persons already registered as data users at the time of commencement of the new Act (1 March 2000). Such persons are exempt from notification until the end of their registration period.

A further transitional exemption relates to automated processing which was already under way immediately before 24 October 1998 in the following categories:

(a)   Payroll and accounts — see sch. 8, para. 6;
(b)   Unincorporated members clubs — see sch. 8, para. 7;
(c)   Mailing list — see sch. 8, para. 8.

Such processing need not be notified until 24 October 2001.

THE REGISTER

Section 19 requires the Commissioner to maintain a register of notifications by data controllers. The register will consist of the registrable particulars (see above) and the following further information:

(a) a registration number;

(b) the date of entry (or deemed entry) of the registrable particulars on the register;

(c) the date of expiry of the register entry; and

(d) such further information as the Commissioner feels necessary for the purpose of assisting persons consulting the register to communicate with any data controller.

The date of deemed entry on the register depends upon the method chosen by the data controller for dispatch of the registrable particulars to the Commissioner. For registered post or recorded delivery, the date of entry will be treated as the day after posting. For all other methods entry is deemed to be the date of receipt by the Commissioner.

A fee (currently £35) must accompany a notification. This fee covers registration for an initial period of one year only, although the Secretary does have the power to change the length of this period. A further fee (currently £35) is payable on the expiry of that period and each subsequent period, i.e., every year.

The Commissioner must include an entry in the register in respect of each person who is exempt from the requirement to notify by virtue of the fact that such a person is already registered under the 1984 Act.

Within 28 days of making an entry in the register (or of altering an entry as a result of a notification of change by the data controller — see below) the Commissioner must send a notice to the data controller setting out the deemed date of registration (or the date of receipt in the case of a notification of change). The notice should also include the information entered on the register and the date of expiry of the entry.

A significant change from the regime under the 1984 Act is that under the 1998 Act only one entry is permitted in the register in respect of each data controller. However, the Commissioner may make provision for large organisations with many processing functions to be able to subdivide their entry in the interest of clarity.

Public inspection

The Commissioner is obliged to make the register open to the public for inspection at reasonable hours without charge. The register can be inspected at the premises of the Commissioner (Wyecliffe House, Water Lane, Wilmslow, Cheshire SK9 5AF) and is also available at http://www.dataprotection.gov.uk. The office of the Commissioner will normally provide photocopies of register entries by post free of charge. Certified copies are available subject to a fee of £2 each.

NOTIFICATION OF CHANGES

Section 20 of the Act puts every registered data controller under a duty to inform the Commissioner of any change in his operations which leads to his register entry being inaccurate or incomplete in respect of:

(a) the registrable particulars; or

(b) the measures taken to comply with the Seventh Data Protection Principle.

The data controller's notification should also set out the changes which need to be made to his entry in order to make it accurate and complete.

The notification of change must be sent by the data controller to the Commissioner within 28 days of the entry becoming inaccurate or incomplete. This requirement may be seen to be burdensome on a business undergoing a series of operational changes and imposes a continuous obligation on data controllers to monitor their data processing activities. Failure to meet the 28-day deadline is a criminal offence — see below.

Upon receiving notification of the alterations in the registrable particulars, the Commissioner must ensure that the register is updated to reflect the change.

Criminal offence

By virtue of s. 21(2), failure to notify the Commissioner of changes as required by s. 20 is a criminal offence. It is a defence for the person charged to show that he exercised all due diligence to comply with the duty.

NOTIFICATION OF CHANGES — TRANSITIONAL PROVISIONS

The rules on notification of changes are different for those persons who are exempt from notification by virtue of the fact that the data controller is registered under the 1984 Act. It will be remembered that this exemption will expire on the date of expiry of the registered entry.

In the time leading up to the expiry of the exemption, the data controller must notify the Commissioner of any change in his name or address. The remaining obligations to notify changes depend upon whether or not a registered controller's processing relates to eligible data (i.e., data which was subject to processing that was already under way immediately before 24 October 1998).

Eligible data

As far as an entry relating to eligible data is concerned, unless the information or particulars is included in the entry, the data controller must give the Commissioner a notice giving:

(a)   a description of any eligible data being or to be processed by him, or on his behalf;

(b)   a description of the category or categories of data subject to which eligible data relate;

(c)   a description of the purpose or purposes for which eligible data are being or are to be processed;

(d)   a description of the source or sources from which he intends or may wish to obtain eligible data;

(e)   a description of any recipient or recipients to whom he intends or may wish to disclose eligible data; and

(f)   the names, or a description of, any countries or territories outside the United Kingdom to which he directly or indirectly transfers or intends or may wish to directly or indirectly transfer, eligible data.

Non-eligible data

If the data being processed are non-eligible (i.e., subject to new processing commenced after 24 October 1998) the data controller must, in respect of which the entry is inaccurate or incomplete, notify the following:

(a)   a statement of his current registrable particulars as far as the descriptions, purpose and intended recipients of personal data and category of data subjects are concerned;

(b)   a description of the source or sources from which he currently intends or may wish to obtain personal data; and

(c)   the names or a description of any countries or territories outside the United Kingdom to which he currently intends or may wish directly or indirectly to transfer personal data.

In each case the data controller must set out the changes which need to be made to the register entry. All such changes must be notified to the Commissioner within 28 days of their becoming effective.

Changes that must be notified by those registered under the 1984 Act **(transitional provisions applicable until 23 October 2001)**	
Entry relates to eligible data (processing under way 24 October 1998)	**Entry relates to non-eligible data (new processing after 24 October 1998)**
Name and Address	
Where not currently included: Description of eligible data Categories of data subjects Purpose of processing Source of data Countries of transfer outside UK	*Where current entry is inaccurate or incomplete:* Description of data Categories of data subjects Purpose of processing Intended recipients Source of data Countries of transfer outside UK
Notification must be given within 28 days of the data from which any of the above information is not included in the entry	Notification must be given within 28 days of when the relevant entry becomes inaccurate or incomplete

ASSESSABLE PROCESSING

Section 22 of the Data Protection Act 1998 (as amended by the Data Protection (Notification and Notification Fees) Regulations 2000) provides that the Commissioner must, after receiving particulars from the data controller (either by way of initial notification or by a notification of changes), determine whether the processing to be undertaken is assessable processing Assessable processing is defined in s. 22(1) to be processing that appears particularly likely:

(a)   to cause substantial damage or substantial distress to data subjects; or
(b)   otherwise significantly to prejudice the rights and freedoms of data subjects.

The Commissioner has identified the following three types of processing as being particularly likely to constitute assessable processing:

(a)   data matching;
(b)   processing of genetic data;
(c)   processing by private investigators.

If the processing is of a type which is assessable, then the Commissioner must inform the data controller of this fact within ten days of receiving the particulars from the data controller and must specifically indicate processing that he considers to be assessable. The Commissioner must also state whether the assessable processing is likely to comply with the provisions of the Act. It should be noted that entry on the register cannot be refused due to the presence of assessable processing.

The Commissioner's ten-day time limit can be extended (once only) in special circumstances by a maximum of 14 days, at the option of the Commissioner, by notice to the data controller. The Secretary of State may, by order, amend the time limit.

Section 22 requires the Secretary of State to specify, by order, the types of processing that will meet the above test. The Secretary of State had not done so at the time of writing.

Processing which was already under way immediately before 24 October 1998 is not assessable processing for the purposes of s. 22 (sch. 8, para. 19).

Criminal offence

Under s. 22(5) and (6), it is a criminal offence to carry on assessable processing after notification of such processing to the Commissioner unless either:

(a)   the period during which the Commissioner can notify the data controller whether the processing will comply with the Act (ten days unless extended by notice) has elapsed, or
(b)   before the end of the period in (a), the data controller has received a notice from the Commissioner stating the extent to which the Commissioner is of the opinion that the processing is likely or unlikely to comply with the provisions of the Act.

It is unclear from the statute whether, in option (b) above, the s. 22(6) offence will still apply to processing which the Commissioner states to be unlikely to comply with the provisions of the Act.

DATA PROTECTION SUPERVISORS

The Data Protection Act 1998 confers on the Secretary of State the power to make regulations concerning the appointment of data protection supervisors. Such persons are envisaged to be employed by data controllers but would carry out their data protection functions independently. The supervisor would monitor the data controller's data protection activity with a view to ensuring compliance with the legislation. The benefit to the data controller in making such an appointment is that the notification provisions will take effect subject to certain modifications, which will be specified in the regulations.

No such regulations had been made by the Secretary of State at the date of writing.

DUTY OF DISCLOSURE FOR NON-REGISTERED DATA CONTROLLERS

Section 24 imposes a duty on a data controller who chooses not to register with the Commissioner in circumstances where notification is not compulsory because:

(a)   the only personal data being processed are manual data recorded as part of a relevant filing system (and the processing is not assessable processing);

(b)   the only personal data being processed are part of an accessible record (and the processing is not assessable processing); or

(c)   notification regulations provide that processing of that description does not require notification.

The duty under s. 24 is that the data controller must, within 21 days of receiving a written request from any person, make the relevant particulars available in writing to that person free of charge. The relevant particulars are items (a) to (f) of the registrable particulars listed in s. 16(1) (see 'Required information' above). Thus lack of notification, and hence lack of registration, does not mean that a data controller will not be required to make appropriate disclosure to a data subject.

Criminal offence

It is a criminal offence to fail to comply with this duty of disclosure (s. 24(4)). It is a defence to show that all due diligence to comply was exercised by the defendant. Thus a non-negligent accidental failure to set out the relevant particulars fully should escape conviction.

VOLUNTARY NOTIFICATION

A data controller who is exempt from the need to notify due to one of the factors below may nevertheless choose to make a voluntary notification. Data controllers who volunteer in this way will be subject to the full notification regime, including the payment of fees and the need to monitor and notify changes. The factors which qualify a data controller to voluntarily notify are the following:

(a)   the data controller holds manual personal data;

(b)   the notification regulations exempt the data controller from the requirement of notification;

(c)   the holding of personal data for the purposes of maintaining a public register; or

(d)   existing registration under the 1984 Act.

The principal reason for making voluntary notification is that the duty of disclosure provisions in s. 24 (see above) do not apply to data controllers who have made a notification.

EFFECT OF 1984 ACT REGISTRATION

An application for registration under Part II of the 1984 Act which is received by the Commissioner before the commencement of the notification provisions of the 1998 Act will be dealt with under the provisions of the old Act.

Under sch. 14, para. 2, a data controller may treat his 1984 Act registration (and deemed registration by virtue of s. 7(6) of the 1984 Act) as continuing for the purposes of the new Act until the date on which his entry in the register would have fallen to be removed under the old Act.

A data controller may therefore choose not to notify the Commissioner of any processing until the expiry of that period. The data controller will not be subject to the prohibition on processing in s. 17(1) by so doing. It is open to any data controller who could benefit by virtue of these provisions to register voluntarily under s. 18(1). Such registration will terminate the exemption in the above provisions.

The benefit of these provisions will cease in respect of a data controller who is treated as being registered under the old Act by virtue of s. 7(6) of that Act and who receives a notification under s. 7(1) of the 1984 Act of the refusal of his application. The date of such cessation will be:

(a)   if no appeal is brought, the end of the period during which an appeal can be brought against the refusal; or

(b)   the date of the withdrawal or dismissal of the appeal.

DO I NEED
TO NOTIFY?

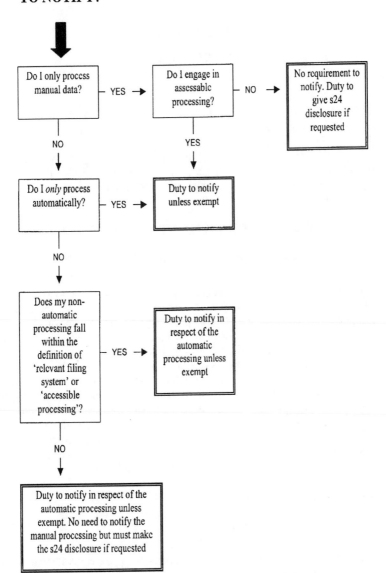

Chapter 9
Exemptions

Both the Data Protection Act 1998 and the regulations which have been made under it, create a great many exemptions from various provisions of the Act for various types of personal data processing.

This chapter is divided into two parts. The first part deals with permanent exemptions from certain provisions of the Data Protection Act 1998. The second part looks at transitional exemptions, i.e., exemptions which are available for a limited period of time only.

PART 1 — PERMANENT EXEMPTIONS

INTRODUCTION AND DEFINITIONS

Exemptions from certain provisions in the Data Protection Act 1998 exist for various purposes. The main exemptions appear in Part IV of the statute. Various miscellaneous exemptions are listed in sch. 7. This part explains the exemptions in both Part IV and sch. 7. Schedule 8 lists transitional exemptions — these are dealt with in Part 2. Each of the exemptions authorises non-compliance with various provisions of the statute. The table below lists the provisions of the Act from which the data controller is exempt in respect of each exemption (with the relevant section or parts in brackets).

The detailed exemption provisions of the Act require an understanding of the definition of two key phrases which have been devised by the drafters of the legislation for ease of reference. Each refers to several of the provisions of the statute in respect of which an exemption might apply. They are 'the subject information provisions' and 'the non-disclosure provisions'. The table also lists exemptions from the 'subject access provisions' and these are also defined below.

Subject information provisions

The 'subject information provisions' are:

(a) the 'information requirements' (see Chapter 4), i.e., the right of the data subject to receive information relating to the identity of the data controller, the purpose of the processing and anything else necessary to ensure fairness (i.e., the First Data Protection Principle to the extent to which it requires compliance with sch. 1, part II, para. 2), and

(b)   the data subject's right of access to personal data (i.e., the rights in s. 7).

The statute gives the subject information provisions special status by providing that any other rule of law that seeks to restrict the giving of the information specified shall not apply (s. 27(5)). The only restrictions that can exist are therefore the exemptions contained in the Act and its regulations.

Non-disclosure provisions

The 'non-disclosure provisions' mean, to the extent that they are inconsistent with the disclosure in question, the following:

(a)   the fair and lawful processing requirement in the First Data Protection Principle (i.e., the First Principle except the need to comply with sch. 2 and sch. 3),
(b)   the Second, Third, Fourth and Fifth Data Protection Principles,
(c)   the right to prevent processing likely to cause damage or distress (s. 10), and
(d)   the right to rectification, blocking, erasure or destruction (s. 14(1) to (3)).

In addition to those listed below, the Secretary of State is empowered to make further exemptions from the subject information provisions and the non-disclosure provisions.

Subject access provisions

The subject access provisions are those provisions contained in s. 7 of the Act which allow a data subject access to certain information which is being processed by the data controller — for further detail see Chapter 2. It will be noted that the subject access provisions are a subset of the subject information provisions.

Exemption	Provisions from which exempt
National security	The Data Protection Principles
	Rights of data subjects (Part II)
	Notification provisions (Part III)
	Enforcement (Part V)
	Unlawful obtaining offence (s. 55)
Crime and taxation	First Data Protection Principle (except sch. 2 and sch. 3)
	The subject access provisions
	The non-disclosure provisions
Health	The subject information provisions
	The subject access provisions
Education	The subject information provisions
	The subject access provisions
Social work	The subject information provisions
	The subject access provisions
Regulatory activity	The subject information provisions
Journalism, literature and art	The Data Protection Principles (except the Seventh)
	The subject access provisions
	Right to prevent processing likely to cause damage or distress (s. 10)

Exemption	Provisions from which exempt
	Rights in relation to automated decision-taking (s. 12)
	Right to rectification, blocking, erasure or destruction (s. 14(1) to (3))
Research, history and statistics	Certain aspects of the Second and Fifth Data Protection Principles
	The subject access provisions
Public inspection	The subject information provisions
	The Fourth Data Protection Principle
	Right to rectification, blocking, erasure or destruction (s. 14(1) to (3))
	The non-disclosure provisions
Corporate finance	The subject information provisions
Examination marks	Certain aspects of the subject access provisions
Disclosures required by law	The non-disclosure provisions
Legal proceedings	The non-disclosure provisions
Domestic purposes	The Data Protection Principles
	Rights of data subjects (Part II)
	Notification provisions (Part III)
Confidential references	The subject access provisions
Armed forces	The subject information provisions
Judicial appointments and honours	The subject information provisions
Crown or Ministerial appointments	The subject information provisions
Management forecasts	The subject information provisions
Negotiations	The subject information provisions
Examination scripts	The subject access provisions
Legal professional privilege	The subject information provisions
Self-incrimination	The subject access provisions
Human fertilisation and embryology	The subject access provisions
Adoption records	The subject access provisions
Special educational needs	The subject access provisions
Parental records and reports	The subject access provisions
Public registers	Notification provisions (Part III)
Staff administration	Notification provisions (Part III)
Advertising, marketing and public relations	Notification provisions (Part III)
Accounts and records	Notification provisions (Part III)
Non-profit-making organisations	Notification provisions (Part III)
Public authorities' manual data	(see below)
Parliamentary privilege	(see below)

The remainder of this chapter will examine each of the exemptions in more detail.

NATIONAL SECURITY

Personal data are exempt from the following provisions of the Act where such an exemption is required for the purpose of 'safeguarding national security':

(a)   the Data Protection Principles;
(b)   the rights of data subjects (Part II);

(c)   the notification provisions (Part III);

(d)   enforcement (Part V);

(e)   the offence of unlawful obtaining (s. 55).

A Minister (who must be a member of the Cabinet, the Attorney-General or the Lord Advocate) may certify, under s. 28(2), that any specified processing is required for the purposes of safeguarding national security. The certificate may describe, in general terms, the personal data to which it relates and may be issued in anticipation of future processing. Any person directly affected by the certification may, by virtue of s. 28(4), appeal to the Data Protection Tribunal against its application. The Tribunal will treat the appeal as if it was an application for judicial review, and will revoke the certificate where the Minister did not have reasonable grounds for its issue.

Any party to any proceedings under the Act concerning a generally worded certificate may appeal to the Tribunal on the basis that the Minister's certification does not cover the personal data in question. The decision of the Tribunal is conclusive. Any party wishing to challenge the authenticity of a certificate has the burden of proving that it is not a s. 28(2) certificate. A certified copy of a certificate is admissible in the same way as the original.

Detailed procedural rules for appeals under s. 28 may be found in the Data Protection Tribunal (National Security Appeals) Rules 2000 — see Appendix 3.

CRIME AND TAXATION

Section 29 gives an exemption to the processing of personal data for the following purposes:

(a)   the prevention or detection of crime,

(b)   the apprehension or prosecution of offenders, or

(c)   the assessment or collection of any tax or duty or of any imposition of a similar nature.

Such personal data are exempt from:

(a)   the First Data Protection Principle (except sch. 2 and sch. 3),

(b)   the subject access provisions in s. 7.

Personal data which are processed with a view to compliance with a statutory function, and which have been obtained from a person who possessed it for one of the purposes in (a) to (c) above, are exempt from the subject information provisions.

Personal data are exempt from the non-disclosure provisions where the disclosure is for one of the purposes in (a) to (c) above and the application of those provisions would be likely to prejudice those purposes.

Where the data controller is a government department or local authority (or any other authority administering council tax or housing benefits), certain personal data are exempt from the subject access provisions in s. 7 so far as is necessary for the smooth running of a risk assessment system. The exempt personal data for this purpose are defined in s. 29(4) as those which:

(a)   consist of a classification applied to the data subject as part of a system of risk assessment which is operated by the authority for either of the following purposes—

(i)   the assessment or collection of any tax or duty or any imposition of a similar nature, or

(ii)   the prevention or detection of crime, or apprehension or prosecution of offenders, where the offence concerned involves any unlawful claim for any payment out of, or any unlawful application of, public funds [including funds provided by any Community institution: s. 29(5)], and

(b)   are processed for either of those purposes.

HEALTH

The Data Protection (Subjects Access Modification) (Health) Order 2000 provides partial exemptions from the subject information provisions and from the subject access provisions in s. 7 for personal data which relate to the physical health or mental state or condition of the data subject.

Subject information provisions

Such health data which are processed by a court from information deriving from a local authority, Health and Social Services Board, Health and Social Services Trust, probation officer or other person in the course of most child proceedings, are exempt from the subject information provisions.

Subject access request

Health data are exempt from s. 7 where granting a subject access request would be likely to cause serious harm to the physical or mental health or condition of the data subject or any other person. The exemption does not apply where the data controller is not a health professional unless it has consulted the appropriate health professional on the question of whether or not the exemption applies. For these purposes 'the appropriate health professional' means:

(a)   the health professional who is currently or was most recently responsible for the clinical care of the data subject in connection with the matters to which the information which is the subject of the request relates; or

(b)   where there is more than one such health professional, the health professional who is the most suitable to advise on the matters to which the information which is the subject of the request relates; or

(c)   where—

(i)   there is no health professional falling within (a) or (b) available, or

(ii)   the data controller is the Secretary of State and the data are processed by him in connection with child support, social security or war pensions a health professional who has the necessary experience and qualifications to advise on the matters to which the information which is the subject of the request relates.

Where a subject access request is made on behalf of a data subject who is a child (or, in Scotland, a person under the age of sixteen) by a person who has parental responsibility or on behalf of a person who is incapable of managing his own affairs by a court appointee, health data are exempt from such a request where compliance with the request would disclose information—

(a) provided by the data subject in the expectation that it would not be disclosed to the person making the request;

(b) obtained as a result of any examination or investigation to which the data subject consented in the expectation that the information would not be so disclosed; or

(c) which the data subject has expressly indicated should not be so disclosed.

A data controller cannot refuse a subject access request for health data on the grounds that the identity of a third party would be disclosed where the third party is a health professional who has compiled or contributed to that health record or has been involved in the care of the data subject in his capacity as a health professional unless serious harm to that health professional's physical or mental health or condition is likely to be caused by giving such access.

EDUCATION

The Data Protection (Subject Access Modification) (Education) Order 2000 makes exemptions from the subject access provisions for the following types of personal data:

(a) in England and Wales, any record of information relating to a pupil which is processed by or on behalf of a teacher (other than for the teacher's sole use) or governing body and which originated from one or more of a number of specified persons including the pupil, his parent and an employee of the local education authority that maintains the relevant school (see sch. II, para. 4 for the full list of such persons);

(b) in Scotland, any record of information which is processed by an education authority other than information which is processed by a teacher for the teacher's sole use; and

(c) in Northern Ireland, any record of information which relates to a pupil and which is processed by or on behalf of the Board of Governors of or a teacher (other than information processed by a teacher for his sole use) at any grant-aided school which was supplied by a teacher, an employee of an education and library board, the pupil or his parent.

Subject information provisions

Exemption from the subject information provisions exists for the above types of education data which are processed by a court from information given to the court in children's proceedings.

Subject access provisions

Such education data are exempt from s. 7 where granting a subject access request would be likely to cause serious harm to the mental or physical health or condition of the data subject or any other person.

Where a rule of law enables a parent (or someone with parental responsibility) or court appointee (in respect of a person who is incapable of managing his own affairs) to make a subject access request on behalf of the data subject, the data controller is exempt from the need to comply with that request in circumstances where the data consists of information as to actual or potential child abuse and such compliance would not be in the interests of the data subject.

A data controller cannot refuse access to education data merely by virtue of the fact that disclosure of the data would identify a teacher or other relevant third party (see para. 7 of the Data Protection (Subject Access Modification) (Education) Order 2000) unless serious harm to that person's physical or mental health or condition is likely to result.

SOCIAL WORK

The Data Protection (Subject Access Modification) (Social Work) Order 2000 relates to data processed by local authorities and other data controllers (for the full list see the Schedule to the above Order) for the purposes of social work.

Subject information provisions

Such data are exempt from the subject information provisions unless they consist of health or education data (see above).

Subject access provisions

Exemption from the operation of s. 7 exists for social work data where granting a subject access request would be likely to prejudice the carrying on of social work by virtue of resultant serious harm to the physical or mental conditon of the data subject or any other person.

A person empowered by virtue of parental responsibility (in the case of a child in England and Wales or Northern Ireland or a person under sixteen in Scotland) or being a court appointee (in the case of a person who is incapable of managing his own affairs) to make a subject access request on behalf of the data subject shall not be entitled to the information under s. 7 where the granting of such request would disclose information:

(a) provided by the data subject in the expectation that it would not be disclosed to the person making the request;

(b) obtained as a result of any examination or investigation to which the data subject consented in the expectation that the information would not be so disclosed; or

(c) which the data subject has expressly indicated should not be so disclosed.

REGULATORY ACTIVITY

Certain functions are given special status by s. 31, which provides that personal data processed for the purpose of such functions will be exempt from the subject information provisions where compliance with those provisions would prejudice those functions.

The section provides an exhaustive list of the functions to which the exemption relates. Examples are any relevant function which is designed:

(a) for protecting members of the public against—

    (i) financial loss due to dishonesty, malpractice or other seriously improper conduct by, or the unfitness or incompetence of, persons concerned in the provision of banking, insurance, investment or other financial services or in the management of bodies corporate,
    (ii) financial loss due to the conduct of discharged or undischarged bankrupts, or
    (iii) dishonesty, malpractice or other seriously improper conduct by, or the unfitness or incompetence of, persons authorised to carry on any profession or other activity,

(b) to protect charities against misconduct or mismanagement;
(c) to protect the property of charities from loss or misapplication;
(d) for the recovery of the property of charities;
(e) for ensuring the health and safety of persons at work;
(f) to protect non-employees against health and safety risks arising out of the activities of persons at work.

A relevant function is defined in s. 31(3) as:

(a) any function conferred on any person by virtue of a statute,
(b) any function of the Crown or a Minister or government department, or
(c) any other public function which is exercised in the public interest.

Section 31(4) lists further exemptions (from the subject information provisions) for personal data which are processed for the protection of the public by persons such as:

(a) the Parliamentary Commissioner for Administration,
(b) the Local Administration Commissioners for England, Wales and Scotland,
(c) the Welsh Administration Ombudsman,
(d) the Assembly Ombudsman for Northern Ireland,
(e) the Northern Ireland Commissioner for Complaints,
(f) the Health Service Commissioner for England, Wales and Scotland.

Section 31(5) exempts from the subject information provisions personal data processed by the Director General of Fair Trading for the purpose of:

(a)   protecting members of the public against conduct which may adversely affect their interests by persons carrying on a business,

(b)   regulating agreements or conduct which have as their object or effect the prevention, restriction or distortion of competition in connection with any commercial activity, or

(c)   regulating conduct on the part of one or more undertakings which amounts to the abuse of a dominant position in a market,

to the extent to which the application of those provisions to the data would be likely to prejudice the proper discharge of the duties.

JOURNALISM, LITERATURE AND ART

Data protection legislation is founded in a desire to preserve the right of privacy. Although there is no such right in English law, this legislation and other statutes in the pipeline in 1998 were expected to create substantial privacy rights. However, the media proved to be a powerful lobby during the course of the creation of the legislation and the so-called media exemption in the Data Protection Act 1998, s. 32, preserves, at least in part, the freedom of the press.

Journalists invariably hold on computers personal data on living individuals. In many cases this is sensitive personal data within the meaning of the Act, being information relating to, for example, a person's racial origin, political opinion or sex life. By virtue of this exemption, none of the conditions for the processing of sensitive personal data in sch. 3 are required to be met by the media. Investigative journalism would clearly be hampered if the consent of the data subject was a requirement of processing.

The following provisions of the Act will not apply to the media where the exemption operates:

(a)   the Data Protection Principles (except the Seventh);
(b)   the subject access provisions in s. 7;
(c)   right to prevent processing likely to cause damage or distress (s. 10);
(d)   rights in relation to automated decision-taking (s. 12);
(e)   the transitional rights in s. 12A (see Chapter 2, 'Transitional rights');
(f)   right to rectification, blocking, erasure or destruction (s. 14(1) to (3)).

To benefit from the exemption, personal data must be processed for the 'special purposes' and each of the following three prerequisites must be satisfied:

(a)   the processing must be undertaken with a view to the publication by any person of any journalistic, literary or artistic material;
(b)   the data controller must reasonably believe that, having regard in particular to the special importance of the public interest in freedom of expression, publication would be in the public interest; and
(c)   the data controller must reasonably believe that, in all the circumstances, compliance with the provision in question is incompatible with the special purposes.

The 'special purposes' are defined in s. 3 as meaning any one or more of the following:

(a)   the purposes of journalism,
(b)   artistic purposes, and
(c)   literary purposes.

In considering whether the data controller reasonably believes the publication to be in the public interest, he or she may have regard to compliance with the provisions of 'any relevant code of practice'. The following table shows the code to be considered in relation to each relevant medium:

Medium	Code
Newspapers and magazines	Press Complaints Commission's Code of Practice
BBC Television	The Producer's Guidelines
Other Television	Broadcasting Standards Commission's Fairness, Privacy and Standards Codes Independant Television Commission's Programme Code
Radio	Radio Authority's Radio Code

Section 32(4) seems to prevent so-called gagging orders within 24 hours prior to publication by providing that proceedings against a data controller under any of the provisions to which the exemption relates will be stayed if the relevant personal data are being processed:

(a)   only for the special purposes; and
(b)   with a view to the publication of special purposes material which had not, excluding the 24-hour period prior to the proceedings, previously been published by the data controller.

The stay will remain in place until either the Commissioner makes a determination (under s. 45) that the personal data are not being processed in compliance with (a) and (b) above or the data controller withdraws his claim to have complied with (a) and (b) above. For further detail on the s. 45 determination procedure see Chapter 10, 'Special information notice'.

RESEARCH, HISTORY AND STATISTICS

Those engaged in historical and other research, and in the preparation of certain statistics, will be able to escape some of the provisions of the Data Protection Act 1998, under s. 33 of the Act. This exemption relates to personal data which are processed 'only for research purposes'. 'Research purposes' is not defined in the Act but is stated to include statistical or historical purposes (s. 33(1)). A disclosure of personal data to any person for research purposes does not prevent the exemptions from applying, nor does a disclosure to a data subject or a person acting on his or her behalf. The research exemptions concern the following provisions of the Act:

(a)   the Second Data Protection Principle;
(b)   the Fifth Data Protection Principle; and
(c)   the subject access provisions.

The Second Data Protection Principle requires that data must not be processed in a manner which is incompatible with the purpose for which it was obtained. Section 33(2) provides that the processing of personal data for research purposes will not breach the Second Principle if the processing complies with certain 'relevant conditions' (see below). Further, personal data processed (in compliance with the same conditions) for research purposes can be kept indefinitely, notwithstanding the provisions against the keeping of 'old' data in the Fifth Principle.

An exemption from the subject access provisions is available for personal data which are processed for research purposes and the processing complies with the relevant conditions where 'the results of the research or any resulting statistics are not made available in a form which identifies data subjects or any of them' (s. 33(4)).

The relevant conditions mentioned in the three exemptions above are negatively defined in s. 33(1) as follows:

(a)   that the data are not processed to support measures or decisions with respect to particular individuals, and
(b)   that the data are not processed in such a way that substantial damage or substantial distress is, or is likely to be, caused to any data subject.

See further transitional exemptions for historical research in part 2 of this chapter.

PUBLIC INSPECTION

If a data controller is obliged by statute to make any disclosure of personal data to the public (whether by charging a fee or not) then the personal data are exempt from the following provisions:

(a)   the subject information provisions;
(b)   the Fourth Data Protection Principle;
(c)   the right to rectification, blocking, erasure or destruction (s. 14(1) to (3));
(d)   the transitional rights in s. 12A (see Chapter 2, 'Transitional rights'); and
(e)   the non-disclosure provisions.

CORPORATE FINANCE

This exemption, contained in sch. 7, para. 6, concerns a corporate finance service, which is defined as:

a service consisting in:
(a)   underwriting in respect of issues of, or the placing of issues of, any instrument,
(b)   advice to undertakings on capital structure, industrial strategy and related matters and advice and service relating to mergers and the purchase of undertakings, or
(c)   services relating to such underwriting as is mentioned in paragraph (a).

The exemption is designed to ensure that the market price or value of financial instruments, such as stocks, futures or annuities, is unaffected by knowledge of any dealings. Personal data processed for the purpose of a corporate finance service are exempt from the subject information provisions where the application of those provisions could affect the price of any instrument, or where the data controller reasonably believes an instrument could be so affected. The provisions cover both existing instruments and those to be created. Where the data are not exempt by virtue of the above, they nevertheless will benefit from a further exemption where required to safeguard an important economic or financial interest of the United Kingdom.

By virtue of the Data Protection (Corporate Finance Exemption) Order 2000 the matter to be taken into account in determining whether exemption from the subject information provisions is required for the purpose of safeguarding an important economic or financial interest of the UK, is the inevitable prejudicial effect on the orderly functioning of financial markets or the efficient allocation of capital within the economy which will result from supplying information as to:

(a)   any decision of any person whether or not to deal in, subscribe for or issue any instrument; or

(b)   any decision of any person to act or not act in a way likely to have an effect on any business activity.

In order for the exemption to operate, the corporate finance service must be provided by a specific type of person. The list of relevant persons appears in sch. 7, para. 6(3), and includes persons authorised to provide services under certain provisions of the Financial Services Act 1986 and certain European investment firms.

EXAMINATION MARKS

Paragraph 8 of sch. 7 modifies the time limit for compliance with the subject access provisions where the personal data consist of examination results.

Where personal data are processed for the purpose of determining examination results (or any consequence of such determination) the s. 7 time limits are extended. If the relevant day (commonly, the day the data controller receives the request for subject access — see Chapter 2, 'Basic rights of access') falls before the day of the announcement of the examination results then the time period for compliance is extended until the earlier of:

(a)   the end of five months from the relevant day, or

(b)   the end of 40 days from the date of the announcement.

In certain cases the above provisions will inevitably result in a request under s. 7 being complied with after the expiry of the normal s. 7 time limits. Where this occurs the data supplied must not only be the data relevant to the date of the request but also must take account of any alterations in the data from that date until actual compliance.

OTHER EXEMPTIONS

This section lists further miscellaneous exemptions.

Disclosures required by law

Where the disclosure of personal data is required by law, whether statute, case law or court order, those personal data are exempt from the non-disclosure provisions (s. 35(1)).

Legal proceedings

Personal data are exempt from the non-disclosure provisions where the disclosure in question is necessary for the purpose of legal proceedings or for the obtaining of legal advice or for establishing, exercising or defending legal rights (s. 35(2)).

Domestic purposes

Personal data processed as part of household or domestic activities should not be subject to a rigid data protection regime. A Christmas card list, for example, would come under this exemption. Section 36 gives such personal data an exemption from the following provisions of the statute:

(a)   the Data Protection Principles,
(b)   the rights of data subjects (Part II),
(c)   the notification provisions (Part III).

Confidential references

The statutory provisions recognise the importance to be attached to the confidential nature of references (sch. 7, para. 1). The value of an employer's reference would be diminished if the subject of the reference was able to obtain a copy of the personal data it contained.

Personal data are exempt from the subject access provisions if they are included as part of a confidential reference given or to be given by the data controller for the purpose of:

(a)   the education, training or employment, or prospective education, training or employment, of the data subject,
(b)   the appointment, or prospective appointment, of the data subject to any office, or
(c)   the provision, or prospective provision, by the data subject of any service.

Armed forces

Personal data are exempt from the subject information provisions to the extent that those provisions are likely to prejudice the 'combat effectiveness' of the armed forces of the Crown (sch. 7, para. 2).

Judicial appointments and honours

An exemption from the subject information provisions is available in respect of personal data processed for determining the suitability of a person for appointment as a judge or Queen's Counsel or for the conferring of any honour by the Crown.

Crown or Ministerial appointments

The Secretary of State is empowered to produce subject information exemptions for personal data which are processed for the purpose of assessing the suitability of any person for appointment as a Minister or other government employee. No such exemptions exist at the time of writing.

Management forecasts

Where it would be of assistance to the data controller in 'the conduct of any business or other activity', personal data are exempt from the subject information provisions (to the extent that those provisions would be prejudicial to that business or other activity) where processed for the following purposes:

(a)   management forecasting, or
(b)   management planning (sch. 7, para. 5).

Negotiations

Where the data controller makes a record of his intentions in respect of negotiations with a data subject, then that record is exempt from the subject information provisions to the extent that those provisions would be likely to prejudice the negotiation (sch. 7, para. 7).

Examination scripts

In certain circumstances the information given by students in examinations will consist of personal data. The exemption in sch. 7, para. 9, provides that anything written down by candidates in a professional or academic examination is exempt from the subject access provisions.

Legal professional privilege

Personal data are exempt from the subject information provisions in so far as they consist of material for which legal professional privilege can be claimed.

Self-incrimination

A data controller is exempted from complying with any request or order for information under s. 7 where such compliance would expose the controller to proceedings for any offence. The exemption relates to all criminal offences except offences under the Data Protection Act 1998 itself. But if a controller does make information available to another under s. 7, the information cannot be used in any criminal proceedings against that controller for an offence under the 1998 Act (sch. 7, para, 11).

Human fertilisation and embryology

Exemption from the subject access provisions contained in s. 7 exist for the following types of personal data information:

(a) information about the provision of treatment services;
(b) the keeping or use of gametes or embryos; and
(c) whether identifiable individuals were born in consequence of treatment services.

Adoption records and reports

Adoption records and reports are exempt from the subject access provisions.

Special education needs

Statements and records of the special educational needs of children are exempt from the subject access provisions.

Parental records and reports

Certain parental records and reports are exempt from the subject access provisions (see The Data Protection (Miscellaneous Subject Access Exemptions) Order 2000).

Manual data held by public authorities

By virtue of the Freedom of Information Bill, personal data falling within paragraph (e) of the definition of data (manual information held by pulic authorities) will be exempt from:

(a) the First, Second, Third, Fifth, Seventh and Eighth Data Protection Principles;
(b) the Sixth Data Protection Principle except insofar as it relates to data subject access and the rights to rectification, blocking, erasure and destruction;
(c) the right to prevent processing leading to damage or distress, and processing for direct marketing and automated decision-taking;
(d) the right to compensation for damage or distress except where such is caused by breach of the subject access provisions or the Fourth Data Protection Principle;
(e) Part III of the Act; and
(f) the criminal offence of unlawful obtaining or disclosure of personal data.

Parliamentary privilege

Where such an exemption is required for the purpose of avoiding an infringement of the privileges of either House of Parliament, personal data are exempt from:

(a) the First Data Protection Principle, except to the extent that it requires compliance with the conditions in schs 2 and 3;

(b)   the Second, Third, Fourth and Fifth Data Protection Principles;

(c)   the subject access provisions; and

(d)   the right to prevent processing likely to cause damage and distress and to a court order for rectification, blocking, erasure or destruction.

PART 2 — TRANSITIONAL EXEMPTIONS

INTRODUCTION AND DEFINITIONS

This part looks at certain exemptions which result from limited-duration modifications to the Act — all of which are contained in sch. 8. The two most important dates for these purposes are 23 October 2001 (the end of the *first transitional period*) and 23 October 2007 (the end of the *second transitional period*). The first transitional period began when sch. 8 was brought into force on 1 March 2000. The second transitional period commences on 24 October 2001.

The exemptions in sch. 8 relate to 'eligible data'. Personal data are eligible data if they are subject to processing which was already under way immediately before 24 October 1998. There is no definition of the phrase 'already under way' in the Act. Many transitional exemptions operate by reference to the relevant parts of the 1998 Act. For ease of reference the following parts deal with the following subject matter:

- Part II — Rights of data subjects
- Part III — Notification requirements

Eligible automated data

'Eligible automated data' means eligible data which consists of information that is being processed by means of equipment operating automatically in response to instructions given for that purpose or which is recorded with the intention that it should be so processed (this is the first two parts of the definition of 'data' in s. 1(1)). During the first transitional period, eligible automated data are not to be regarded as 'processed' unless the processing is by reference to the data subject.

In addition to the specific exemptions listed in the remainder of this chapter, eligible automated data are exempt from the following provisions of the Act during the *first transitional period*:

(a)   the First Data Protection Principle in so far as it requires compliance with sch. 2 and sch. 3 (this exemption does not remove the obligation on the data controller to ensure that the processing is fair);

(b)   that part of the Seventh Data Protection Principle which requires any processing carried out by a data processor on behalf of a data controller to be carried out under certain contractual provisions (see Chapter 3);

(c)   the Eighth Data Protection Principle (but any transfer of data abroad must comply with the fairness requirement in the First Principle);

(d)   those parts of the subject access provisions (s. 7) which require the data subject to be given descriptions of the data, its purpose and likely recipients, the source of the data and the logic involved in automated decision-taking;

(e)   the right in s. 10 to prevent processing likely to cause damage or distress (this does not remove the obligation on the data controller to process fairly as required by the First Principle);

(f)   the right in s. 11 to prevent direct marketing processing (such processing must be fair as required by the First Principle);

(g)   the right to request that a decision affecting the data subject is not taken solely by automated means (s. 12);

(h)   the right to compensation (s. 13) except where relating to:

(i)   a contravention of the Fourth Data Protection Principle,
(ii)   a disclosure without the consent of the data controller,
(iii)   loss or destruction of data without the consent of the data controller, or
(iv)   processing for the special purposes.

Eligible manual data

Processing which was already under way immediately before 24 October 1998 is not assessable processing for the purposes of s. 22 (sch. 8, para. 19).

'Eligible manual data' means eligible data not falling within the definition of eligible automated data (i.e., personal data which are recorded or intended to be recorded as part of a relevant filing system or which forms part of an accessible record — see Chapter 2, 'Initial definitions').

MANUAL DATA

Subject to the two exceptions below, eligible manual data are exempt from the following provisions of the Act during the *first transitional period*:

(a)   the Data Protection Principles;

(b)   Part II of the Act (the data subject's rights of access, rights to prevent processing and rights to rectification, blocking, erasure, destruction and compensation);

(c)   Part III of the Act (the notification provisions).

The two types of data which do not benefit from the above transitional exemption are:

(a)   data forming part of an accessible record; and
(b)   data held by a credit reference agency (sch. 8, para. 3).

Data forming part of an accessible record

Eligible manual data forming part of an accessible record (whether or not processing was already under way on 24 October 1998) are exempt from the following provisions during the *first transitional period*:

(a)   the Data Protection Principles, except the Sixth Principle so far as relating to ss. 7 and 12A;

(b)   Part II of the Act, except ss. 7, 12A and 15; and
(c)   Part III of the Act.

See s. 68 for the definition of 'accessible record'.

Credit reference agency

Eligible manual data which consist of information relevant to the financial standing of the data subject and in respect of which the data controller is a credit reference agency (see definition in Chapter 2) are exempt from the following provisions during the *first transitional period*:

(a) the Data Protection Principles, except the Sixth Principle so far as relating to ss. 7 and 12A;
(b) Part II of the Act, except ss. 7, 12A and 15; and
(c) Part III of the Act.

Second transitional period

Eligible manual data (other than data which are processed only for the purpose of historical research) which were held immediately before 24 October 1998 and any other personal data forming part of an accessible record are exempt from the following provisions of the Act during the *second transitional period*:

(a) the First Data Protection Principle except to the extent to which it requires compliance with sch. 1, Part II, para. 2;
(b) the Second Data Protection Principle;
(c) the Third Data Protection Principle;
(d) the Fourth Data Protection Principle;
(e) the Fifth Data Protection Principle; and
(f) the rights in respect of court orders for rectification, blocking, erasure and destruction under s. 14(1) to (3).

PAYROLLS

Under sch. 8, para. 6, eligible automated data processed for the purpose of calculating salaries, wages or pensions are exempt (provided that the processing was done only for one or more of those purposes or the data controller took reasonable steps to ensure that was the case) from the following provisions during the *first transitional period*:

(a) the Data Protection Principles;
(b) Part II of the Act; and
(c) Part III of the Act.

Data which are processed only for the above purposes may be disclosed:

(a) to any person (other than the data controller) by whom the remuneration or pensions in question are payable;
(b) for the purpose of obtaining actuarial advice;
(c) for the purpose of giving information as to the persons in any employment or office for use in medical research into the health of, or injuries suffered by, persons engaged in particular occupations or working in particular places or areas;

(d)   if the data subject (or a person acting on his or her behalf) has requested or consented to the disclosure of the data either generally or in the circumstances in which the disclosure in question is made;

(e)   if the person making the disclosure has reasonable grounds for believing that the disclosure falls within paragraph (d); or

(f)   for the purpose of audit or where the disclosure is for the purpose only of giving information about the data controller's financial affairs.

ACCOUNTS

Eligible automated data processed for the purpose of keeping business or other accounts or keeping records of purchases, sales or other transactions for the purpose of making or receiving payment or of making management forecasts are exempt (provided that the processing was done only for one or more of those purposes or the data controller took reasonable steps to ensure that was the case) from the following provisions during the *first transitional period*:

(a)   the Data Protection Principles;
(b)   Part II of the Act; and
(c)   Part III of the Act.

Data which are processed only for the above purposes may be disclosed for the purpose of audit or where the disclosure is for the purpose only of giving information about the data controller's financial affairs.

UNINCORPORATED MEMBERS' CLUBS

Subject to the conditions below, eligible automated data processed by an unincorporated members' club are exempt from the following of the Act's provisions during the *first transitional period*:

(a)   the Data Protection Principles;
(b)   Part II of the Act; and
(c)   Part III of the Act.

This transitional exemption does not apply unless the data subject has indicated to the club that there is no objection to the processing of his or her personal data. If the data subject does object then the processing cannot benefit from the exemption.

A further condition on the operation of the exemption is that the data must not be disclosed unless one of the following apply:

(a)   the data subject (or a person acting on his or her behalf) has requested or consented to the disclosure of the data either generally or in the circumstances in which the disclosure in question is made; or

(b)   the person making the disclosure has reasonable grounds for believing that the disclosure falls within paragraph (a).

Any disclosure otherwise than in accordance with (a) or (b) above will not result in the loss of the transitional exemption where the data controller is able to show that reasonable care was taken to prevent the disclosure.

MAILING LISTS

Subject to the conditions below, eligible automated data consisting only of names, addresses and other particulars necessary for ensuring delivery and processed only for the purposes of distribution of information or articles are exempt from the following of the Act's provisions during the *first transitional period*:

(a)   the Data Protection Principles;
(b)   Part II of the Act; and
(c)   Part III of the Act.

This transitional exemption does not apply unless the data subject has indicated to the data controller that there is no objection to the processing of his or her personal data. If the data subject does object, the processing cannot benefit from the exemption.

A further condition on the operation of the exemption is that the data must not be disclosed unless one of the following applies:

(a)   the data subject (or a person acting on his or her behalf) has requested or consented to the disclosure of the data, either generally or in the circumstances in which the disclosure in question is made;
(b)   the person making the disclosure has reasonable grounds for believing that the disclosure falls within paragraph (a);
(c)   disclosure would be permitted by any other provision of sch. 8, part II, if the provision giving the mailing list exemption were included among the non-disclosure provisions.

Any disclosure otherwise than in accordance with (a) or (b) above will not result in the loss of the transitional exemption where the data controller is able to show that reasonable care was taken to prevent the disclosure.

BACK-UP DATA

Eligible automated data which are processed only for the purpose of replacing other data in the event of the data being lost, destroyed or impaired are exempt from the subject access provisions in s. 7 during the *first transitional period*.

HISTORICAL RESEARCH

Both eligible manual and eligible automated data processed for the purposes of historical research are exempt from certain provisions of the Act after 23 October 2001. The benefit of this exemption (in the case of both manual and automated data) will not be lost merely because the data concerned are disclosed:

(a)   to any person, for the purpose of historical research only;
(b)   to the data subject or a person acting on his behalf;
(c)   at the request, or with the consent, of the data subject or a person acting on his behalf; or
(d)   in circumstances in which the person making the disclosure has reasonable grounds for believing that the disclosure falls within paragraph (a), (b) or (c).

A further condition of the operation of the exemption (for both manual and automated data) is that the processing must be in compliance with the 'relevant conditions'. These conditions are the same as the relevant conditions in s. 33, which relate to the permanent exemptions for research, history and statistics, i.e.:

(a)   that the data are not processed to support measures or decisions with respect to particular individuals; and
(b)   that the data are not processed in such a way that substantial damage or substantial distress is, or is likely to be, caused to any data subject.

Manual data

Eligible manual data which are processed only for the purpose of historical research in compliance with the relevant conditions (see above) are exempt from the following provisions of the Act *after 23 October 2001*:

(a)   the First Data Protection Principle except to the extent to which it requires compliance with sch. 1, part II, para. 2;
(b)   the Second Data Protection Principle;
(c)   the Third Data Protection Principle;
(d)   the Fourth Data Protection Principle;
(e)   the Fifth Data Protection Principle; and
(f)   the rights in respect of court orders for rectification, blocking, erasure and destruction under s. 14(1) to (3).

Automated data

Eligible automated data which are processed only for the purpose of historical research in compliance with the relevant conditions (see above) are exempt from the following provision of the Act *after 23 October 2001*:

(a)   the First Data Protection Principle in so far as it requires compliance with the conditions in sch. 2 and sch. 3.

Where such data are processed otherwise than by reference to the data subject they are also exempt from the following provisions:

(b)   the First Data Protection Principle except to the extent to which it requires compliance with sch. 1, part II, para. 2;
(c)   the Second Data Protection Principle;
(d)   the Third Data Protection Principle;
(e)   the Fourth Data Protection Principle;
(f)   the Fifth Data Protection Principle;
(g)   the rights in respect of court orders for rectification, blocking, erasure and destruction under s. 14(1) to (3).

Chapter 10
Enforcement

INTRODUCTION

Part V of the Data Protection Act 1998 provides methods by which the Commissioner can seek to ensure that data controllers comply with the provisions of the Act. The Commissioner's powers revolve around serving notices on data controllers. Information and special information notices require data controllers to supply information to the Commissioner, while enforcement notices require data controllers to comply with measures which they list. It is a criminal offence to fail to respond appropriately to any of the notices.

A notice is unlikely to be served on a data controller unless the Commissioner has received some information concerning a potential compliance issue. This may occur in a number of ways. Section 42, for example, provides that any person may apply to the Commissioner for an assessment of whether any processing concerning him or her is being carried out lawfully. The mechanics of such a request are examined below.

The processing of special purposes material is examined here in some detail as it gives rise to a more complex notice procedure.

REQUEST FOR ASSESSMENT

Any person who believes that he or she is being directly affected by the processing of personal data may apply to the Commissioner for an assessment of whether that processing is being carried out in compliance with the Act (s. 42). Such a request will usually be made where the person concerned feels that the processing is being carried out in contravention of the Act. The request should contain details of the applicant's name and of any other relevant information sufficient to enable the Commissioner to identify the processing in question. In determining the appropriate manner in which to make an assessment, the Commissioner will consider all relevant information including:

(a) the extent to which the request appears to her to raise a matter of substance;
(b) any undue delay in making the request; and
(c) whether or not the person making the request is entitled to make an application under s. 7 in respect of the personal data in question.

Section 7 contains the provisions which enable a data subject to gain access to information concerning personal data held by a data controller (see Chapter 2).

Section 42(4) requires the Commissioner to notify the applicant whether an assessment has been made and to inform the applicant of any view formed or action taken as a result of the request. In determining the appropriateness of the Commissioner's response under s. 42(4), the Commissioner shall bear in mind the extent to which the personal data concerned are exempt from the provisions of s. 7. For a discussion of the exemptions, see Chapter 5.

INFORMATION NOTICE

Under s. 43 the Commissioner may serve a document, known as an information notice, on any data controller requiring the data controller to furnish certain information to the Commissioner within a time limit specified in the notice. The purpose of the notice is to allow the Commissioner to gather sufficient information to determine whether the data controller is processing in contravention of the statutory provisions.

Service of an information notice on any particular data controller must be for one of two reasons:

(a)   that the Commissioner has received an application for an assessment under s. 42 (see above); or

(b)   that the Commissioner reasonably requires the information requested in the information notice for the purpose of determining whether the data controller has complied, or is complying, with the Data Protection Principles.

If the Commissioner has served an information notice following an application for an assessment, she must inform the data controller of that fact and must specify the particular processing in question. In all other cases, the information notice must state why the Commissioner regards the information requested as being relevant for the purpose of determining whether the data controller is complying with the Data Protection Principles.

In every case the information notice must contain particulars of the s. 48 rights of appeal to the Data Protection Tribunal (s. 43(3)). See below for further information on the appeal process.

Time limit for compliance

The time limit imposed on a data controller by the Commissioner for compliance with the information notice starts to run from the day the notice is served. In most cases it cannot expire before the day on which the rights of appeal against the notice elapse (see below) and, where an appeal is brought, will not expire until the determination or withdrawal of the appeal. Exceptionally, and where the Commissioner requires the information as a matter of urgency, the time limit specified in the notice can be shorter than the above but must not be less than seven days. In this event the Commissioner must make a statement why she considers the matter to be urgent. There is a right of appeal to the tribunal against the Commissioner's decision to include such a statement and against its effect (see below, 'Appeals').

Section 43(9) allows the Commissioner to withdraw (in writing) an information notice. Compliance is not required after such a withdrawal.

Exemptions from compliance

A person may choose not to comply with an information notice where compliance would reveal one or more of the following:

(a)   the content of any communication between a lawyer and his or her client where the subject of such communication is advice in respect of the client's rights, obligations or liabilities under the Act;

(b)   the content of any communication between a lawyer and his or her client, or between a lawyer or his or her client and any other person, made in connection with or in contemplation of proceedings (including proceedings before the Tribunal) under the Act; or

(c)   the commission by that person of an actionable criminal offence (except a criminal offence under the Act).

Special purposes

Section 46(3) prevents the Commissioner from serving an information notice on a data controller which relates to processing for the special purposes (see Chapter 9, 'Journalism, literature and art') unless the Commissioner has made a determination (under s. 45) that the personal data:

(a)   are not being processed only for the special purposes; or

(b)   are not being processed with a view to the publication by any person of any journalistic, literary or artistic material which has not previously been published by the data controller.

Criminal offences

It is an offence to fail to comply with an information notice (s. 47(1)). It is a defence to show that the accused exercised all due diligence to comply with the notice.

Further, it is an offence to make a false statement (knowingly or recklessly) in response to an information notice (s. 47(2)).

SPECIAL INFORMATION NOTICE

The exemption relating to processing for the special purposes, i.e., for journalistic, literary or artistic purposes, was discussed in Chapter 9. It is a significant exemption which preserves freedom of speech and writing for those who publish public interest material. The Commissioner's powers under the special information notice procedure exist to ensure that the exemption is used only in appropriate circumstances.

Where the Commissioner wishes to ascertain whether personal data are being processed only for the special purposes or with a view to publication of journalistic, literary or artistic material which has not previously been published by the data controller (i.e., the grounds for a stay under s. 32(4) — see Chapter 9, 'Journalism, literature and art') she may serve a notice (a 'special information notice') on the data controller which requests the data controller to supply certain information.

Under s. 44(1), a special information notice may only be served where the Commissioner:

(a) has received a request for an assessment under s. 42, or
(b) has reasonable grounds for suspecting that, in a case in which proceedings have been stayed under s. 32, the personal data to which the proceedings relate:

(i) are not being processed only for the special purposes, or
(ii) are not being processed with a view to the publication by any person of any journalistic, literary or artistic material which has not previously been published by the data controller.

The notice must state the grounds upon which it is served, the time limit for compliance and particulars of the rights of appeal conferred by s. 48 (see below). The prerequisite of either a request for assessment or a stay should mean that a special information notice is a relatively rarely used device.

Time limit for compliance

The time limit imposed on a data controller by the Commissioner for compliance with a special information notice starts to run from the day the notice is served. Subject to the limited exception below it cannot expire before the day on which the rights of appeal against the notice elapse and, where an appeal is brought, will not expire until the determination or withdrawal of the appeal. Exceptionally, and where the Commissioner requires the information as a matter of urgency, the time limit specified in the notice can be shorter than the above but must not be less than seven days. In this event the Commissioner must state why she considers the matter to be urgent. There is a right of appeal to the Tribunal against the Commissioner's decision to include such a statement and against its effect (see below, 'Appeals').

A special information notice may be cancelled by the Commissioner after it has been served (s. 44(10)). Compliance is not required after such a cancellation.

Exemptions from compliance

A person may choose not to comply with a special information notice where compliance would reveal one or more of the following:

(a) the content of any communication between a lawyer and his or her client where the subject of such communication is advice in respect of the client's rights, obligations or liabilities under the Act;
(b) the content of any communication between a lawyer and his or her client, or between a lawyer or his or her client and any other person, made in connection with or in contemplation of proceedings (including proceedings before the Tribunal) under the Act; or
(c) the commission by that person of an actionable criminal offence (except a criminal offence under the Act).

Determination by the Commissioner

Under s. 45 the Commissioner may, at any time, make a determination in writing to the data controller that certain specified processing is not being carried out only for the special purposes or with a view to publication of journalistic, literary or artistic material not previously published by the data controller. This will usually be done where the Commissioner has served a special information notice, but is not limited to such cases. The purpose of such a determination is to allow the Commissioner to serve an enforcement notice — one of the prerequisites for serving an enforcement notice in respect of processing for the special purposes is the service by the Commissioner of a s. 45 determination on the data controller (for further detail see below, 'Enforcement notice — Special purposes').

Notice of a determination under s. 45 must be given to the data controller together with a statement of the rights of appeal covered by s. 48. The determination will not take effect until the end of the period in which an appeal can be brought. Where an appeal is brought the determination will have no effect until after the conclusion or withdrawal of the appeal.

Criminal offences

It is an offence to fail to comply with a special information notice (s. 47(1)). It is a defence to show that the defendant exercised all due diligence to comply with the notice.

Further, it is an offence to make a false statement (knowingly or recklessly) in response to a special information notice (s. 47(2)).

ENFORCEMENT NOTICE

Where the Commissioner is satisfied that a data controller has contravened or is contravening any of the Data Protection Principles she may serve on the data controller a notice (an 'enforcement notice') requiring the data controller to take specific steps to rectify the contravention or to refrain from processing certain specified personal data (s. 40(1)). An enforcement notice is more likely to be served in cases where the contravention in question is causing (or is likely to cause) a person damage or distress.

Where the enforcement notice requires the data controller to rectify, block, erase or destroy any personal data, the Commissioner may require the data controller to notify third parties of that rectification, blocking, erasure or destruction. The same is true where the Commissioner is satisfied that personal data which have been rectified, blocked, erased or destroyed had been processed in contravention of any of the Data Protection Principles. In each case the requirement to notify third parties will not be imposed where this is not reasonably practicable (e.g., where there are a large number of such persons).

An enforcement notice which is concerned with a contravention of the Fourth Data Protection Principle (the obligation to keep personal data accurate and up to date) may, in addition to requiring the rectification, blocking, erasure or destruction of inaccurate personal data, impose a similar requirement in respect of any expression of opinion which appears to be based on the inaccurate data (s. 40(3)). Where, in the case of such a Fourth Principle enforcement notice, the data accurately portray information conveyed to the data controller by the data subject or a third party, the enforcement notice may require the data controller either:

(a)   to rectify, block, erase or destroy any inaccurate data and any other data containing an expression of opinion, and
(b)   to take specified steps to check the accuracy of the data and (if relevant) to supplement the data with a statement reflecting the data subject's view of the inaccuracy of the data.

Every enforcement notice must contain a list of the Data Protection Principles that are alleged to have been contravened and the grounds for that belief. The time limit for compliance should be given, along with a statement of the rights of appeal under s. 48.

An enforcement notice may be cancelled or varied by the Commissioner in writing to the data controller (s. 41(1)). A data controller who has received an enforcement notice may apply in writing to the Commissioner for the cancellation or variation of the notice. This may be done only where a change of circumstances of the data controller means that some or all of the requirements of the notice need not be complied with to ensure compliance with the Data Protection Principles and only where the time limit for the bringing of an appeal has expired (s. 41(2)). An appeal is available against the decision of the Commissioner not to allow an application under s. 41(2) (see below, 'Appeals').

Time limit for compliance

The time limit imposed on a data controller by the Commissioner for compliance with an enforcement notice starts to run from the day the notice is served. Subject to the limited exception below, it cannot expire before the day on which the rights of appeal against the notice elapse and, where an appeal is brought, will not expire until the determination or withdrawal of the appeal. Where the Commissioner requires the information as a matter of urgency, the time limit specified in the notice can be shorter than the above but must not be less than seven days. In this event the Commissioner must state why she considers the matter to be urgent. There is a right of appeal to the Tribunal against the Commissioner's decision to include such a statement and against its effect (see below, 'Appeals').

Special purposes

Section 46(1) prevents the Commissioner from serving an enforcement notice on a data controller which relates to processing for the special purposes unless the court has granted leave for the notice to be served and the Commissioner has made a determination (under s. 45) that the personal data:

(a)   are not being processed only for the special purposes, or
(b)   are not being processed with a view to the publication by any person of any journalistic, literary or artistic material which has not previously been published by the data controller.

The court will not grant leave for this purpose unless it is satisfied that the Commissioner has reason to suspect that the contravention of the Data Protection Principles in question is of substantial public importance (s. 46(2)(a)). Additionally, the court must be satisfied that the data controller has been given notice of the application for leave, which will not be necessary where the case is one of urgency (s. 46(2)(b)).

Criminal offence

It is an offence to fail to comply with an enforement notice (s. 47(1)). It is a defence to show that the defendant exercised all due diligence to comply with the notice.

APPEALS

Safeguards on the operation of powers by the Commissioner allow a data controller to appeal against certain decisions and procedures. Section 48 confers the following types of appeal.

(a)   Any person on whom an information, special information or enforcement notice has been served may appeal against it.

On such an appeal the Tribunal may review any question of fact on which the service of the notice was based. The Tribunal must dismiss the appeal unless it considers that one of the following two factors is true:

(i)   that the notice against which the appeal is brought does not accord with some legal provision, or

(ii)   that the Commissioner ought to have exercised her discretion (if any) differently.

If either factor is made out by the appellant then the Tribunal must allow the appeal or substitute the notice with any other notice which the Commissioner could have served.

(b)   A person who has been served with an enforcement notice may appeal against the refusal of an application under s. 41(2) for cancellation or variation of the notice.

Section 41(2) allows an application to the Commissioner for cancellation or variation of an enforcement notice (due to change of circumstances) where the time limit for an appeal against the notice has expired. Notwithstanding the expiry of the right to appeal against the notice itself, this provision allows an appeal against the decision of the Commissioner not to grant such variation or cancellation.

The Tribunal may cancel or vary the notice due to a change of circumstances where it feels it appropriate to do so.

(c)   A person who has been served with an information, special information or enforcement notice containing a statement of urgency for the purposes of imposing a shorter than normal time limit for compliance may appeal against the Commissioner's decision to include such a statement in the notice.

The Tribunal may abolish the effect of the statement.

(d)   A person who has been served with an information, special information or enforcement notice containing a statement of urgency for the purposes of imposing a shorter than normal time limit for compliance may appeal against the effect of the inclusion of the statement in respect of any part of the notice.

The Tribunal may direct that the inclusion of the statement shall not have effect in relation to any part of the notice.

(e)   A data controller may appeal against a determination under s. 45 that personal data are not being processed only for the special purposes or with a view to publication by any person of any journalistic, literary or artistic material which has not previously been published by the data controller.

The Tribunal may cancel the determination of the Commissioner.

Appeals from any decision of the Tribunal are available to either party and will be heard by the High Court of Justice (or the Court of Session where the appellant's address is in Scotland; the High Court of Justice of Northern Ireland where the appellant's address is in Northern Ireland).

For further detail on procedural aspects of appeals see The Data Protection Tribunal (Enforcement Appeals) Rules 2000 — Appendix 3.

Chapter 11
Criminal Offences

INTRODUCTION

The Data Protection Act 1998 creates a number of criminal offences which are contained in various parts of the Act. This chapter examines each of the offences in turn. Some have been dealt with in the text of Chapters 2 and 10 where they have been relevant to the material contained in those chapters. Other offences are of a more general nature and will be dealt with here for the first time.

Criminal proceedings cannot be instituted except by the Commissioner or by or with the consent of the Director of Public Prosecutions (in Northern Ireland the Director of Public Prosecutions for Northern Ireland).

All offences contained in the Act are punishable only with a fine — imprisonment is not a possibility for contraventions of the Act. The offence contained in sch. 9, para. 12, is a summary-only offence punishable with a fine not exceeding level 5 on the standard scale. All other offences in the Act are either-way offences which may be tried in a magistrates' court or by jury in the Crown Court. The maximum fine on summary conviction is £5,000. In the Crown Court there is no maximum limit.

In certain offences, the court has power to order the forfeiture, destruction or erasure of a document, computer disk or other material used in connection with the processing of personal data. Where the owner of such a document, computer disk or other material is not the offender, that person must be given the opportunity of making representations before the making of such an order for forfeiture, destruction or erasure.

UNLAWFUL OBTAINING OR DISCLOSURE OF PERSONAL DATA

By virtue of s. 55(1), a person must not knowingly or recklessly, without the consent of the data controller:

(a)   obtain or disclose personal data or the information contained in personal data, or

(b)   procure the disclosure to another person of the information contained in personal data.

For these purposes only, the definition of personal data does not include any personal data which are exempt on national security grounds (s. 55(8)).

Section 55(3) makes the contravention of s. 55(1) a criminal offence. A defence is available to any person charged with such an offence who shows:

(a) that the obtaining, disclosing or procuring was necessary for the purpose of preventing or detecting crime, or was required or authorised by or under any enactment, by any rule of law or by the order of a court,

(b) that the actions said to constitute the offence were taken in the reasonable belief of having in law the right to obtain or disclose the data or information or, as the case may be, to procure the disclosure of the information to the other person,

(c) that the actions said to constitute the offence were taken in the reasonable belief that the consent of the data controller would have been given if the data controller had known of the obtaining, disclosing or procuring and the circumstances of it, or

(d) that in the particular circumstances the obtaining, disclosing or procuring was justified as being in the public interest.

The creation of this offence deals with some of the problems created by the unsuccessful prosecution in *R v Brown* [1996] 2 WLR 203. In that case a police officer, in an attempt to assist a friend who ran a debt collection agency (Capital Investigations Ltd.), asked a colleague to call to a computer screen certain information held on the police national computer database. There was no evidence that the personal data revealed by the search was ever communicated by the officer to Capital Investigations or used by him in any other way. The officer was charged with the 1984 Act offence of using personal data for a purpose other than that described in the register. The police registration with the Registrar anticipated use of data for police purposes and did not cover the suspected activities of the officer in question.

The key to the prosecution lay in the word 'use' as it appeared in the 1984 Act. If the officer could be said to be using data then he was guilty. The defence case was that the officer was not using data, as he had merely read information appearing on a computer screen. He was found guilty by a jury but the conviction was overturned on appeal. The House of Lords held that 'use' was to be given its ordinary meaning and that the concept of use did not extend to mere retrieval of information from a database.

Section 55 of the Act makes it an offence to 'obtain' or 'disclose' information contained in personal data (or procure the disclosure to another person of the information contained in personal data). A person who acted today as Mr Brown had done would be guilty of this offence.

SELLING AND OFFERING TO SELL PERSONAL DATA

Section 55(4) creates an offence where a person sells personal data having obtained them in contravention of s. 55(1), which is discussed above.

Section 55(5) creates an offence which will be committed where a person offers to sell personal data and:

(a) the person has obtained the data in contravention of s. 55(1), or

(b) the person subsequently obtains the data in contravention of s. 55(1).

Subsections (4) and (5) of s. 55 cover the situations of both sale and offering for sale. A person may be guilty of offering for sale even where, at the point of offer, there has been no obtaining in contravention of s. 55(1) — the later obtaining of personal data in contravention of that subsection will outlaw the earlier offer.

The distinction between an offer and an invitation to treat is purely academic in relation to advertisements: by virtue of s. 55(6) all indications of the availability for sale of personal data which are contained in advertisements are to be treated as offers for sale for the purpose of this offence.

ENFORCED SUBJECT ACCESS

The criminal offence of 'enforced subject access' does not appear in the Directive. It was included in the 1998 Act by the UK Parliament in an attempt to combat the practice which had become common under the 1984 Act, namely the requiring of a data subject, usually a prospective employee, to obtain a copy of the details held in him or her by another, usually the police. In this way an employer would be able to obtain a copy of a candidate's criminal record.

By virtue of s. 56(1), a person must not require another person (or a third party) to supply him or her with a relevant record (see definition below) or to produce a relevant record in connection with:

(a)   the recruitment of that other person as an employee;
(b)   the continued employment of that other person; or
(c)   any contract for the provision of services to him or her by that other person.

Section 56(2) provides that a person who is concerned with the provision of goods, facilities or services to the public must not, as a condition of such provision, require that other person or a third party to supply him with a relevant record or to produce a relevant record to him.

Section 56(5) makes the contravention of s. 56(1) or (2) a criminal offence. However, it will be a defence for a person charged with either offence to show that:

(a)   the imposition of the requirement was required or authorised by or under any enactment, by any rule of law or by the order of a court, or
(b)   in the particular circumstances the imposition of the requirement was justified as being in the public interest.

Subsection (4) of s. 56 makes it clear that the imposition of a requirement is not to be regarded as being justified as being in the public interest merely on the ground that it would assist in the prevention or detection of crime, and contains a cross-reference to Part V of the Police Act 1997.

'Relevant record' is defined, somewhat confusingly, by reference to a table (reproduced below) which consists of two columns. The left-hand column lists various data controllers, and the right-hand column, various types of relevant subject matter. A 'relevant record' is any record which:

(a)   has been or is to be obtained by a data subject from any data controller specified in the first column of the table in exercise of the subject access provisions in s. 7, and
(b)   contains information relating to any matter specified in relation to that data controller in the second column,

and includes a copy of such a record or a part of such a record.

At the time of writing s. 56 was yet to be brought into force. It cannot come into force until ss. 112, 113 and 115 of the Police Act 1997 are all in force.

Data controller	Subject-matter
1. Any of the following persons— (a) a chief officer of police of a police force in England and Wales, (b) a chief constable of a police force in Scotland, (c) the Chief Constable of the Royal Ulster Constabulary, (d) the Director General of the National Criminal Intelligence Service, (e) the Director General of the National Crime Squad,	(a) Convictions. (b) Cautions.
2. The Secretary of State.	(a) Convictions. (b) Cautions. (c) His functions under section 53 of the Children and Young Persons Act 1933, section 205(2) or 208 of the Criminal Procedure (Scotland) Act 1995 or section 73 of the Children and Young Persons Act (Northern Ireland) 1968 in relation to any person sentenced to detention. (d) His functions under the Prison Act 1952, the Prisons (Scotland) Act 1989 or the Prison Act (Northern Ireland) 1953 in relation to any person imprisoned or detained. (e) His functions under the Social Security Contributions and Benefits Act 1992, the Social Security Administration Act 1992 or the Jobseekers Act 1995. (f) His functions under Part V of the Police Act 1997.
3. The Department of Health and Social Services for Northern Ireland.	Its functions under the Social Security Contributions and Benefits (Northern Ireland) Act 1992, the Social Security Administration (Northern Ireland) Act 1992 or the Jobseekers (Northern Ireland) Order 1995.

This table may be amended by the Secretary of State by order.

DISCLOSING THE COMMISSIONER'S INFORMATION

Section 59(1) contains a prohibition on the disclosing of certain information which has been provided to the office of the Commissioner. It is an offence knowingly or recklessly to disclose such information (s. 59(3)). The prohibition exists in relation to the following persons only:

(a)   the Commissioner,
(b)   a member of the Commissioner's staff,
(c)   an agent of the Commissioner.

The information which cannot be disclosed (unless the disclosure is made with lawful authority — see below) is that which:

(a)   has been obtained by, or furnished to, the Commissioner under or for the purposes of the Act,
(b)   relates to an identified or identifiable individual or business, and
(c)   is not at the time of the disclosure, and has not previously been, available to the public from other sources.

A disclosure is made with lawful authority only if one or more of the following apply:

(a)   the disclosure is made with the consent of the individual or of the person for the time being carrying on the business,
(b)   the information was provided for the purpose of its being made available to the public (in whatever manner) under any provision of the Act,
(c)   the disclosure is made for the purposes of, and is necessary for, the discharge of any function under the Act or any Community obligation,
(d)   the disclosure is made for the purposes of any proceedings, whether criminal or civil and whether arising under, or by virtue of, this Act or otherwise, or
(e)   having regard to the rights and freedoms or legitimate interests of any person, the disclosure is necessary in the public interest.

OBSTRUCTING OR FAILING TO ASSIST IN THE EXECUTION OF A WARRANT

Schedule 9 contains provisions allowing the application for a warrant to enter and inspect premises where there is a suspicion of contravention of the Data Protection Principles or of a criminal offence having been committed under the Act. Paragraph 12 of that schedule makes it a criminal offence:

(a)   to intentionally obstruct a person in the execution of such a warrant, or
(b)   to fail without reasonable cause to give any person executing such a warrant such assistance as he or she may reasonably require for the execution of the warrant.

The offence is summary only and punishable only by a fine not exceeding level 5 on the standard scale.

PROCESSING WITHOUT A REGISTER ENTRY

Section 21(1) makes it a criminal offence to process personal data where all of the following apply:

(a)   an entry in the register maintained by the Commissioner has not been made,
(b)   the notification regulations (if any) relating to deemed registration do not apply,
(c)   notification regulations (if any) giving authority to certain specified types of processing without the need for notification do not apply, and
(d)   it is not the case that the sole purpose of the processing is the maintenance of a public register.

Manual records (and accessible records), even if they fall within the definition of data, are not subject to notification to the Commissioner and, therefore, processing them will not be a criminal offence under this provision (see Chapter 8, 'Prohibition on processing without notification').

FAILING TO NOTIFY CHANGES

Under s. 21(1) a data controller is under a duty to inform the Commissioner of any change in:

(a)   the registrable particulars, or
(b)   the measures taken to comply with the Seventh Principle.

What will and will not constitute a change for these purposes is to be set out in the notification regulations.

By virtue of s. 21(2), failure to notify the Commissioner of these changes constitutes the commission of a criminal offence. It is a defence to show that the defendant exercised all due diligence to comply with the duty.

CARRYING ON ASSESSABLE PROCESSING

Under s. 22(6) it is a criminal offence to carry on assessable processing (see Chapter 8, 'Assessable processing') after the data controller has notified the Commissioner of processing unless either:

(a)   the relevant period of 28 days (within which the Commissioner must send to the data controller a notice opining on whether the processing is accessible) has elapsed; or
(b)   before the end of the period in (a) the data controller has received a notice from the Commissioner stating the extent to which the Commissioner is of the opinion that the processing is likely or unlikely to comply with the provisions of the Act.

In other words, where the Commissioner has not informed the data controller, within 28 days of receiving a notification, that in her opinion the data controller is carrying on assessable processing, no offence will be committed under s. 26.

The types of processing that are most likely to fall within the category of assessable processing are the following:

(a) data matching;
(b) processing of genetic data; and
(c) processing by private investigations.

FAILING TO MAKE CERTAIN PARTICULARS AVAILABLE

Section 24 imposes a duty on a data controller who chooses not to register with the Commissioner where notification is not compulsory because:

(a) the only personal data being processed are manual data recorded as part of a relevant filing system (and the processing is not assessable processing); or
(b) the only personal data being processed are part of an accessible record (and the processing is not assessable processing); or
(c) notification regulations provide that processing of that description does not require notification.

The duty under s. 24 is that the data controller must, within 21 days of receiving a written request from any person, make the relevant particulars available in writing to that person free of charge. The relevant particulars are items (a) to (f) of the registrable particulars listed in s. 16(1) (see Chapter 8). Thus lack of notification, and hence lack of registration, does not mean that a data controller will not be required to make the appropriate disclosure to a data subject.

It is a criminal offence to fail to comply with this duty of disclosure (s. 24(4)). It is a defence to show that the defendant exercised all due diligence to comply. Thus an accidental failure to set out the relevant particulars fully should escape conviction.

FAILING TO COMPLY WITH A NOTICE

By virtue of s. 47(1) it is an offence to fail to comply with an enforcement, an information or a special information notice (see Chapter 10). It is a defence to show that the defendant exercised all due diligence to comply with the notice.

MAKING A FALSE STATEMENT IN RESPONSE TO A NOTICE

Under s. 47(2) it is an offence to make a false statement, knowingly or recklessly, in response to an information or special information notice (see Chapter 10).

LIABILITY OF CORPORATE OFFICERS

Under s. 61(1) a director, manager, secretary or other similar officer of a corporate body may be liable to be punished for the same offence as that which has been proved against the corporate body by whom they are employed. In order to be found guilty of the offence the director etc. must be involved in the offence committed by the corporate body by virtue of some connivance or neglect. Similar rules exist in relation to a Scottish partnership (s. 61(3)).

A charge under s. 61(1) may be brought against a person who is a member of a corporate body where that body is managed by its members.

IMMUNITY FROM PROSECUTION

Although the Crown is subject to the provisions of the Data Protection Act 1998 in the same way as other persons, s. 63(5) provides that neither a government department nor a person who acts on behalf of the Royal Household, the Duchy of Lancaster or the Duchy of Cornwall in respect of certain types of data (see s. 63(3)) can be prosecuted for any offences contained in the Act.

Chapter 12
Telecommunications

INTRODUCTION

As a direct result of the explosion in the provision and availability of telecommunications services in the 1980s and early 1990s, concerns arose over the privacy of individuals when using and operating telephones and related devices. Such concerns have been multiplied with the advent of digital technology, the availability of calling line identification and the proliferation of related Internet services. Although data protection legislation applies to the telecommunications sector in the same way as it does to other industries, the European Union (EU) considered that extra safeguards were required.

The Telecommunications (Data Protection and Privacy) Regulations 1999 (SI 1999, No. 2093) (the 1999 Regulations) were produced to give effect to Directive 97/66/EC concerning the 'processing of personal data and the protection of privacy in the telecommunications sector'. They repeal and replace the Telecommunications (Data Protection and Privacy) (Direct Marketing) Regulations 1998 (that came into force on 1 May 1999), dealing with unsolicited direct marketing telephone calls and faxes. However, the provisions relating to unsolicited direct marketing telephone calls or faxes contained in the 1999 Regulations do not differ from the provisions of the 1998 Regulations. The 1999 Regulations, as amended by the Telecommunications (Data Protection and Privacy) (Amendment) Regulations 2000 (SI 2000, No. 157), came into force on 1 March 2000.

The 1999 Regulations create rights for individuals and companies over and above those under the Data Protection Act 1998. They also make compulsory the supply to telephone subscribers of certain services or facilities and allow telecommunications providers to make a reasonable charge for those services or facilities.

Key provisions of the new Regulations

- Restrictions on the processing of traffic and billing data.
- Withholding of calling or called line identification (CLI).
- Rights related to entries in public telephone directories of subscribers.
- Unsolicited direct marketing telephone calls and faxes.
- Security standards.
- Right of subscribers to receive non-itemised bills.
- Entries in telephone directories.

DEFINITIONS

The 1999 Regulations provide a legal regime for the protection of the privacy of individuals when using telecommunications equipment. The regulations can be seen as being complementary to the general data protection provisions contained in the Data Protection Act 1998. Indeed, much of the terminology of the regulations is imported from the Act. However, certain additional words and phrases require definition:

'bill' includes an invoice, account, statement or other instrument of the like character;

'individual' means a living individual and includes an unincorporated body of such individuals;

'public telecommunications network' means any transmission system, and any associated switching equipment and other resources, which (in either case)—

(a)   permit the conveyance of signals between defined termination points by wire, by radio, by optical or by other electro-magnetic means, and

(b)   are used, in whole or in part, for the provision of publicly available telecommunications services;

'subscriber' means a person who is a party to a contract with a telecommunications service provider for the supply of publicly available telecommunications services;

'telecommunications network provider' means a person who provides a public telecommunications network (whether or not he is also a telecommunications service provider);

'telecommunications service provider' means a person who provides publicly available telecommunications services (whether or not he is also a telecommunications network provider);

'telecommunications services' means services the provision of which consists, in whole or in part, of the transmission and routing of signals on telecommunications networks, not being services by way of radio or television broadcasting;

'user' means an individual using a publicly available telecommunications service (whether or not he is a subscriber).

LIMITATIONS ON PROCESSING OF DATA

Part II of the 1999 Regulations places restrictions on the processing of data concerning telecommunications traffic and billing. Although different rules apply to each of these two types of data, it should be noted that the definitions of each are not mutually exclusive. In many cases information that constitutes billing data will also be traffic data, and vice versa. In addition to the specific restrictions detailed below, both traffic data and billing data may only be processed for the following purposes:

(a)   the management of billing or traffic;
(b)   customer enquiries;
(c)   the detection of fraud; and
(d)   the marketing of telecommunications services.

The prerequisite in Directive 97/66/EC that the subscriber must give his *consent* to the processing for marketing purposes in paragraph (d) above is missing in the UK regulations.

Traffic data

Subject to two exceptions, personal data which are processed to secure the connection of a call and which are stored for that purpose must be erased or depersonalised by the telecommunications provider as soon as the call is terminated. There is no definition of 'depersonalised' in the 1999 Regulations, but help with the meaning can be gleaned from the use of the words 'made anonymous' in the Directive. It seems clear that a telecommunication services provider is able to keep all data relating to the connection of a call as long as the personal details of the individual concerned are removed from such data. Thus, by way of example, a telecommunications provider may keep figures relating to call duration and billing for statistical purposes.

Interestingly, the limitation on the storage of personal data extends, unlike the 1998 Act itself, to data relating to *corporate* subscribers to telecommunications services. The name of the company who made the call concerned must, therefore, be removed from the other call data before it is stored for any purpose.

Traffic data are those data which:

(a) are in respect of traffic handled by a telecommunications network provider or a telecommunications service provider;

(b) are processed to secure the connection of a call and held by the provider concerned; and

(c) constitute personal data whereof the data subject is a subscriber to, or user of, any publicly available telecommunications service or, in the case of a corporate subscriber, would constitute such personal data if that subscriber were an individual.

The exceptions, which allow the storage of non-depersonalised call connection data in respect of both individual and corporate subscribers, are contained in paras 7(2) and 8(2) of the 1999 Regulations. The first relates to the marketing of telecommunications services (with the consent of the subscriber) and the second to the settling of disputes. Little detail is given in the Regulations save that the dispute concerned may be by way of 'legal proceedings'. The Directive clearly contemplates interconnection or billing disputes as being the specific beneficiaries from this provision. It is clear then that non-depersonalised traffic and billing data can be furnished to a court or other competent authority for the purposes of litigation.

Billing data

The processing of billing data is allowed for purposes connected with the payment of sums either by a subscriber or by way of interconnection charges. Interconnection charges are the amounts of money charged by one provider to another for the use of connections. But where the data are personal data (individual or corporate) processing is allowed only until the expiry of the period during which legal proceedings may be brought or appealed. Billing data for these purposes are defined, in sch. 1 to the Regulations, as data that comprise information in respect of all or any of the following matters:

(a)   the number or other identification of the subscriber's station;

(b)   the subscriber's address and the type of the station;

(c)   the total number of units of use by reference to which the sum payable in respect of any accounting period is calculated;

(d)   the type, date, starting time and duration of calls and the volume of data transmissions in respect of which sums are payable by the subscriber and the numbers or other identification of the stations to which they were made;

(e)   the date of the provision of any service not falling within sub-paragraph (d); and

(f)   other matters concerning payments including, in particular, advance payments, payments by instalments, reminders and disconnections.

Marketing

Where billing or traffic data are processed for the purposes of marketing telecommunications services provided by the telecommunications service provider, such processing can only take place with the consent of the subscriber concerned. Such consent may be implied, but then only where the implication results from some action. Silence or lack of activity cannot amount to consent for these purposes.

CALLING AND CALLED LINE IDENTIFICATION

In several countries of Europe it has been possible for some time to identify the telephone number of a person making a call. Calling Line Identification (CLI), as this service is known, provides a number of benefits, including allowing a called person the freedom to choose whether to accept a particular call before it is answered and giving information to emergency services on the location of distressed callers who may not be able to give such information.

Outgoing calls

Under the 1999 Regulations, a subscriber is entitled to be able to prevent CLI attaching to his *outgoing* call whether or not he is the subscriber to the line from which he is calling. In the UK this is possible by dialling 141 immediately prior to the number of the person being called. Additionally, a subscriber has the right to block CLI on all outgoing calls on his line or on individual calls on a call-by-call basis. Both services must be made available free of charge by the relevant telecommunications service provider.

Incoming calls

A person is entitled to prevent his or her telecommunications equipment from providing information identifying any *incoming* call. Such identification may be made available in two ways — by a display device or by a call return service. Further, where telecommunications equipment makes details of the telephone number of a subscriber being called available to the caller, the subscriber must be able to prevent presentation of his or her number. Both services must be made available free of charge.

Where incoming caller identification is available, it must be possible for the person being called to reject any call where the caller has withheld his or her number before it has been answered.

999 or 112 calls

Both 999 (UK emergency services) and 112 (the single European emergency call number) calls are subject to the following rules:

(a)   no CLI shall be permitted to attach to these calls by the caller; and
(b)   the identity of the calling line cannot be withheld by the person being called.

Malicious or nuisance calls

Paragraph 14 of the 1999 Regulations permit a telecommunications provider to override any attempt by a person who makes malicious or nuisance calls from withholding the identity of the calling line.

DIRECT MARKETING USING TELECOMMUNICATIONS SYSTEMS

Telephone marketing, whether by voice or fax, has proved to be a highly successful sales technique. But it has also led to considerable numbers of complaints. The 1999 Regulations seek to address this concern by regulating the use of telecommunications equipment for direct marketing (defined for the purposes of the Regulations as 'communication of any advertising or marketing material on a particular line'). It should be noted that the Regulations apply to anyone who uses a publicly available telecommunications network for direct marketing, not just to data controllers.

Use of automated calling systems

Automated systems which operate direct-marketing functions without human intervention are unlawful unless the subscriber (whether individual or corporate) has notified the caller that he or she consents to such communications being made.

Use of fax for unsolicited direct marketing

The automated use of faxes for direct marketing is subject to the same rules as that of automated calling (see above). This section, therefore, concerns only non-automated faxing.

The Director General of Telecommunications (an official set up under the Telecommunications Act 1984) is obliged to keep a record of both individual and corporate subscribers who have notified the Director that they do not wish to receive direct marketing by fax. It is unlawful to send such a fax to any number listed in that record or to any person who has informed the caller that he or she does not wish to receive such communications. Further, it is unlawful to send a direct marketing fax to an *individual* subscriber unless the individual has notified the caller that he or she consents to such communications.

The record maintained by the Director General may be searched by any person upon payment of a fee.

Unsolicited calls

It is unlawful to make unsolicited calls to an individual for the purposes of direct marketing where such an individual's name appears on the record maintained by the Director General or where the individual has notified the caller that he or she does not wish to receive such communications.

TELEPHONE DIRECTORIES

The 1999 Regulations give certain rights to individual and corporate subscribers in relation to entries in publicly available telephone directories (whether available in paper form or on-line). Both an individual and a corporate subscriber are entitled to request that no entry of their telephone number appears in a directory (i.e., ex-directory status). Where a subscriber is an individual he or she may additionally request that any entry relating to the subscriber does not reveal either or both of the following:

(a)   the subscriber's sex; or
(b)   the subscriber's address.

Any directory entry relating to an individual must not contain any personal data other than data which are necessary to identify the individual and the number allocated to him or her, unless the individual has consented to the inclusion of such additional material.

SECURITY

A telecommunications service provider is under a duty to undertake appropriate technical and organisational measures to ensure the security of the service provided. A telecommunications network provider must comply with any reasonable request of the service provider in this regard.

NON-ITEMISED BILLS

Any subscriber is entitled to receive telecommunication bills which are not itemised. This provision is designed to protect the privacy of a person in relation to other members of his or her household.

TERMINATION OF UNWANTED CALL FORWARDING

Where calls are automatically forwarded to a subscriber's number, the subscriber is entitled to the termination of that forwarding at no cost and without delay.

ENFORCEMENT

The 1999 Regulations are enforceable by the Data Protection Commissioner and most of her powers and functions under the 1998 Act are extended to the provisions of the Regulations.

TRANSITIONAL PROVISIONS

Most of the provisions of the 1999 Regulations came into force on 1 March 2000. The transitional provisions apply only to billing data used for marketing purposes. Such data will be eligible data under the Regulations if they were subject to processing which was already under way immediately before 1 March 2000.

THE FUTURE

Directive 97/66/EC applies to the processing of personal data in the 'telecommunications sector'. Concern that the extra safeguards in the Directive, over and above those applicable to other types of processing under the Act, led to the Commission, on 12 July 2000, publishing a 'Proposal for a Directive concerning the processing of personal data and the protection of privacy in the electronic communications sector'. This new Directive, when eventually implemented in Member States, will apply the existing telecommunications regulations to all electronic communications. The aim of the Directive is to ensure that data protection measures apply uniformly and in a technology-neutral fashion to all electronic communications, including those conducted via the Internet.

Chapter 13
Employment

INTRODUCTION

Data protection legislation is of particular relevance in the field of employment. Employers process a great deal of personal data about their employees, including name, address, date of birth, payroll details and, where relevant, CCTV images. In some cases employers will also process sensitive personal data such as lists of criminal convictions, physical and mental health data and trade union membership information. The 1998 Act encourages employers to be proactive in respect of their data protection obligations, to allow employees access to data held about them in manual files and to refrain from enforced subject access and unauthorised data matching.

Large- and medium-sized employers would be best advised to immediately put in place a Data Protection Officer to ensure compliance with the Act. Such a person should be effectively trained on the ramifications of the 1998 Act and in the design of procedures to ensure compliance. One of the first tasks of the Data Protection Officer should be to undertake a thorough review of all personal data held by the employer and to set up procedures and policies for governing the relationship between the employer and its employees. In most cases separate initiatives will be required for sensitive personal data (see below).

This chapter considers those aspects of the law that will be of particular significance to employers, personnel departments and human resources officers. It then goes on to look at some procedures that are recommended for ensuring compliance with the legislation. In this chapter the data controller will be the employer, and data subjects will be the employees or prospective employees. Where an employer has been engaged in processing employee data since before 24 October 1998 it is likely that it will not have to comply with the new provisions discussed in this chapter until 24 October 2001. Employers are referred to other statutory constraints affecting employment information contained in the Human Rights Act 1998, the Public Interests Disclosure Act 1998 and the Trades Union and Labour Relations (Consolidation) Act 1992.

NOTIFICATION

In contrast to the registration system under the 1984 Act, the notification regime does not require an employer to notify processing for 'staff administration' to the

Commissioner. The Data Protection (Notification and Notification Fees) Regulations 2000 list the following purposes of processing employee details as falling within the staff administration provisions and thus being exempt from the requirement of notification:

- appointments or removals;
- pay;
- discipline;
- superannuation;
- work management; and
- other personnel matters.

To benefit from the exemption the processing must:

    (a)   be of personal data in respect of which the data subject is—
       (i)   a past, existing or prospective member of staff of the data controller; or
       (ii)   any person the processing of whose personal data is necessary for one or more of the above six purposes;
    (b)   be of personal data consisting of the name, address and other identifiers of the data subject or information as to—
       (i)   qualifications, work experience or pay;
       (ii)   or other matters the processing of which is necessary for one or more of the above six purposes;
    (c)   not involve disclosure of the personal data to any third party other than—
       (i)   with the consent of the data subject; or
       (ii)   where it is necessary to make such disclosure for one or more of the above six purposes; and
    (d)   not involve keeping the personal data after the relationship between the data controller and staff member ends, unless and for so long as it is necessary to do so for one of the above six purposes.

It can be seen then that provided the employer has put procedures in place to ensure that employee data processing falls within the above provisions, the employer need not notify its employee data processing to the Commissioner. There are two observations that should, however, be made: first, exemption from notification of staff administration processing does not mean that the employer will not need to notify its other types of personal data processing; and second, that exemption from notification does not absolve the employer from complying with all other relevant aspects of the legislation such as the Data Protection Principles and the data subject access rights.

SENSITIVE DATA

Of particular concern to employers will be the new category of sensitive personal data introduced in the 1998 Act. It will be remembered that sensitive personal data are those data which relate to one or more of the following categories of information concerning the employee:

(a)   the racial or ethnic origin of the employee;
(b)   the employee's political opinions;
(c)   the employee's religious beliefs or other beliefs of a similar nature;
(d)   whether the employee is a member of a trade union;
(e)   the employee's physical or mental health or condition;
(f)   the employee's sexual life;
(g)   the commission or alleged commission by the employee of any offence.

Employers will commonly keep records of employee trade union membership as well as criminal convictions and certain health data (e.g., doctors' notes) — all of which are sensitive personal data. Schedule 3 to the Act states that sensitive data may not be processed unless one of a number of pre-conditions is in existence (see Chapter 5). One of those pre-conditions is the 'explicit consent' of the data subject. Although yet to be tested in the courts, it is most unlikely that explicit consent will ever be made out where an employee has not been fully informed of the type of processing being undertaken and given his or her unambiguous and freely-given consent to such processing. The safest course of action for an employer is therefore to obtain employees' consent in writing, and the most logical place to do this is in the contract of employment. Consideration should therefore be given to amending standard employment contracts so as to obtain the requisite consent; it would also be prudent to draw a prospective employee's attention specifically to the relevant clause and give examples of its operation. As far as existing employees are concerned, their consent to amendment of their contracts should be obtained. As an alternative, specific consent to sensitive data processing could be obtained by distributing a form explaining the requirements of the employer and requesting the employee's signature by way of agreement to the uses proposed. It should of course be remembered that not only must an employee be informed that the employer wishes to process sensitive data (and the employee's consent obtained), but also that the employer must inform the employee of all the *purposes* for such processing.

EMPLOYEE DATA SECURITY

The Seventh Data Protection Principle requires employers to take appropriate care during employee data processing to ensure that the data are not lost, destroyed, damaged or accessed by unauthorised third parties. Employers should bear in mind the technical security measures that are currently available in the market, as well as the cost of such measures in making a determination of the appropriate steps that should be taken. The Personnel Policy Research Unit has suggested that it is appropriate for employers to comply with BS7799 in their employee data processing (see Chapter 8).

OUTSOURCING EMPLOYER FUNCTIONS

It may be, particularly in the case of larger employers, that employee personal data are processed by a third-party on behalf of the employer. Such a situation most commonly arises where the employer out-sources his payroll function. Where the third-party has no control over the determination of the purposes of processing but merely undertakes the processing on behalf of the employer, the third-party will be, for the purposes of the legislation, a 'data processor'.

In this case, as with any third-party data processing, there must be a contract in place between the employer and the data processor. The contract should be in writing and must oblige the processor to take such measures in respect of the personal data processing as would comply with the requirements of the Seventh Data Protection Principle. The employer must check that the processor is complying with this contractual obligation.

EMPLOYEE RIGHTS

Under the data subject access provisions in s. 7 of the Act, an employee is entitled to gain access to data held by the employer concerning the employee. Similarly, a job applicant is entitled to see the record (if any) of the reasons for being refused the job applied for (see Chapter 2 for further detail). There are specific limits on employee access which benefit the employer where the information relates to 'management forecasting' or negotiations which the employer is planning to carry out with the employee (see Chapter 9). An employee is entitled to compensation where employer processing has caused unwarranted and substantial damage or unwarranted and substantial distress (see Chapter 2).

Manual data

Employers should take care when writing comments on an employee's file. Under the 1998 Act an employee is entitled to see manual records which concern the employee and may therefore learn that he or she is 'not suitable for promotion' or 'frequently sleeps on the job'. The Data Protection Officer (or personnel department) must be ready, from 24 October 2001, to comply with data subject access requests which relate to manual data. In many cases this will require an assessment of whether any hardwritten records exist which concern the employee anywhere in the employer's premises. In larger organisations such records may be kept by line managers and other members of staff, as well as by the personnel and/or HR departments themselves. For further detail on the definition of manual records, see Chapter 7.

AUTOMATED DECISIONS

Where any substantial decision is taken by an employer solely by automated means (e.g., computer processed psychometric testing or automated CV scanning for job applicants), the subject of the automated decision must be informed that the decision has been taken by automated means. Commentators have argued that no employer decisions are ever taken purely by automated means due to there always being some human input in the design of the systems and the programming of software. Such arguments are ingenious but unlikely to meet with success in the courts.

ENFORCED SUBJECT ACCESS

Section 56 of the Act provides that an employer will commit a criminal offence where, in connection with the recruitment of any person or other employment matters, the employer requires an employee or prospective employee to make a subject access request to the police. So-called 'enforced subject access', a practice which this offence is designed to combat, grew out of the subject access rights provisions originally conferred under the 1984 Act. Employers have sought to obtain records of employee criminal convictions by insisting that the employee makes a subject access request of the police.

Section 56 provides that:

A person must not in connection with—

    (a)   the recruitment of that other person as an employee,
    (b)   the continued employment of that other person, or
    (c)   any contract for the provision of services to him by that other person

require that other person (or a third party) to supply him with a relevant record or to produce a relevant record to him.

The definition of 'relevant record' is complex (see the table in Chapter 11) but generally means information concerning criminal convictions and cautions.

Section 56 is not in force at the time of writing. It cannot come into force until sections 112, 113 and 115 of the Police Act 1997 come into force.

TRANSFERRING EMPLOYEE DATA ABROAD

The Eighth Data Protection Principle outlaws the export of personal data to countries outside the European Economic Area (EEA) unless such a country ensures an adequate level of protection for the rights and freedoms of data subjects. Employers must therefore generally not transfer personnel files outside the EEA. Similarly, names of job applicants should not be transferred to non-EEA countries (unless an appropriate exemption applies). In each case the export of such data will be permitted where the country of the transferee has adequate data protection legislation in place (only Hungary and Switzerland have thus far been approved by the EU for this purpose) or where one of the exemptions in sch. 4 to the Act (e.g., consent of the employee) applies to the transfer. The Eighth Principle will have greatest effect on multi-national companies who wish to transfer employee records between branches internationally.

One of the exemptions to the operation of the export ban allows the transfer of personal data to non-EEA countries where the Commissioner has specifically authorised the transfer. The UK Commissioner has yet to exercise this power but it is interesting to note that the German Data Protection Commissioner recently acted to give Citibank permission to transfer personal data from Germany to the United States.

EMPLOYEE SURVEILLANCE

Employers may carry out surveillance of their employees for a number of reasons. A particular employee may be suspected of fraudulent activity. Or it may be that an employer wishes to monitor the amount of time being spent by employees surfing the Internet or to review the content of e-mails to check for matters such as discrimination or defamation. Employee surveillance may take a number of forms including the following:

- visible CCTV;
- covert surveillance cameras;
- e-mail diversion and interception ('dataveillance');
- telephone tapping;
- reviewing the destination of telephone calls; and
- recording the number of photocopies being made (in circumstances where photocopying requires an ID card).

In most cases employee surveillance will amount to processing of personal data, and will therefore be subject to the provisions of the Act. The First Data Protection Principle requires that surveillance must be undertaken fairly and lawfully. In most cases this will require the consent of the employee. Such consent could conceivably be obtained in the contract of employment. If the surveillance is obvious (such as CCTV cameras) then there are some grounds for maintaining that employees have given their implied consent to processing for normal CCTV purposes. But it must be remembered that an employee is able to withdraw his consent to any type of processing at any time. The Fifth Data Protection Principle requires that data must not be kept for longer than is necessary for the purpose for which they are required. It is therefore a responsibility of employers to destroy or erase data obtained through surveillance as soon as it is clear that such data is not required for any disciplinary or other action against the employee, or for other related purposes.

Public sector employees have the additional safeguard of art. 8 of the European Human Rights Convention which guarantees the right to privacy of correspondence (including e-mails and telephone calls). Where employees have consented to surveillance then it is unlikely that they would benefit from art. 8 as they will be taken to have waived such a right.

Chapter 14
The Internet

INTRODUCTION

The Internet, as a means of communication, facilitates intra- and inter-state commerce on a hitherto unprecedented scale. Although there are no specific provisions in the Data Protection Act 1998 on Internet or World Wide Web processing, data protection legislation applies as much to processing using this medium as to any other form of communication. Websites that offer information services frequently require users to 'register' with the site. The personal data thus provided by individuals is valuable for obvious commercial reasons. But data controllers should take care to ensure that their processing complies with the Data Protection Principles — for example, data must be processed fairly and lawfully, data requested must not be excessive for its purpose and data must not be transferred outside the European Economic Area (EEA).

This chapter sets out some specific points that should be borne in mind by data controllers who utilise the Internet, whether for data capture or transfer, website processing (including e-commerce) or merely for sending and receiving e-mails.

LOCATION OF SERVER

One of the considerations for data controllers who operate e-commerce businesses is where to locate their server. The geographical location of the server will be important, not only for tax reasons, but also for data protection purposes. As far as website processing is concerned, the location of the server is the place where the processing is undertaken. If the server is located outside the EEA and is controlled from a third (i.e., non-European Union) country, then the Data Protection Act 1998 does not apply to the processing.

The 1998 Act will apply to website processing where one of the following applies:

(a) *The operator of the website is established in the UK.* This will be the case where the operator is either an individual who is ordinarily resident or is a UK company, partnership or unincorporated association. The presence of an office, branch or agency which carries on any activity or business practice within the UK will also be caught by this provision.

(b) *The operator of the website is not established in the EEA but uses equipment in the EEA for processing data (other than data that are merely in transit).* Although this provision is controversial, the better view is that such 'equipment' must be owned by the data controller for the Act to apply.

E-MAIL ADDRESSES

It is far from clear whether e-mail addresses themselves should be dealt with under personal data protection legislation. The question will be of fundamental importance to website owners, particularly those whose processing of an individual's details extends only to an e-mail address. Take, for example, a website that allows surfers to put themselves on a mailing list. It may be a site which provides news stories on a specialist subject or a service which gives the latest prices or information on new products. Such sites as these work by requesting an e-mail address from the user. That address is then stored and later used to send material specifically to the individual concerned.

If an e-mail address is personal data, then the owners of websites that request users' e-mail addresses are subject to the provisions of the 1998 Act. If, on the other hand, an e-mail address does not constitute personal data and no other personal information is taken, then the Act is of no relevance to the website in question.

Personal data

It will be remembered that the definition of personal data in the 1998 Act is as follows:

data which relate to a living individual who can be identified—
    (a)   from those data, or
    (b)   from those data and other information which is in the possession of, or
is likely to come into the possession of, the data controller.

The common element of these definitions is *identification*. The question is thus: can a data subject be identified from an e-mail address? The answer would seem to be: it depends on the e-mail address! To take an example, suppose Joseph Bloggs supplies his business e-mail address, 'Joe.Bloggs@Ritz-Hotel.co.uk'. Few people would argue that Joseph cannot be identified from this address. His name is clearly stated, as is that of his employer, the Ritz Hotel, using a corporate domain name in the UK. Use of the Yellow Pages (or even a good general knowledge of London) would lead to the discovery of his whereabouts on a daily basis. This potential for invasion of an individual's personal privacy is exactly the sort of thing that the legislation is designed to obviate.

But what of other types of e-mail address? My e-mail address, 'peterwc@cr-law.co.uk', may not be one which would readily lead to the identification of me. My full name is not stated and so we cannot look it up in the telephone directory, even if we knew where I lived or worked. It would not be clear on the face of it that the domain 'cr-law' related to a law firm (although we could have a good guess at this!) nor which law firm it might be. It is thus arguable whether I could be identified from my e-mail address alone. To take a third example, 'Simon@yahoo.com', all we know about the person with this e-mail address is that he seems to call himself Simon, and that he uses Yahoo Mail as his e-mail service provider. This person most certainly *cannot be identified* by his e-mail address alone.

It follows from the above examples that certain types of e-mail address will fall within the strict definition of personal data, but that others will not. Such a position is not without its difficulties, particularly bearing in mind the desire for legal provisions to apply uniformly. Two categories of e-mail address with vastly differing legal principles applying to each, is not a practical arrangement for data controllers to cope with, and is not an easy system to regulate. It is doubtless this latter factor that has led the Office of the Data Protection Commissioner to advise that *all* e-mail addresses should be treated as personal data.

Of course the view of the Commissioner is extremely significant in practice, and data controllers would be well advised to take the view as law unless and until it is overturned by the courts. Thus, any company or organisation processing e-mail addresses should notify their activities (unless exempt — see Chapter 9) to the Data Protection Commissioner and comply with the Data Protection Principles. Failure to register data processing is a criminal offence, as US Robotics discovered when it was convicted of failing to register website processing of personal data in January 1997. The fact that the e-mail addresses alone are to be treated as personal data will have obvious implications for businesses generally and website owners in particular.

Sensitive personal data

Given that most, if not all, e-mail addresses are effectively deemed for the time being to amount to personal data, and that in many cases significantly more information is taken from an individual by owners of e-commerce websites, e-businesses should check whether the personal data they hold also amounts to *sensitive* personal data. It will be remembered that the processing of sensitive personal data cannot be undertaken unless one of a number of pre-conditions is in existence (see Chapter 5). Sensitive personal data is personal data consisting of information as to:

(a)   the racial or ethnic origin of the data subject;
(b)   the political opinions of the data subject;
(c)   the religious beliefs or other beliefs of a similar nature of the data subject;
(d)   membership of a trade union;
(e)   physical or mental health or condition;
(f)   the sexual life of the data subject;
(g)   the commission or alleged commission by the data subject of any offence, or any proceedings for any offence committed or alleged to have been committed by the data subject, the disposal of such proceedings or the sentence of any court in such proceedings.

There is some difference of opinion as to whether an e-mail address alone could disclose one or more of the above types of information and hence constitute sensitive personal data. Those addresses that consist of a person's name may do so, if the name is indicative of racial or ethnic origin. Examples might be Abdullah, MacTavish, Singh, etc. Further, it is possible for a domain name to indicate a person's political opinions, religious beliefs or sexual orientation. But is a *mere indication* of one of the above factors enough for an e-mail address to constitute sensitive personal data? Take the e-mail address 'david.jones@conservative-party.co.uk'. This may be an indication of David's political opinions, but is not conclusive of them. David may work for the Conservative Party but vote Labour at general elections. However, there is no express requirement in the Act for the indication to be conclusive. The correct position would seem to turn on the meaning of 'as to' in the definition of sensitive personal data, and it would be surprising if this was not one of the matters that the courts were asked to interpret when the new law comes into force. The better view

must surely be that sensitivity requires neither certainty nor a
of the above factors, but something in between which, as yet,
list of conditions permitting the processing of sensitive perso
sch. 3 to the 1998 Act — see Chapter 5.

INFORMATION REQUESTED BY WE

The section above describes the implications of requesting and processing
individual e-mail addresses. Websites, however, frequently request significantly
more information than merely an e-mail address. Where a street address is required
for goods delivery, for example, or where the website requests address and other
information for the purposes of selling the information for profit, the total package
of information will clearly constitute personal data. Some sites require further
'survey' information or track a surfer's movements, thus building up a picture of a
person's interests and attitudes — such information is an extremely valuable
commodity in the hands of commercial organisations.

It will be remembered that the Third Data Protection Principle provides that no
more data may be gathered from an individual than is relevant to the processing in
question. A website that provides on-line prices for hi-fi equipment, for example,
does not need a person's full name and street address merely to provide a price. The
Third Principle provides as follows:

Personal data shall be adequate, relevant and not excessive in relation to the
purpose or purposes for which they are processed.

Data controllers should carefully consider the purpose of requesting data from
individuals on-line. Guidance from the Data Protection Commissioner provides the
following: 'Never collect or retain personal data unless it is strictly necessary for your
purposes.' If the further information is required for the purposes of marketing
products or services, then this should be made clear on the site and its provision by
the individual should be optional. Where the data collected are to be transferred to
third parties for their own marketing purposes, then consent must be obtained.

AUTOMATED DECISIONS

E-commerce websites often utilise software that incorporates a decision-making
function. For example, an on-line bank may offer credit card applications on its site
or an insurance company may provide insurance policies on-line. In effect, the
outcome of the transaction between the user and the operator of the website will be
determined by software rather than by a person.

It will be remembered that persons who have decisions concerning them taken by
automated means have the right to require the decision to be re-evaluated with some
human input. Data controllers should therefore be prepared to retake web-based
automated decisions by human means. See Chapter 2 for further detail on the rights
of individuals concerning automated decision-taking.

DATA EXPORTS

The Eighth Data Protection Principle provides that data must not be transferred to countries outside the EEA, except in certain limited circumstances (see Chapter 6). Due to the global accessibility of the Internet, operators of websites must therefore ensure that personal data are not available on their sites unless an appropriate exemption can be claimed. Any personal data that can be accessed in the UK can also be accessed in the United States, as well as in Iraq and North Korea — and none of these countries have adequate data protection laws which protect the privacy of data subjects.

Whether the Data Protection Commissioner would take enforcement action largely depends upon what types of data are available on any particular site. Non-sensitive data processing will be treated more leniently than its sensitive counterpart. Similarly, material that is already in the public domain may be transferred abroad on the basis that it is already publicly available, and therefore further public availability does little to affect the position. Take for example a UK site which displays the names, photographs and ages of famous actresses — the fact that the site is accessible from countries without an adequate data protection regime makes little difference to the privacy of the actresses concerned.

Data controllers should check whether e-mails containing personal data are sent to third countries and instigate a policy of banning such practices unless the country of the transferee ensures an 'adequate level of protection for the rights and freedoms of data subjects' (or one of the exemptions in sch. 4 of the Act applies).

PRIVACY POLICIES

It will be remembered that processing of personal data is unlawful unless one of a number of conditions (contained in sch. 2 to the Act) is satisfied. Inserting appropriate clauses in website privacy policies, and taking appropriate steps to ensure that each user reviews the policy, is one method of obtaining the necessary consent for Internet processing.

Constructing a privacy policy

Data controllers will need to consider the purpose of requesting data from individuals. Questions that should be asked are shown in the box below.

1.	Is the data being requested so that a user may be identified on returning to the site?
2.	Is it hoped to utilise that data for commercial reasons, such as informing the user of special offers or services that the data controller may provide?
3.	Will the data be passed to third parties in any circumstances? If so, for what reason?
4.	Are cookies used to track users' movements and to store other information?
5.	Will personal data be exported to countries outside the EEA?
6.	What security procedures are in place to prevent unauthorised access to personal data?

Once the uses for the data have been ascertained, an appropriate privacy policy can be drafted. The next consideration is the method of notification to the user of the presence on the site of a privacy policy. There are a number of possibilities. There could be a link to the privacy policy on the home page, or users could be asked (or, better still, obliged) to 'click through' the privacy policy as a prerequisite to registration on the site. The latter is most preferable from the point of view of compliance with the legislation.

If the site will be requesting sensitive personal data from the user then, in most cases, the 'explicit consent' of the data subject will be required. In this case, mere notice of the privacy policy will be insufficient. The policy should be designed so that its access is obligatory and it must list all uses and anticipated future uses of any such data requested. If the sensitive data are to be deleted from the data controller's system on completion of the transaction, then this should be stated. Ideally, the processing of sensitive personal data should be undertaken only with a signature from the data subject. As this is not currently practicable on the Internet, an appropriate click box should be established which enables the data subject to convey consent to the processing.

COOKIES

'Cookies' are devices which are inserted on a user's hard-drive when visiting a website and which can identify that user on a return to the site, as well as track a surfer's movements through the Internet generally. The use of cookies for marketing and selling purposes will amount to 'direct marketing' within the meaning of the Act. A user has the right to request that data controllers do not process his personal data for the purposes of direct marketing. Data controllers must react to such a request within 21 days and will need to have procedures in place to either:

(a) disable the cookie in relation to the specific customer who made the request; or

(b) flag the specific customer's account so that no further attempts at direct marketing are made to that person.

From a user's point of view, the implications for personal privacy of the use of cookies are enormous. In many cases the tracking of a surfer's movements around the Web will amount to sensitive personal data processing. Users can make subject access requests of website hosts to check what information is being stored on them. If the information stored is unrelated to their visit to the site, or where they have not given consent for its storage, a user could make a justified complaint to the Data Protection Commissioner.

DATA SECURITY

The Seventh Data Protection Principle requires that appropriate security measures be undertaken so as to ensure that personal data are not lost, damaged or destroyed during processing. Data controllers are required to undertake reviews of available technology from time to time to ensure that the systems currently being deployed are capable of dealing with security breaches. In most cases, websites should employ a password protection system for user data to ensure that such data are secure from tampering by third persons.

Chapter 15
CCTV

INTRODUCTION

The use of closed-circuit television (CCTV) is now prevalent in the UK. When walking down the street in urban areas one has only to gaze upwards to see CCTV cameras on the corner of many street blocks. Use of cameras by the police for the detection and prevention of crime is now widespread, and it is growing rapidly in city centres. Shopkeepers routinely employ CCTV cameras inside their premises to detect shoplifting. Employers use cameras (hidden or otherwise) to detect suspected fraud by employees. The use of CCTV technology has led to a reduction in certain types of crime in some areas of the UK. But there are growing concerns that the prevalence of cameras in public places is leading to 'Big Brother' surveillance on an unprecedented scale.

DOES THE LEGISLATION APPLY?

It will be remembered that the definition of personal data is 'those data from which a living individual can be identified'. Thus images produced by CCTV cameras, whether digital or analogue, will amount to 'personal data' where any identifiable individual is depicted on-screen. The filming of unknown persons will not be personal data processing unless some cross-referencing is possible so as to achieve identification. This may occur, for example, where CCTV cameras film persons sitting in a stadium or theatre — seat records can be matched with the filmed images of persons sitting in the relevant seat. Shops can match images of customers paying with credit cards with the records of credit card transactions. The use of digital technology and image-matching systems potentially allows the identification of individuals filmed by the police and others in public places (automatic facial recognition systems). Further, the wider definition of personal data contained in the European Directive means that the ability to be able to distinguish an individual's features from the images will amount to personal data processing.

Recital (16) of the Directive should however be borne in mind in respect of certain types of processing:

> whereas the processing of sound and image data, such as in cases of video surveillance, does not come within the scope of this Directive if it is carried out for the purposes of public security, defence, National Security or in the course of State activities relating to the area of criminal law or of other activities which do not come within the scope of Community law.

The filming, recording, storing, adapting, transferring and viewing of images from CCTV equipment all constitute 'processing' under current data protection legislation. The processor of the images will be the 'data controller' for the purposes of the Data Protection Act 1998. If a third-party security company is used to run the cameras then that person will be a 'data processor'. It can be seen then that UK data protection legislation does apply to many uses of CCTV surveillance equipment.

USE OF CCTV CAMERAS

It will be remembered that the processing of personal data (including any CCTV image from which a living individual can be identified) is unlawful unless certain rules have been observed. Data controllers who use CCTV should carefully consider the following.

1. Notification

Data controllers must notify the processing of CCTV images to the Data Protection Commissioner. Failure to notify CCTV use will mean that any processing of CCTV images will be unlawful.

2. Conditions for processing

Processing may only be undertaken where it complies with one of the conditions contained in sch. 2 to the Act. The first potentially relevant condition is the consent of the data subject. A shop, for example, could clearly display a notice on its door and elsewhere to the effect that CCTV cameras are in use on the premises — an individual could then be taken to be consenting to his or her image being filmed by the action of entering the shop. The notice should clearly state the purpose of the cameras (e.g., crime prevention and public safety) and ideally should state where further information may be obtained about the processing. It could also be argued that the use of cameras (to prevent theft and other criminal activity) is necessary as part of the legitimate activities of the owner of any relevant premises.

3. Sensitive personal data

The processing of 'sensitive personal data' (see definition in Chapter 5) may only be undertaken where one of the conditions in sch. 3 to the Act applies to the processing. In many cases the use of CCTV cameras will amount to the processing of sensitive personal data — it will be clear in relevant cases that the individual who is being filmed is disabled or is a Sikh. The obvious condition that will apply, and thus allow the processing of such sensitive data, is that the information contained in the personal data has been made public as a result of steps deliberately taken by the data subject. The argument here is that the filming of sensitive data is permitted by the very fact that the relevant individual has chosen to appear in a public place.

Where the images record the commission of a crime, the sensitive personal data processing thus being undertaken will benefit from at least one of the list of permitted purposes for processing, namely the processing being necessary for the 'legitimate interests of the data controller' or the processing being in the 'substantial public interest and necessary for the detection of an unlawful act'.

4. Fair processing

The concept of fair processing as encapsulated in the First Data Protection Principle requires consideration of a number of factors (see Chapter 4). One of the First Principle's requirements is that at the point of first processing the data controller must supply (or make available) to the data subject the following information:

(a) the identity of the data controller (and of his or her representative if relevant);
(b) the purpose or purposes for which the data are to be processed; and
(c) any other information to enable the processing to be fair.

Consideration should therefore be given to the siting and content of a suitable sign (which, according to guidance from the Commissioner, should be at least A3 in size) which provides the above information to the public unless one of the exemptions to this requirement applies to the CCTV processing. The most relevant exemption is likely to be that the processing of CCTV images is undertaken for the 'prevention and detection of crime' — for further detail see Chapter 9.

Usage of the CCTV images must not extend beyond that for which they were originally obtained. This provision of the legislation would prevent a shopkeeper selling a CCTV surveillance video to a film production company for use in a documentary about shoplifting.

5. Lawful processing

The use of CCTV surveillance must comply with the law generally, not just the provisions of the 1998 Act. There are circumstances where filming could constitute a breach of confidence, such as, for example, where it was undertaken in a doctor's surgery.

6. Relevant processing

Any data processed must be adequate, relevant and not excessive for its relevant purpose. The application of this principle depends on the type of surveillance being undertaken. By way of example, cameras placed on roads for the purposes of detecting bad driving should not have private dwellings within their field of vision.

7. Data exports

Personal data must not be transferred to countries outside the European Economic Area unless certain conditions apply (see Chapter 6). In most cases this restriction will not be relevant to the processing of CCTV images.

8. Data security

Appropriate technical and organisational measures must be undertaken by the processor of CCTV images to ensure that there is no unauthorised access to the images and to secure the images from accidental loss or destruction. Data controllers should consider the following factors in devising appropriate procedures for the security of their CCTV processing:

(a) security of the central control room;
(b) monitoring of access to the central control room;
(c) selection and recruitment of staff;
(d) ongoing training in data protection and privacy issues;
(e) monitoring of access to recorded material; and
(f) security of storage of recorded material.

9. Storage of images

Personal data may only be kept for as long as is necessary for its purpose. Video cassettes or other storage media should therefore be purged of footage containing personal data on a regular basis. In most cases it will be unlawful to keep the images for longer than a fairly short period (i.e., 28 days) and a rolling process of tape reusage should be employed. If footage is required as evidence of a crime then it may be kept until after disposal of the proceedings (including appeals). However, it is arguable that images on the tape which do not relate to the relevant incident should be erased at an earlier stage. An alternative would be to transfer the images to a secure system. In this event a careful note should be taken by the operator of the system of the date on which the images were removed from the system and the reason for such removal together with any other relevant information, such as a crime reference number.

10. Subject access

Appropriate procedures must be established to allow individuals to gain access to any CCTV images from which they can be identified. Staff should be trained so that they are able to identify a subject access request. See Chapter 2 for further detail on the information that must be supplied to a data subject following a subject access request. There are a number of limited exemptions that could apply to the right of an individual to request to see a copy of the CCTV image on which he or she appears. The most relevant is likely to be the exemption relating to the 'prevention and detection of crime' and the 'apprehension and prosecution of offenders'. This enables a data controller to refuse to comply with a subject access request where such compliance would prejudice one of those purposes — for further details on exemptions see Chapter 9.

CODE OF CONDUCT

The Data Protection Commissioner has published a code of practice that should be observed by processors of CCTV images. The code can be obtained in full from the Commissioner's website — see Appendix 6.

Appendix 1
Directive 95/46/EC

DIRECTIVE 95/46/EC OF THE EUROPEAN PARLIAMENT AND OF THE COUNCIL OF 24 OCTOBER 1995 ON THE PROTECTION OF INDIVIDUALS WITH REGARD TO THE PROCESSING OF PERSONAL DATA AND ON THE FREE MOVEMENT OF SUCH DATA

THE EUROPEAN PARLIAMENT AND THE COUNCIL OF THE EUROPEAN UNION,

Having regard to the Treaty establishing the European Community, and in particular Article 100a thereof,

Having regard to the proposal from the Commission,[1]

Having regard to the opinion of the Economic and Social Committee,[2]

Acting in accordance with the procedure referred to in Article 189b of the Treaty,[3]

(1) Whereas the objectives of the Community, as laid down in the Treaty, as amended by the Treaty on European Union, include creating an ever closer union among the peoples of Europe, fostering closer relations between the States belonging to the Community, ensuring economic and social progress by common action to eliminate the barriers which divide Europe, encouraging the constant improvement of the living conditions of its peoples, preserving and strengthening peace and liberty and promoting democracy on the basis of the fundamental rights recognised in the constitution and laws of the Member States and in the European Convention for the Protection of Human Rights and Fundamental Freedoms;

(2) Whereas data-processing systems are designed to serve man; whereas they must, whatever the nationality or residence of natural persons, respect their fundamental rights and freedoms, notably the right to privacy, and contribute to economic and social progress, trade expansion and the well-being of individuals;

(3) Whereas the establishment and functioning of an internal market in which, in accordance with Article 7a of the Treaty, the free movement of goods, persons, services and capital is ensured require not only that personal data should be able to

Notes

[1] OJ No. C277, 5.11.1990, p. 3 and OJ No. C311, 27.11.1992, p. 30.

[2] OJ No. C159, 17.6.1991, p. 38.

[3] Opinion of the European Parliament of 11 March 1992 (OJ No. C94, 13.4.1992, p. 198), confirmed on 2 December 1993 (OJ No. C342, 20.12.1993, p. 30); Council common position of 20 February 1995 (OJ No. C93, 13.4.1995, p. 1) and Decision of the European Parliament of 15 June 1995 (OJ No. C166, 3.7.1995).

flow freely from one Member State to another, but also that the fundamental rights of individuals should be safeguarded;

(4)   Whereas increasingly frequent recourse is being had in the Community to the processing of personal data in the various spheres of economic and social activity; whereas the progress made in information technology is making the processing and exchange of such data considerably easier;

(5)   Whereas the economic and social integration resulting from the establishment and functioning of the internal market within the meaning of Article 7a of the Treaty will necessarily lead to a substantial increase in cross-border flows of personal data between all those involved in a private or public capacity in economic and social activity in the Member States; whereas the exchange of personal data between undertakings in different Member States is set to increase; whereas the national authorities in the various Member States are being called upon by virtue of Community law to collaborate and exchange personal data so as to be able to perform their duties or carry out tasks on behalf of an authority in another Member State within the context of the area without internal frontiers as constituted by the internal market;

(6)   Whereas, furthermore, the increase in scientific and technical cooperation and the coordinated introduction of new telecommunications networks in the Community necessitate and facilitate cross-border flows of personal data;

(7)   Whereas the difference in levels of protection of the rights and freedoms of individuals, notably the right to privacy, with regard to the processing of personal data afforded in the Member States may prevent the transmission of such data from the territory of one Member State to that of another Member State; whereas this difference may therefore constitute an obstacle to the pursuit of a number of economic activities at Community level, distort competition and impede authorities in the discharge of their responsibilities under Community law; whereas this difference in levels of protection is due to the existence of a wide variety of national laws, regulations and administrative provisions;

(8)   Whereas, in order to remove the obstacles to flows of personal data, the level of protection of the rights and freedoms of individuals with regard to the processing of such data must be equivalent in all Member States; whereas this objective is vital to the internal market but cannot be achieved by the Member States alone, especially in view of the scale of the divergences which currently exist between the relevant laws in the Member States and the need to coordinate the laws of the Member States so as to ensure that the cross-border flow of personal data is regulated in a consistent manner that is in keeping with the objective of the internal market as provided for in Article 7a of the Treaty; whereas Community action to approximate those laws is therefore needed;

(9)   Whereas, given the equivalent protection resulting from the approximation of national laws, the Member States will no longer be able to inhibit the free movement between them of personal data on grounds relating to protection of the rights and freedoms of individuals, and in particular the right to privacy; whereas Member States will be left a margin for manoeuvre, which may, in the context of implementation of the Directive, also be exercised by the business and social partners; whereas Member States will therefore be able to specify in their national law the general conditions governing the lawfulness of data processing; whereas in doing so the Member States shall strive to improve the protection currently provided by their legislation; whereas, within the limits of this margin for manoeuvre and in

accordance with Community law, disparities could arise in the implementation of the Directive and this could have an effect on the movement of data within a Member State as well as within the Community;

(10)   Whereas the object of the national laws on the processing of personal data is to protect fundamental rights and freedoms, notably the right to privacy, which is recognised both in Article 8 of the European Convention for the Protection of Human Rights and Fundamental Freedoms and in the general principles of Community law; whereas, for that reason, the approximation of those laws must not result in any lessening of the protection they afford but must, on the contrary, seek to ensure a high level of protection in the Community;

(11)   Whereas the principles of the protection of the rights and freedoms of individuals, notably the right to privacy, which are contained in this Directive, give substance to and amplify those contained in the Council of Europe Convention of 28 January 1981 for the Protection of Individuals with regard to Automatic Processing of Personal Data;

(12)   Whereas the protection principles must apply to all processing of personal data by any person whose activities are governed by Community law; whereas there should be excluded the processing of data carried out by a natural person in the exercise of activities which are exclusively personal or domestic, such as correspondence and the holding of records of addresses;

(13)   Whereas the activities referred to in Titles V and VI of the Treaty on European Union regarding public safety, defence, State security or the activities of the State in the area of criminal laws fall outside the scope of Community law, without prejudice to the obligations incumbent upon Member States under Article 56 (2), Article 57 or Article 100a of the Treaty establishing the European Community; whereas the processing of personal data that is necessary to safeguard the economic well-being of the State does not fall within the scope of this Directive where such processing relates to State security matters;

(14)   Whereas, given the importance of the developments under way, in the framework of the information society, of the techniques used to capture, transmit, manipulate, record, store or communicate sound and image data relating to natural persons, this Directive should be applicable to processing involving such data;

(15)   Whereas the processing of such data is covered by this Directive only if it is automated or if the data processed are contained or are intended to be contained in a filing system structured according to specific criteria relating to individuals, so as to permit easy access to the personal data in question;

(16)   Whereas the processing of sound and image data, such as in cases of video surveillance, does not come within the scope of this Directive if it is carried out for the purposes of public security, defence, national security or in the course of State activities relating to the area of criminal law or of other activities which do not come within the scope of Community law;

(17)   Whereas, as far as the processing of sound and image data carried out for purposes of journalism or the purposes of literary or artistic expression is concerned, in particular in the audiovisual field, the principles of the Directive are to apply in a restricted manner according to the provisions laid down in Article 9;

(18)   Whereas, in order to ensure that individuals are not deprived of the protection to which they are entitled under this Directive, any processing of personal data in the Community must be carried out in accordance with the law of one of the

Member States; whereas, in this connection, processing carried out under the responsibility of a controller who is established in a Member State should be governed by the law of that State;

(19) Whereas establishment on the territory of a Member State implies the effective and real exercise of activity through stable arrangements; whereas the legal form of such an establishment, whether simply branch or a subsidiary with a legal personality, is not the determining factor in this respect; whereas, when a single controller is established on the territory of several Member States, particularly by means of subsidiaries, he must ensure, in order to avoid any circumvention of national rules, that each of the establishments fulfils the obligations imposed by the national law applicable to its activities;

(20) Whereas the fact that the processing of data is carried out by a person established in a third country must not stand in the way of the protection of individuals provided for in this Directive; whereas in these cases, the processing should be governed by the law of the Member State in which the means used are located, and there should be guarantees to ensure that the rights and obligations provided for in this Directive are respected in practice;

(21) Whereas this Directive is without prejudice to the rules of territoriality applicable in criminal matters;

(22) Whereas Member States shall more precisely define in the laws they enact or when bringing into force the measures taken under this Directive the general circumstances in which processing is lawful; whereas in particular Article 5, in conjunction with Articles 7 and 8, allows Member States, independently of general rules, to provide for special processing conditions for specific sectors and for the various categories of data covered by Article 8;

(23) Whereas Member States are empowered to ensure the implementation of the protection of individuals both by means of a general law on the protection of individuals as regards the processing of personal data and by sectorial laws such as those relating, for example, to statistical institutes;

(24) Whereas the legislation concerning the protection of legal persons with regard to the processing data which concerns them is not affected by this Directive;

(25) Whereas the principles of protection must be reflected, on the one hand, in the obligations imposed on persons, public authorities, enterprises, agencies or other bodies responsible for processing, in particular regarding data quality, technical security, notification to the supervisory authority, and the circumstances under which processing can be carried out, and, on the other hand, in the right conferred on individuals, the data on whom are the subject of processing, to be informed that processing is taking place, to consult the data, to request corrections and even to object to processing in certain circumstances;

(26) Whereas the principles of protection must apply to any information concerning an identified or identifiable person; whereas, to determine whether a person is identifiable, account should be taken of all the means likely reasonably to be used either by the controller or by any other person to identify the said person; whereas the principles of protection shall not apply to data rendered anonymous in such a way that the data subject is no longer identifiable; whereas codes of conduct within the meaning of Article 27 may be a useful instrument for providing guidance as to the ways in which data may be rendered anonymous and retained in a form in which identification of the data subject is no longer possible;

(27)   Whereas the protection of individuals must apply as much to automatic processing of data as to manual processing; whereas the scope of this protection must not in effect depend on the techniques used, otherwise this would create a serious risk of circumvention; whereas, nonetheless, as regards manual processing, this Directive covers only filing systems, not unstructured files; whereas, in particular, the content of a filing system must be structured according to specific criteria relating to individuals allowing easy access to the personal data; whereas, in line with the definition in Article 2(c), the different criteria for determining the constituents of a structured set of personal data, and the different criteria governing access to such a set, may be laid down by each Member State; whereas files or sets of files as well as their cover pages, which are not structured according to specific criteria, shall under no circumstances fall within the scope of this Directive;

(28)   Whereas any processing of personal data must be lawful and fair to the individuals concerned; whereas, in particular, the data must be adequate, relevant and not excessive in relation to the purposes for which they are processed; whereas such purposes must be explicit and legitimate and must be determined at the time of collection of the data; whereas the purposes of processing further to collection shall not be incompatible with the purposes as they were originally specified;

(29)   Whereas the further processing of personal data for historical, statistical or scientific purposes is not generally to be considered incompatible with the purposes for which the data have previously been collected provided that Member States furnish suitable safeguards; whereas these safeguards must in particular rule out the use of the data in support of measures or decisions regarding any particular individual;

(30)   Whereas, in order to be lawful, the processing of personal data must in addition be carried out with the consent of the data subject or be necessary for the conclusion or performance of a contract binding on the data subject, or as a legal requirement, or for the performance of a task carried out in the public interest or in the exercise of official authority, or in the legitimate interests of a natural or legal person, provided that the interests or the rights and freedoms of the data subject are not overriding; whereas, in particular, in order to maintain a balance between the interests involved while guaranteeing effective competition, Member States may determine the circumstances in which personal data may be used or disclosed to a third party in the context of the legitimate ordinary business activities of companies and other bodies; whereas Member States may similarly specify the conditions under which personal data may be disclosed to a third party for the purposes of marketing whether carried out commercially or by a charitable organisation or by any other association or foundation, of a political nature for example, subject to the provisions allowing a data subject to object to the processing of data regarding him, at no cost and without having to state his reasons;

(31)   Whereas the processing of personal data must equally be regarded as lawful where it is carried out in order to protect an interest which is essential for the data subject's life;

(32)   Whereas it is for national legislation to determine whether the controller performing a task carried out in the public interest or in the exercise of official authority should be a public administration or another natural or legal person governed by public law, or by private law such as a professional association;

(33)   Whereas data which are capable by their nature of infringing fundamental freedoms or privacy should not be processed unless the data subject gives his explicit consent; whereas, however, derogations from this prohibition must be explicitly provided for in respect of specific needs, in particular where the processing of these data is carried out for certain health-related purposes by persons subject to a legal obligation of professional secrecy or in the course of legitimate activities by certain associations or foundations the purpose of which is to permit the exercise of fundamental freedoms;

(34)   Whereas Member States must also be authorised, when justified by grounds of important public interest, to derogate from the prohibition on processing sensitive categories of data where important reasons of public interest so justify in areas such as public health and social protection — especially in order to ensure the quality and cost-effectiveness of the procedures used for settling claims for benefits and services in the health insurance system — scientific research and government statistics; whereas it is incumbent on them, however, to provide specific and suitable safeguards so as to protect the fundamental rights and the privacy of individuals;

(35)   Whereas, moreover, the processing of personal data by official authorities for achieving aims, laid down in constitutional law or international public law, of officially recognised religious associations is carried out on important grounds of public interest;

(36)   Whereas where, in the course of electoral activities, the operation of the democratic system requires in certain Member States that political parties compile data on people's political opinion, the processing of such data may be permitted for reasons of important public interest, provided that appropriate safeguards are established;

(37)   Whereas the processing of personal data for purposes of journalism or for purposes of literary or artistic expression, in particular in the audiovisual field, should qualify for exemption from the requirements of certain provisions of this Directive in so far as this is necessary to reconcile the fundamental rights of individuals with freedom of information and notably the right to receive and impart information, as guaranteed in particular in Article 10 of the European Convention for the Protection of Human Rights and Fundamental Freedoms; whereas Member States should therefore lay down exemptions and derogations necessary for the purpose of balance between fundamental rights as regards general measures on the legitimacy of data processing, measures on the transfer of data to third countries and the power of the supervisory authority; whereas this should not, however, lead Member States to lay down exemptions from the measures to ensure security of processing; whereas at least the supervisory authority responsible for this sector should also be provided with certain ex-post powers, e.g., to publish a regular report or to refer matters to the judicial authorities;

(38)   Whereas, if the processing of data is to be fair, the data subject must be in a position to learn of the existence of a processing operation and, where data are collected from him, must be given accurate and full information, bearing in mind the circumstances of the collection;

(39)   Whereas certain processing operations involve data which the controller has not collected directly from the data subject; whereas, furthermore, data can be legitimately disclosed to a third party, even if the disclosure was not anticipated at the time the data were collected from the data subject; whereas, in all these cases, the

data subject should be informed when the data are recorded or at the latest when the data are first disclosed to a third party;

(40)　Whereas, however, it is not necessary to impose this obligation of the data subject who already has the information; whereas, moreover, there will be no such obligation if the recording or disclosure are expressly provided for by law or if the provision of information to the data subject proves impossible or would involve disproportionate efforts, which could be the case where processing is for historical, statistical or scientific purposes; whereas, in this regard, the number of data subjects, the age of the data, and any compensatory measures adopted may be taken into consideration;

(41)　Whereas any person must be able to exercise the right of access to data relating to him which are being processed, in order to verify in particular the accuracy of the data and the lawfulness of the processing; whereas, for the same reasons, every data subject must also have the right to know the logic involved in the automatic processing of data concerning him, at least in the case of the automated decisions referred to in Article 15(1); whereas this right must not adversely affect trade secrets or intellectual property and in particular the copyright protecting the software; whereas these considerations must not, however, result in the data subject being refused all information;

(42)　Whereas Member States may, in the interest of the data subject or so as to protect the rights and freedoms of others, restrict rights of access and information; whereas they may, for example, specify that access to medical data may be obtained only through a health professional;

(43)　Whereas restrictions on the rights of access and information and on certain obligations of the controller may similarly be imposed by Member States in so far as they are necessary to safeguard, for example, national security, defence, public safety, or important economic or financial interests of a Member State or the Union, as well as criminal investigations and prosecutions and action in respect of breaches of ethics in the regulated professions; whereas the list of exceptions and limitations should include the tasks of monitoring, inspection or regulation necessary in the three last-mentioned areas concerning public security, economic or financial interests and crime prevention; whereas the listing of tasks in these three areas does not affect the legitimacy of exceptions or restrictions for reasons of State security or defence;

(44)　Whereas Member States may also be led, by virtue of the provisions of Community law, to derogate from the provisions of this Directive concerning the right of access, the obligation to inform individuals, and the quality of data, in order to secure certain of the purposes referred to above;

(45)　Whereas, in cases where data might lawfully be processed on grounds of public interest, official authority or the legitimate interests of a natural or legal person, any data subject should nevertheless be entitled, on legitimate and compelling grounds relating to his particular situation, to object to the processing of any data relating to himself; whereas Member States may nevertheless lay down national provisions to the contrary;

(46)　Whereas the protection of the rights and freedoms of data subjects with regard to the processing of personal data requires that appropriate technical and organisational measures be taken, both at the time of the design of the processing system and at the time of the processing itself, particularly in order to maintain security and thereby to prevent any unauthorised processing; whereas it is incumbent on the Member States to ensure that controllers comply with these measures; whereas these measures must ensure an appropriate level of security, taking into account the state of the art and the costs of their implementation in relation to the risks inherent in the processing and the nature of the data to be protected;

(47)   Whereas where a message containing personal data is transmitted by means of a telecommunications or electronic mail service, the sole purpose of which is the transmission of such messages, the controller in respect of the personal data contained in the message will normally be considered to be the person from whom the message originates, rather than the person offering the transmission services; whereas, nevertheless, those offering such services will normally be considered controllers in respect of the processing of the additional personal data necessary for the operation of the service;

(48)   Whereas the procedures for notifying the supervisory authority are designed to ensure disclosure of the purposes and main features of any processing operation for the purpose of verification that the operation is in accordance with the national measures taken under this Directive;

(49)   Whereas, in order to avoid unsuitable administrative formalities, exemptions from the obligation to notify and simplification of the notification required may be provided for by Member States in cases where processing is unlikely adversely to affect the rights and freedoms of data subjects, provided that it is in accordance with a measure taken by a Member State specifying its limits; whereas exemption or simplification may similarly be provided for by Member States where a person appointed by the controller ensures that the processing carried out is not likely adversely to affect the rights and freedoms of data subjects; whereas such a data protection official, whether or not an employee of the controller, must be in a position to exercise his functions in complete independence;

(50)   Whereas exemption or simplification could be provided for in cases of processing operations whose sole purpose is the keeping of a register intended, according to national law, to provide information to the public and open to consultation by the public or by any person demonstrating a legitimate interest;

(51)   Whereas, nevertheless, simplification or exemption from the obligation to notify shall not release the controller from any of the other obligations resulting from this Directive;

(52)   Whereas, in this context, ex post facto verification by the competent authorities must in general be considered a sufficient measure;

(53)   Whereas, however, certain processing operation are likely to pose specific risks to the rights and freedoms of data subjects by virtue of their nature, their scope or their purposes, such as that of excluding individuals from a right, benefit or a contract, or by virtue of the specific use of new technologies; whereas it is for Member States, if they so wish, to specify such risks in their legislation;

(54)   Whereas with regard to all the processing undertaken in society, the amount posing such specific risks should be very limited; whereas Member States must provide that the supervisory authority, or the data protection official in cooperation with the authority, check such processing prior to it being carried out; whereas following this prior check, the supervisory authority may, according to its national law, give an opinion or an authorisation regarding the processing; whereas such checking may equally take place in the course of the preparation either of a measure of the national parliament or of a measure based on such a legislative measure, which defines the nature of the processing and lays down appropriate safeguards;

(55)   Whereas, if the controller fails to respect the rights of data subjects, national legislation must provide for a judicial remedy; whereas any damage which a person may suffer as a result of unlawful processing must be compensated for by the controller, who may be exempted from liability if he proves that he is not responsible for the damage, in particular in cases where he establishes fault on the part of the data subject or in case of force majeure; whereas sanctions must be imposed on any person, whether governed by private or public law, who fails to comply with the national measures taken under this Directive;

(56)   Whereas cross-border flows of personal data are necessary to the expansion of international trade; whereas the protection of individuals guaranteed in the Community by this Directive does not stand in the way of transfers of personal data to third countries which ensure an adequate level of protection; whereas the adequacy of the level of protection afforded by a third country must be assessed in the light of all the circumstances surrounding the transfer operation or set of transfer operations;

(57)   Whereas, on the other hand, the transfer of personal data to a third country which does not ensure an adequate level of protection must be prohibited;

(58)   Whereas provisions should be made for exemptions from this prohibition in certain circumstances where the data subject has given his consent, where the transfer is necessary in relation to a contract or a legal claim, where protection of an important public interest so requires, for example in cases of international transfers of data between tax or customs administrations or between services competent for social security matters, or where the transfer is made from a register established by law and intended for consultation by the public or persons having a legitimate interest; whereas in this case such a transfer should not involve the entirety of the data or entire categories of the data contained in the register and, when the register is intended for consultation by persons having a legitimate interest, the transfer should be made only at the request of those persons or if they are to be the recipients;

(59)   Whereas particular measures may be taken to compensate for the lack of protection in a third country in cases where the controller offers appropriate safeguards; whereas, moreover, provision must be made for procedures for negotiations between the Community and such third countries;

(60)   Whereas, in any event, transfers to third countries may be effected only in full compliance with the provisions adopted by the Member States pursuant to this Directive, and in particular Article 8 thereof;

(61)   Whereas Member States and the Commission, in their respective spheres of competence, must encourage the trade associations and other representative organisations concerned to draw up codes of conduct so as to facilitate the application of this Directive, taking account of the specific characteristics of the processing carried out in certain sectors, and respecting the national provisions adopted for its implementation;

(62)   Whereas the establishment in Member States of supervisory authorities, exercising their functions with complete independence, is an essential component of the protection of individuals with regard to the processing of personal data;

(63)   Whereas such authorities must have the necessary means to perform their duties, including powers of investigation and intervention, particularly in cases of complaints from individuals, and powers to engage in legal proceedings; whereas such authorities must help to ensure transparency of processing in the Member States within whose jurisdiction they fall;

(64)   Whereas the authorities in the different Member States will need to assist one another in performing their duties so as to ensure that the rules of protection are properly respected throughout the European Union;

(65)   Whereas, at Community level, a Working Party on the Protection of Individuals with regard to the Processing of Personal Data must be set up and be completely independent in the performance of its functions; whereas, having regard to its specific nature, it must advise the Commission and, in particular, contribute to the uniform application of the national rules adopted pursuant to this Directive;

(66)   Whereas, with regard to the transfer of data to third countries, the application of this Directive calls for the conferment of powers of implementation on the Commission and the establishment of a procedure as laid down in Council Decision 87/373/EEC;[1]

(67)   Whereas an agreement on a modus vivendi between the European Parliament, the Council and the Commission concerning the implementing measures for acts adopted in accordance with the procedure laid down in Article 189b of the EC Treaty was reached on 20 December 1994;

(68)   Whereas the principles set out in this Directive regarding the protection of the rights and freedoms of individuals, notably their right to privacy, with regard to the processing of personal data may be supplemented or clarified, in particular as far as certain sectors are concerned, by specific rules based on those principles;

(69)   Whereas Member States should be allowed a period of not more than three years from the entry into force of the national measures transposing this Directive in which to apply such new national rules progressively to all processing operations already under way; whereas, in order to facilitate their cost-effective implementation, a further period expiring 12 years after the date on which this Directive is adopted will be allowed to Member States to ensure the conformity of existing manual filing systems with certain of the Directive's provisions; whereas, where data contained in such filing systems are manually processed during this extended transition period, those systems must be brought into conformity with these provisions at the time of such processing;

(70)   Whereas it is not necessary for the data subject to give his consent again so as to allow the controller to continue to process, after the national provisions taken pursuant to this Directive enter into force, any sensitive data necessary for the performance of a contract concluded on the basis of free and informed consent before the entry into force of these provisions;

(71)   Whereas this Directive does not stand in the way of a Member State's regulating marketing activities aimed at consumers residing in territory in so far as such regulation does not concern the protection of individuals with regard to the processing of personal data;

(72)   Whereas this Directive allows the principle of public access to official documents to be taken into account when implementing the principles set out in this Directive,

HAVE ADOPTED THIS DIRECTIVE:

Note
[1] OJ No. L197, 18.7.1987, p. 33.

CHAPTER I   GENERAL PROVISIONS

Article 1   Object of the Directive

1.   In accordance with this Directive, Member States shall protect the fundamental rights and freedoms of natural persons, and in particular their right to privacy with respect to the processing of personal data.

2.   Member States shall neither restrict nor prohibit the free flow of personal data between Member States for reasons connected with the protection afforded under paragraph 1.

Article 2   Definitions

For the purposes of this Directive:

(a)   'personal data' shall mean any information relating to an identified or identifiable natural person ('data subject'); an identifiable person is one who can be identified, directly or indirectly, in particular by reference to an identification number or to one or more factors specific to his physical, physiological, mental, economic, cultural or social identity;

(b)   'processing of personal data' ('processing') shall mean any operation or set of operations which is performed upon personal data, whether or not by automatic means, such as collection, recording, organisation, storage, adaptation or alteration, retrieval, consultation, use, disclosure by transmission, dissemination or otherwise making available, alignment or combination, blocking, erasure or destruction;

(c)   'personal data filing system' ('filing system') shall mean any structured set of personal data which are accessible according to specific criteria, whether centralised, decentralised or dispersed on a functional or geographical basis;

(d)   'controller' shall mean the natural or legal person, public authority, agency or any other body which alone or jointly with others determines the purposes and means of the processing of personal data; where the purposes and means of processing are determined by national or Community laws or regulations, the controller or the specific criteria for his nomination may be designated by national or Community law;

(e)   'processor' shall mean a natural or legal person, public authority, agency or any other body which processes personal data on behalf of the controller;

(f)   'third party' shall mean any natural or legal person, public authority, agency or any other body other than the data subject, the controller, the processor and the persons who, under the direct authority of the controller or the processor, are authorised to process the data;

(g)   'recipient' shall mean a natural or legal person, public authority, agency or any other body to whom data are disclosed, whether a third party or not; however, authorities which may receive data in the framework of a particular inquiry shall not be regarded as recipients;

(h)   'the data subject's consent' shall mean any freely given specific and informed indication of his wishes by which the data subject signifies his agreement to personal data relating to him being processed.

Article 3   Scope

1.   This Directive shall apply to the processing of personal data wholly or partly by automatic means, and to the processing otherwise than by automatic means of personal data which form part of a filing system or are intended to form part of a filing system.

2. This Directive shall not apply to the processing of personal data:
— in the course of an activity which falls outside the scope of Community law, such as those provided for by Titles V and VI of the Treaty on European Union and in any case to processing operations concerning public security, defence, State security (including the economic well-being of the State when the processing operation relates to State security matters) and the activities of the State in areas of criminal law,
— by a natural person in the course of a purely personal or household activity.

Article 4   National law applicable
1. Each Member State shall apply the national provisions it adopts pursuant to this Directive to the processing of personal data where:
(a) the processing is carried out in the context of the activities of an establishment of the controller on the territory of the Member State; when the same controller is established on the territory of several Member States, he must take the necessary measures to ensure that each of these establishments complies with the obligations laid down by the national law applicable;
(b) the controller is not established on the Member State's territory, but in a place where its national law applies by virtue of international public law;
(c) the controller is not established on Community territory and, for purposes of processing personal data makes use of equipment, automated or otherwise, situated on the territory of the said Member State, unless such equipment is used only for purposes of transit through the territory of the Community.
2. In the circumstances referred to in paragraph 1(c), the controller must designate a representative established in the territory of that Member State, without prejudice to legal actions which could be initiated against the controller himself.

CHAPTER II   GENERAL RULES ON THE LAWFULNESS OF THE PROCESSING OF PERSONAL DATA

Article 5
Member States shall, within the limits of the provisions of this Chapter, determine more precisely the conditions under which the processing of personal data is lawful.

SECTION I
PRINCIPLES RELATING TO DATA QUALITY

Article 6
1. Member States shall provide that personal data must be:
(a) processed fairly and lawfully;
(b) collected for specified, explicit and legitimate purposes and not further processed in a way incompatible with those purposes. Further processing of data for historical, statistical or scientific purposes shall not be considered as incompatible provided that Member States provide appropriate safeguards;
(c) adequate, relevant and not excessive in relation to the purposes for which they are collected and/or further processed;
(d) accurate and, where necessary, kept up to date; every reasonable step must be taken to ensure that data which are inaccurate or incomplete, having regard to the purposes for which they were collected or for which they are further processed, are erased or rectified;

(e)   kept in a form which permits identification of data subjects for no longer than is necessary for the purposes for which the data were collected or for which they are further processed. Member States shall lay down appropriate safeguards for personal data stored for longer periods for historical, statistical or scientific use.

2.   It shall be for the controller to ensure that paragraph 1 is complied with.

SECTION II
CRITERIA FOR MAKING DATA PROCESSING LEGITIMATE

Article 7

Member States shall provide that personal data may be processed only if:

(a)   the data subject has unambiguously given his consent; or

(b)   processing is necessary for the performance of a contract to which the data subject is party or in order to take steps at the request of the data subject prior to entering into a contract; or

(c)   processing is necessary for compliance with a legal obligation to which the controller is subject; or

(d)   processing is necessary in order to protect the vital interests of the data subject; or

(e)   processing is necessary for the performance of a task carried out in the public interest or in the exercise of official authority vested in the controller or in a third party to whom the data are disclosed; or

(f)   processing is necessary for the purposes of the legitimate interests pursued by the controller or by the third party or parties to whom the data are disclosed, except where such interests are overridden by the interests for fundamental rights and freedoms of the data subject which require protection under Article 1(1).

SECTION III
SPECIAL CATEGORIES OF PROCESSING

Article 8   The processing of special categories of data

1.   Member States shall prohibit the processing of personal data revealing racial or ethnic origin, political opinions, religious or philosophical beliefs, trade-union membership, and the processing of data concerning health or sex life.

2.   Paragraph 1 shall not apply where:

(a)   the data subject has given his explicit consent to the processing of those data, except where the laws of the Member State provide that the prohibition referred to in paragraph 1 may not be lifted by the data subject's giving his consent; or

(b)   processing is necessary for the purposes of carrying out the obligations and specific rights of the controller in the field of employment law in so far as it is authorised by national law providing for adequate safeguards; or

(c)   processing is necessary to protect the vital interests of the data subject or of another person where the data subject is physically or legally incapable of giving his consent; or

(d)   processing is carried out in the course of its legitimate activities with appropriate guarantees by a foundation, association or any other non-profit-seeking body with a political, philosophical, religious or trade-union aim and on condition that the processing relates solely to the members of the body or to persons who have regular contact with it in connection with its purposes and that the data are not disclosed to a third party without the consent of the data subjects; or

(e)   the processing relates to data which are manifestly made public by the data subject or is necessary for the establishment, exercise or defence of legal claims.

3.   Paragraph 1 shall not apply where processing of the data is required for the purposes of preventive medicine, medical diagnosis, the provision of care or treatment or the management of health-care services, and where those data are processed by a health professional subject under national law or rules established by national competent bodies to the obligation of professional secrecy or by another person also subject to an equivalent obligation of secrecy.

4.   Subject to the provision of suitable safeguards, Member States may, for reasons of substantial public interest, lay down exemptions in addition to those laid down in paragraph 2 either by national law or by decision of the supervisory authority.

5.   Processing of data relating to offences, criminal convictions or security measures may be carried out only under the control of official authority, or if suitable specific safeguards are provided under national law, subject to derogations which may be granted by the Member State under national provisions providing suitable specific safeguards. However, a complete register of criminal convictions may be kept only under the control of official authority.

Member States may provide that data relating to administrative sanctions or judgements in civil cases shall also be processed under the control of official authority.

6.   Derogations from paragraph 1 provided for in paragraphs 4 and 5 shall be notified to the Commission.

7.   Member States shall determine the conditions under which a national identification number or any other identifier of general application may be processed.

Article 9   Processing of personal data and freedom of expression

Member States shall provide for exemptions or derogations from the provisions of this Chapter, Chapter IV and Chapter VI for the processing of personal data carried out solely for journalistic purposes or the purpose of artistic or literary expression only if they are necessary to reconcile the right to privacy with the rules governing freedom of expression.

SECTION IV
INFORMATION TO BE GIVEN TO THE DATA SUBJECT

Article 10   Information in cases of collection of data from the data subject

Member States shall provide that the controller or his representative must provide a data subject from whom data relating to himself are collected with at least the following information, except where he already has it:

(a)   the identity of the controller and of his representative, if any;

(b)   the purposes of the processing for which the data are intended;

(c)   any further information such as

— the recipients or categories of recipients of the data,

— whether replies to the questions are obligatory or voluntary, as well as the possible consequences of failure to reply,

— the existence of the right of access to and the right to rectify the data concerning him in so far as such further information is necessary, having regard to the specific circumstances in which the data are collected, to guarantee fair processing in respect of the data subject.

Article 11   Information where the data have not been obtained from the data subject

1.   Where the data have not been obtained from the data subject, Member States shall provide that the controller or his representative must at the time of undertaking the recording of personal data or if a disclosure to a third party is envisaged, no later than the time when the data are first disclosed provide the data subject with at least the following information, except where he already has it:

   (a)   the identity of the controller and of his representative, if any;

   (b)   the purposes of the processing;

   (c)   any further information such as

— the categories of data concerned,

— the recipients or categories of recipients,

— the existence of the right of access to and the right to rectify the data concerning him

in so far as such further information is necessary, having regard to the specific circumstances in which the data are processed, to guarantee fair processing in respect of the data subject.

2.   Paragraph 1 shall not apply where, in particular for processing for statistical purposes or for the purposes of historical or scientific research, the provision of such information proves impossible or would involve a disproportionate effort or if recording or disclosure is expressly laid down by law. In these cases Member States shall provide appropriate safeguards.

SECTION V
THE DATA SUBJECT'S RIGHT OF ACCESS TO DATA

Article 12   Right of access

Member States shall guarantee every data subject the right to obtain from the controller:

   (a)   without constraint at reasonable intervals and without excessive delay or expense:

— confirmation as to whether or not data relating to him are being processed and information at least as to the purposes of the processing, the categories of data concerned, and the recipients or categories of recipients to whom the data are disclosed,

— communication to him in an intelligible form of the data undergoing processing and of any available information as to their source,

— knowledge of the logic involved in any automatic processing of data concerning him at least in the case of the automated decisions referred to in Article 15(1);

   (b)   as appropriate the rectification, erasure or blocking of data the processing of which does not comply with the provisions of this Directive, in particular because of the incomplete or inaccurate nature of the data;

   (c)   notification to third parties to whom the data have been disclosed of any rectification, erasure or blocking carried out in compliance with (b), unless this proves impossible or involves a disproportionate effort.

SECTION VI
EXEMPTIONS AND RESTRICTIONS

Article 13   Exemptions and restrictions
1.   Member States may adopt legislative measures to restrict the scope of the obligations and rights provided for in Articles 6(1), 10, 11(1), 12 and 21 when such a restriction constitutes a necessary measure to safeguard:

(a)   national security;

(b)   defence;

(c)   public security;

(d)   the prevention, investigation, detection and prosecution of criminal offences, or of breaches of ethics for regulated professions;

(e)   an important economic or financial interest of a Member State or of the European Union, including monetary, budgetary and taxation matters;

(f)   a monitoring, inspection or regulatory function connected, even occasionally, with the exercise of official authority in cases referred to in (c), (d) and (e);

(g)   the protection of the data subject or of the rights and freedoms of others.

2.   Subject to adequate legal safeguards, in particular that the data are not used for taking measures or decisions regarding any particular individual, Member States may, where there is clearly no risk of breaching the privacy of the data subject, restrict by a legislative measure the rights provided for in Article 12 when data are processed solely for purposes of scientific research or are kept in personal form for a period which does not exceed the period necessary for the sole purpose of creating statistics.

SECTION VII
THE DATA SUBJECT'S RIGHT TO OBJECT

Article 14   The data subject's right to object
Member States shall grant the data subject the right:

(a)   at least in the cases referred to in Article 7(e) and (f), to object at any time on compelling legitimate grounds relating to his particular situation to the processing of data relating to him, save where otherwise provided by national legislation. Where there is a justified objection, the processing instigated by the controller may no longer involve those data;

(b)   to object, on request and free of charge, to the processing of personal data relating to him which the controller anticipates being processed for the purposes of direct marketing, or to be informed before personal data are disclosed for the first time to third parties or used on their behalf for the purposes of direct marketing, and to be expressly offered the right to object free of charge to such disclosures or uses.

Member States shall take the necessary measures to ensure that data subjects are aware of the existence of the right referred to in the first subparagraph of (b).

Article 15   Automated individual decisions
1.   Member States shall grant the right to every person not to be subject to a decision which produces legal effects concerning him or significantly affects him and which is based solely on automated processing of data intended to evaluate certain personal aspects relating to him, such as his performance at work, creditworthiness, reliability, conduct, etc.

2.   Subject to the other Articles of this Directive, Member States shall provide that a person may be subjected to a decision of the kind referred to in paragraph 1 if that decision:

(a)   is taken in the course of the entering into or performance of a contract, provided the request for the entering into or the performance of the contract, lodged by the data subject, has been satisfied or that there are suitable measures to safeguard his legitimate interests, such as arrangements allowing him to put his point of view; or

(b)   is authorised by a law which also lays down measures to safeguard the data subject's legitimate interests.

SECTION VIII
CONFIDENTIALITY AND SECURITY OF PROCESSING

Article 16   Confidentiality of processing

Any person acting under the authority of the controller or of the processor, including the processor himself, who has access to personal data must not process them except on instructions from the controller, unless he is required to do so by law.

Article 17   Security of processing

1.   Member States shall provide that the controller must implement appropriate technical and organisational measures to protect personal data against accidental or unlawful destruction or accidental loss, alteration, unauthorised disclosure or access, in particular where the processing involves the transmission of data over a network, and against all other unlawful forms of processing.

Having regard to the state of the art and the cost of their implementation, such measures shall ensure a level of security appropriate to the risks represented by the processing and the nature of the data to be protected.

2.   The Member States shall provide that the controller must, where processing is carried out on his behalf, choose a processor providing sufficient guarantees in respect of the technical security measures and organisational measures governing the processing to be carried out, and must ensure compliance with those measures.

3.   The carrying out of processing by way of a processor must be governed by a contract or legal act binding the processor to the controller and stipulating in particular that:

— the processor shall act only on instructions from the controller,

— the obligations set out in paragraph 1, as defined by the law of the Member State in which the processor is established, shall also be incumbent on the processor.

4.   For the purposes of keeping proof, the parts of the contract or the legal act relating to data protection and the requirements relating to the measures referred to in paragraph 1 shall be in writing or in another equivalent form.

SECTION IX
NOTIFICATION

Article 18   Obligation to notify the supervisory authority

1.   Member States shall provide that the controller or his representative, if any, must notify the supervisory authority referred to in Article 28 before carrying out any wholly or partly automatic processing operation or set of such operations intended to serve a single purpose or several related purposes.

2. Member States may provide for the simplification of or exemption from notification only in the following cases and under the following conditions:

— where, for categories of processing operations which are unlikely, taking account of the data to be processed, to affect adversely the rights and freedoms of data subjects, they specify the purposes of the processing, the data or categories of data undergoing processing, the category or categories of data subject, the recipients or categories of recipient to whom the data are to be disclosed and the length of time the data are to be stored, and/or

— where the controller, in compliance with the national law which governs him, appoints a personal data protection official, responsible in particular:

— for ensuring in an independent manner the internal application of the national provisions taken pursuant to this Directive

— for keeping the register of processing operations carried out by the controller, containing the items of information referred to in Article 21(2),

thereby ensuring that the rights and freedoms of the data subjects are unlikely to be adversely affected by the processing operations.

3. Member States may provide that paragraph 1 does not apply to processing whose sole purpose is the keeping of a register which according to laws or regulations is intended to provide information to the public and which is open to consultation either by the public in general or by any person demonstrating a legitimate interest.

4. Member States may provide for an exemption from the obligation to notify or a simplification of the notification in the case of processing operations referred to in Article 8(2)(d).

5. Member States may stipulate that certain or all non-automatic processing operations involving personal data shall be notified, or provide for these processing operations to be subject to simplified notification.

Article 19   Contents of notification

1. Member States shall specify the information to be given in the notification. It shall include at least:

(a)   the name and address of the controller and of his representative, if any;

(b)   the purpose or purposes of the processing;

(c)   a description of the category or categories of data subject and of the data or categories of data relating to them;

(d)   the recipients or categories of recipient to whom the data might be disclosed;

(e)   proposed transfers of data to third countries;

(f)   a general description allowing a preliminary assessment to be made of the appropriateness of the measures taken pursuant to Article 17 to ensure security of processing.

2. Member States shall specify the procedures under which any change affecting the information referred to in paragraph 1 must be notified to the supervisory authority.

Article 20   Prior checking

1. Member States shall determine the processing operations likely to present specific risks to the rights and freedoms of data subjects and shall check that these processing operations are examined prior to the start thereof.

2.   Such prior checks shall be carried out by the supervisory authority following receipt of a notification from the controller or by the data protection official, who, in cases of doubt, must consult the supervisory authority.

3.   Member States may also carry out such checks in the context of preparation either of a measure of the national parliament or of a measure based on such a legislative measure, which define the nature of the processing and lay down appropriate safeguards.

Article 21   Publicising of processing operations

1.   Member States shall take measures to ensure that processing operations are publicised.

2.   Member States shall provide that a register of processing operations notified in accordance with Article 18 shall be kept by the supervisory authority.

The register shall contain at least the information listed in Article 19(1)(a) to (e).

The register may be inspected by any person.

3.   Member States shall provide, in relation to processing operations not subject to notification, that controllers or another body appointed by the Member States make available at least the information referred to in Article 19(1)(a) to (e) in an appropriate form to any person on request.

Member States may provide that this provision does not apply to processing whose sole purpose is the keeping of a register which according to laws or regulations is intended to provide information to the public and which is open to consultation either by the public in general or by any person who can provide proof of a legitimate interest.

CHAPTER III   JUDICIAL REMEDIES, LIABILITY AND SANCTIONS

Article 22   Remedies

Without prejudice to any administrative remedy for which provision may be made, inter alia before the supervisory authority referred to in Article 28, prior to referral to the judicial authority, Member States shall provide for the right of every person to a judicial remedy for any breach of the rights guaranteed him by the national law applicable to the processing in question.

Article 23   Liability

1.   Member States shall provide that any person who has suffered damage as a result of an unlawful processing operation or of any act incompatible with the national provisions adopted pursuant to this Directive is entitled to receive compensation from the controller for the damage suffered.

2.   The controller may be exempted from this liability, in whole or in part, if he proves that he is not responsible for the event giving rise to the damage.

Article 24   Sanctions

The Member States shall adopt suitable measures to ensure the full implementation of the provisions of this Directive and shall in particular lay down the sanctions to be imposed in case of infringement of the provisions adopted pursuant to this Directive.

CHAPTER IV   TRANSFER OF PERSONAL DATA TO THIRD COUNTRIES

Article 25   Principles

1.   The Member States shall provide that the transfer to a third country of personal data which are undergoing processing or are intended for processing after transfer may take place only if, without prejudice to compliance with the national provisions adopted pursuant to the other provisions of this Directive, the third country in question ensures an adequate level of protection.

2.   The adequacy of the level of protection afforded by a third country shall be assessed in the light of all the circumstances surrounding a data transfer operation or set of data transfer operations; particular consideration shall be given to the nature of the data, the purpose and duration of the proposed processing operation or operations, the country of origin and country of final destination, the rules of law, both general and sectoral, in force in the third country in question and the professional rules and security measures which are complied with in that country.

3.   The Member States and the Commission shall inform each other of cases where they consider that a third country does not ensure an adequate level of protection within the meaning of paragraph 2.

4.   Where the Commission finds, under the procedure provided for in Article 31(2), that a third country does not ensure an adequate level of protection within the meaning of paragraph 2 of this Article, Member States shall take the measures necessary to prevent any transfer of data of the same type to the third country in question.

5.   At the appropriate time, the Commission shall enter into negotiations with a view to remedying the situation resulting from the finding made pursuant to paragraph 4.

6.   The Commission may find, in accordance with the procedure referred to in Article 31(2), that a third country ensures an adequate level of protection within the meaning of paragraph 2 of this Article, by reason of its domestic law or of the international commitments it has entered into, particularly upon conclusion of the negotiations referred to in paragraph 5, for the protection of the private lives and basic freedoms and rights of individuals.

Member States shall take the measures necessary to comply with the Commission's decision.

Article 26   Derogations

1.   By way of derogation from Article 25 and save where otherwise provided by domestic law governing particular cases, Member States shall provide that a transfer or a set of transfers of personal data to a third country which does not ensure an adequate level of protection within the meaning of Article 25(2) may take place on condition that:

(a)   the data subject has given his consent unambiguously to the proposed transfer; or

(b)   the transfer is necessary for the performance of a contract between the data subject and the controller or the implementation of precontractual measures taken in response to the data subject's request; or

(c)   the transfer is necessary for the conclusion or performance of a contract concluded in the interest of the data subject between the controller and a third party; or

(d)   the transfer is necessary or legally required on important public interest grounds, or for the establishment, exercise or defence of legal claims; or

(e)   the transfer is necessary in order to protect the vital interests of the data subject; or

(f)   the transfer is made from a register which according to laws or regulations is intended to provide information to the public and which is open to consultation either by the public in general or by any person who can demonstrate legitimate interest, to the extent that the conditions laid down in law for consultation are fulfilled in the particular case.

2.   Without prejudice to paragraph 1, a Member State may authorise a transfer or a set of transfers of personal data to a third country which does not ensure an adequate level of protection within the meaning of Article 25(2), where the controller adduces adequate safeguards with respect to the protection of the privacy and fundamental rights and freedoms of individuals and as regards the exercise of the corresponding rights; such safeguards may in particular result from appropriate contractual clauses.

3.   The Member State shall inform the Commission and the other Member States of the authorisations it grants pursuant to paragraph 2.

If a Member State or the Commission objects on justified grounds involving the protection of the privacy and fundamental rights and freedoms of individuals, the Commission shall take appropriate measures in accordance with the procedure laid down in Article 31(2).

Member States shall take the necessary measures to comply with the Commission's decision.

4.   Where the Commission decides, in accordance with the procedure referred to in Article 31(2), that certain standard contractual clauses offer sufficient safeguards as required by paragraph 2, Member States shall take the necessary measures to comply with the Commission's decision.

CHAPTER V   CODES OF CONDUCT

Article 27

1.   The Member States and the Commission shall encourage the drawing up of codes of conduct intended to contribute to the proper implementation of the national provisions adopted by the Member States pursuant to this Directive, taking account of the specific features of the various sectors.

2.   Member States shall make provision for trade associations and other bodies representing other categories of controllers which have drawn up draft national codes or which have the intention of amending or extending existing national codes to be able to submit them to the opinion of the national authority.

Member States shall make provision for this authority to ascertain, among other things, whether the drafts submitted to it are in accordance with the national provisions adopted pursuant to this Directive. If it sees fit, the authority shall seek the views of data subjects or their representatives.

3.   Draft Community codes, and amendments or extensions to existing Community codes, may be submitted to the Working Party referred to in Article 29. This Working Party shall determine, among other things, whether the drafts submitted to it are in accordance with the national provisions adopted pursuant to this Directive. If it sees fit, the authority shall seek the views of data subjects or their representatives.

The Commission may ensure appropriate publicity for the codes which have been approved by the Working Party.

CHAPTER VI SUPERVISORY AUTHORITY AND WORKING PARTY ON THE PROTECTION OF INDIVIDUALS WITH REGARD TO THE PROCESSING OF PERSONAL DATA

Article 28 Supervisory authority

1. Each Member State shall provide that one or more public authorities are responsible for monitoring the application within its territory of the provisions adopted by the Member States pursuant to this Directive.

These authorities shall act with complete independence in exercising the functions entrusted to them.

2. Each Member State shall provide that the supervisory authorities are consulted when drawing up administrative measures or regulations relating to the protection of individuals' rights and freedoms with regard to the processing of personal data.

3. Each authority shall in particular be endowed with:

— investigative powers, such as powers of access to data forming the subject-matter of processing operations and powers to collect all the information necessary for the performance of its supervisory duties,

— effective powers of intervention, such as, for example, that of delivering opinions before processing operations are carried out, in accordance with Article 20, and ensuring appropriate publication of such opinions, of ordering the blocking, erasure or destruction of data, of imposing a temporary or definitive ban on processing, of warning or admonishing the controller, or that of referring the matter to national parliaments or other political institutions,

— the power to engage in legal proceedings where the national provisions adopted pursuant to this Directive have been violated or to bring these violations to the attention of the judicial authorities.

Decisions by the supervisory authority which give rise to complaints may be appealed against through the courts.

4. Each supervisory authority shall hear claims lodged by any person, or by an association representing that person, concerning the protection of his rights and freedoms in regard to the processing of personal data. The person concerned shall be informed of the outcome of the claim.

Each supervisory authority shall, in particular, hear claims for checks on the lawfulness of data processing lodged by any person when the national provisions adopted pursuant to Article 13 of this Directive apply. The person shall at any rate be informed that a check has taken place.

5. Each supervisory authority shall draw up a report on its activities at regular intervals. The report shall be made public.

6. Each supervisory authority is competent, whatever the national law applicable to the processing in question, to exercise, on the territory of its own Member State, the powers conferred on it in accordance with paragraph 3. Each authority may be requested to exercise its powers by an authority of another Member State.

The supervisory authorities shall cooperate with one another to the extent necessary for the performance of their duties, in particular by exchanging all useful information.

7. Member States shall provide that the members and staff of the supervisory authority, even after their employment has ended, are to be subject to a duty of professional secrecy with regard to confidential information to which they have access.

Article 29 Working Party on the Protection of Individuals with regard to the Processing of Personal Data

1. A Working Party on the Protection of Individuals with regard to the Processing of Personal Data, hereinafter referred to as 'the Working Party', is hereby set up.

It shall have advisory status and act independently.

2. The Working Party shall be composed of a representative of the supervisory authority or authorities designated by each Member State and of a representative of the authority or authorities established for the Community institutions and bodies, and of a representative of the Commission.

Each member of the Working Party shall be designated by the institution, authority or authorities which he represents. Where a Member State has designated more than one supervisory authority, they shall nominate a joint representative. The same shall apply to the authorities established for Community institutions and bodies.

3. The Working Party shall take decisions by a simple majority of the representatives of the supervisory authorities.

4. The Working Party shall elect its chairman. The chairman's term of office shall be two years. His appointment shall be renewable.

5. The Working Party's secretariat shall be provided by the Commission.

6. The Working Party shall adopt its own rules of procedure.

7. The Working Party shall consider items placed on its agenda by its chairman, either on his own initiative or at the request of a representative of the supervisory authorities or at the Commission's request.

Article 30

1. The Working Party shall:

(a) examine any question covering the application of the national measures adopted under this Directive in order to contribute to the uniform application of such measures;

(b) give the Commission an opinion on the level of protection in the Community and in third countries;

(c) advise the Commission on any proposed amendment of this Directive, on any additional or specific measures to safeguard the rights and freedoms of natural persons with regard to the processing of personal data and on any other proposed Community measures affecting such rights and freedoms;

(d) give an opinion on codes of conduct drawn up at Community level.

2. If the Working Party finds that divergences likely to affect the equivalence of protection for persons with regard to the processing of personal data in the Community are arising between the laws or practices of Member States, it shall inform the Commission accordingly.

3. The Working Party may, on its own initiative, make recommendations on all matters relating to the protection of persons with regard to the processing of personal data in the Community.

4. The Working Party's opinions and recommendations shall be forwarded to the Commission and to the committee referred to in Article 31.

5. The Commission shall inform the Working Party of the action it has taken in response to its opinions and recommendations. It shall do so in a report which shall also be forwarded to the European Parliament and the Council. The report shall be made public.

6. The Working Party shall draw up an annual report on the situation regarding the protection of natural persons with regard to the processing of personal data in the Community and in third countries, which it shall transmit to the Commission, the European Parliament and the Council. The report shall be made public.

CHAPTER VII   COMMUNITY IMPLEMENTING MEASURES

Article 31   The Committee

1. The Commission shall be assisted by a committee composed of the representatives of the Member States and chaired by the representative of the Commission.

2. The representative of the Commission shall submit to the committee a draft of the measures to be taken. The committee shall deliver its opinion on the draft within a time limit which the chairman may lay down according to the urgency of the matter.

The opinion shall be delivered by the majority laid down in Article 148 (2) of the Treaty. The votes of the representatives of the Member States within the committee shall be weighted in the manner set out in that Article. The chairman shall not vote.

The Commission shall adopt measures which shall apply immediately. However, if these measures are not in accordance with the opinion of the committee, they shall be communicated by the Commission to the Council forthwith. In that event:

— the Commission shall defer application of the measures which it has decided for a period of three months from the date of communication,

— the Council, acting by a qualified majority, may take a different decision within the time limit referred to in the first indent.

FINAL PROVISIONS

Article 32

1. Member States shall bring into force the laws, regulations and administrative provisions necessary to comply with this Directive at the latest at the end of a period of three years from the date of its adoption.

When Member States adopt these measures, they shall contain a reference to this Directive or be accompanied by such reference on the occasion of their official publication. The methods of making such reference shall be laid down by the Member States.

2. Member States shall ensure that processing already under way on the date the national provisions adopted pursuant to this Directive enter into force, is brought into conformity with these provisions within three years of this date.

By way of derogation from the preceding subparagraph, Member States may provide that the processing of data already held in manual filing systems on the date of entry into force of the national provisions adopted in implementation of this Directive shall be brought into conformity with Articles 6, 7 and 8 of this Directive within 12 years of the date on which it is adopted. Member States shall, however, grant the data subject the right to obtain, at his request and in particular at the time of exercising his right of access, the rectification, erasure or blocking of data which are incomplete, inaccurate or stored in a way incompatible with the legitimate purposes pursued by the controller.

3. By way of derogation from paragraph 2, Member States may provide, subject to suitable safeguards, that data kept for the sole purpose of historical research need not be brought into conformity with Articles 6, 7 and 8 of this Directive.

4. Member States shall communicate to the Commission the text of the provisions of domestic law which they adopt in the field covered by this Directive.

Article 33

The Commission shall report to the Council and the European Parliament at regular intervals, starting not later than three years after the date referred to in Article 32(1), on the implementation of this Directive, attaching to its report, if necessary, suitable proposals for amendments. The report shall be made public.

The Commission shall examine, in particular, the application of this Directive to the data processing of sound and image data relating to natural persons and shall submit any appropriate proposals which prove to be necessary, taking account of developments in information technology and in the light of the state of progress in the information society.

Article 34

This Directive is addressed to the Member States.

Done at Luxembourg, 24 October 1995.

For the European Parliament
The President
K. HAENSCH

For the Council
The President
L. ATIENZA SERNA

Appendix 2
Data Protection Act 1998

CHAPTER 29

ARRANGEMENT OF SECTIONS

PART I
PRELIMINARY

Unlawful obtaining etc. of personal data

55.   Unlawful obtaining etc. of personal data.

Records obtained under data subject's right of access

56.   Prohibition of requirement as to production of certain records.
57.   Avoidance of certain contractual terms relating to health records.

Information provided to Commissioner or Tribunal

58.   Disclosure of information.
59.   Confidentiality of information.

General provisions relating to offences

60.   Prosecutions and penalties.
61.   Liability of directors etc.

Amendments of Consumer Credit Act 1974

62.   Amendments of Consumer Credit Act 1974.

General

63.   Application to Crown.
64.   Transmission of notices etc. by electronic or other means.
65.   Service of notices by Commissioner.
66.   Exercise of rights in Scotland by children.
67.   Orders, regulations and rules.
68.   Meaning of 'accessible record'.
69.   Meaning of 'health professional'.
70.   Supplementary definitions.
71.   Index of defined expressions.
72.   Modifications of Act.
73.   Transitional provisions and savings.
74.   Minor and consequential amendments and repeals and revocations.
75.   Short title, commencement and extent.

SCHEDULES:

Schedule 1—The data protection principles.
   Part I—The principles.
   Part II—Interpretation of the principles in Part I.
Schedule 2—Conditions relevant for purposes of the first principle: processing
   of any personal data.
Schedule 3—Conditions relevant for purposes of the first principle: processing
   of sensitive personal data.
Schedule 4—Cases where the eighth principle does not apply.
Schedule 5—The Data Protection Commissioner and the Data Protection
   Tribunal.
   Part I—The Commissioner.
   Part II—The Tribunal.
   Part III—Transitional provisions.

Data Protection Act 1998

1998 CHAPTER 29

An Act to make new provision for the regulation of the processing of information relating to individuals, including the obtaining, holding, use or disclosure of such information. [16th July 1998]

BE IT ENACTED by the Queen's most Excellent Majesty, by and with the advice and consent of the Lords Spiritual and Temporal, and Commons, in this present Parliament assembled, and by the authority of the same, as follows:

PART I

PRELIMINARY

1. Basic interpretative provisions

(1)   In this Act, unless the context otherwise requires—

'data' means information which—

(a)   is being processed by means of equipment operating automatically in response to instructions given for that purpose,

(b)   is recorded with the intention that it should be processed by means of such equipment,

(c)   is recorded as part of a relevant filing system or with the intention that it should form part of a relevant filing system, or

(d)   does not fall within paragraph (a), (b) or (c) but forms part of an accessible record as defined by section 68;

'data controller' means, subject to subsection (4), a person who (either alone or jointly or in common with other persons) determines the purposes for which and the manner in which any personal data are, or are to be, processed;

'data processor', in relation to personal data, means any person (other than an employee of the data controller) who processes the data on behalf of the data controller;

'data subject' means an individual who is the subject of personal data;

'personal data' means data which relate to a living individual who can be identified—

(a)   from those data, or

(b)   from those data and other information which is in the possession of, or is likely to come into the possession of, the data controller,

and includes any expression of opinion about the individual and any indication of the intentions of the data controller or any other person in respect of the individual;

'processing', in relation to information or data, means obtaining, recording or holding the information or data or carrying out any operation or set of operations on the information or data, including—

(a)   organisation, adaptation or alteration of the information or data,

(b)   retrieval, consultation or use of the information or data,

(c)   disclosure of the information or data by transmission, dissemination or otherwise making available, or

(d)   alignment, combination, blocking, erasure or destruction of the information or data;

'relevant filing system' means any set of information relating to individuals to the extent that, although the information is not processed by means of equipment operating automatically in response to instructions given for that purpose, the set is structured, either by reference to individuals or by reference to criteria relating to individuals, in such a way that specific information relating to a particular individual is readily accessible.

(2)   In this Act, unless the context otherwise requires—

(a)   'obtaining' or 'recording', in relation to personal data, includes obtaining or recording the information to be contained in the data, and

(b)   'using' or 'disclosing', in relation to personal data, includes using or disclosing the information contained in the data.

(3)   In determining for the purposes of this Act whether any information is recorded with the intention—

(a)   that it should be processed by means of equipment operating automatically in response to instructions given for that purpose, or

(b)   that it should form part of a relevant filing system,

it is immaterial that it is intended to be so processed or to form part of such a system only after being transferred to a country or territory outside the European Economic Area.

(4)   Where personal data are processed only for purposes for which they are required by or under any enactment to be processed, the person on whom the obligation to process the data is imposed by or under that enactment is for the purposes of this Act the data controller.

2.   Sensitive personal data

In this Act 'sensitive personal data' means personal data consisting of information as to—

(a)   the racial or ethnic origin of the data subject,

(b)   his political opinions,

(c)   his religious beliefs or other beliefs of a similar nature,

(d)   whether he is a member of a trade union (within the meaning of the Trade Union and Labour Relations (Consolidation) Act 1992),

(e)   his physical or mental health or condition,

(f)   his sexual life,

(g)   the commission or alleged commission by him of any offence, or

(h) any proceedings for any offence committed or alleged to have been committed by him, the disposal of such proceedings or the sentence of any court in such proceedings.

3. The special purposes
In this Act 'the special purposes' means any one or more of the following—
(a) the purposes of journalism,
(b) artistic purposes, and
(c) literary purposes.

4. The data protection principles
(1) References in this Act to the data protection principles are to the principles set out in Part I of Schedule 1.
(2) Those principles are to be interpreted in accordance with Part II of Schedule 1.
(3) Schedule 2 (which applies to all personal data) and Schedule 3 (which applies only to sensitive personal data) set out conditions applying for the purposes of the first principle; and Schedule 4 sets out cases in which the eighth principle does not apply.
(4) Subject to section 27(1), it shall be the duty of a data controller to comply with the data protection principles in relation to all personal data with respect to which he is the data controller.

5. Application of Act
(1) Except as otherwise provided by or under section 54, this Act applies to a data controller in respect of any data only if—
(a) the data controller is established in the United Kingdom and the data are processed in the context of that establishment, or
(b) the data controller is established neither in the United Kingdom nor in any other EEA State but uses equipment in the United Kingdom for processing the data otherwise than for the purposes of transit through the United Kingdom.
(2) A data controller falling within subsection (1)(b) must nominate for the purposes of this Act a representative established in the United Kingdom.
(3) For the purposes of subsections (1) and (2), each of the following is to be treated as established in the United Kingdom—
(a) an individual who is ordinarily resident in the United Kingdom,
(b) a body incorporated under the law of, or of any part of, the United Kingdom,
(c) a partnership or other unincorporated association formed under the law of any part of the United Kingdom, and
(d) any person who does not fall within paragraph (a), (b) or (c) but maintains in the United Kingdom—
(i) an office, branch or agency through which he carries on any activity, or
(ii) a regular practice;
and the reference to establishment in any other EEA State has a corresponding meaning.

6. The Commissioner and the Tribunal
(1) The office originally established by section 3(1)(a) of the Data Protection Act 1984 as the office of Data Protection Registrar shall continue to exist for the purposes

of this Act but shall be known as the office of Data Protection Commissioner; and in this Act the Data Protection Commissioner is referred to as 'the Commissioner'.

(2) The Commissioner shall be appointed by Her Majesty by Letters Patent.

(3) For the purposes of this Act there shall continue to be a Data Protection Tribunal (in this Act referred to as 'the Tribunal').

(4) The Tribunal shall consist of—

(a) a chairman appointed by the Lord Chancellor after consultation with the Lord Advocate,

(b) such number of deputy chairmen so appointed as the Lord Chancellor may determine, and

(c) such number of other members appointed by the Secretary of State as he may determine.

(5) The members of the Tribunal appointed under subsection (4)(a) and (b) shall be—

(a) persons who have a 7 year general qualification, within the meaning of section 71 of the Courts and Legal Services Act 1990,

(b) advocates or solicitors in Scotland of at least 7 years' standing, or

(c) members of the bar of Northern Ireland or solicitors of the Supreme Court of Northern Ireland of at least 7 years' standing.

(6) The members of the Tribunal appointed under subsection (4)(c) shall be—

(a) persons to represent the interests of data subjects, and

(b) persons to represent the interests of data controllers.

(7) Schedule 5 has effect in relation to the Commissioner and the Tribunal.

PART II
RIGHTS OF DATA SUBJECTS AND OTHERS

7. Right of access to personal data

(1) Subject to the following provisions of this section and to sections 8 and 9, an individual is entitled—

(a) to be informed by any data controller whether personal data of which that individual is the data subject are being processed by or on behalf of that data controller,

(b) if that is the case, to be given by the data controller a description of—

(i) the personal data of which that individual is the data subject,

(ii) the purposes for which they are being or are to be processed, and

(iii) the recipients or classes of recipients to whom they are or may be disclosed,

(c) to have communicated to him in an intelligible form—

(i) the information constituting any personal data of which that individual is the data subject, and

(ii) any information available to the data controller as to the source of those data, and

(d) where the processing by automatic means of personal data of which that individual is the data subject for the purpose of evaluating matters relating to him such as, for example, his performance at work, his creditworthiness, his reliability or his conduct, has constituted or is likely to constitute the sole basis for any decision significantly affecting him, to be informed by the data controller of the logic involved in that decision-taking.

(2)   A data controller is not obliged to supply any information under subsection (1) unless he has received—

(a)   a request in writing, and

(b)   except in prescribed cases, such fee (not exceeding the prescribed maximum) as he may require.

(3)   A data controller is not obliged to comply with a request under this section unless he is supplied with such information as he may reasonably require in order to satisfy himself as to the identity of the person making the request and to locate the information which that person seeks.

(4)   Where a data controller cannot comply with the request without disclosing information relating to another individual who can be identified from that information, he is not obliged to comply with the request unless—

(a)   the other individual has consented to the disclosure of the information to the person making the request, or

(b)   it is reasonable in all the circumstances to comply with the request without the consent of the other individual.

(5)   In subsection (4) the reference to information relating to another individual includes a reference to information identifying that individual as the source of the information sought by the request; and that subsection is not to be construed as excusing a data controller from communicating so much of the information sought by the request as can be communicated without disclosing the identity of the other individual concerned, whether by the omission of names or other identifying particulars or otherwise.

(6)   In determining for the purposes of subsection (4)(b) whether it is reasonable in all the circumstances to comply with the request without the consent of the other individual concerned, regard shall be had, in particular, to—

(a)   any duty of confidentiality owed to the other individual,

(b)   any steps taken by the data controller with a view to seeking the consent of the other individual,

(c)   whether the other individual is capable of giving consent, and

(d)   any express refusal of consent by the other individual.

(7)   An individual making a request under this section may, in such cases as may be prescribed, specify that his request is limited to personal data of any prescribed description.

(8)   Subject to subsection (4), a data controller shall comply with a request under this section promptly and in any event before the end of the prescribed period beginning with the relevant day.

(9)   If a court is satisfied on the application of any person who has made a request under the foregoing provisions of this section that the data controller in question has failed to comply with the request in contravention of those provisions, the court may order him to comply with the request.

(10)   In this section—

'prescribed' means prescribed by the Secretary of State by regulations;

'the prescribed maximum' means such amount as may be prescribed;

'the prescribed period' means forty days or such other period as may be prescribed;

'the relevant day', in relation to a request under this section, means the day on which the data controller receives the request or, if later, the first day on which the data controller has both the required fee and the information referred to in subsection (3).

(11)   Different amounts or periods may be prescribed under this section in relation to different cases.

8.   Provisions supplementary to section 7

(1)   The Secretary of State may by regulations provide that, in such cases as may be prescribed, a request for information under any provision of subsection (1) of section 7 is to be treated as extending also to information under other provisions of that subsection.

(2)   The obligation imposed by section 7(1)(c)(i) must be complied with by supplying the data subject with a copy of the information in permanent form unless—

(a)   the supply of such a copy is not possible or would involve disproportionate effort, or

(b)   the data subject agrees otherwise;

and where any of the information referred to in section 7(1)(c)(i) is expressed in terms which are not intelligible without explanation the copy must be accompanied by an explanation of those terms.

(3)   Where a data controller has previously complied with a request made under section 7 by an individual, the data controller is not obliged to comply with a subsequent identical or similar request under that section by that individual unless a reasonable interval has elapsed between compliance with the previous request and the making of the current request.

(4)   In determining for the purposes of subsection (3) whether requests under section 7 are made at reasonable intervals, regard shall be had to the nature of the data, the purpose for which the data are processed and the frequency with which the data are altered.

(5)   Section 7(1)(d) is not to be regarded as requiring the provision of information as to the logic involved in any decision-taking if, and to the extent that, the information constitutes a trade secret.

(6)   The information to be supplied pursuant to a request under section 7 must be supplied by reference to the data in question at the time when the request is received, except that it may take account of any amendment or deletion made between that time and the time when the information is supplied, being an amendment or deletion that would have been made regardless of the receipt of the request.

(7)   For the purposes of section 7(4) and (5) another individual can be identified from the information being disclosed if he can be identified from that information, or from that and any other information which, in the reasonable belief of the data controller, is likely to be in, or to come into, the possession of the data subject making the request.

9.   Application of section 7 where data controller is credit reference agency

(1)   Where the data controller is a credit reference agency, section 7 has effect subject to the provisions of this section.

(2)   An individual making a request under section 7 may limit his request to personal data relevant to his financial standing, and shall be taken to have so limited his request unless the request shows a contrary intention.

(3)   Where the data controller receives a request under section 7 in a case where personal data of which the individual making the request is the data subject are being

processed by or on behalf of the data controller, the obligation to supply information under that section includes an obligation to give the individual making the request a statement, in such form as may be prescribed by the Secretary of State by regulations, of the individual's rights—

    (a)   under section 159 of the Consumer Credit Act 1974, and

    (b)   to the extent required by the prescribed form, under this Act.

10.   Right to prevent processing likely to cause damage or distress

    (1)   Subject to subsection (2), an individual is entitled at any time by notice in writing to a data controller to require the data controller at the end of such period as is reasonable in the circumstances to cease, or not to begin, processing, or processing for a specified purpose or in a specified manner, any personal data in respect of which he is the data subject, on the ground that, for specified reasons—

    (a)   the processing of those data or their processing for that purpose or in that manner is causing or is likely to cause substantial damage or substantial distress to him or to another, and

    (b)   that damage or distress is or would be unwarranted.

    (2)   Subsection (1) does not apply—

    (a)   in a case where any of the conditions in paragraphs 1 to 4 of Schedule 2 is met, or

    (b)   in such other cases as may be prescribed by the Secretary of State by order.

    (3)   The data controller must within twenty-one days of receiving a notice under subsection (1) ('the data subject notice') give the individual who gave it a written notice—

    (a)   stating that he has complied or intends to comply with the data subject notice, or

    (b)   stating his reasons for regarding the data subject notice as to any extent unjustified and the extent (if any) to which he has complied or intends to comply with it.

    (4)   If a court is satisfied, on the application of any person who has given a notice under subsection (1) which appears to the court to be justified (or to be justified to any extent), that the data controller in question has failed to comply with the notice, the court may order him to take such steps for complying with the notice (or for complying with it to that extent) as the court thinks fit.

    (5)   The failure by a data subject to exercise the right conferred by subsection (1) or section 11 (1) does not affect any other right conferred on him by this Part.

11.   Right to prevent processing for purposes of direct marketing

    (1)   An individual is entitled at any time by notice in writing to a data controller to require the data controller at the end of such period as is reasonable in the circumstances to cease, or not to begin, processing for the purposes of direct marketing personal data in respect of which he is the data subject.

    (2)   If the court is satisfied, on the application of any person who has given a notice under subsection (1), that the data controller has failed to comply with the notice, the court may order him to take such steps for complying with the notice as the court thinks fit.

    (3)   In this section 'direct marketing' means the communication (by whatever means) of any advertising or marketing material which is directed to particular individuals.

12. Rights in relation to automated decision-taking

(1) An individual is entitled at any time, by notice in writing to any data controller, to require the data controller to ensure that no decision taken by or on behalf of the data controller which significantly affects that individual is based solely on the processing by automatic means of personal data in respect of which that individual is the data subject for the purpose of evaluating matters relating to him such as, for example, his performance at work, his creditworthiness, his reliability or his conduct.

(2) Where, in a case where no notice under subsection (1) has effect, a decision which significantly affects an individual is based solely on such processing as is mentioned in subsection (1)—

(a) the data controller must as soon as reasonably practicable notify the individual that the decision was taken on that basis, and

(b) the individual is entitled, within twenty-one days of receiving that notification from the data controller, by notice in writing to require the data controller to reconsider the decision or to take a new decision otherwise than on that basis.

(3) The data controller must, within twenty-one days of receiving a notice under subsection (2)(b) ('the data subject notice') give the individual a written notice specifying the steps that he intends to take to comply with the data subject notice.

(4) A notice under subsection (1) does not have effect in relation to an exempt decision; and nothing in subsection (2) applies to an exempt decision.

(5) In subsection (4) 'exempt decision' means any decision—

(a) in respect of which the condition in subsection (6) and the condition in subsection (7) are met, or

(b) which is made in such other circumstances as may be prescribed by the Secretary of State by order.

(6) The condition in this subsection is that the decision—

(a) is taken in the course of steps taken—

(i) for the purpose of considering whether to enter into a contract with the data subject,

(ii) with a view to entering into such a contract, or

(iii) in the course of performing such a contract, or

(b) is authorised or required by or under any enactment.

(7) The condition in this subsection is that either—

(a) the effect of the decision is to grant a request of the data subject, or

(b) steps have been taken to safeguard the legitimate interests of the data subject (for example, by allowing him to make representations).

(8) If a court is satisfied on the application of a data subject that a person taking a decision in respect of him ('the responsible person') has failed to comply with subsection (1) or (2)(b), the court may order the responsible person to reconsider the decision, or to take a new decision which is not based solely on such processing as is mentioned in subsection (1).

(9) An order under subsection (8) shall not affect the rights of any person other than the data subject and the responsible person.

13. Compensation for failure to comply with certain requirements

(1) An individual who suffers damage by reason of any contravention by a data controller of any of the requirements of this Act is entitled to compensation from the data controller for that damage.

(2)   An individual who suffers distress by reason of any contravention by a data controller of any of the requirements of this Act is entitled to compensation from the data controller for that distress if—

(a)   the individual also suffers damage by reason of the contravention, or

(b)   the contravention relates to the processing of personal data for the special purposes.

(3)   In proceedings brought against a person by virtue of this section it is a defence to prove that he had taken such care as in all the circumstances was reasonably required to comply with the requirement concerned.

14.   Rectification, blocking, erasure and destruction

(1)   If a court is satisfied on the application of a data subject that personal data of which the applicant is the subject are inaccurate, the court may order the data controller to rectify, block, erase or destroy those data and any other personal data in respect of which he is the data controller and which contain an expression of opinion which appears to the court to be based on the inaccurate data.

(2)   Subsection (1) applies whether or not the data accurately record information received or obtained by the data controller from the data subject or a third party but where the data accurately record such information, then—

(a)   if the requirements mentioned in paragraph 7 of Part II of Schedule 1 have been complied with, the court may, instead of making an order under subsection (1), make an order requiring the data to be supplemented by such statement of the true facts relating to the matters dealt with by the data as the court may approve, and

(b)   if all or any of those requirements have not been complied with, the court may, instead of making an order under that subsection, make such order as it thinks fit for securing compliance with those requirements with or without a further order requiring the data to be supplemented by such a statement as is mentioned in paragraph (a).

(3)   Where the court—

(a)   makes an order under subsection (1), or

(b)   is satisfied on the application of a data subject that personal data of which he was the data subject and which have been rectified, blocked, erased or destroyed were inaccurate,

it may, where it considers it reasonably practicable, order the data controller to notify third parties to whom the data have been disclosed of the rectification, blocking, erasure or destruction.

(4)   If a court is satisfied on the application of a data subject—

(a)   that he has suffered damage by reason of any contravention by a data controller of any of the requirements of this Act in respect of any personal data, in circumstances entitling him to compensation under section 13, and

(b)   that there is a substantial risk of further contravention in respect of those data in such circumstances,

the court may order the rectification, blocking, erasure or destruction of any of those data.

(5)   Where the court makes an order under subsection (4) it may, where it considers it reasonably practicable, order the data controller to notify third parties to whom the data have been disclosed of the rectification, blocking, erasure or destruction.

(6)   In determining whether it is reasonably practicable to require such notification as is mentioned in subsection (3) or (5) the court shall have regard, in particular, to the number of persons who would have to be notified.

15.   Jurisdiction and procedure

(1)   The jurisdiction conferred by sections 7 to 14 is exercisable by the High Court or a county court or, in Scotland, by the Court of Session or the sheriff.

(2)   For the purpose of determining any question whether an applicant under subsection (9) of section 7 is entitled to the information which he seeks (including any question whether any relevant data are exempt from that section by virtue of Part IV) a court may require the information constituting any data processed by or on behalf of the data controller and any information as to the logic involved in any decision-taking as mentioned in section 7(1)(d) to be made available for its own inspection but shall not, pending the determination of that question in the applicant's favour, require the information sought by the applicant to be disclosed to him or his representatives whether by discovery (or, in Scotland, recovery) or otherwise.

PART III
NOTIFICATION BY DATA CONTROLLERS

16.   Preliminary

(1)   In this Part 'the registrable particulars', in relation to a data controller, means—

(a)   his name and address,

(b)   if he has nominated a representative for the purposes of this Act, the name and address of the representative,

(c)   a description of the personal data being or to be processed by or on behalf of the data controller and of the category or categories of data subject to which they relate,

(d)   a description of the purpose or purposes for which the data are being or are to be processed,

(e)   a description of any recipient or recipients to whom the data controller intends or may wish to disclose the data,

(f)   the names, or a description of, any countries or territories outside the European Economic Area to which the data controller directly or indirectly transfers, or intends or may wish directly or indirectly to transfer, the data, and

(g)   in any case where—

(i)   personal data are being, or are intended to be, processed in circumstances in which the prohibition in subsection (1) of section 17 is excluded by subsection (2) or (3) of that section, and

(ii)   the notification does not extend to those data,

a statement of that fact.

(2)   In this Part—

'fees regulations' means regulations made by the Secretary of State under section 18(5) or 19(4) or (7);

'notification regulations' means regulations made by the Secretary of State under the other provisions of this Part;

'prescribed', except where used in relation to fees regulations, means prescribed by notification regulations.

(3)   For the purposes of this Part, so far as it relates to the addresses of data controllers—
  (a)   the address of a registered company is that of its registered office, and
  (b)   the address of a person (other than a registered company) carrying on a business is that of his principal place of business in the United Kingdom.

17.   Prohibition on processing without registration

(1)   Subject to the following provisions of this section, personal data must not be processed unless an entry in respect of the data controller is included in the register maintained by the Commissioner under section 19 (or is treated by notification regulations made by virtue of section 19(3) as being so included).

(2)   Except where the processing is assessable processing for the purposes of section 22, subsection (1) does not apply in relation to personal data consisting of information which falls neither within paragraph (a) of the definition of 'data' in section 1(1) nor within paragraph (b) of that definition.

(3)   If it appears to the Secretary of State that processing of a particular description is unlikely to prejudice the rights and freedoms of data subjects, notification regulations may provide that, in such cases as may be prescribed, subsection (1) is not to apply in relation to processing of that description.

(4)   Subsection (1) does not apply in relation to any processing whose sole purpose is the maintenance of a public register.

18.   Notification by data controllers

(1)   Any data controller who wishes to be included in the register maintained under section 19 shall give a notification to the Commissioner under this section.

(2)   A notification under this section must specify in accordance with notification regulations—
  (a)   the registrable particulars, and
  (b)   a general description of measures to be taken for the purpose of complying with the seventh data protection principle.

(3)   Notification regulations made by virtue of subsection (2) may provide for the determination by the Commissioner, in accordance with any requirements of the regulations, of the form in which the registrable particulars and the description mentioned in subsection (2)(b) are to be specified, including in particular the detail required for the purposes of section 16(1)(c), (d), (e) and (f) and subsection (2)(b).

(4)   Notification regulations may make provision as to the giving of notification—
  (a)   by partnerships, or
  (b)   in other cases where two or more persons are the data controllers in respect of any personal data.

(5)   The notification must be accompanied by such fee as may be prescribed by fees regulations.

(6)   Notification regulations may provide for any fee paid under subsection (5) or section 19(4) to be refunded in prescribed circumstances.

19.   Register of notifications

(1)   The Commissioner shall—
  (a)   maintain a register of persons who have given notification under section 18, and

(b)   make an entry in the register in pursuance of each notification received by him under that section from a person in respect of whom no entry as data controller was for the time being included in the register.

(2)   Each entry in the register shall consist of—

(a)   the registrable particulars notified under section 18 or, as the case requires, those particulars as amended in pursuance of section 20(4), and

(b)   such other information as the Commissioner may be authorised or required by notification regulations to include in the register.

(3)   Notification regulations may make provision as to the time as from which any entry in respect of a data controller is to be treated for the purposes of section 17 as having been made in the register.

(4)   No entry shall be retained in the register for more than the relevant time except on payment of such fee as may be prescribed by fees regulations.

(5)   In subsection (4) 'the relevant time' means twelve months or such other period as may be prescribed by notification regulations; and different periods may be prescribed in relation to different cases.

(6)   The Commissioner—

(a)   shall provide facilities for making the information contained in the entries in the register available for inspection (in visible and legible form) by members of the public at all reasonable hours and free of charge, and

(b)   may provide such other facilities for making the information contained in those entries available to the public free of charge as he considers appropriate.

(7)   The Commissioner shall, on payment of such fee, if any, as may be prescribed by fees regulations, supply any member of the public with a duly certified copy in writing of the particulars contained in any entry made in the register.

20.   Duty to notify changes

(1)   For the purpose specified in subsection (2), notification regulations shall include provision imposing on every person in respect of whom an entry as a data controller is for the time being included in the register maintained under section 19 a duty to notify to the Commissioner, in such circumstances and at such time or times and in such form as may be prescribed, such matters relating to the registrable particulars and measures taken as mentioned in section 18(2)(b) as may be prescribed.

(2)   The purpose referred to in subsection (1) is that of ensuring, so far as practicable, that at any time—

(a)   the entries in the register maintained under section 19 contain current names and addresses and describe the current practice or intentions of the data controller with respect to the processing of personal data, and

(b)   the Commissioner is provided with a general description of measures currently being taken as mentioned in section 18(2)(b).

(3)   Subsection (3) of section 18 has effect in relation to notification regulations made by virtue of subsection (1) as it has effect in relation to notification regulations made by virtue of subsection (2) of that section.

(4)   On receiving any notification under notification regulations made by virtue of subsection (1), the Commissioner shall make such amendments of the relevant entry in the register maintained under section 19 as are necessary to take account of the notification.

21. Offences

(1)   If section 17(1) is contravened, the data controller is guilty of an offence.

(2)   Any person who fails to comply with the duty imposed by notification regulations made by virtue of section 20(1) is guilty of an offence.

(3)   It shall be a defence for a person charged with an offence under subsection (2) to show that he exercised all due diligence to comply with the duty.

22. Preliminary assessment by Commissioner

(1)   In this section 'assessable processing' means processing which is of a description specified in an order made by the Secretary of State as appearing to him to be particularly likely—

(a)   to cause substantial damage or substantial distress to data subjects, or

(b)   otherwise significantly to prejudice the rights and freedoms of data subjects.

(2)   On receiving notification from any data controller under section 18 or under notification regulations made by virtue of section 20 the Commissioner shall consider—

(a)   whether any of the processing to which the notification relates is assessable processing, and

(b)   if so, whether the assessable processing is likely to comply with the provisions of this Act.

(3)   Subject to subsection (4), the Commissioner shall, within the period of twenty-eight days beginning with the day on which he receives a notification which relates to assessable processing, give a notice to the data controller stating the extent to which the Commissioner is of the opinion that the processing is likely or unlikely to comply with the provisions of this Act.

(4)   Before the end of the period referred to in subsection (3) the Commissioner may, by reason of special circumstances, extend that period on one occasion only by notice to the data controller by such further period not exceeding fourteen days as the Commissioner may specify in the notice.

(5)   No assessable processing in respect of which a notification has been given to the Commissioner as mentioned in subsection (2) shall be carried on unless either—

(a)   the period of twenty-eight days beginning with the day on which the notification is received by the Commissioner (or, in a case falling within subsection (4), that period as extended under that subsection) has elapsed, or

(b)   before the end of that period (or that period as so extended) the data controller has received a notice from the Commissioner under subsection (3) in respect of the processing.

(6)   Where subsection (5) is contravened, the data controller is guilty of an offence.

(7)   The Secretary of State may by order amend subsections (3), (4) and (5) by substituting for the number of days for the time being specified there a different number specified in the order.

23. Power to make provision for appointment of data protection supervisors

(1)   The Secretary of State may by order—

(a)   make provision under which a data controller may appoint a person to act as a data protection supervisor responsible in particular for monitoring in an independent manner the data controller's compliance with the provisions of this Act, and

(b)   provide that, in relation to any data controller who has appointed a data protection supervisor in accordance with the provisions of the order and who complies with such conditions as may be specified in the order, the provisions of this Part are to have effect subject to such exemptions or other modifications as may be specified in the order.

(2)   An order under this section may—

(a)   impose duties on data protection supervisors in relation to the Commissioner, and

(b)   confer functions on the Commissioner in relation to data protection supervisors.

24.   Duty of certain data controllers to make certain information available

(1)   Subject to subsection (3), where personal data are processed in a case where—

(a)   by virtue of subsection (2) or (3) of section 17, subsection (1) of that section does not apply to the processing, and

(b)   the data controller has not notified the relevant particulars in respect of that processing under section 18,

the data controller must, within twenty-one days of receiving a written request from any person, make the relevant particulars available to that person in writing free of charge.

(2)   In this section 'the relevant particulars' means the particulars referred to in paragraphs (a) to (f) of section 16(1).

(3)   This section has effect subject to any exemption conferred for the purposes of this section by notification regulations.

(4)   Any data controller who fails to comply with the duty imposed by subsection (1) is guilty of an offence.

(5)   It shall be a defence for a person charged with an offence under subsection (4) to show that he exercised all due diligence to comply with the duty.

25.   Functions of Commissioner in relation to making of notification regulations

(1)   As soon as practicable after the passing of this Act, the Commissioner shall submit to the Secretary of State proposals as to the provisions to be included in the first notification regulations.

(2)   The Commissioner shall keep under review the working of notification regulations and may from time to time submit to the Secretary of State proposals as to amendments to be made to the regulations.

(3)   The Secretary of State may from time to time require the Commissioner to consider any matter relating to notification regulations and to submit to him proposals as to amendments to be made to the regulations in connection with that matter.

(4)   Before making any notification regulations, the Secretary of State shall—

(a)   consider any proposals made to him by the Commissioner under subsection (1), (2) or (3), and

(b)   consult the Commissioner.

26.   Fees regulations

(1)   Fees regulations prescribing fees for the purposes of any provision of this Part may provide for different fees to be payable in different cases.

(2)   In making any fees regulations, the Secretary of State shall have regard to the desirability of securing that the fees payable to the Commissioner are sufficient to offset—

(a)   the expenses incurred by the Commissioner and the Tribunal in discharging their functions and any expenses of the Secretary of State in respect of the Commissioner or the Tribunal, and

(b)   to the extent that the Secretary of State considers appropriate—

(i)   any deficit previously incurred (whether before or after the passing of this Act) in respect of the expenses mentioned in paragraph (a), and

(ii)   expenses incurred or to be incurred by the Secretary of State in respect of the inclusion of any officers or staff of the Commissioner in any scheme under section 1 of the Superannuation Act 1972.

PART IV
EXEMPTIONS

27. Preliminary

(1)   References in any of the data protection principles or any provision of Parts II and III to personal data or to the processing of personal data do not include references to data or processing which by virtue of this Part are exempt from that principle or other provision.

(2)   In this Part 'the subject information provisions' means—

(a)   the first data protection principle to the extent to which it requires compliance with paragraph 2 of Part II of Schedule 1, and

(b)   section 7.

(3)   In this Part 'the non-disclosure provisions' means the provisions specified in subsection (4) to the extent to which they are inconsistent with the disclosure in question.

(4)   The provisions referred to in subsection (3) are—

(a)   the first data protection principle, except to the extent to which it requires compliance with the conditions in Schedules 2 and 3,

(b)   the second, third, fourth and fifth data protection principles, and

(c)   sections 10 and 14(1) to (3).

(5)   Except as provided by this Part, the subject information provisions shall have effect notwithstanding any enactment or rule of law prohibiting or restricting the disclosure, or authorising the withholding, of information.

28. National security

(1)   Personal data are exempt from any of the provisions of—

(a)   the data protection principles,

(b)   Parts II, III and V, and

(c)   section 55,

if the exemption from that provision is required for the purpose of safeguarding national security.

(2)   Subject to subsection (4), a certificate signed by a Minister of the Crown certifying that exemption from all or any of the provisions mentioned in subsection (1) is or at any time was required for the purpose there mentioned in respect of any personal data shall be conclusive evidence of that fact.

(3)   A certificate under subsection (2) may identify the personal data to which it applies by means of a general description and may be expressed to have prospective effect.

(4)   Any person directly affected by the issuing of a certificate under subsection (2) may appeal to the Tribunal against the certificate.

(5)   If on an appeal under subsection (4), the Tribunal finds that, applying the principles applied by the court on an application for judicial review, the Minister did not have reasonable grounds for issuing the certificate, the Tribunal may allow the appeal and quash the certificate.

(6)   Where in any proceedings under or by virtue of this Act it is claimed by a data controller that a certificate under subsection (2) which identifies the personal data to which it applies by means of a general description applies to any personal data, any other party to the proceedings may appeal to the Tribunal on the ground that the certificate does not apply to the personal data in question and, subject to any determination under subsection (7), the certificate shall be conclusively presumed so to apply.

(7)   On any appeal under subsection (6), the Tribunal may determine that the certificate does not so apply.

(8)   A document purporting to be a certificate under subsection (2) shall be received in evidence and deemed to be such a certificate unless the contrary is proved.

(9)   A document which purports to be certified by or on behalf of a Minister of the Crown as a true copy of a certificate issued by that Minister under subsection (2) shall in any legal proceedings be evidence (or, in Scotland, sufficient evidence) of that certificate.

(10)   The power conferred by subsection (2) on a Minister of the Crown shall not be exercisable except by a Minister who is a member of the Cabinet or by the Attorney General or the Lord Advocate.

(11)   No power conferred by any provision of Part V may be exercised in relation to personal data which by virtue of this section are exempt from that provision.

(12)   Schedule 6 shall have effect in relation to appeals under subsection (4) or (6) and the proceedings of the Tribunal in respect of any such appeal.

29.   Crime and taxation

(1)   Personal data processed for any of the following purposes—
   (a)   the prevention or detection of crime,
   (b)   the apprehension or prosecution of offenders, or
   (c)   the assessment or collection of any tax or duty or of any imposition of a similar nature,
are exempt from the first data protection principle (except to the extent to which it requires compliance with the conditions in Schedules 2 and 3) and section 7 in any case to the extent to which the application of those provisions to the data would be likely to prejudice any of the matters mentioned in this subsection.

(2)   Personal data which—
   (a)   are processed for the purpose of discharging statutory functions, and
   (b)   consist of information obtained for such a purpose from a person who had it in his possession for any of the purposes mentioned in subsection (1),
are exempt from the subject information provisions to the same extent as personal data processed for any of the purposes mentioned in that subsection.

(3)   Personal data are exempt from the non-disclosure provisions in any case in which—

    (a)   the disclosure is for any of the purposes mentioned in subsection (1), and

    (b)   the application of those provisions in relation to the disclosure would be likely to prejudice any of the matters mentioned in that subsection.

(4)   Personal data in respect of which the data controller is a relevant authority and which—

    (a)   consist of a classification applied to the data subject as part of a system of risk assessment which is operated by that authority for either of the following purposes—

        (i)   the assessment or collection of any tax or duty or any imposition of a similar nature, or

        (ii)   the prevention or detection of crime, or apprehension or prosecution of offenders, where the offence concerned involves any unlawful claim for any payment out of, or any unlawful application of, public funds, and

    (b)   are processed for either of those purposes,

are exempt from section 7 to the extent to which the exemption is required in the interests of the operation of the system.

(5)   In subsection (4)—

'public funds' includes funds provided by any Community institution;

'relevant authority' means—

    (a)   a government department,

    (b)   a local authority, or

    (c)   any other authority administering housing benefit or council tax benefit.

30.   Health, education and social work

(1)   The Secretary of State may by order exempt from the subject information provisions, or modify those provisions in relation to, personal data consisting of information as to the physical or mental health or condition of the data subject.

(2)   The Secretary of State may by order exempt from the subject information provisions, or modify those provisions in relation to—

    (a)   personal data in respect of which the data controller is the proprietor of, or a teacher at, a school, and which consist of information relating to persons who are or have been pupils at the school, or

    (b)   personal data in respect of which the data controller is an education authority in Scotland, and which consist of information relating to persons who are receiving, or have received, further education provided by the authority.

(3)   The Secretary of State may by order exempt from the subject information provisions, or modify those provisions in relation to, personal data of such other descriptions as may be specified in the order, being information—

    (a)   processed by government departments or local authorities or by voluntary organisations or other bodies designated by or under the order, and

    (b)   appearing to him to be processed in the course of, or for the purposes of, carrying out social work in relation to the data subject or other individuals;

but the Secretary of State shall not under this subsection confer any exemption or make any modification except so far as he considers that the application to the data of those provisions (or of those provisions without modification) would be likely to prejudice the carrying out of social work.

(4)   An order under this section may make different provision in relation to data consisting of information of different descriptions.

(5)   In this section—

'education authority' and 'further education' have the same meaning as in the Education (Scotland) Act 1980 ('the 1980 Act'), and

'proprietor'—

(a)   in relation to a school in England or Wales, has the same meaning as in the Education Act 1996,

(b)   in relation to a school in Scotland, means—

(i)   in the case of a self-governing school, the board of management within the meaning of the Self-Governing Schools etc. (Scotland) Act 1989,

(ii)   in the case of an independent school, the proprietor within the meaning of the 1980 Act,

(iii)   in the case of a grant-aided school, the managers within the meaning of the 1980 Act, and

(iv)   in the case of a public school, the education authority within the meaning of the 1980 Act, and

(c)   in relation to a school in Northern Ireland, has the same meaning as in the Education and Libraries (Northern Ireland) Order 1986 and includes, in the case of a controlled school, the Board of Governors of the school.

31.   Regulatory activity

(1)   Personal data processed for the purposes of discharging functions to which this subsection applies are exempt from the subject information provisions in any case to the extent to which the application of those provisions to the data would be likely to prejudice the proper discharge of those functions.

(2)   Subsection (1) applies to any relevant function which is designed—

(a)   for protecting members of the public against—

(i)   financial loss due to dishonesty, malpractice or other seriously improper conduct by, or the unfitness or incompetence of, persons concerned in the provision of banking, insurance, investment or other financial services or in the management of bodies corporate,

(ii)   financial loss due to the conduct of discharged or undischarged bankrupts, or

(iii)   dishonesty, malpractice or other seriously improper conduct by, or the unfitness or incompetence of, persons authorised to carry on any profession or other activity,

(b)   for protecting charities against misconduct or mismanagement (whether by trustees or other persons) in their administration,

(c)   for protecting the property of charities from loss or misapplication,

(d)   for the recovery of the property of charities,

(e)   for securing the health, safety and welfare of persons at work, or

(f)   for protecting persons other than persons at work against risk to health or safety arising out of or in connection with the actions of persons at work.

(3)   In subsection (2) 'relevant function' means—

(a)   any function conferred on any person by or under any enactment,

(b)   any function of the Crown, a Minister of the Crown or a government department, or

(c)   any other function which is of a public nature and is exercised in the public interest.

(4)   Personal data processed for the purpose of discharging any function which—

(a)   is conferred by or under any enactment on—

(i)   the Parliamentary Commissioner for Administration,

(ii)   the Commission for Local Administration in England, the Commission for Local Administration in Wales or the Commissioner for Local Administration in Scotland,

(iii)   the Health Service Commissioner for England, the Health Service Commissioner for Wales or the Health Service Commissioner for Scotland,

(iv)   the Welsh Administration Ombudsman,

(v)   the Assembly Ombudsman for Northern Ireland, or

(vi)   the Northern Ireland Commissioner for Complaints, and

(b)   is designed for protecting members of the public against—

(i)   maladministration by public bodies,

(ii)   failures in services provided by public bodies, or

(iii)   a failure of a public body to provide a service which it was a function of the body to provide,

are exempt from the subject information provisions in any case to the extent to which the application of those provisions to the data would be likely to prejudice the proper discharge of that function.

(5)   Personal data processed for the purpose of discharging any function which—

(a)   is conferred by or under any enactment on the Director General of Fair Trading, and

(b)   is designed—

(i)   for protecting members of the public against conduct which may adversely affect their interests by persons carrying on a business,

(ii)   for regulating agreements or conduct which have as their object or effect the prevention, restriction or distortion of competition in connection with any commercial activity, or

(iii)   for regulating conduct on the part of one or more undertakings which amounts to the abuse of a dominant position in a market,

are exempt from the subject information provisions in any case to the extent to which the application of those provisions to the data would be likely to prejudice the proper discharge of that function.

32.   Journalism, literature and art

(1)   Personal data which are processed only for the special purposes are exempt from any provision to which this subsection relates if—

(a)   the processing is undertaken with a view to the publication by any person of any journalistic, literary or artistic material,

(b)   the data controller reasonably believes that, having regard in particular to the special importance of the public interest in freedom of expression, publication would be in the public interest, and

(c)   the data controller reasonably believes that, in all the circumstances, compliance with that provision is incompatible with the special purposes.

(2)   Subsection (1) relates to the provisions of—

(a)   the data protection principles except the seventh data protection principle,

(b)   section 7,

(c)   section 10,

(d)   section 12, and

(e)   section 14(1) to (3).

(3)   In considering for the purposes of subsection (1)(b) whether the belief of a data controller that publication would be in the public interest was or is a reasonable one, regard may be had to his compliance with any code of practice which—

(a)   is relevant to the publication in question, and

(b)   is designated by the Secretary of State by order for the purposes of this subsection.

(4)   Where at any time ('the relevant time') in any proceedings against a data controller under section 7(9), 10(4), 12(8) or 14 or by virtue of section 13 the data controller claims, or it appears to the court, that any personal data to which the proceedings relate are being processed—

(a)   only for the special purposes, and

(b)   with a view to the publication by any person of any journalistic, literary or artistic material which, at the time twenty-four hours immediately before the relevant time, had not previously been published by the data controller,

the court shall stay the proceedings until either of the conditions in subsection (5) is met.

(5)   Those conditions are—

(a)   that a determination of the Commissioner under section 45 with respect to the data in question takes effect, or

(b)   in a case where the proceedings were stayed on the making of a claim, that the claim is withdrawn.

(6)   For the purposes of this Act 'publish', in relation to journalistic, literary or artistic material, means make available to the public or any section of the public.

33.   Research, history and statistics

(1)   In this section—

'research purposes' includes statistical or historical purposes;

'the relevant conditions', in relation to any processing of personal data, means the conditions—

(a)   that the data are not processed to support measures or decisions with respect to particular individuals, and

(b)   that the data are not processed in such a way that substantial damage or substantial distress is, or is likely to be, caused to any data subject.

(2)   For the purposes of the second data protection principle, the further processing of personal data only for research purposes in compliance with the relevant conditions is not to be regarded as incompatible with the purposes for which they were obtained.

(3)   Personal data which are processed only for research purposes in compliance with the relevant conditions may, notwithstanding the fifth data protection principle, be kept indefinitely.

(4)   Personal data which are processed only for research purposes are exempt from section 7 if—

(a)   they are processed in compliance with the relevant conditions, and

(b)   the results of the research or any resulting statistics are not made available in a form which identifies data subjects or any of them.

(5)   For the purposes of subsections (2) to (4) personal data are not to be treated as processed otherwise than for research purposes merely because the data are disclosed—
(a)   to any person, for research purposes only,
(b)   to the data subject or a person acting on his behalf,
(c)   at the request, or with the consent, of the data subject or a person acting on his behalf, or
(d)   in circumstances in which the person making the disclosure has reasonable grounds for believing that the disclosure falls within paragraph (a), (b) or (c).

34.   Information available to the public by or under enactment
Personal data are exempt from—
(a)   the subject information provisions,
(b)   the fourth data protection principle and section 14(1) to (3), and
(c)   the non-disclosure provisions,
if the data consist of information which the data controller is obliged by or under any enactment to make available to the public, whether by publishing it, by making it available for inspection, or otherwise and whether gratuitously or on payment of a fee.

35.   Disclosures required by law or made in connection with legal proceedings etc.
(1)   Personal data are exempt from the non-disclosure provisions where the disclosure is required by or under any enactment, by any rule of law or by the order of a court.
(2)   Personal data are exempt from the non-disclosure provisions where the disclosure is necessary—
(a)   for the purpose of, or in connection with, any legal proceedings (including prospective legal proceedings), or
(b)   for the purpose of obtaining legal advice,
or is otherwise necessary for the purposes of establishing, exercising or defending legal rights.

36.   Domestic purposes
Personal data processed by an individual only for the purposes of that individual's personal, family or household affairs (including recreational purposes) are exempt from the data protection principles and the provisions of Parts II and III.

37.   Miscellaneous exemptions
Schedule 7 (which confers further miscellaneous exemptions) has effect.

38.   Powers to make further exemptions by order
(1)   The Secretary of State may by order exempt from the subject information provisions personal data consisting of information the disclosure of which is prohibited or restricted by or under any enactment if and to the extent that he considers it necessary for the safeguarding of the interests of the data subject or the rights and freedoms of any other individual that the prohibition or restriction ought to prevail over those provisions.
(2)   The Secretary of State may by order exempt from the non-disclosure provisions any disclosures of personal data made in circumstances specified in the order, if he considers the exemption is necessary for the safeguarding of the interests of the data subject or the rights and freedoms of any other individual.

39. Transitional relief
Schedule 8 (which confers transitional exemptions) has effect.

PART V

ENFORCEMENT

40. Enforcement notices

(1)   If the Commissioner is satisfied that a data controller has contravened or is contravening any of the data protection principles, the Commissioner may serve him with a notice (in this Act referred to as 'an enforcement notice') requiring him, for complying with the principle or principles in question, to do either or both of the following—

(a)   to take within such time as may be specified in the notice, or to refrain from taking after such time as may be so specified, such steps as are so specified, or

(b)   to refrain from processing any personal data, or any personal data of a description specified in the notice, or to refrain from processing them for a purpose so specified or in a manner so specified, after such time as may be so specified.

(2)   In deciding whether to serve an enforcement notice, the Commissioner shall consider whether the contravention has caused or is likely to cause any person damage or distress.

(3)   An enforcement notice in respect of a contravention of the fourth data protection principle which requires the data controller to rectify, block, erase or destroy any inaccurate data may also require the data controller to rectify, block, erase or destroy any other data held by him and containing an expression of opinion which appears to the Commissioner to be based on the inaccurate data.

(4)   An enforcement notice in respect of a contravention of the fourth data protection principle, in the case of data which accurately record information received or obtained by the data controller from the data subject or a third party, may require the data controller either—

(a)   to rectify, block, erase or destroy any inaccurate data and any other data held by him and containing an expression of opinion as mentioned in subsection (3), or

(b)   to take such steps as are specified in the notice for securing compliance with the requirements specified in paragraph 7 of Part II of Schedule 1 and, if the Commissioner thinks fit, for supplementing the data with such statement of the true facts relating to the matters dealt with by the data as the Commissioner may approve.

(5)   Where—

(a)   an enforcement notice requires the data controller to rectify, block, erase or destroy any personal data, or

(b)   the Commissioner is satisfied that personal data which have been rectified, blocked, erased or destroyed had been processed in contravention of any of the data protection principles,

an enforcement notice may, if reasonably practicable, require the data controller to notify third parties to whom the data have been disclosed of the rectification, blocking, erasure or destruction; and in determining whether it is reasonably practicable to require such notification regard shall be had, in particular, to the number of persons who would have to be notified.

(6)   An enforcement notice must contain—

(a)   a statement of the data protection principle or principles which the Commissioner is satisfied have been or are being contravened and his reasons for reaching that conclusion, and

(b)   particulars of the rights of appeal conferred by section 48.

(7)   Subject to subsection (8), an enforcement notice must not require any of the provisions of the notice to be complied with before the end of the period within which an appeal can be brought against the notice and, if such an appeal is brought, the notice need not be complied with pending the determination or withdrawal of the appeal.

(8)   If by reason of special circumstances the Commissioner considers that an enforcement notice should be complied with as a matter of urgency he may include in the notice a statement to that effect and a statement of his reasons for reaching that conclusion; and in that event subsection (7) shall not apply but the notice must not require the provisions of the notice to be complied with before the end of the period of seven days beginning with the day on which the notice is served.

(9)   Notification regulations (as defined by section 16(2)) may make provision as to the effect of the service of an enforcement notice on any entry in the register maintained under section 19 which relates to the person on whom the notice is served.

(10)   This section has effect subject to section 46(1).

41.   Cancellation of enforcement notice

(1)   If the Commissioner considers that all or any of the provisions of an enforcement notice need not be complied with in order to ensure compliance with the data protection principle or principles to which it relates, he may cancel or vary the notice by written notice to the person on whom it was served.

(2)   A person on whom an enforcement notice has been served may, at any time after the expiry of the period during which an appeal can be brought against that notice, apply in writing to the Commissioner for the cancellation or variation of that notice on the ground that, by reason of a change of circumstances, all or any of the provisions of that notice need not be complied with in order to ensure compliance with the data protection principle or principles to which that notice relates.

42.   Request for assessment

(1)   A request may be made to the Commissioner by or on behalf of any person who is, or believes himself to be, directly affected by any processing of personal data for an assessment as to whether it is likely or unlikely that the processing has been or is being carried out in compliance with the provisions of this Act.

(2)   On receiving a request under this section, the Commissioner shall make an assessment in such manner as appears to him to be appropriate, unless he has not been supplied with such information as he may reasonably require in order to—

(a)   satisfy himself as to the identity of the person making the request, and

(b)   enable him to identify the processing in question.

(3)   The matters to which the Commissioner may have regard in determining in what manner it is appropriate to make an assessment include—

(a)   the extent to which the request appears to him to raise a matter of substance,

(b)   any undue delay in making the request, and

(c)   whether or not the person making the request is entitled to make an application under section 7 in respect of the personal data in question.

(4)   Where the Commissioner has received a request under this section he shall notify the person who made the request—

(a)   whether he has made an assessment as a result of the request, and

(b)   to the extent that he considers appropriate, having regard in particular to any exemption from section 7 applying in relation to the personal data concerned, of any view formed or action taken as a result of the request.

43.   Information notices

(1)   If the Commissioner—

(a)   has received a request under section 42 in respect of any processing of personal data, or

(b)   reasonably requires any information for the purpose of determining whether the data controller has complied or is complying with the data protection principles,

he may serve the data controller with a notice (in this Act referred to as 'an information notice') requiring the data controller, within such time as is specified in the notice, to furnish the Commissioner, in such form as may be so specified, with such information relating to the request or to compliance with the principles as is so specified.

(2)   An information notice must contain—

(a)   In a case falling within subsection (1)(a), a statement that the Commissioner has received a request under section 42 in relation to the specified processing, or

(b)   in a case falling within subsection (1)(b), a statement that the Commissioner regards the specified information as relevant for the purpose of determining whether the data controller has complied, or is complying, with the data protection principles and his reasons for regarding it as relevant for that purpose.

(3)   An information notice must also contain particulars of the rights of appeal conferred by section 48.

(4)   Subject to subsection (5), the time specified in an information notice shall not expire before the end of the period within which an appeal can be brought against the notice and, if such an appeal is brought, the information need not be furnished pending the determination or withdrawal of the appeal.

(5)   If by reason of special circumstances the Commissioner considers that the information is required as a matter of urgency, he may include in the notice a statement to that effect and a statement of his reasons for reaching that conclusion; and in that event subsection (4) shall not apply, but the notice shall not require the information to be furnished before the end of the period of seven days beginning with the day on which the notice is served.

(6)   A person shall not be required by virtue of this section to furnish the Commissioner with any information in respect of—

(a)   any communication between a professional legal adviser and his client in connection with the giving of legal advice to the client with respect to his obligations, liabilities or rights under this Act, or

(b)   any communication between a professional legal adviser and his client, or between such an adviser or his client and any other person, made in connection with or in contemplation of proceedings under or arising out of this Act (including proceedings before the Tribunal) and for the purposes of such proceedings.

(7)   In subsection (6) references to the client of a professional legal adviser include references to any person representing such a client.

(8)   A person shall not be required by virtue of this section to furnish the Commissioner with any information if the furnishing of that information would, by revealing evidence of the commission of any offence other than an offence under this Act, expose him to proceedings for that offence.

(9)   The Commissioner may cancel an information notice by written notice to the person on whom it was served.

(10)   This section has effect subject to section 46(3).

44.   Special information notices

(1)   If the Commissioner—

(a)   has received a request under section 42 in respect of any processing of personal data, or

(b)   has reasonable grounds for suspecting that, in a case in which proceedings have been stayed under section 32, the personal data to which the proceedings relate—

(i)   are not being processed only for the special purposes, or

(ii)   are not being processed with a view to the publication by any person of any journalistic, literary or artistic material which has not previously been published by the data controller,

he may serve the data controller with a notice (in this Act referred to as a 'special information notice') requiring the data controller, within such time as is specified in the notice, to furnish the Commissioner, in such form as may be so specified, with such information as is so specified for the purpose specified in subsection (2).

(2)   That purpose is the purpose of ascertaining—

(a)   whether the personal data are being processed only for the special purposes, or

(b)   whether they are being processed with a view to the publication by any person of any journalistic, literary or artistic material which has not previously been published by the data controller.

(3)   A special information notice must contain—

(a)   in a case falling within paragraph (a) of subsection (1), a statement that the Commissioner has received a request under section 42 in relation to the specified processing, or

(b)   in a case falling within paragraph (b) of that subsection, a statement of the Commissioner's grounds for suspecting that the personal data are not being processed as mentioned in that paragraph.

(4)   A special information notice must also contain particulars of the rights of appeal conferred by section 48.

(5)   Subject to subsection (6), the time specified in a special information notice shall not expire before the end of the period within which an appeal can be brought against the notice and, if such an appeal is brought, the information need not be furnished pending the determination or withdrawal of the appeal.

(6)   If by reason of special circumstances the Commissioner considers that the information is required as a matter of urgency, he may include in the notice a statement to that effect and a statement of his reasons for reaching that conclusion; and in that event subsection (5) shall not apply, but the notice shall not require the

information to be furnished before the end of the period of seven days beginning with the day on which the notice is served.

(7) A person shall not be required by virtue of this section to furnish the Commissioner with any information in respect of—

(a) any communication between a professional legal adviser and his client in connection with the giving of legal advice to the client with respect to his obligations, liabilities or rights under this Act, or

(b) any communication between a professional legal adviser and his client, or between such an adviser or his client and any other person, made in connection with or in contemplation of proceedings under or arising out of this Act (including proceedings before the Tribunal) and for the purposes of such proceedings.

(8) In subsection (7) references to the client of a professional legal adviser include references to any person representing such a client.

(9) A person shall not be required by virtue of this section to furnish the Commissioner with any information if the furnishing of that information would, by revealing evidence of the commission of any offence other than an offence under this Act, expose him to proceedings for that offence.

(10) The Commissioner may cancel a special information notice by written notice to the person on whom it was served.

45. Determination by Commissioner as to the special purposes

(1) Where at any time it appears to the Commissioner (whether as a result of the service of a special information notice or otherwise) that any personal data—

(a) are not being processed only for the special purposes, or

(b) are not being processed with a view to the publication by any person of any journalistic, literary or artistic material which has not previously been published by the data controller,

he may make a determination in writing to that effect.

(2) Notice of the determination shall be given to the data controller; and the notice must contain particulars of the right of appeal conferred by section 48.

(3) A determination under subsection (1) shall not take effect until the end of the period within which an appeal can be brought and, where an appeal is brought, shall not take effect pending the determination or withdrawal of the appeal.

46. Restriction on enforcement in case of processing for the special purposes

(1) The Commissioner may not at any time serve an enforcement notice on a data controller with respect to the processing of personal data for the special purposes unless—

(a) a determination under section 45(1) with respect to those data has taken effect, and

(b) the court has granted leave for the notice to be served.

(2) The court shall not grant leave for the purposes of subsection (1)(b) unless it is satisfied—

(a) that the Commissioner has reason to suspect a contravention of the data protection principles which is of substantial public importance, and

(b) except where the case is one of urgency, that the data controller has been given notice, in accordance with rules of court, of the application for leave.

(3)   The Commissioner may not serve an information notice on a data controller with respect to the processing of personal data for the special purposes unless a determination under section 45(1) with respect to those data has taken effect.

47.   Failure to comply with notice

(1)   A person who fails to comply with an enforcement notice, an information notice or a special information notice is guilty of an offence.

(2)   A person who, in purported compliance with an information notice or a special information notice—

   (a)   makes a statement which he knows to be false in a material respect, or

   (b)   recklessly makes a statement which is false in a material respect, is guilty of an offence.

(3)   It is a defence for a person charged with an offence under subsection (1) to prove that he exercised all due diligence to comply with the notice in question.

48.   Rights of appeal

(1)   A person on whom an enforcement notice, an information notice or a special information notice has been served may appeal to the Tribunal against the notice.

(2)   A person on whom an enforcement notice has been served may appeal to the Tribunal against the refusal of an application under section 41(2) for cancellation or variation of the notice.

(3)   Where an enforcement notice, an information notice or a special information notice contains a statement by the Commissioner in accordance with section 40(8), 43(5) or 44(6) then, whether or not the person appeals against the notice, he may appeal against—

   (a)   the Commissioner's decision to include the statement in the notice, or

   (b)   the effect of the inclusion of the statement as respects any part of the notice.

(4)   A data controller in respect of whom a determination has been made under section 45 may appeal to the Tribunal against the determination.

(5)   Schedule 6 has effect in relation to appeals under this section and the proceedings of the Tribunal in respect of any such appeal.

49.   Determination of appeals

(1)   If on an appeal under section 48(1) the Tribunal considers—

   (a)   that the notice against which the appeal is brought is not in accordance with the law, or

   (b)   to the extent that the notice involved an exercise of discretion by the Commissioner, that he ought to have exercised his discretion differently,

the Tribunal shall allow the appeal or substitute such other notice or decision as could have been served or made by the Commissioner; and in any other case the Tribunal shall dismiss the appeal.

(2)   On such an appeal, the Tribunal may review any determination of fact on which the notice in question was based.

(3)   If on an appeal under section 48(2) the Tribunal considers that the enforcement notice ought to be cancelled or varied by reason of a change in circumstances, the Tribunal shall cancel or vary the notice.

(4)   On an appeal under subsection (3) of section 48 the Tribunal may direct—

   (a)   that the notice in question shall have effect as if it did not contain any such statement as is mentioned in that subsection, or

(b)   that the inclusion of the statement shall not have effect in relation to any part of the notice,

and may make such modifications in the notice as may be required for giving effect to the direction.

(5)   On an appeal under section 48(4), the Tribunal may cancel the determination of the Commissioner.

(6)   Any party to an appeal to the Tribunal under section 48 may appeal from the decision of the Tribunal on a point of law to the appropriate court; and that court shall be—

(a)   the High Court of Justice in England if the address of the person who was the appellant before the Tribunal is in England or Wales,

(b)   the Court of Session if that address is in Scotland, and

(c)   the High Court of Justice in Northern Ireland if that address is in Northern Ireland.

(7)   For the purposes of subsection (6)—

(a)   the address of a registered company is that of its registered office, and

(b)   the address of a person (other than a registered company) carrying on a business is that of his principal place of business in the United Kingdom.

50.   Powers of entry and inspection

Schedule 9 (powers of entry and inspection) has effect.

PART VI
MISCELLANEOUS AND GENERAL

Functions of Commissioner

51.   General duties of Commissioner

(1)   It shall be the duty of the Commissioner to promote the following of good practice by data controllers and, in particular, so to perform his functions under this Act as to promote the observance of the requirements of this Act by data controllers.

(2)   The Commissioner shall arrange for the dissemination in such form and manner as he considers appropriate of such information as it may appear to him expedient to give to the public about the operation of this Act, about good practice, and about other matters within the scope of his functions under this Act, and may give advice to any person as to any of those matters.

(3)   Where—

(a)   the Secretary of State so directs by order, or

(b)   the Commissioner considers it appropriate to do so,

the Commissioner shall, after such consultation with trade associations, data subjects or persons representing data subjects as appears to him to be appropriate, prepare and disseminate to such persons as he considers appropriate codes of practice for guidance as to good practice.

(4)   The Commissioner shall also—

(a)   where he considers it appropriate to do so, encourage trade associations to prepare, and to disseminate to their members, such codes of practice, and

(b)   where any trade association submits a code of practice to him for his consideration, consider the code and, after such consultation with data subjects or persons representing data subjects as appears to him to be appropriate, notify the trade association whether in his opinion the code promotes the following of good practice.

(5)   An order under subsection (3) shall describe the personal data or processing to which the code of practice is to relate, and may also describe the persons or classes of persons to whom it is to relate.

(6)   The Commissioner shall arrange for the dissemination in such form and manner as he considers appropriate of—

   (a)   any Community finding as defined by paragraph 15(2) of Part II of Schedule 1,

   (b)   any decision of the European Commission, under the procedure provided for in Article 31(2) of the Data Protection Directive, which is made for the purposes of Article 26(3) or (4) of the Directive, and

   (c)   such other information as it may appear to him to be expedient to give to data controllers in relation to any personal data about the protection of the rights and freedoms of data subjects in relation to the processing of personal data in countries and territories outside the European Economic Area.

(7)   The Commissioner may, with the consent of the data controller, assess any processing of personal data for the following of good practice and shall inform the data controller of the results of the assessment.

(8)   The Commissioner may charge such sums as he may with the consent of the Secretary of State determine for any services provided by the Commissioner by virtue of this Part.

(9)   In this section—

'good practice' means such practice in the processing of personal data as appears to the Commissioner to be desirable having regard to the interests of data subjects and others, and includes (but is not limited to) compliance with the requirements of this Act;

'trade association' includes any body representing data controllers.

52.   Reports and codes of practice to be laid before Parliament

(1)   The Commissioner shall lay annually before each House of Parliament a general report on the exercise of his functions under this Act.

(2)   The Commissioner may from time to time lay before each House of Parliament such other reports with respect to those functions as he thinks fit.

(3)   The Commissioner shall lay before each House of Parliament any code of practice prepared under section 51(3) for complying with a direction of the Secretary of State, unless the code is included in any report laid under subsection (1) or (2).

53.   Assistance by Commissioner in cases involving processing for the special purposes

(1)   An individual who is an actual or prospective party to any proceedings under section 7(9), 10(4), 12(8) or 14 or by virtue of section 13 which relate to personal data processed for the special purposes may apply to the Commissioner for assistance in relation to those proceedings.

(2)   The Commissioner shall, as soon as reasonably practicable after receiving an application under subsection (1), consider it and decide whether and to what extent to grant it, but he shall not grant the application unless, in his opinion, the case involves a matter of substantial public importance.

(3)   If the Commissioner decides to provide assistance, he shall, as soon as reasonably practicable after making the decision, notify the applicant, stating the extent of the assistance to be provided.

(4)   If the Commissioner decides not to provide assistance, he shall, as soon as reasonably practicable after making the decision, notify the applicant of his decision and, if he thinks fit, the reasons for it.

(5)   In this section—

(a)   references to 'proceedings' include references to prospective proceedings, and

(b)   'applicant', in relation to assistance under this section, means an individual who applies for assistance.

(6)   Schedule 10 has effect for supplementing this section.

54.   International co-operation

(1)   The Commissioner—

(a)   shall continue to be the designated authority in the United Kingdom for the purposes of Article 13 of the Convention, and

(b)   shall be the supervisory authority in the United Kingdom for the purposes of the Data Protection Directive.

(2)   The Secretary of State may by order make provision as to the functions to be discharged by the Commissioner as the designated authority in the United Kingdom for the purposes of Article 13 of the Convention.

(3)   The Secretary of State may by order make provision as to co-operation by the Commissioner with the European Commission and with supervisory authorities in other EEA States in connection with the performance of their respective duties and, in particular, as to—

(a)   the exchange of information with supervisory authorities in other EEA States or with the European Commission, and

(b)   the exercise within the United Kingdom at the request of a supervisory authority in another EEA State, in cases excluded by section 5 from the application of the other provisions of this Act, of functions of the Commissioner specified in the order.

(4)   The Commissioner shall also carry out any data protection functions which the Secretary of State may by order direct him to carry out for the purpose of enabling Her Majesty's Government in the United Kingdom to give effect to any international obligations of the United Kingdom.

(5)   The Commissioner shall, if so directed by the Secretary of State, provide any authority exercising data protection functions under the law of a colony specified in the direction with such assistance in connection with the discharge of those functions as the Secretary of State may direct or approve, on such terms (including terms as to payment) as the Secretary of State may direct or approve.

(6)   Where the European Commission makes a decision for the purposes of Article 26(3) or (4) of the Data Protection Directive under the procedure provided for in Article 31(2) of the Directive, the Commissioner shall comply with that decision in exercising his functions under paragraph 9 of Schedule 4 or, as the case may be, paragraph 8 of that Schedule.

(7)   The Commissioner shall inform the European Commission and the supervisory authorities in other EEA States—

   (a)   of any approvals granted for the purposes of paragraph 8 of Schedule 4, and

   (b)   of any authorisations granted for the purposes of paragraph 9 of that Schedule.

(8)   In this section—

'the Convention' means the Convention for the Protection of Individuals with regard to Automatic Processing of Personal Data which was opened for signature on 28th January 1981;

'data protection functions' means functions relating to the protection of individuals with respect to the processing of personal information.

Unlawful obtaining etc. of personal data

55. Unlawful obtaining etc. of personal data

(1)   A person must not knowingly or recklessly, without the consent of the data controller—

   (a)   obtain or disclose personal data or the information contained in personal data, or

   (b)   procure the disclosure to another person of the information contained in personal data.

(2)   Subsection (1) does not apply to a person who shows—

   (a)   that the obtaining, disclosing or procuring—

      (i)   was necessary for the purpose of preventing or detecting crime, or

      (ii)   was required or authorised by or under any enactment, by any rule of law or by the order of a court,

   (b)   that he acted in the reasonable belief that he had in law the right to obtain or disclose the data or information or, as the case may be, to procure the disclosure of the information to the other person,

   (c)   that he acted in the reasonable belief that he would have had the consent of the data controller if the data controller had known of the obtaining, disclosing or procuring and the circumstances of it, or

   (d)   that in the particular circumstances the obtaining, disclosing or procuring was justified as being in the public interest.

(3)   A person who contravenes subsection (1) is guilty of an offence.

(4)   A person who sells personal data is guilty of an offence if he has obtained the data in contravention of subsection (1).

(5)   A person who offers to sell personal data is guilty of an offence if—

   (a)   he has obtained the data in contravention of subsection (1), or

   (b)   he subsequently obtains the data in contravention of that subsection.

(6)   For the purposes of subsection (5), an advertisement indicating that personal data are or may be for sale is an offer to sell the data.

(7)   Section 1(2) does not apply for the purposes of this section; and for the purposes of subsections (4) to (6), 'personal data' includes information extracted from personal data.

(8)   References in this section to personal data do not include references to personal data which by virtue of section 28 are exempt from this section.

Records obtained under data subject's right of access

56. Prohibition of requirement as to production of certain records

(1)   A person must not, in connection with—

(a)   the recruitment of another person as an employee,

(b)   the continued employment of another person, or

(c)   any contract for the provision of services to him by another person,

require that other person or a third party to supply him with a relevant record or to produce a relevant record to him.

(2)   A person concerned with the provision (for payment or not) of goods, facilities or services to the public or a section of the public must not, as a condition of providing or offering to provide any goods, facilities or services to another person, require that other person or a third party to supply him with a relevant record or to produce a relevant record to him.

(3)   Subsections (1) and (2) do not apply to a person who shows—

(a)   that the imposition of the requirement was required or authorised by or under any enactment, by any rule of law or by the order of a court, or

(b)   that in the particular circumstances the imposition of the requirement was justified as being in the public interest.

(4)   Having regard to the provisions of Part V of the Police Act 1997 (certificates of criminal records etc.), the imposition of the requirement referred to in subsection (1) or (2) is not to be regarded as being justified as being in the public interest on the ground that it would assist in the prevention or detection of crime.

(5)   A person who contravenes subsection (1) or (2) is guilty of an offence.

(6)   In this section 'a relevant record' means any record which—

(a)   has been or is to be obtained by a data subject from any data controller specified in the first column of the Table below in the exercise of the right conferred by section 7, and

(b)   contains information relating to any matter specified in relation to that data controller in the second column,

and includes a copy of such a record or a part of such a record.

TABLE

Data controller	Subject-matter
1. Any of the following persons— (a) a chief officer of police of a police force in England and Wales. (b) a chief constable of a police force in Scotland. (c) the Chief Constable of the Royal Ulster Constabulary. (d) the Director General of the National Criminal Intelligence Service. (e) the Director General of the National Crime Squad.	(a) Convictions. (b) Cautions.
2. The Secretary of State.	(a) Convictions. (b) Cautions. (c) His functions under section 53 of the Children and Young Persons Act 1933, section 205(2) or 208 of the Criminal Procedure (Scotland) Act 1995 or section 73 of the Children and Young Persons Act (Northern Ireland) 1968 in relation to any person sentenced to detention. (d) His functions under the Prison Act 1952, the Prisons (Scotland) Act 1989 or the Prison Act (Northern Ireland) 1953 in relation to any person imprisoned or detained. (e) His functions under the Social Security Contributions and Benefits Act 1992, the Social Security Administration Act 1992 or the Jobseekers Act 1995. (f) His functions under Part V of the Police Act 1997.
3. The Department of Health and Social Services for Northern Ireland.	Its functions under the Social Security Contributions and Benefits (Northern Ireland) Act 1992, the Social Security Administration (Northern Ireland) Act 1992 or the Jobseekers (Northern Ireland) Order 1995.

(7)   In the Table in subsection (6)—

'caution' means a caution given to any person in England and Wales or Northern Ireland in respect of an offence which, at the time when the caution is given, is admitted;

'conviction' has the same meaning as in the Rehabilitation of Offenders Act 1974 or the Rehabilitation of Offenders (Northern Ireland) Order 1978.

(8)   The Secretary of State may by order amend—

    (a)   the Table in subsection (6), and

    (b)   subsection (7).

(9)   For the purposes of this section a record which states that a data controller is not processing any personal data relating to a particular matter shall be taken to be a record containing information relating to that matter.

(10)   In this section 'employee' means an individual who—

    (a)   works under a contract of employment, as defined by section 230(2) of the Employment Rights Act 1996, or

    (b)   holds any office,

whether or not he is entitled to remuneration; and 'employment' shall be construed accordingly.

57.   Avoidance of certain contractual terms relating to health records

(1)   Any term or condition of a contract is void in so far as it purports to require an individual—

    (a)   to supply any other person with a record to which this section applies, or with a copy of such a record or a part of such a record, or

    (b)   to produce to any other person such a record, copy or part.

(2)   This section applies to any record which—

    (a)   has been or is to be obtained by a data subject in the exercise of the right conferred by section 7, and

    (b)   consists of the information contained in any health record as defined by section 68(2).

Information provided to Commissioner or Tribunal

58.   Disclosure of information

No enactment or rule of law prohibiting or restricting the disclosure of information shall preclude a person from furnishing the Commissioner or the Tribunal with any information necessary for the discharge of their functions under this Act.

59.   Confidentiality of information

(1)   No person who is or has been the Commissioner, a member of the Commissioner's staff or an agent of the Commissioner shall disclose any information which—

    (a)   has been obtained by, or furnished to, the Commissioner under or for the purposes of this Act,

    (b)   relates to an identified or identifiable individual or business, and

    (c)   is not at the time of the disclosure, and has not previously been, available to the public from other sources,

unless the disclosure is made with lawful authority.

(2)   For the purposes of subsection (1) a disclosure of information is made with lawful authority only if, and to the extent that—

    (a)   the disclosure is made with the consent of the individual or of the person for the time being carrying on the business,

    (b)   the information was provided for the purpose of its being made available to the public (in whatever manner) under any provision of this Act,

    (c)   the disclosure is made for the purposes of, and is necessary for, the discharge of—

        (i)   any functions under this Act, or

        (ii)   any Community obligation,

    (d)   the disclosure is made for the purposes of any proceedings, whether criminal or civil and whether arising under, or by virtue of, this Act or otherwise, or

    (e)   having regard to the rights and freedoms or legitimate interests of any person, the disclosure is necessary in the public interest.

(3)   Any person who knowingly or recklessly discloses information in contravention of subsection (1) is guilty of an offence.

General provisions relating to offences

60.   Prosecutions and penalties

(1)   No proceedings for an offence under this Act shall be instituted—

    (a)   in England or Wales, except by the Commissioner or by or with the consent of the Director of Public Prosecutions;

    (b)   in Northern Ireland, except by the Commissioner or by or with the consent of the Director of Public Prosecutions for Northern Ireland.

(2)   A person guilty of an offence under any provision of this Act other than paragraph 12 of Schedule 9 is liable—

    (a)   on summary conviction, to a fine not exceeding the statutory maximum, or

    (b)   on conviction on indictment, to a fine.

(3)   A person guilty of an offence under paragraph 12 of Schedule 9 is liable on summary conviction to a fine not exceeding level 5 on the standard scale.

(4)   Subject to subsection (5), the court by or before which a person is convicted of—

    (a)   an offence under section 21(1), 22(6), 55 or 56,

    (b)   an offence under section 21(2) relating to processing which is assessable processing for the purposes of section 22, or

    (c)   an offence under section 47(1) relating to an enforcement notice,

may order any document or other material used in connection with the processing of personal data and appearing to the court to be connected with the commission of the offence to be forfeited, destroyed or erased.

(5)   The court shall not make an order under subsection (4) in relation to any material where a person (other than the offender) claiming to be the owner of or otherwise interested in the material applies to be heard by the court, unless an opportunity is given to him to show cause why the order should not be made.

61.   Liability of directors etc.

(1)   Where an offence under this Act has been committed by a body corporate and is proved to have been committed with the consent or connivance of or to be attributable to any neglect on the part of any director, manager, secretary or similar

officer of the body corporate or any person who was purporting to act in any such capacity, he as well as the body corporate shall be guilty of that offence and be liable to be proceeded against and punished accordingly.

(2)   Where the affairs of a body corporate are managed by its members subsection (1) shall apply in relation to the acts and defaults of a member in connection with his functions of management as if he were a director of the body corporate.

(3)   Where an offence under this Act has been committed by a Scottish partnership and the contravention in question is proved to have occurred with the consent or connivance of, or to be attributable to any neglect on the part of, a partner, he as well as the partnership shall be guilty of that offence and shall be liable to be proceeded against and punished accordingly.

Amendments of Consumer Credit Act 1974

62.   Amendments of Consumer Credit Act 1974

(1)   In section 158 of the Consumer Credit Act 1974 (duty of agency to disclose filed information)—

(a)   in subsection (1)—

(i)   in paragraph (a) for 'individual' there is substituted 'partnership or other unincorporated body of persons not consisting entirely of bodies corporate', and

(ii)   for 'him' there is substituted 'it',

(b)   in subsection (2), for 'his' there is substituted 'the consumer's', and

(c)   in subsection (3), for 'him' there is substituted 'the consumer'.

(2)   In section 159 of that Act (correction of wrong information) for subsection (1) there is substituted—

'(1)   Any individual (the 'objector') given—

(a)   information under section 7 of the Data Protection Act 1998 by a credit reference agency, or

(b)   information under section 158,

who considers that an entry in his file is incorrect, and that if it is not corrected he is likely to be prejudiced, may give notice to the agency requiring it either to remove the entry from the file or amend it.'

(3)   In subsections (2) to (6) of that section—

(a)   for 'consumer', wherever occurring, there is substituted 'objector', and

(b)   for 'Director', wherever occurring, there is substituted 'the relevant authority'.

(4)   After subsection (6) of that section there is inserted—

'(7)   The Data Protection Commissioner may vary or revoke any order made by him under this section.

(8)   In this section 'the relevant authority' means—

(a)   where the objector is a partnership or other unincorporated body of persons, the Director, and

(b)   in any other case, the Data Protection Commissioner.'

(5)   In section 160 of that Act (alternative procedure for business consumers)—

(a)   in subsection (4)—

(i)   for 'him' there is substituted 'to the consumer', and

(ii)   in paragraphs (a) and (b) for 'he' there is substituted 'the consumer' and for 'his' there is substituted 'the consumer's', and

(b)   after subsection (6) there is inserted—

'(7)   In this section 'consumer' has the same meaning as in section 158.'

General

63.   Application to Crown
(1)   This Act binds the Crown.

(2)   For the purposes of this Act each government department shall be treated as a person separate from any other government department.

(3)   Where the purposes for which and the manner in which any personal data are, or are to be, processed are determined by any person acting on behalf of the Royal Household, the Duchy of Lancaster or the Duchy of Cornwall, the data controller in respect of those data for the purposes of this Act shall be—

    (a)   in relation to the Royal Household, the Keeper of the Privy Purse,

    (b)   in relation to the Duchy of Lancaster, such person as the Chancellor of the Duchy appoints, and

    (c)   in relation to the Duchy of Cornwall, such person as the Duke of Cornwall, or the possessor for the time being of the Duchy of Cornwall, appoints.

(4)   Different persons may be appointed under subsection (3)(b) or (c) for different purposes.

(5)   Neither a government department nor a person who is a data controller by virtue of subsection (3) shall be liable to prosecution under this Act, but section 55 and paragraph 12 of Schedule 9 shall apply to a person in the service of the Crown as they apply to any other person.

64.   Transmission of notices etc. by electronic or other means
(1)   This section applies to—

    (a)   a notice or request under any provision of Part II,

    (b)   a notice under subsection (1) of section 24 or particulars made available under that subsection, or

    (c)   an application under section 41(2),

but does not apply to anything which is required to be served in accordance with rules of court.

(2)   The requirement that any notice, request, particulars or application to which this section applies should be in writing is satisfied where the text of the notice, request, particulars or application—

    (a)   is transmitted by electronic means,

    (b)   is received in legible form, and

    (c)   is capable of being used for subsequent reference.

(3)   The Secretary of State may by regulations provide that any requirement that any notice, request, particulars or application to which this section applies should be in writing is not to apply in such circumstances as may be prescribed by the regulations.

65.   Service of notices by Commissioner
(1)   Any notice authorised or required by this Act to be served on or given to any person by the Commissioner may—

    (a)   if that person is an individual, be served on him—

       (i)   by delivering it to him, or

(ii)   by sending it to him by post addressed to him at his usual or last-known place of residence or business, or

(iii)   by leaving it for him at that place;

(b)   if that person is a body corporate or unincorporate, be served on that body—

(i)   by sending it by post to the proper officer of the body at its principal office, or

(ii)   by addressing it to the proper officer of the body and leaving it at that office;

(c)   if that person is a partnership in Scotland, be served on that partnership—

(i)   by sending it by post to the principal office of the partnership, or

(ii)   by addressing it to that partnership and leaving it at that office.

(2)   In subsection (1)(b) 'principal office', in relation to a registered company, means its registered office and 'proper officer', in relation to any body, means the secretary or other executive officer charged with the conduct of its general affairs.

(3)   This section is without prejudice to any other lawful method of serving or giving a notice.

66.   Exercise of rights in Scotland by children

(1)   Where a question falls to be determined in Scotland as to the legal capacity of a person under the age of sixteen years to exercise any right conferred by any provision of this Act, that person shall be taken to have that capacity where he has a general understanding of what it means to exercise that right.

(2)   Without prejudice to the generality of subsection (1), a person of twelve years of age or more shall be presumed to be of sufficient age and maturity to have such understanding as is mentioned in that subsection.

67.   Orders, regulations and rules

(1)   Any power conferred by this Act on the Secretary of State to make an order, regulations or rules shall be exercisable by statutory instrument.

(2)   Any order, regulations or rules made by the Secretary of State under this Act may—

(a)   make different provision for different cases, and

(b)   make such supplemental, incidental, consequential or transitional provision or savings as the Secretary of State considers appropriate;

and nothing in section 7(11), 19(5), 26(1) or 30(4) limits the generality of paragraph (a).

(3)   Before making—

(a)   an order under any provision of this Act other than section 75(3),

(b)   any regulations under this Act other than notification regulations (as defined by section 16(2)),

the Secretary of State shall consult the Commissioner.

(4)   A statutory instrument containing (whether alone or with other provisions) an order under—

section 10(2)(b),

section 12(5)(b),

section 22(1),

section 30,

section 32(3),

section 38,

section 56(8),

paragraph 10 of Schedule 3, or

paragraph 4 of Schedule 7,

shall not be made unless a draft of the instrument has been laid before and approved by a resolution of each House of Parliament.

(5) A statutory instrument which contains (whether alone or with other provisions)—

(a) an order under—

section 22(7),

section 23,

section 51(3),

section 54(2), (3) or (4),

paragraph 3, 4 or 14 of Part II of Schedule 1,

paragraph 6 of Schedule 2,

paragraph 2, 7 or 9 of Schedule 3,

paragraph 4 of Schedule 4,

paragraph 6 of Schedule 7,

(b) regulations under section 7 which—

   (i)   prescribe cases for the purposes of subsection (2)(b),

  (ii)   are made by virtue of subsection (7), or

 (iii)   relate to the definition of 'the prescribed period',

(c) regulations under section 8(1) or 9(3),

(d) regulations under section 64,

(e) notification regulations (as defined by section 16(2)), or

(f) rules under paragraph 7 of Schedule 6,

and which is not subject to the requirement in subsection (4) that a draft of the instrument be laid before and approved by a resolution of each House of Parliament, shall be subject to annulment in pursuance of a resolution of either House of Parliament.

(6) A statutory instrument which contains only—

(a) regulations prescribing fees for the purposes of any provision of this Act, or

(b) regulations under section 7 prescribing fees for the purposes of any other enactment,

shall be laid before Parliament after being made.

68. Meaning of 'accessible record'

(1) In this Act 'accessible record' means—

(a) a health record as defined by subsection (2),

(b) an educational record as defined by Schedule 11, or

(c) an accessible public record as defined by Schedule 12.

(2) In subsection (1)(a) 'health record' means any record which—

(a) consists of information relating to the physical or mental health or condition of an individual, and

(b) has been made by or on behalf of a health professional in connection with the care of that individual.

69. Meaning of 'health professional'

(1) In this Act 'health professional' means any of the following—

(a)　a registered medical practitioner,

(b)　a registered dentist as defined by section 53(1) of the Dentists Act 1984,

(c)　a registered optician as defined by section 36(1) of the Opticians Act 1989,

(d)　a registered pharmaceutical chemist as defined by section 24(1) of the Pharmacy Act 1954 or a registered person as defined by Article 2(2) of the Pharmacy (Northern Ireland) Order 1976,

(e)　a registered nurse, midwife or health visitor,

(f)　a registered osteopath as defined by section 41 of the Osteopaths Act 1993,

(g)　a registered chiropractor as defined by section 43 of the Chiropractors Act 1994,

(h)　any person who is registered as a member of a profession to which the Professions Supplementary to Medicine Act 1960 for the time being extends,

(i)　a clinical psychologist, child psychotherapist or speech therapist,

(j)　a music therapist employed by a health service body, and

(k)　a scientist employed by such a body as head of a department.

(2)　In subsection (1)(a) 'registered medical practitioner' includes any person who is provisionally registered under section 15 or 21 of the Medical Act 1983 and is engaged in such employment as is mentioned in subsection (3) of that section.

(3)　In subsection (1) 'health service body' means—

(a)　a Health Authority established under section 8 of the National Health Service Act 1977,

(b)　a Special Health Authority established under section 11 of that Act,

(c)　a Health Board within the meaning of the National Health Service (Scotland) Act 1978,

(d)　a Special Health Board within the meaning of that Act,

(e)　the managers of a State Hospital provided under section 102 of that Act,

(f)　a National Health Service trust first established under section 5 of the National Health Service and Community Care Act 1990 or section 12A of the National Health Service (Scotland) Act 1978,

(g)　a Health and Social Services Board established under Article 16 of the Health and Personal Social Services (Northern Ireland) Order 1972,

(h)　a special health and social services agency established under the Health and Personal Social Services (Special Agencies) (Northern Ireland) Order 1990, or

(i)　a Health and Social Services trust established under Article 10 of the Health and Personal Social Services (Northern Ireland) Order 1991.

70.　Supplementary definitions

(1)　In this Act, unless the context otherwise requires—

'business' includes any trade or profession;

'the Commissioner' means the Data Protection Commissioner;

'credit reference agency' has the same meaning as in the Consumer Credit Act 1974;

'the Data Protection Directive' means Directive 95/46/EC on the protection of individuals with regard to the processing of personal data and on the free movement of such data;

'EEA State' means a State which is a contracting party to the Agreement on the European Economic Area signed at Oporto on 2nd May 1992 as adjusted by the Protocol signed at Brussels on 17th March 1993;

'enactment' includes an enactment passed after this Act;

'government department' includes a Northern Ireland department and any body or authority exercising statutory functions on behalf of the Crown;

'Minister of the Crown' has the same meaning as in the Ministers of the Crown Act 1975;

'public register' means any register which pursuant to a requirement imposed—

    (a)   by or under any enactment, or

    (b)   in pursuance of any international agreement,

is open to public inspection or open to inspection by any person having a legitimate interest;

'pupil'—

    (a)   in relation to a school in England and Wales, means a registered pupil within the meaning of the Education Act 1996,

    (b)   in relation to a school in Scotland, means a pupil within the meaning of the Education (Scotland) Act 1980, and

    (c)   in relation to a school in Northern Ireland, means a registered pupil within the meaning of the Education and Libraries (Northern Ireland) Order 1986;

'recipient', in relation to any personal data, means any person to whom the data are disclosed, including any person (such as an employee or agent of the data controller, a data processor or an employee or agent of a data processor) to whom they are disclosed in the course of processing the data for the data controller, but does not include any person to whom disclosure is or may be made as a result of, or with a view to, a particular inquiry by or on behalf of that person made in the exercise of any power conferred by law;

'registered company' means a company registered under the enactments relating to companies for the time being in force in the United Kingdom;

'school'—

    (a)   in relation to England and Wales, has the same meaning as in the Education Act 1996,

    (b)   in relation to Scotland, has the same meaning as in the Education (Scotland) Act 1980, and

    (c)   in relation to Northern Ireland, has the same meaning as in the Education and Libraries (Northern Ireland) Order 1986;

'teacher' includes—

    (a)   in Great Britain, head teacher, and

    (b)   in Northern Ireland, the principal of a school;

'third party', in relation to personal data, means any person other than—

    (a)   the data subject,

    (b)   the data controller, or

    (c)   any data processor or other person authorised to process data for the data controller or processor;

'the Tribunal' means the Data Protection Tribunal.

(2)   For the purposes of this Act data are inaccurate if they are incorrect or misleading as to any matter of fact.

71. Index of defined expressions

The following Table shows provisions defining or otherwise explaining expressions used in this Act (other than provisions defining or explaining an expression only used in the same section or Schedule)—

accessible record	section 68
address (in Part III)	section 16(3)
business	section 70(1)
the Commissioner	section 70(1)
credit reference agency	section 70(1)
data	section 1(1)
data controller	sections 1(1) and (4) and 63(3)
data processor	section 1(1)
the Data Protection Directive	section 70(1)
data protection principles	section 4 and Schedule 1
data subject	section 1(1)
disclosing (of personal data)	section 1(2)(b)
EEA State	section 70(1)
enactment	section 70(1)
enforcement notice	section 40(1)
fees regulations (in Part III)	section 16(2)
government department	section 70(1)
health professional	section 69
inaccurate (in relation to data)	section 70(2)
information notice	section 43(1)
Minister of the Crown	section 70(1)
the non-disclosure provisions (in Part IV)	section 27(3)
notification regulations (in Part III)	section 16(2)
obtaining (of personal data)	section 1(2)(a)
personal data	section 1(1)
prescribed (in Part III)	section 16(2)
processing (of information or data)	section 1(1) and paragraph 5 of Schedule 8
public register	section 70(1)
publish (in relation to journalistic, literary or artistic material)	section 32(6)
pupil (in relation to a school)	section 70(1)
recipient (in relation to personal data)	section 70(1)
recording (of personal data)	section 1(2)(a)
registered company	section 70(1)
registrable particulars (in Part III)	section 16(1)
relevant filing system	section 1(1)
school	section 70(1)
sensitive personal data	section 2
special information notice	section 44(1)

the special purposes	section 3
the subject information provisions (in Part IV)	section 27(2)
teacher	section 70(1)
third party (in relation to processing of personal data)	section 70(1)
the Tribunal	section 70(1)
using (of personal data)	section 1(2)(b).

72. Modifications of Act

During the period beginning with the commencement of this section and ending with 23rd October 2007, the provisions of this Act shall have effect subject to the modifications set out in Schedule 13.

73. Transitional provisions and savings

Schedule 14 (which contains transitional provisions and savings) has effect.

74. Minor and consequential amendments and repeals and revocations

(1)   Schedule 15 (which contains minor and consequential amendments) has effect.

(2)   The enactments and instruments specified in Schedule 16 are repealed or revoked to the extent specified.

75. Short title, commencement and extent

(1)   This Act may be cited as the Data Protection Act 1998.

(2)   The following provisions of this Act—

   (a)   sections 1 to 3,

   (b)   section 25(1) and (4),

   (c)   section 26,

   (d)   sections 67 to 71,

   (e)   this section,

   (f)   paragraph 17 of Schedule 5,

   (g)   Schedule 11,

   (h)   Schedule 12, and

   (i)   so much of any other provision of this Act as confers any power to make subordinate legislation,

shall come into force on the day on which this Act is passed.

(3)   The remaining provisions of this Act shall come into force on such day as the Secretary of State may by order appoint; and different days may be appointed for different purposes.

(4)   The day appointed under subsection (3) for the coming into force of section 56 must not be earlier than the first day on which sections 112, 113 and 115 of the Police Act 1997 (which provide for the issue by the Secretary of State of criminal conviction certificates, criminal record certificates and enhanced criminal record certificates) are all in force.

(5)   Subject to subsection (6), this Act extends to Northern Ireland.

(6)   Any amendment, repeal or revocation made by Schedule 15 or 16 has the same extent as that of the enactment or instrument to which it relates.

SCHEDULES

Section 4(1) and (2)   SCHEDULE 1
THE DATA PROTECTION PRINCIPLES

PART I
THE PRINCIPLES

1. Personal data shall be processed fairly and lawfully and, in particular, shall not be processed unless—

  (a) at least one of the conditions in Schedule 2 is met, and

  (b) in the case of sensitive personal data, at least one of the conditions in Schedule 3 is also met.

2. Personal data shall be obtained only for one or more specified and lawful purposes, and shall not be further processed in any manner incompatible with that purpose or those purposes.

3. Personal data shall be adequate, relevant and not excessive in relation to the purpose or purposes for which they are processed.

4. Personal data shall be accurate and, where necessary, kept up to date.

5. Personal data processed for any purpose or purposes shall not be kept for longer than is necessary for that purpose or those purposes.

6. Personal data shall be processed in accordance with the rights of data subjects under this Act.

7. Appropriate technical and organisational measures shall be taken against unauthorised or unlawful processing of personal data and against accidental loss or destruction of, or damage to, personal data.

8. Personal data shall not be transferred to a country or territory outside the European Economic Area unless that country or territory ensures an adequate level of protection for the rights and freedoms of data subjects in relation to the processing of personal data.

PART II
INTERPRETATION OF THE PRINCIPLES IN PART I

The first principle

1.—(1) In determining for the purposes of the first principle whether personal data are processed fairly, regard is to be had to the method by which they are obtained, including in particular whether any person from whom they are obtained is deceived or misled as to the purpose or purposes for which they are to be processed.

(2) Subject to paragraph 2, for the purposes of the first principle data are to be treated as obtained fairly if they consist of information obtained from a person who—

  (a) is authorised by or under any enactment to supply it, or

  (b) is required to supply it by or under any enactment or by any convention or other instrument imposing an international obligation on the United Kingdom.

2.—(1) Subject to paragraph 3, for the purposes of the first principle personal data are not to be treated as processed fairly unless—

  (a) in the case of data obtained from the data subject, the data controller ensures so far as practicable that the data subject has, is provided with, or has made readily available to him, the information specified in subparagraph (3), and

(b)   in any other case, the data controller ensures so far as practicable that, before the relevant time or as soon as practicable after that time, the data subject has, is provided with, or has made readily available to him, the information specified in sub-paragraph (3).

(2)   In sub-paragraph (1)(b) 'the relevant time' means—

(a)   the time when the data controller first processes the data, or

(b)   in a case where at that time disclosure to a third party within a reasonable period is envisaged—

(i)   if the data are in fact disclosed to such a person within that period, the time when the data are first disclosed,

(ii)   if within that period the data controller becomes, or ought to become, aware that the data are unlikely to be disclosed to such a person within that period, the time when the data controller does become, or ought to become, so aware, or

(iii)   in any other case, the end of that period.

(3)   The information referred to in sub-paragraph (1) is as follows, namely—

(a)   the identity of the data controller,

(b)   if he has nominated a representative for the purposes of this Act, the identity of that representative,

(c)   the purpose or purposes for which the data are intended to be processed, and

(d)   any further information which is necessary, having regard to the specific circumstances in which the data are or are to be processed, to enable processing in respect of the data subject to be fair.

3.—(1)   Paragraph 2(1)(b) does not apply where either of the primary conditions in sub-paragraph (2), together with such further conditions as may be prescribed by the Secretary of State by order, are met.

(2)   The primary conditions referred to in sub-paragraph (1) are—

(a)   that the provision of that information would involve a disproportionate effort, or

(b)   that the recording of the information to be contained in the data by, or the disclosure of the data by, the data controller is necessary for compliance with any legal obligation to which the data controller is subject, other than an obligation imposed by contract.

4.—(1)   Personal data which contain a general identifier falling within a description prescribed by the Secretary of State by order are not to be treated as processed fairly and lawfully unless they are processed in compliance with any conditions so prescribed in relation to general identifiers of that description.

(2)   In sub-paragraph (1) 'a general identifier' means any identifier (such as, for example, a number or code used for identification purposes) which—

(a)   relates to an individual, and

(b)   forms part of a set of similar identifiers which is of general application.

The second principle

5.   The purpose or purposes for which personal data are obtained may in particular be specified—

(a)   in a notice given for the purposes of paragraph 2 by the data controller to the data subject, or

(b)   in a notification given to the Commissioner under Part III of this Act.

6.   In determining whether any disclosure of personal data is compatible with the purpose or purposes for which the data were obtained, regard is to be had to the purpose or purposes for which the personal data are intended to be processed by any person to whom they are disclosed.

The fourth principle

7.   The fourth principle is not to be regarded as being contravened by reason of any inaccuracy in personal data which accurately record information obtained by the data controller from the data subject or a third party in a case where—

(a)   having regard to the purpose or purposes for which the data were obtained and further processed, the data controller has taken reasonable steps to ensure the accuracy of the data, and

(b)   if the data subject has notified the data controller of the data subject's view that the data are inaccurate, the data indicate that fact.

The sixth principle

8.   A person is to be regarded as contravening the sixth principle if, but only if—

(a)   he contravenes section 7 by failing to supply information in accordance with that section,

(b)   he contravenes section 10 by failing to comply with a notice given under subsection (1) of that section to the extent that the notice is justified or by failing to give a notice under subsection (3) of that section,

(c)   he contravenes section 11 by failing to comply with a notice given under subsection (1) of that section, or

(d)   he contravenes section 12 by failing to comply with a notice given under subsection (1) or (2)(b) of that section or by failing to give a notification under subsection (2)(a) of that section or a notice under subsection (3) of that section.

The seventh principle

9.   Having regard to the state of technological development and the cost of implementing any measures, the measures must ensure a level of security appropriate to—

(a)   the harm that might result from such unauthorised or unlawful processing or accidental loss, destruction or damage as are mentioned in the seventh principle, and

(b)   the nature of the data to be protected.

10.   The data controller must take reasonable steps to ensure the reliability of any employees of his who have access to the personal data.

11.   Where processing of personal data is carried out by a data processor on behalf of a data controller, the data controller must in order to comply with the seventh principle—

(a)   choose a data processor providing sufficient guarantees in respect of the technical and organisational security measures governing the processing to be carried out, and

(b)   take reasonable steps to ensure compliance with those measures.

12.   Where processing of personal data is carried out by a data processor on behalf of a data controller, the data controller is not to be regarded as complying with the seventh principle unless—

(a)   the processing is carried out under a contract—

   (i)   which is made or evidenced in writing, and

   (ii)   under which the data processor is to act only on instructions from the data controller, and

(b)   the contract requires the data processor to comply with obligations equivalent to those imposed on a data controller by the seventh principle.

The eighth principle

13.   An adequate level of protection is one which is adequate in all the circumstances of the case, having regard in particular to—

(a)   the nature of the personal data,

(b)   the country or territory of origin of the information contained in the data,

(c)   the country or territory of final destination of that information,

(d)   the purposes for which and period during which the data are intended to be processed,

(e)   the law in force in the country or territory in question,

(f)   the international obligations of that country or territory,

(g)   any relevant codes of conduct or other rules which are enforceable in that country or territory (whether generally or by arrangement in particular cases), and

(h)   any security measures taken in respect of the data in that country or territory.

14.   The eighth principle does not apply to a transfer falling within any paragraph of Schedule 4, except in such circumstances and to such extent as the Secretary of State may by order provide.

15.—(1)   Where—

(a)   in any proceedings under this Act any question arises as to whether the requirement of the eighth principle as to an adequate level of protection is met in relation to the transfer of any personal data to a country or territory outside the European Economic Area, and

(b)   a Community finding has been made in relation to transfers of the kind in question,

that question is to be determined in accordance with that finding.

(2)   In sub-paragraph (1) 'Community finding' means a finding of the European Commission, under the procedure provided for in Article 31(2) of the Data Protection Directive, that a country or territory outside the European Economic Area does, or does not, ensure an adequate level of protection within the meaning of Article 25(2) of the Directive.

Section 4(3)   SCHEDULE 2
CONDITIONS RELEVANT FOR PURPOSES OF THE FIRST PRINCIPLE:
PROCESSING OF ANY PERSONAL DATA

1.   The data subject has given his consent to the processing.

2.   The processing is necessary—

(a)   for the performance of a contract to which the data subject is a party, or

(b)   for the taking of steps at the request of the data subject with a view to entering into a contract.

3.   The processing is necessary for compliance with any legal obligation to which the data controller is subject, other than an obligation imposed by contract.

4.   The processing is necessary in order to protect the vital interests of the data subject.

5.   The processing is necessary—

(a)   for the administration of justice,

(b)   for the exercise of any functions conferred on any person by or under any enactment,

(c)   for the exercise of any functions of the Crown, a Minister of the Crown or a government department, or

(d)   for the exercise of any other functions of a public nature exercised in the public interest by any person.

6.—(1)   The processing is necessary for the purposes of legitimate interests pursued by the data controller or by the third party or parties to whom the data are disclosed, except where the processing is unwarranted in any particular case by reason of prejudice to the rights and freedoms or legitimate interests of the data subject.

(2)   The Secretary of State may by order specify particular circumstances in which this condition is, or is not, to be taken to be satisfied.

Section 4(3)   SCHEDULE 3
CONDITIONS RELEVANT FOR PURPOSES OF THE FIRST PRINCIPLE:
PROCESSING OF SENSITIVE PERSONAL DATA

1.   The data subject has given his explicit consent to the processing of the personal data.

2.—(1)   The processing is necessary for the purposes of exercising or performing any right or obligation which is conferred or imposed by law on the data controller in connection with employment.

(2)   The Secretary of State may by order—

(a)   exclude the application of sub-paragraph (1) in such cases as may be specified, or

(b)   provide that, in such cases as may be specified, the condition in sub-paragraph (1) is not to be regarded as satisfied unless such further conditions as may be specified in the order are also satisfied.

3.   The processing is necessary—

(a)   in order to protect the vital interests of the data subject or another person, in a case where—

(i)   consent cannot be given by or on behalf of the data subject, or

(ii)   the data controller cannot reasonably be expected to obtain the consent of the data subject, or

(b)   in order to protect the vital interests of another person, in a case where consent by or on behalf of the data subject has been unreasonably withheld.

4.   The processing—

(a)   is carried out in the course of its legitimate activities by any body or association which—

(i)   is not established or conducted for profit, and

(ii)   exists for political, philosophical, religious or trade-union purposes,

(b)   is carried out with appropriate safeguards for the rights and freedoms of data subjects,

(c)   relates only to individuals who either are members of the body or association or have regular contact with it in connection with its purposes, and

(d)   does not involve disclosure of the personal data to a third party without the consent of the data subject.

5.   The information contained in the personal data has been made public as a result of steps deliberately taken by the data subject.

6.   The processing—

(a)   is necessary for the purpose of, or in connection with, any legal proceedings (including prospective legal proceedings),

(b)   is necessary for the purpose of obtaining legal advice, or

(c)   is otherwise necessary for the purposes of establishing, exercising or defending legal rights.

7.—(1)   The processing is necessary—

(a)   for the administration of justice,

(b)   for the exercise of any functions conferred on any person by or under an enactment, or

(c)   for the exercise of any functions of the Crown, a Minister of the Crown or a government department.

(2)   The Secretary of State may by order—

(a)   exclude the application of sub-paragraph (1) in such cases as may be specified, or

(b)   provide that, in such cases as may be specified, the condition in sub-paragraph (1) is not to be regarded as satisfied unless such further conditions as may be specified in the order are also satisfied.

8.—(1)   The processing is necessary for medical purposes and is undertaken by—

(a)   a health professional, or

(b)   a person who in the circumstances owes a duty of confidentiality which is equivalent to that which would arise if that person were a health professional.

(2)   In this paragraph 'medical purposes' includes the purposes of preventative medicine, medical diagnosis, medical research, the provision of care and treatment and the management of healthcare services.

9.—(1)   The processing—

(a)   is of sensitive personal data consisting of information as to racial or ethnic origin,

(b)   is necessary for the purpose of identifying or keeping under review the existence or absence of equality of opportunity or treatment between persons of different racial or ethnic origins, with a view to enabling such equality to be promoted or maintained, and

(c)   is carried out with appropriate safeguards for the rights and freedoms of data subjects.

(2)   The Secretary of State may by order specify circumstances in which processing falling within sub-paragraph (1)(a) and (b) is, or is not, to be taken for the purposes of sub-paragraph (1)(c) to be carried out with appropriate safeguards for the rights and freedoms of data subjects.

10.   The personal data are processed in circumstances specified in an order made by the Secretary of State for the purposes of this paragraph.

Section 4(3)　　　　　　SCHEDULE 4
CASES WHERE THE EIGHTH PRINCIPLE DOES NOT APPLY

1.　The data subject has given his consent to the transfer.

2.　The transfer is necessary—

　(a)　for the performance of a contract between the data subject and the data controller, or

　(b)　for the taking of steps at the request of the data subject with a view to his entering into a contract with the data controller.

3.　The transfer is necessary—

　(a)　for the conclusion of a contract between the data controller and a person other than the data subject which—

　　(i)　is entered into at the request of the data subject, or

　　(ii)　is in the interests of the data subject, or

　(b)　for the performance of such a contract.

4.—(1)　The transfer is necessary for reasons of substantial public interest.

(2)　The Secretary of State may by order specify—

　(a)　circumstances in which a transfer is to be taken for the purposes of sub-paragraph (1) to be necessary for reasons of substantial public interest, and

　(b)　circumstances in which a transfer which is not required by or under an enactment is not to be taken for the purpose of sub-paragraph (1) to be necessary for reasons of substantial public interest.

5.　The transfer—

　(a)　is necessary for the purpose of, or in connection with, any legal proceedings (including prospective legal proceedings),

　(b)　is necessary for the purpose of obtaining legal advice, or

　(c)　is otherwise necessary for the purposes of establishing, exercising or defending legal rights.

6.　The transfer is necessary in order to protect the vital interests of the data subject.

7.　The transfer is of part of the personal data on a public register and any conditions subject to which the register is open to inspection are complied with by any person to whom the data are or may be disclosed after the transfer.

8.　The transfer is made on terms which are of a kind approved by the Commissioner as ensuring adequate safeguards for the rights and freedoms of data subjects.

9.　The transfer has been authorised by the Commissioner as being made in such a manner as to ensure adequate safeguards for the rights and freedoms of data subjects.

Section 6(7)　　　　　　SCHEDULE 5
THE DATA PROTECTION COMMISSIONER AND THE DATA PROTECTION TRIBUNAL

PART I
THE COMMISSIONER

Status and capacity

1.—(1)　The corporation sole by the name of the Data Protection Registrar established by the Data Protection Act 1984 shall continue in existence by the name of the Data Protection Commissioner.

(2)   The Commissioner and his officers and staff are not to be regarded as servants or agents of the Crown.

Tenure of office

2.—(1)   Subject to the provisions of this paragraph, the Commissioner shall hold office for such term not exceeding five years as may be determined at the time of his appointment.

(2)   The Commissioner may be relieved of his office by Her Majesty at his own request.

(3)   The Commissioner may be removed from office by Her Majesty in pursuance of an Address from both Houses of Parliament.

(4)   The Commissioner shall in any case vacate his office—

  (a)   on completing the year of service in which he attains the age of sixty-five years, or

  (b)   if earlier, on completing his fifteenth year of service.

(5)   Subject to sub-paragraph (4), a person who ceases to be Commissioner on the expiration of his term of office shall be eligible for re-appointment, but a person may not be re-appointed for a third or subsequent term as Commissioner unless, by reason of special circumstances, the person's re-appointment for such a term is desirable in the public interest.

Salary etc.

3.—(1)   There shall be paid—

  (a)   to the Commissioner such salary, and

  (b)   to or in respect of the Commissioner such pension,

as may be specified by a resolution of the House of Commons.

(2)   A resolution for the purposes of this paragraph may—

  (a)   specify the salary or pension,

  (b)   provide that the salary or pension is to be the same as, or calculated on the same basis as, that payable to, or to or in respect of, a person employed in a specified office under, or in a specified capacity in the service of, the Crown, or

  (c)   specify the salary or pension and provide for it to be increased by reference to such variables as may be specified in the resolution.

(3)   A resolution for the purposes of this paragraph may take effect from the date on which it is passed or from any earlier or later date specified in the resolution.

(4)   A resolution for the purposes of this paragraph may make different provision in relation to the pension payable to or in respect of different holders of the office of Commissioner.

(5)   Any salary or pension payable under this paragraph shall be charged on and issued out of the Consolidated Fund.

(6)   In this paragraph 'pension' includes an allowance or gratuity and any reference to the payment of a pension includes a reference to the making of payments towards the provision of a pension.

Officers and staff

4.—(1)   The Commissioner—

  (a)   shall appoint a deputy commissioner, and

(b)   may appoint such number of other officers and staff as he may determine.

(2)   The remuneration and other conditions of service of the persons appointed under this paragraph shall be determined by the Commissioner.

(3)   The Commissioner may pay such pensions, allowances or gratuities to or in respect of the persons appointed under this paragraph, or make such payments towards the provision of such pensions, allowances or gratuities, as he may determine.

(4)   The references in sub-paragraph (3) to pensions, allowances or gratuities to or in respect of the persons appointed under this paragraph include references to pensions, allowances or gratuities by way of compensation to or in respect of any of those persons who suffer loss of office or employment.

(5)   Any determination under sub-paragraph (1)(b), (2) or (3) shall require the approval of the Secretary of State.

(6)   The Employers' Liability (Compulsory Insurance) Act 1969 shall not require insurance to be effected by the Commissioner.

5.—(1)   The deputy commissioner shall perform the functions conferred by this Act on the Commissioner during any vacancy in that office or at any time when the Commissioner is for any reason unable to act.

(2)   Without prejudice to sub-paragraph (1), any functions of the Commissioner under this Act may, to the extent authorised by him, be performed by any of his officers or staff.

Authentication of seal of the Commissioner

6.   The application of the seal of the Commissioner shall be authenticated by his signature or by the signature of some other person authorised for the purpose.

Presumption of authenticity of documents issued by the Commissioner

7.   Any document purporting to be an instrument issued by the Commissioner and to be duly executed under the Commissioner's seal or to be signed by or on behalf of the Commissioner shall be received in evidence and shall be deemed to be such an instrument unless the contrary is shown.

Money

8.   The Secretary of State may make payments to the Commissioner out of money provided by Parliament.

9.—(1)   All fees and other sums received by the Commissioner in the exercise of his functions under this Act or section 159 of the Consumer Credit Act 1974 shall be paid by him to the Secretary of State.

(2)   Sub-paragraph (1) shall not apply where the Secretary of State, with the consent of the Treasury, otherwise directs.

(3)   Any sums received by the Secretary of State under sub-paragraph (1) shall be paid into the Consolidated Fund.

Accounts

10.—(1)   It shall be the duty of the Commissioner—

(a)   to keep proper accounts and other records in relation to the accounts,

(b)   to prepare in respect of each financial year a statement of account in such form as the Secretary of State may direct, and

(c)   to send copies of that statement to the Comptroller and Auditor General on or before 31st August next following the end of the year to which the statement relates or on or before such earlier date after the end of that year as the Treasury may direct.

(2)   The Comptroller and Auditor General shall examine and certify any statement sent to him under this paragraph and lay copies of it together with his report thereon before each House of Parliament.

(3)   In this paragraph 'financial year' means a period of twelve months beginning with 1st April.

Application of Part I in Scotland

11.   Paragraphs 1(1), 6 and 7 do not extend to Scotland.

PART II
THE TRIBUNAL

Tenure of office

12.—(1)   Subject to the following provisions of this paragraph, a member of the Tribunal shall hold and vacate his office in accordance with the terms of his appointment and shall, on ceasing to hold office, be eligible for re-appointment.

(2)   Any member of the Tribunal may at any time resign his office by notice in writing to the Lord Chancellor (in the case of the chairman or a deputy chairman) or to the Secretary of State (in the case of any other member).

(3)   A person who is the chairman or deputy chairman of the Tribunal shall vacate his office on the day on which he attains the age of seventy years; but this sub-paragraph is subject to section 26(4) to (6) of the Judicial Pensions and Retirement Act 1993 (power to authorise continuance in office up to the age of seventy-five years).

Salary etc.

13.   The Secretary of State shall pay to the members of the Tribunal out of money provided by Parliament such remuneration and allowances as he may determine.

Officers and staff

14.   The Secretary of State may provide the Tribunal with such officers and staff as he thinks necessary for the proper discharge of its functions.

Expenses

15.   Such expenses of the Tribunal as the Secretary of State may determine shall be defrayed by the Secretary of State out of money provided by Parliament.

PART III
TRANSITIONAL PROVISIONS

16.   Any reference in any enactment, instrument or other document to the Data Protection Registrar shall be construed, in relation to any time after the commencement of section 6(1), as a reference to the Commissioner.

17.   Any reference in this Act or in any instrument under this Act to the Commissioner shall be construed, in relation to any time before the commencement of section 6(1), as a reference to the Data Protection Registrar.

Sections 28(12), 48(5)   SCHEDULE 6
                                 APPEAL PROCEEDINGS

Hearing of appeals

1.   For the purpose of hearing and determining appeals or any matter preliminary or incidental to an appeal the Tribunal shall sit at such times and in such places as the chairman or a deputy chairman may direct and may sit in two or more divisions.

Constitution of Tribunal in national security cases

2.—(1)   The Lord Chancellor shall from time to time designate, from among the chairman and deputy chairmen appointed by him under section 6(4)(a) and (b), those persons who are to be capable of hearing appeals under section 28(4) or (6).

(2)   A designation under sub-paragraph (1) may at any time be revoked by the Lord Chancellor.

3.   In any case where the application of paragraph 6(1) is excluded by rules under paragraph 7, the Tribunal shall be duly constituted for an appeal under section 28(4) or (6) if it consists of three of the persons designated under paragraph 2(1), of whom one shall be designated by the Lord Chancellor to preside.

Constitution of Tribunal in other cases

4.—(1)   Subject to any rules made under paragraph 7, the Tribunal shall be duly constituted for an appeal under section 48(1), (2) or (4) if it consists of—

(a)   the chairman or a deputy chairman (who shall preside), and

(b)   an equal number of the members appointed respectively in accordance with paragraphs (a) and (b) of section 6(6).

(2)   The members who are to constitute the Tribunal in accordance with subparagraph (1) shall be nominated by the chairman or, if he is for any reason unable to act, by a deputy chairman.

Determination of questions by full Tribunal

5.   The determination of any question before the Tribunal when constituted in accordance with paragraph 3 or 4 shall be according to the opinion of the majority of the members hearing the appeal.

Ex parte proceedings

6.—(1)   Subject to any rules made under paragraph 7, the jurisdiction of the Tribunal in respect of an appeal under section 28(4) or (6) shall be exercised ex parte by one or more persons designated under paragraph 2(1).

(2)   Subject to any rules made under paragraph 7, the jurisdiction of the Tribunal in respect of an appeal under section 48(3) shall be exercised ex parte by the chairman or a deputy chairman sitting alone.

Rules of procedure

7.—(1)   The Secretary of State may make rules for regulating the exercise of the rights of appeal conferred by sections 28(4) or (6) and 48 and the practice and procedure of the Tribunal.

(2)   Rules under this paragraph may in particular make provision—

(a)   with respect to the period within which an appeal can be brought and the burden of proof on an appeal,

(b)   for the summoning (or, in Scotland, citation) of witnesses and the administration of oaths,

(c)   for securing the production of documents and material used for the processing of personal data,

(d)   for the inspection, examination, operation and testing of any equipment or material used in connection with the processing of personal data,

(e)   for the hearing of an appeal wholly or partly in camera,

(f)   for hearing an appeal in the absence of the appellant or for determining an appeal without a hearing,

(g)   for enabling an appeal under section 48(1) against an information notice to be determined by the chairman or a deputy chairman,

(h)   for enabling any matter preliminary or incidental to an appeal to be dealt with by the chairman or a deputy chairman,

(i)   for the awarding of costs or, in Scotland, expenses,

(j)   for the publication of reports of the Tribunal's decisions, and

(k)   for conferring on the Tribunal such ancillary powers as the Secretary of State thinks necessary for the proper discharge of its functions.

(3)   In making rules under this paragraph which relate to appeals under section 28(4) or (6) the Secretary of State shall have regard, in particular, to the need to secure that information is not disclosed contrary to the public interest.

Obstruction etc.

8.—(1)   If any person is guilty of any act or omission in relation to proceedings before the Tribunal which, if those proceedings were proceedings before a court having power to commit for contempt, would constitute contempt of court, the Tribunal may certify the offence to the High Court or, in Scotland, the Court of Session.

(2)   Where an offence is so certified, the court may inquire into the matter and, after hearing any witness who may be produced against or on behalf of the person charged with the offence, and after hearing any statement that may be offered in defence, deal with him in any manner in which it could deal with him if he had committed the like offence in relation to the court.

Section 37   SCHEDULE 7
                    MISCELLANEOUS EXEMPTIONS

Confidential references given by the data controller

1.   Personal data are exempt from section 7 if they consist of a reference given or to be given in confidence by the data controller for the purposes of—

(a)   the education, training or employment, or prospective education, training or employment, of the data subject,

(b)   the appointment, or prospective appointment, of the data subject to any office, or

(c)   the provision, or prospective provision, by the data subject of any service.

Armed forces

2.   Personal data are exempt from the subject information provisions in any case to the extent to which the application of those provisions would be likely to prejudice the combat effectiveness of any of the armed forces of the Crown.

Judicial appointments and honours

3.   Personal data processed for the purposes of—
   (a)   assessing any person's suitability for judicial office or the office of Queen's Counsel, or
   (b)   the conferring by the Crown of any honour,
are exempt from the subject information provisions.

Crown employment and Crown or Ministerial appointments

4.   The Secretary of State may by order exempt from the subject information provisions personal data processed for the purposes of assessing any person's suitability for—
   (a)   employment by or under the Crown, or
   (b)   any office to which appointments are made by Her Majesty, by a Minister of the Crown or by a Northern Ireland department.

Management forecasts etc.

5.   Personal data processed for the purposes of management forecasting or management planning to assist the data controller in the conduct of any business or other activity are exempt from the subject information provisions in any case to the extent to which the application of those provisions would be likely to prejudice the conduct of that business or other activity.

Corporate finance

6.—(1)   Where personal data are processed for the purposes of, or in connection with, a corporate finance service provided by a relevant person—
   (a)   the data are exempt from the subject information provisions in any case to the extent to which either—
       (i)   the application of those provisions to the data could affect the price of any instrument which is already in existence or is to be or may be created, or
       (ii)   the data controller reasonably believes that the application of those provisions to the data could affect the price of any such instrument, and
   (b)   to the extent that the data are not exempt from the subject information provisions by virtue of paragraph (a), they are exempt from those provisions if the exemption is required for the purpose of safeguarding an important economic or financial interest of the United Kingdom.
   (2)   For the purposes of sub-paragraph (1)(b) the Secretary of State may by order specify—
   (a)   matters to be taken into account in determining whether exemption from the subject information provisions is required for the purpose of safeguarding an important economic or financial interest of the United Kingdom, or
   (b)   circumstances in which exemption from those provisions is, or is not, to be taken to be required for that purpose.

(3)   In this paragraph—
'corporate finance service' means a service consisting in—
    (a)   underwriting in respect of issues of, or the placing of issues of, any instrument,
    (b)   advice to undertakings on capital structure, industrial strategy and related matters and advice and service relating to mergers and the purchase of undertakings, or
    (c)   services relating to such underwriting as is mentioned in paragraph (a);
'instrument' means any instrument listed in section B of the Annex to the Council Directive on investment services in the securities field (93/22/EEC), as set out in Schedule 1 to the Investment Services Regulations 1995;
'price' includes value;
'relevant person' means—
    (a)   any person who is authorised under Chapter III of Part I of the Financial Services Act 1986 or is an exempted person under Chapter IV of Part I of that Act,
    (b)   any person who, but for Part III or IV of Schedule 1 to that Act, would require authorisation under that Act,
    (c)   any European investment firm within the meaning given by Regulation 3 of the Investment Services Regulations 1995,
    (d)   any person who, in the course of his employment, provides to his employer a service falling within paragraph (b) or (c) of the definition of 'corporate finance service', or
    (e)   any partner who provides to other partners in the partnership a service falling within either of those paragraphs.

Negotiations

7.   Personal data which consist of records of the intentions of the data controller in relation to any negotiations with the data subject are exempt from the subject information provisions in any case to the extent to which the application of those provisions would be likely to prejudice those negotiations.

Examination marks

8.—(1)   Section 7 shall have effect subject to the provisions of sub-paragraphs (2) to (4) in the case of personal data consisting of marks or other information processed by a data controller—
    (a)   for the purpose of determining the results of an academic, professional or other examination or of enabling the results of any such examination to be determined, or
    (b)   in consequence of the determination of any such results.
(2)   Where the relevant day falls before the day on which the results of the examination are announced, the period mentioned in section 7(8) shall be extended until—
    (a)   the end of five months beginning with the relevant day, or
    (b)   the end of forty days beginning with the date of the announcement,
whichever is the earlier.
(3)   Where by virtue of sub-paragraph (2) a period longer than the prescribed period elapses after the relevant day before the request is complied with, the

information to be supplied pursuant to the request shall be supplied both by reference to the data in question at the time when the request is received and (if different) by reference to the data as from time to time held in the period beginning when the request is received and ending when it is complied with.

(4)   For the purposes of this paragraph the results of an examination shall be treated as announced when they are first published or (if not published) when they are first made available or communicated to the candidate in question.

(5)   In this paragraph—

'examination' includes any process for determining the knowledge, intelligence, skill or ability of a candidate by reference to his performance in any test, work or other activity;

'the prescribed period' means forty days or such other period as is for the time being prescribed under section 7 in relation to the personal data in question;

'relevant day' has the same meaning as in section 7.

Examination scripts etc.

9.—(1)   Personal data consisting of information recorded by candidates during an academic, professional or other examination are exempt from section 7.

(2)   In this paragraph 'examination' has the same meaning as in paragraph 8.

Legal professional privilege

10.   Personal data are exempt from the subject information provisions if the data consist of information in respect of which a claim to legal professional privilege or, in Scotland, to confidentiality as between client and professional legal adviser, could be maintained in legal proceedings.

Self-incrimination

11.—(1)   A person need not comply with any request or order under section 7 to the extent that compliance would, by revealing evidence of the commission of any offence other than an offence under this Act, expose him to proceedings for that offence.

(2)   Information disclosed by any person in compliance with any request or order under section 7 shall not be admissible against him in proceedings for an offence under this Act.

Section 39   SCHEDULE 8
                                TRANSITIONAL RELIEF

                                      PART I
                        INTERPRETATION OF SCHEDULE

1.—(1)   For the purposes of this Schedule, personal data are 'eligible data' at any time if, and to the extent that, they are at that time subject to processing which was already under way immediately before 24th October 1998.

(2)   In this Schedule—

'eligible automated data' means eligible data which fall within paragraph (a) or (b) of the definition of 'data' in section 1(1);

'eligible manual data' means eligible data which are not eligible automated data;

'the first transitional period' means the period beginning with the commencement of this Schedule and ending with 23rd October 2001;

'the second transitional period' means the period beginning with 24th October 2001 and ending with 23rd October 2007.

PART II
EXEMPTIONS AVAILABLE BEFORE 24TH OCTOBER 2001

Manual data

2.—(1) Eligible manual data, other than data forming part of an accessible record, are exempt from the data protection principles and Parts II and III of this Act during the first transitional period.

(2) This paragraph does not apply to eligible manual data to which paragraph 4 applies.

3.—(1) This paragraph applies to—

(a) eligible manual data forming part of an accessible record, and

(b) personal data which fall within paragraph (d) of the definition of 'data' in section 1(1) but which, because they are not subject to processing which was already under way immediately before 24th October 1998, are not eligible data for the purposes of this Schedule.

(2) During the first transitional period, data to which this paragraph applies are exempt from—

(a) the data protection principles, except the sixth principle so far as relating to sections 7 and 12A,

(b) Part II of this Act, except—

(i) section 7 (as it has effect subject to section 8) and section 12A, and

(ii) section 15 so far as relating to those sections, and

(c) Part III of this Act.

4.—(1) This paragraph applies to eligible manual data which consist of information relevant to the financial standing of the data subject and in respect of which the data controller is a credit reference agency.

(2) During the first transitional period, data to which this paragraph applies are exempt from—

(a) the data protection principles, except the sixth principle so far as relating to sections 7 and 12A,

(b) Part II of this Act, except—

(i) section 7 (as it has effect subject to sections 8 and 9) and section 12A, and

(ii) section 15 so far as relating to those sections, and

(c) Part III of this Act.

Processing otherwise than by reference to the data subject

5. During the first transitional period, for the purposes of this Act (apart from paragraph 1), eligible automated data are not to be regarded as being 'processed' unless the processing is by reference to the data subject.

Payrolls and accounts

6.—(1)　Subject to sub-paragraph (2), eligible automated data processed by a data controller for one or more of the following purposes—

(a)　calculating amounts payable by way of remuneration or pensions in respect of service in any employment or office or making payments of, or of sums deducted from, such remuneration or pensions, or

(b)　keeping accounts relating to any business or other activity carried on by the data controller or keeping records of purchases, sales or other transactions for the purpose of ensuring that the requisite payments are made by or to him in respect of those transactions or for the purpose of making financial or management forecasts to assist him in the conduct of any such business or activity,

are exempt from the data protection principles and Parts II and III of this Act during the first transitional period.

(2)　It shall be a condition of the exemption of any eligible automated data under this paragraph that the data are not processed for any other purpose, but the exemption is not lost by any processing of the eligible data for any other purpose if the data controller shows that he had taken such care to prevent it as in all the circumstances was reasonably required.

(3)　Data processed only for one or more of the purposes mentioned in sub-paragraph (1)(a) may be disclosed—

(a)　to any person, other than the data controller, by whom the remuneration or pensions in question are payable,

(b)　for the purpose of obtaining actuarial advice,

(c)　for the purpose of giving information as to the persons in any employment or office for use in medical research into the health of, or injuries suffered by, persons engaged in particular occupations or working in particular places or areas,

(d)　if the data subject (or a person acting on his behalf) has requested or consented to the disclosure of the data either generally or in the circumstances in which the disclosure in question is made, or

(e)　if the person making the disclosure has reasonable grounds for believing that the disclosure falls within paragraph (d).

(4)　Data processed for any of the purposes mentioned in sub-paragraph (1) may be disclosed—

(a)　for the purpose of audit or where the disclosure is for the purpose only of giving information about the data controller's financial affairs, or

(b)　in any case in which disclosure would be permitted by any other provision of this Part of this Act if sub-paragraph (2) were included among the non-disclosure provisions.

(5)　In this paragraph 'remuneration' includes remuneration in kind and 'pensions' includes gratuities or similar benefits.

Unincorporated members' clubs and mailing lists

7.　Eligible automated data processed by an unincorporated members' club and relating only to the members of the club are exempt from the data protection principles and Parts II and III of this Act during the first transitional period.

8.　Eligible automated data processed by a data controller only for the purposes of distributing, or recording the distribution of, articles or information to the data subjects and consisting only of their names, addresses or other particulars necessary for effecting the distribution, are exempt from the data protection principles and Parts II and III of this Act during the first transitional period.

9.   Neither paragraph 7 nor paragraph 8 applies to personal data relating to any data subject unless he has been asked by the club or data controller whether he objects to the data relating to him being processed as mentioned in that paragraph and has not objected.

10.   It shall be a condition of the exemption of any data under paragraph 7 that the data are not disclosed except as permitted by paragraph 11 and of the exemption under paragraph 8 that the data are not processed for any purpose other than that mentioned in that paragraph or as permitted by paragraph 11, but—

(a)   the exemption under paragraph 7 shall not be lost by any disclosure in breach of that condition, and

(b)   the exemption under paragraph 8 shall not be lost by any processing in breach of that condition,

if the data controller shows that he had taken such care to prevent it as in all the circumstances was reasonably required.

11.   Data to which paragraph 10 applies may be disclosed—

(a)   if the data subject (or a person acting on his behalf) has requested or consented to the disclosure of the data either generally or in the circumstances in which the disclosure in question is made,

(b)   if the person making the disclosure has reasonable grounds for believing that the disclosure falls within paragraph (a), or

(c)   in any case in which disclosure would be permitted by any other provision of this Part of this Act if paragraph 8 were included among the non-disclosure provisions.

Back-up data

12.   Eligible automated data which are processed only for the purpose of replacing other data in the event of the latter being lost, destroyed or impaired are exempt from section 7 during the first transitional period.

Exemption of all eligible automated data from certain requirements

13.—(1)   During the first transitional period, eligible automated data are exempt from the following provisions—

(a)   the first data protection principle to the extent to which it requires compliance with—

(i)   paragraph 2 of Part II of Schedule 1,

(ii)   the conditions in Schedule 2, and

(iii)   the conditions in Schedule 3,

(b)   the seventh data protection principle to the extent to which it requires compliance with paragraph 12 of Part II of Schedule 1;

(c)   the eighth data protection principle,

(d)   in section 7(1), paragraphs (b), (c)(ii) and (d),

(e)   sections 10 and 11,

(f)   section 12, and

(g)   section 13, except so far as relating to—

(i)   any contravention of the fourth data protection principle,

(ii)   any disclosure without the consent of the data controller,

(iii)   loss or destruction of data without the consent of the data controller, or

(iv)   processing for the special purposes.

(2)   The specific exemptions conferred by sub-paragraph (1)(a), (c) and (e) do not limit the data controller's general duty under the first data protection principle to ensure that processing is fair.

PART III
EXEMPTIONS AVAILABLE AFTER 23RD OCTOBER 2001 BUT BEFORE 24TH OCTOBER 2007

14.—(1)   This paragraph applies to—

(a)   eligible manual data which were held immediately before 24th October 1998, and

(b)   personal data which fall within paragraph (d) of the definition of 'data' in section 1(1) but do not fall within paragraph (a) of this sub-paragraph, but does not apply to eligible manual data to which the exemption in paragraph 16 applies.

(2)   During the second transitional period, data to which this paragraph applies are exempt from the following provisions—

(a)   the first data protection principle except to the extent to which it requires compliance with paragraph 2 of Part II of Schedule 1,

(b)   the second, third, fourth and fifth data protection principles, and

(c)   section 14(1) to (3).

PART IV
EXEMPTIONS AFTER 23RD OCTOBER 2001 FOR HISTORICAL RESEARCH

15.   In this Part of this Schedule 'the relevant conditions' has the same meaning as in section 33.

16.—(1)   Eligible manual data which are processed only for the purpose of historical research in compliance with the relevant conditions are exempt from the provisions specified in sub-paragraph (2) after 23rd October 2001.

(2)   The provisions referred to in sub-paragraph (1) are—

(a)   the first data protection principle except in so far as it requires compliance with paragraph 2 of Part II of Schedule 1,

(b)   the second, third, fourth and fifth data protection principles, and

(c)   section 14(1) to (3).

17.—(1)   After 23rd October 2001 eligible automated data which are processed only for the purpose of historical research in compliance with the relevant conditions are exempt from the first data protection principle to the extent to which it requires compliance with the conditions in Schedules 2 and 3.

(2)   Eligible automated data which are processed—

(a)   only for the purpose of historical research,

(b)   in compliance with the relevant conditions, and

(c)   otherwise than by reference to the data subject,

are also exempt from the provisions referred to in sub-paragraph (3) after 23rd October 2001.

(3)   The provisions referred to in sub-paragraph (2) are—

(a)   the first data protection principle except in so far as it requires compliance with paragraph 2 of Part II of Schedule 1,

(b)   the second, third, fourth and fifth data protection principles, and

(c)   section 14(1) to (3).

18.   For the purposes of this Part of this Schedule personal data are not to be treated as processed otherwise than for the purpose of historical research merely because the data are disclosed—

(a)   to any person, for the purpose of historical research only,

(b)   to the data subject or a person acting on his behalf,

(c)   at the request, or with the consent, of the data subject or a person acting on his behalf, or

(d)   in circumstances in which the person making the disclosure has reasonable grounds for believing that the disclosure falls within paragraph (a), (b) or (c).

PART V
EXEMPTION FROM SECTION 22

19.   Processing which was already under way immediately before 24th October 1998 is not assessable processing for the purposes of section 22.

Section 50   SCHEDULE 9
                          POWERS OF ENTRY AND INSPECTION

Issue of warrants

1.—(1)   If a circuit judge is satisfied by information on oath supplied by the Commissioner that there are reasonable grounds for suspecting—

(a)   that a data controller has contravened or is contravening any of the data protection principles, or

(b)   that an offence under this Act has been or is being committed,

and that evidence of the contravention or of the commission of the offence is to be found on any premises specified in the information, he may, subject to subparagraph (2) and paragraph 2, grant a warrant to the Commissioner.

(2)   A judge shall not issue a warrant under this Schedule in respect of any personal data processed for the special purposes unless a determination by the Commissioner under section 45 with respect to those data has taken effect.

(3)   A warrant issued under sub-paragraph (1) shall authorise the Commissioner or any of his officers or staff at any time within seven days of the date of the warrant to enter the premises, to search them, to inspect, examine, operate and test any equipment found there which is used or intended to be used for the processing of personal data and to inspect and seize any documents or other material found there which may be such evidence as is mentioned in that sub-paragraph.

2.—(1)   A judge shall not issue a warrant under this Schedule unless he is satisfied—

(a)   that the Commissioner has given seven days' notice in writing to the occupier of the premises in question demanding access to the premises, and

(b)   that either—

(i)   access was demanded at a reasonable hour and was unreasonably refused, or

(ii)   although entry to the premises was granted, the occupier unreasonably refused to comply with a request by the Commissioner or any of the Commissioner's officers or staff to permit the Commissioner or the officer or member of staff to do any of the things referred to in paragraph 1(3), and

(c)   that the occupier, has, after the refusal, been notified by the Commissioner of the application for the warrant and has had an opportunity of being heard by the judge on the question whether or not it should be issued.

(2)   Sub-paragraph (1) shall not apply if the judge is satisfied that the case is one of urgency or that compliance with those provisions would defeat the object of the entry.

3.   A judge who issues a warrant under this Schedule shall also issue two copies of it and certify them clearly as copies.

Execution of warrants

4.   A person executing a warrant issued under this Schedule may use such reasonable force as may be necessary.

5.   A warrant issued under this Schedule shall be executed at a reasonable hour unless it appears to the person executing it that there are grounds for suspecting that the evidence in question would not be found if it were so executed.

6.   If the person who occupies the premises in respect of which a warrant is issued under this Schedule is present when the warrant is executed, he shall be shown the warrant and supplied with a copy of it; and if that person is not present a copy of the warrant shall be left in a prominent place on the premises.

7.—(1)   A person seizing anything in pursuance of a warrant under this Schedule shall give a receipt for it if asked to do so.

(2)   Anything so seized may be retained for so long as is necessary in all the circumstances but the person in occupation of the premises in question shall be given a copy of anything that is seized if he so requests and the person executing the warrant considers that it can be done without undue delay.

Matters exempt from inspection and seizure

8.   The powers of inspection and seizure conferred by a warrant issued under this Schedule shall not be exercisable in respect of personal data which by virtue of section 28 are exempt from any of the provisions of this Act.

9.—(1)   Subject to the provisions of this paragraph, the powers of inspection and seizure conferred by a warrant issued under this Schedule shall not be exercisable in respect of—

(a)   any communication between a professional legal adviser and his client in connection with the giving of legal advice to the client with respect to his obligations, liabilities or rights under this Act, or

(b)   any communication between a professional legal adviser and his client, or between such an adviser or his client and any other person, made in connection with or in contemplation of proceedings under or arising out of this Act (including proceedings before the Tribunal) and for the purposes of such proceedings.

(2)   Sub-paragraph (1) applies also to—

(a)   any copy or other record of any such communication as is there mentioned, and

(b)   any document or article enclosed with or referred to in any such communication if made in connection with the giving of any advice or, as the case may be, in connection with or in contemplation of and for the purposes of such proceedings as are there mentioned.

(3)   This paragraph does not apply to anything in the possession of any person other than the professional legal adviser or his client or to anything held with the intention of furthering a criminal purpose.

(4)   In this paragraph references to the client of a professional legal adviser include references to any person representing such a client.

10.   If the person in occupation of any premises in respect of which a warrant is issued under this Schedule objects to the inspection or seizure under the warrant of any material on the grounds that it consists partly of matters in respect of which those powers are not exercisable, he shall, if the person executing the warrant so requests, furnish that person with a copy of so much of the material as is not exempt from those powers.

Return of warrants

11.   A warrant issued under this Schedule shall be returned to the court from which it was issued—

(a)   after being executed, or

(b)   if not executed within the time authorised for its execution;

and the person by whom any such warrant is executed shall make an endorsement on it stating what powers have been exercised by him under the warrant.

Offences

12.   Any person who—

(a)   intentionally obstructs a person in the execution of a warrant issued under this Schedule, or

(b)   fails without reasonable excuse to give any person executing such a warrant such assistance as he may reasonably require for the execution of the warrant, is guilty of an offence.

Vessels, vehicles etc.

13.   In this Schedule 'premises' includes any vessel, vehicle, aircraft or hovercraft, and references to the occupier of any premises include references to the person in charge of any vessel, vehicle, aircraft or hovercraft.

Scotland and Northern Ireland

14.   In the application of this Schedule to Scotland—

(a)   for any reference to a circuit judge there is substituted a reference to the sheriff,

(b)   for any reference to information on oath there is substituted a reference to evidence on oath, and

(c)   for the reference to the court from which the warrant was issued there is substituted a reference to the sheriff clerk.

15.   In the application of this Schedule to Northern Ireland—

(a)   for any reference to a circuit judge there is substituted a reference to a county court judge, and

(b)   for any reference to information on oath there is substituted a reference to a complaint on oath.

Section 53(6)   SCHEDULE 10
FURTHER PROVISIONS RELATING TO ASSISTANCE
UNDER SECTION 53

1.   In this Schedule 'applicant' and 'proceedings' have the same meaning as in section 53.

2.   The assistance provided under section 53 may include the making of arrangements for, or for the Commissioner to bear the costs of—

(a)   the giving of advice or assistance by a solicitor or counsel, and

(b)   the representation of the applicant, or the provision to him of such assistance as is usually given by a solicitor or counsel—

(i)   in steps preliminary or incidental to the proceedings, or

(ii)   in arriving at or giving effect to a compromise to avoid or bring an end to the proceedings.

3.   Where assistance is provided with respect to the conduct of proceedings—

(a)   it shall include an agreement by the Commissioner to indemnify the applicant (subject only to any exceptions specified in the notification) in respect of any liability to pay costs or expenses arising by virtue of any judgment or order of the court in the proceedings,

(b)   it may include an agreement by the Commissioner to indemnify the applicant in respect of any liability to pay costs or expenses arising by virtue of any compromise or settlement arrived at in order to avoid the proceedings or bring the proceedings to an end, and

(c)   it may include an agreement by the Commissioner to indemnify the applicant in respect of any liability to pay damages pursuant to an undertaking given on the grant of interlocutory relief (in Scotland, an interim order) to the applicant.

4.   Where the Commissioner provides assistance in relation to any proceedings, he shall do so on such terms, or make such other arrangements, as will secure that a person against whom the proceedings have been or are commenced is informed that assistance has been or is being provided by the Commissioner in relation to them.

5.   In England and Wales or Northern Ireland, the recovery of expenses incurred by the Commissioner in providing an applicant with assistance (as taxed or assessed in such manner as may be prescribed by rules of court) shall constitute a first charge for the benefit of the Commissioner—

(a)   on any costs which, by virtue of any judgment or order of the court, are payable to the applicant by any other person in respect of the matter in connection with which the assistance is provided, and

(b)   on any sum payable to the applicant under a compromise or settlement arrived at in connection with that matter to avoid or bring to an end any proceedings.

6.   In Scotland, the recovery of such expenses (as taxed or assessed in such manner as may be prescribed by rules of court) shall be paid to the Commissioner, in priority to other debts—

(a)   out of any expenses which, by virtue of any judgment or order of the court, are payable to the applicant by any other person in respect of the matter in connection with which the assistance is provided, and

(b)   out of any sum payable to the applicant under a compromise or settlement arrived at in connection with that matter to avoid or bring to an end any proceedings.

Section 68(1)(6)   SCHEDULE 11
                            EDUCATIONAL RECORDS

Meaning of 'educational record'

1.   For the purposes of section 68 'educational record' means any record to which paragraph 2, 5 or 7 applies.

England and Wales

2.   This paragraph applies to any record of information which—
     (a)   is processed by or on behalf of the governing body of, or a teacher at, any school in England and Wales specified in paragraph 3,
     (b)   relates to any person who is or has been a pupil at the school, and
     (c)   originated from or was supplied by or on behalf of any of the persons specified in paragraph 4,
other than information which is processed by a teacher solely for the teacher's own use.

3.   The schools referred to in paragraph 2(a) are—
     (a)   a school maintained by a local education authority, and
     (b)   a special school, as defined by section 6(2) of the Education Act 1996, which is not so maintained.

4.   The persons referred to in paragraph 2(c) are—
     (a)   an employee of the local education authority which maintains the school,
     (b)   in the case of—
         (i)   a voluntary aided, foundation or foundation special school (within the meaning of the School Standards and Framework Act 1998), or
         (ii)   a special school which is not maintained by a local education authority,
     a teacher or other employee at the school (including an educational psychologist engaged by the governing body under a contract for services),
     (c)   the pupil to whom the record relates, and
     (d)   a parent, as defined by section 576(1) of the Education Act 1996, of that pupil.

Scotland

5.   This paragraph applies to any record of information which is processed—
     (a)   by an education authority in Scotland, and
     (b)   for the purpose of the relevant function of the authority,
other than information which is processed by a teacher solely for the teacher's own use.

6.   For the purposes of paragraph 5—
     (a)   'education authority' means an education authority within the meaning of the Education (Scotland) Act 1980 ('the 1980 Act') or, in relation to a self-governing school, the board of management within the meaning of the Self-Governing Schools etc. (Scotland) Act 1989 ('the 1989 Act'),

(b)   'the relevant function' means, in relation to each of those authorities, their function under section 1 of the 1980 Act and section 7(1) of the 1989 Act, and

(c)   information processed by an education authority is processed for the purpose of the relevant function of the authority if the processing relates to the discharge of that function in respect of a person—

(i)   who is or has been a pupil in a school provided by the authority, or

(ii)   who receives, or has received, further education (within the meaning of the 1980 Act) so provided.

Northern Ireland

7.—(1)   This paragraph applies to any record of information which—

(a)   is processed by or on behalf of the Board of Governors of, or a teacher at, any grant-aided school in Northern Ireland,

(b)   relates to any person who is or has been a pupil at the school, and

(c)   originated from or was supplied by or on behalf of any of the persons specified in paragraph 8,

other than information which is processed by a teacher solely for the teacher's own use.

(2)   In sub-paragraph (1) 'grant-aided school' has the same meaning as in the Education and Libraries (Northern Ireland) Order 1986.

8.   The persons referred to in paragraph 7(1) are—

(a)   a teacher at the school,

(b)   an employee of an education and library board, other than such a teacher,

(c)   the pupil to whom the record relates, and

(d)   a parent (as defined by Article 2(2) of the Education and Libraries (Northern Ireland) Order 1986) of that pupil.

England and Wales: transitory provisions

9.—(1)   Until the appointed day within the meaning of section 20 of the School Standards and Framework Act 1998, this Schedule shall have effect subject to the following modifications.

(2)   Paragraph 3 shall have effect as if for paragraph (b) and the 'and' immediately preceding it there were substituted—

'(aa)   a grant-maintained school, as defined by section 183(1) of the Education Act 1996,

(ab)   a grant-maintained special school, as defined by section 337(4) of that Act, and

(b)   a special school, as defined by section 6(2) of that Act, which is neither a maintained special school, as defined by section 337(3) of that Act, nor a grant-maintained special school.'

(3)   Paragraph 4(b)(i) shall have effect as if for the words from 'foundation', in the first place where it occurs, to '1998)' there were substituted 'or grant-maintained school'.

Section 68(1)(c)   SCHEDULE 12
                     ACCESSIBLE PUBLIC RECORDS

Meaning of 'accessible public record'

1. For the purposes of section 68 'accessible public record' means any record which is kept by an authority specified—
    (a)   as respects England and Wales, in the Table in paragraph 2,
    (b)   as respects Scotland, in the Table in paragraph 4, or
    (c)   as respects Northern Ireland, in the Table in paragraph 6,
and is a record of information of a description specified in that Table in relation to that authority.

Housing and social services records: England and Wales

2. The following is the Table referred to in paragraph 1(a).

TABLE OF AUTHORITIES AND INFORMATION

The authorities	*The accessible information*
Housing Act local authority.	Information held for the purpose of any of the authority's tenancies.
Local social services authority.	Information held for any purpose of the authority's social services functions.

3.—(1)   The following provisions apply for the interpretation of the Table in paragraph 2.
   (2)   Any authority which, by virtue of section 4(e) of the Housing Act 1985, is a local authority for the purpose of any provision of that Act is a 'Housing Act local authority' for the purposes of this Schedule, and so is any housing action trust established under Part III of the Housing Act 1988.
   (3)   Information contained in records kept by a Housing Act local authority is 'held for the purpose of any of the authority's tenancies' if it is held for any purpose of the relationship of landlord and tenant of a dwelling which subsists, has subsisted or may subsist between the authority and any individual who is, has been or, as the case may be, has applied to be, a tenant of the authority.
   (4)   Any authority which, by virtue of section 1 or 12 of the Local Authority Social Services Act 1970, is or is treated as a local authority for the purposes of that Act is a 'local social services authority' for the purposes of this Schedule; and information contained in records kept by such an authority is 'held for any purpose of the authority's social services functions' if it is held for the purpose of any past, current or proposed exercise of such a function in any case.
   (5)   Any expression used in paragraph 2 or this paragraph and in Part II of the Housing Act 1985 or the Local Authority Social Services Act 1970 has the same meaning as in that Act.

Housing and social services records: Scotland

4. The following is the Table referred to in paragraph 1(b).

TABLE OF AUTHORITIES AND INFORMATION

The authorities	The accessible information
Local authority. Scottish Homes.	Information held for the purpose of any of the body's tenancies.
Social work authority.	Information held for any purpose of the the authority's functions under the Social Work (Scotland) Act 1968 and the enactments referred to in section 5(1B) of that Act.

5.—(1)   The following provisions apply for the interpretation of the Table in paragraph 4.

(2)   'Local authority' means—

(a)   a council constituted under section 2 of the Local Government etc. (Scotland) Act 1994,

(b)   a joint board or joint committee of two or more of those councils, or

(c)   any trust under the control of such a council.

(3)   Information contained in records kept by a local authority or Scottish Homes is held for the purpose of any of their tenancies if it is held for any purpose of the relationship of landlord and tenant of a dwelling-house which subsists, has subsisted or may subsist between the authority or, as the case may be, Scottish Homes and any individual who is, has been or, as the case may be, has applied to be a tenant of theirs.

(4)   'Social work authority' means a local authority for the purposes of the Social Work (Scotland) Act 1968, and information contained in records kept by such an authority is held for any purpose of their functions if it is held for the purpose of any past, current or proposed exercise of such a function in any case.

Housing and social services records: Northern Ireland

6.   The following is the Table referred to in paragraph 1(c).

TABLE OF AUTHORITIES AND INFORMATION

The authorities	The accessible information
The Northern Ireland Housing Executive.	Information held for the purpose of any of the Executive's tenancies.
A Health and Social Services Board.	Information held for the purpose of any past, current or proposed exercise by the Board of any function exercisable, by virtue of directions under Article 17(1) of the Health and Personal Social Services (Northern Ireland) Order 1972, by the Board on behalf of the Department of Health and Social Services with respect to the administration of personal social services under—

The authorities	The accessible information
	(a) the Children and Young Persons Act (Northern Ireland) 1968;
	(b) the Health and Personal Social Services (Northern Ireland) Order 1972;
	(c) Article 47 of the Matrimonial Causes (Northern Ireland) Order 1978;
	(d) Article 11 of the Domestic Proceedings (Northern Ireland) Order 1980;
	(e) the Adoption (Northern Ireland) Order 1987; or
	(f) the Children (Northern Ireland) Order 1995.
An HSS trust	Information held for the purpose of any past, current or proposed exercise by the trust of any function exercisable, by virtue of an authorisation under Article 3(1) of the Health and Personal Social Services (Northern Ireland) Order 1994, by the trust on behalf of a Health and Social Services Board with respect to the administration of personal social services under any statutory provision mentioned in the last preceding entry.

7.—(1) This paragraph applies for the interpretation of the Table in paragraph 6.

(2) Information contained in records kept by the Northern Ireland Housing Executive is 'held for the purpose of any of the Executive's tenancies' if it is held for any purpose of the relationship of landlord and tenant of a dwelling which subsists, has subsisted or may subsist between the Executive and any individual who is, has been or, as the case may be, has applied to be, a tenant of the Executive.

Section 72   SCHEDULE 13
MODIFICATIONS OF ACT HAVING EFFECT BEFORE
24TH OCTOBER 2007

1.   After section 12 there is inserted—

'12A.   Rights of data subjects in relation to exempt manual data
    (1)   A data subject is entitled at any time by notice in writing—
        (a)   to require the data controller to rectify, block, erase or destroy exempt manual data which are inaccurate or incomplete, or
        (b)   to require the data controller to cease holding exempt manual data in a way incompatible with the legitimate purposes pursued by the data controller.

(2)   A notice under subsection (1)(a) or (b) must state the data subject's reasons for believing that the data are inaccurate or incomplete or, as the case may be, his reasons for believing that they are held in a way incompatible with the legitimate purposes pursued by the data controller.

(3)   If the court is satisfied, on the application of any person who has given a notice under subsection (1) which appears to the court to be justified (or to be justified to any extent) that the data controller in question has failed to comply with the notice, the court may order him to take such steps for complying with the notice (or for complying with it to that extent) as the court thinks fit.

(4)   In this section 'exempt manual data' means—

(a)   in relation to the first transitional period, as defined by paragraph 1(2) of Schedule 8, data to which paragraph 3 or 4 of that Schedule applies, and

(b)   in relation to the second transitional period, as so defined, data to which paragraph 14 of that Schedule applies.

(5)   For the purposes of this section personal data are incomplete if, and only if, the data, although not inaccurate, are such that their incompleteness would constitute a contravention of the third or fourth data protection principles, if those principles applied to the data.'

2.   In section 32—

(a)   in subsection (2) after 'section 12' there is inserted—

'(dd) section 12A,', and

(b)   in subsection (4) after '12(8)' there is inserted ', 12A(3)'.

3.   In section 34 for 'section 14(1) to (3)' there is substituted 'sections 12A and 14(1) to (3).'

4.   In section 53(1) after '12(8)' there is inserted ', 12A(3)'.

5.   In paragraph 8 of Part II of Schedule 1, the word 'or' at the end of paragraph (c) is omitted and after paragraph (d) there is inserted 'or

(e)   he contravenes section 12A by failing to comply with a notice given under subsection (1) of that section to the extent that the notice is justified.'

Section 73   SCHEDULE 14
                       TRANSITIONAL PROVISIONS AND SAVINGS

Interpretation

1.   In this Schedule—

'the 1984 Act' means the Data Protection Act 1984;

'the old principles' means the data protection principles within the meaning of the 1984 Act;

'the new principles' means the data protection principles within the meaning of this Act.

Effect of registration under Part II of 1984 Act

2.—(1)   Subject to sub-paragraphs (4) and (5) any person who, immediately before the commencement of Part III of this Act—

(a)   is registered as a data user under Part II of the 1984 Act, or

(b)   is treated by virtue of section 7(6) of the 1984 Act as so registered, is exempt from section 17(1) of this Act until the end of the registration period or, if earlier, 24th October 2001.

(2)   In sub-paragraph (1) 'the registration period', in relation to a person, means—

(a)   where there is a single entry in respect of that person as a data user, the period at the end of which, if section 8 of the 1984 Act had remained in force, that entry would have fallen to be removed unless renewed, and

(b)   where there are two or more entries in respect of that person as a data user, the period at the end of which, if that section had remained in force, the last of those entries to expire would have fallen to be removed unless renewed.

(3)   Any application for registration as a data user under Part II of the 1984 Act which is received by the Commissioner before the commencement of Part III of this Act (including any appeal against a refusal of registration) shall be determined in accordance with the old principles and the provisions of the 1984 Act.

(4)   If a person falling within paragraph (b) of sub-paragraph (1) receives a notification under section 7(1) of the 1984 Act of the refusal of his application, sub-paragraph (1) shall cease to apply to him—

(a)   if no appeal is brought, at the end of the period within which an appeal can be brought against the refusal, or

(b)   on the withdrawal or dismissal of the appeal.

(5)   If a data controller gives a notification under section 18(1) at a time when he is exempt from section 17(1) by virtue of sub-paragraph (1), he shall cease to be so exempt.

(6)   The Commissioner shall include in the register maintained under section 19 an entry in respect of each person who is exempt from section 17(1) by virtue of sub-paragraph (1); and each entry shall consist of the particulars which, immediately before the commencement of Part III of this Act, were included (or treated as included) in respect of that person in the register maintained under section 4 of the 1984 Act.

(7)   Notification regulations under Part III of this Act may make provision modifying the duty referred to in section 20(1) in its application to any person in respect of whom an entry in the register maintained under section 19 has been made under sub-paragraph (6).

(8)   Notification regulations under Part III of this Act may make further transitional provision in connection with the substitution of Part III of this Act for Part II of the 1984 Act (registration), including provision modifying the application of provisions of Part III in transitional cases.

Rights of data subjects

3.—(1)   The repeal of section 21 of the 1984 Act (right of access to personal data) does not affect the application of that section in any case in which the request (together with the information referred to in paragraph (a) of subsection (4) of that section and, in a case where it is required, the consent referred to in paragraph (b) of that subsection) was received before the day on which the repeal comes into force.

(2)   Sub-paragraph (1) does not apply where the request is made by reference to this Act.

(3)   Any fee paid for the purposes of section 21 of the 1984 Act before the commencement of section 7 in a case not falling within sub-paragraph (1) shall be taken to have been paid for the purposes of section 7.

4.   The repeal of section 22 of the 1984 Act (compensation for inaccuracy) and the repeal of section 23 of that Act (compensation for loss or unauthorised disclosure) do not affect the application of those sections in relation to damage or distress suffered at any time by reason of anything done or omitted to be done before the commencement of the repeals.

5.   The repeal of section 24 of the 1984 Act (rectification and erasure) does not affect any case in which the application to the court was made before the day on which the repeal comes into force.

6.   Subsection (3)(b) of section 14 does not apply where the rectification, blocking, erasure or destruction occurred before the commencement of that section.

Enforcement and transfer prohibition notices served under Part V of 1984 Act

7.—(1)   If, immediately before the commencement of section 40—

(a)   an enforcement notice under section 10 of the 1984 Act has effect, and

(b)   either the time for appealing against the notice has expired or any appeal has been determined,

then, after that commencement, to the extent mentioned in sub-paragraph (3), the notice shall have effect for the purposes of sections 41 and 47 as if it were an enforcement notice under section 40.

(2)   Where an enforcement notice has been served under section 10 of the 1984 Act before the commencement of section 40 and immediately before that commencement either—

(a)   the time for appealing against the notice has not expired, or

(b)   an appeal has not been determined,

the appeal shall be determined in accordance with the provisions of the 1984 Act and the old principles and, unless the notice is quashed on appeal, to the extent mentioned in sub-paragraph (3) the notice shall have effect for the purposes of sections 41 and 47 as if it were an enforcement notice under section 40.

(3)   An enforcement notice under section 10 of the 1984 Act has the effect described in sub-paragraph (1) or (2) only to the extent that the steps specified in the notice for complying with the old principle or principles in question are steps which the data controller could be required by an enforcement notice under section 40 to take for complying with the new principles or any of them.

8.—(1)   If, immediately before the commencement of section 40—

(a)   a transfer prohibition notice under section 12 of the 1984 Act has effect, and

(b)   either the time for appealing against the notice has expired or any appeal has been determined,

then, on and after that commencement, to the extent specified in sub-paragraph (3), the notice shall have effect for the purposes of sections 41 and 47 as if it were an enforcement notice under section 40.

(2)   Where a transfer prohibition notice has been served under section 12 of the 1984 Act and immediately before the commencement of section 40 either—

(a)   the time for appealing against the notice has not expired, or

(b)   an appeal has not been determined,

the appeal shall be determined in accordance with the provisions of the 1984 Act and the old principles and, unless the notice is quashed on appeal, to the extent mentioned in sub-paragraph (3) the notice shall have effect for the purposes of sections 41 and 47 as if it were an enforcement notice under section 40.

(3)   A transfer prohibition notice under section 12 of the 1984 Act has the effect described in sub-paragraph (1) or (2) only to the extent that the prohibition imposed by the notice is one which could be imposed by an enforcement notice under section 40 for complying with the new principles or any of them.

Notices under new law relating to matters in relation to which 1984 Act had effect

9.   The Commissioner may serve an enforcement notice under section 40 on or after the day on which that section comes into force if he is satisfied that, before that day, the data controller contravened the old principles by reason of any act or omission which would also have constituted a contravention of the new principles if they had applied before that day.

10.   Subsection (5)(b) of section 40 does not apply where the rectification, blocking, erasure or destruction occurred before the commencement of that section.

11.   The Commissioner may serve an information notice under section 43 on or after the day on which that section comes into force if he has reasonable grounds for suspecting that, before that day, the data controller contravened the old principles by reason of any act or omission which would also have constituted a contravention of the new principles if they had applied before that day.

12.   Where by virtue of paragraph 11 an information notice is served on the basis of anything done or omitted to be done before the day on which section 43 comes into force, subsection (2)(b) of that section shall have effect as if the reference to the data controller having complied, or complying, with the new principles were a reference to the data controller having contravened the old principles by reason of any such act or omission as is mentioned in paragraph 11.

Self-incrimination, etc.

13.—(1)   In section 43(8), section 44(9) and paragraph 11 of Schedule 7, any reference to an offence under this Act includes a reference to an offence under the 1984 Act.

(2)   In section 34(9) of the 1984 Act, any reference to an offence under that Act includes a reference to an offence under this Act.

Warrants issued under 1984 Act

14.   The repeal of Schedule 4 to the 1984 Act does not affect the application of that Schedule in any case where a warrant was issued under that Schedule before the commencement of the repeal.

Complaints under section 36(2) of 1984 Act and requests for assessment under section 42

15.   The repeal of section 36(2) of the 1984 Act does not affect the application of that provision in any case where the complaint was received by the Commissioner before the commencement of the repeal.

16.   In dealing with a complaint under section 36(2) of the 1984 Act or a request for an assessment under section 42 of this Act, the Commissioner shall have regard to the provisions from time to time applicable to the processing, and accordingly—

(a)   in section 36(2) of the 1984 Act, the reference to the old principles and the provisions of that Act includes, in relation to any time when the new principles and the provisions of this Act have effect, those principles and provisions, and

(b)   in section 42 of this Act, the reference to the provisions of this Act includes, in relation to any time when the old principles and the provisions of the 1984 Act had effect, those principles and provisions.

Applications under Access to Health Records Act 1990 or corresponding Northern Ireland legislation

17.—(1)   The repeal of any provision of the Access to Health Records Act 1990 does not affect—

(a)   the application of section 3 or 6 of that Act in any case in which the application under that section was received before the day on which the repeal comes into force, or

(b)   the application of section 8 of that Act in any case in which the application to the court was made before the day on which the repeal comes into force.

(2)   Sub-paragraph (1)(a) does not apply in relation to an application for access to information which was made by reference to this Act.

18.—(1)   The revocation of any provision of the Access to Health Records (Northern Ireland) Order 1993 does not affect—

(a)   the application of Article 5 or 8 of that Order in any case in which the application under that Article was received before the day on which the repeal comes into force, or

(b)   the application of Article 10 of that Order in any case in which the application to the court was made before the day on which the repeal comes into force.

(2)   Sub-paragraph (1)(a) does not apply in relation to an application for access to information which was made by reference to this Act.

Applications under regulations under Access to Personal Files Act 1987 or corresponding Northern Ireland legislation

19.—(1)   The repeal of the personal files enactments does not affect the application of regulations under those enactments in relation to—

(a)   any request for information,

(b)   any application for rectification or erasure, or

(c)   any application for review of a decision,

which was made before the day on which the repeal comes into force.

(2)   Sub-paragraph (1)(a) does not apply in relation to a request for information which was made by reference to this Act.

(3)   In sub-paragraph (1) 'the personal files enactments' means—

(a)   in relation to Great Britain, the Access to Personal Files Act 1987, and

(b)   in relation to Northern Ireland, Part II of the Access to Personal Files and Medical Reports (Northern Ireland) Order 1991.

Applications under section 158 of Consumer Credit Act 1974

20.   Section 62 does not affect the application of section 158 of the Consumer Credit Act 1974 in any case where the request was received before the commencement of section 62, unless the request is made by reference to this Act.

Section 74(1)   SCHEDULE 15
            MINOR AND CONSEQUENTIAL AMENDMENTS

Public Records Act 1958 (c. 51)

1.—(1)   In Part II of the Table in paragraph 3 of Schedule 1 to the Public Records Act 1958 (definition of public records) for 'the Data Protection Registrar' there is substituted 'the Data Protection Commissioner'.

(2)   That Schedule shall continue to have effect with the following amendment (originally made by paragraph 14 of Schedule 2 to the Data Protection Act 1984).

(3)   After paragraph 4(1)(n) there is inserted—
'(nn) records of the Data Protection Tribunal'.

Parliamentary Commissioner Act 1967 (c. 13)

2.   In Schedule 2 to the Parliamentary Commissioner Act 1967 (departments etc. subject to investigation) for 'Data Protection Registrar' there is substituted 'Data Protection Commissioner'.

3.   In Schedule 4 to that Act (tribunals exercising administrative functions), in the entry relating to the Data Protection Tribunal, for 'section 3 of the Data Protection Act 1984' there is substituted 'section 6 of the Data Protection Act 1998'.

Superannuation Act 1972 (c. 11)

4.   In Schedule 1 to the Superannuation Act 1972, for 'Data Protection Registrar' there is substituted 'Data Protection Commissioner'.

House of Commons Disqualification Act 1975 (c. 24)

5.—(1)   Part II of Schedule 1 to the House of Commons Disqualification Act 1975 (bodies whose members are disqualified) shall continue to include the entry 'The Data Protection Tribunal' (originally inserted by paragraph 12(1) of Schedule 2 to the Data Protection Act 1984).

(2)   In Part III of that Schedule (disqualifying offices) for 'The Data Protection Registrar' there is substituted 'The Data Protection Commissioner'.

Northern Ireland Assembly Disqualification Act 1975 (c. 25)

6.—(1)   Part II of Schedule 1 to the Northern Ireland Assembly Disqualification Act 1975 (bodies whose members are disqualified) shall continue to include the entry 'The Data Protection Tribunal' (originally inserted by paragraph 12(3) of Schedule 2 to the Data Protection Act 1984).

(2)   In Part III of that Schedule (disqualifying offices) for 'The Data Protection Registrar' there is substituted 'The Data Protection Commissioner'.

Representation of the People Act 1983 (c. 2)

7.   In Schedule 2 of the Representation of the People Act 1983 (provisions which may be included in regulations as to registration etc), in paragraph 11A(2)—
(a)   for 'data user' there is substituted 'data controller' and
(b)   for 'the Data Protection Act 1984' there is substituted 'the Data Protection Act 1998'.

Access to Medical Reports Act 1988 (c. 28)

8.   In section 2(1) of the Access to Medical Reports Act 1988 (interpretation), in the definition of 'health professional', for 'the Data Protection (Subject Access Modification) Order 1987' there is substituted 'the Data Protection Act 1998'.

Football Spectators Act 1989 (c. 37)

9.—(1)   Section 5 of the Football Spectators Act 1989 (national membership scheme: contents and penalties) is amended as follows.

(2)   In subsection (5), for 'paragraph 1(2) of Part II of Schedule 1 to the Data Protection Act 1984' there is substituted 'paragraph 1(2) of Part II of Schedule 1 to the Data Protection Act 1998'.

(3)   In subsection (6), for 'section 28(1) and (2) of the Data Protection Act 1984' there is substituted 'section 29(1) and (2) of the Data Protection Act 1998'.

Education (Student Loans) Act 1990 (c. 6)

10.   Schedule 2 to the Education (Student Loans) Act 1990 (loans for students) so far as that Schedule continues in force shall have effect as if the reference in paragraph 4(2) to the Data Protection Act 1984 were a reference to this Act.

Access to Health Records Act 1990 (c. 23)

11.   For section 2 of the Access to Health Records Act 1990 there is substituted—

'2.   Health professionals
In this Act 'health professional' has the same meaning as in the Data Protection Act 1998.'

12.   In section 3(4) of that Act (cases where fee may be required) in paragraph (a), for 'the maximum prescribed under section 21 of the Data Protection Act 1984' there is substituted 'such maximum as may be prescribed for the purposes of this section by regulations under section 7 of the Data Protection Act 1998'.

13.   In section 5(3) of that Act (cases where right of access may be partially excluded) for the words from the beginning to 'record' in the first place where it occurs there is substituted 'Access shall not be given under section 3(2) to any part of a health record'.

Access to Personal Files and Medical Reports (Northern Ireland) Order 1991
(1991/1707 (N.I. 14))

14.   In Article 4 of the Access to Personal Files and Medical Reports (Northern Ireland) Order 1991 (obligation to give access), in paragraph (2) (exclusion of information to which individual entitled under section 21 of the Data Protection Act 1984) for 'section 21 of the Data Protection Act 1984' there is substituted 'section 7 of the Data Protection Act 1998'.

15.   In Article 6(1) of that Order (interpretation), in the definition of 'health professional', for 'the Data Protection (Subject Access Modification) (Health) Order 1987' there is substituted 'the Data Protection Act 1998'.

Tribunals and Inquiries Act 1992 (c. 53)

16.   In Part 1 of Schedule 1 to the Tribunals and Inquiries Act 1992 (tribunals under direct supervision of Council on Tribunals), for paragraph 14 there is substituted—

'Data protection   14(a) The Data Protection Commissioner appointed under section 6 of the Data Protection Act 1998;
                                              (b) the Data Protection Tribunal constituted under that section, in respect of its jurisdiction under section 48 of that Act.'

Access to Health Records (Northern Ireland) Order 1993 (1993/1250 (N.I. 4))

17.   For paragraphs (1) and (2) of Article 4 of the Access to Health Records (Northern Ireland) Order 1993 there is substituted—

'(1)   In this Order ''health professional'' has the same meaning as in the Data Protection Act 1998.'

18.   In Article 5(4) of that Order (cases where fee may be required) in sub-paragraph (a), for 'the maximum prescribed under section 21 of the Data Protection Act 1984' there is substituted 'such maximum as may be prescribed for the purposes of this Article by regulations under section 7 of the Data Protection Act 1998'.

19.   In Article 7 of that Order (cases where right of access may be partially excluded) for the words from the beginning to 'record' in the first place where it occurs there is substituted 'Access shall not be given under Article 5(2) to any part of a health record'.

Section 74(2)   SCHEDULE 16
                                REPEALS AND REVOCATIONS

PART I
REPEALS

Chapter	Short title	Extent of repeal
1984 c. 35.	The Data Protection Act 1984.	The whole Act.
1986 c. 60.	The Financial Services Act 1986.	Section 190.
1987 c. 37.	The Access to Personal Files Act 1987.	The whole Act.
1988 c. 40.	The Education Reform Act 1988.	Section 223.
1988 c. 50.	The Housing Act 1988.	In Schedule 17, paragraph 80.
1990 c. 23.	The Access to Health Records Act 1990.	In section 1(1), the words from 'but does not' to the end.

Chapter	Short title	Extent of repeal
		In section 3, subsection (1)(a) to (e) and, in subsection (6)(a), the words 'in the case of an application made otherwise than by the patient'. Section 4(1) and (2). In section 5(1)(a)(i), the words 'of the patient or' and the word 'other'. In section 10, in sub-section (2) the words 'or orders' and in subsection (3) the words 'or an order under section 2(3) above'. In section 11, the definitions of 'child' and 'parental responsibility'.
1990 c. 37.	The Human Fertilisation and Embryology Act 1990.	Section 33(8).
1990 c. 41.	The Courts and Legal Services Act 1990.	In Schedule 10, paragraph 58.
1992 c. 13.	The Further and Higher Education Act 1992.	Section 86.
1992 c. 37.	The Further and Higher Education (Scotland) Act 1992.	Section 59.
1993 c. 8.	The Judicial Pensions and Retirement Act 1993.	In Schedule 6, paragraph 50.
1993 c. 10.	The Charities Act 1993.	Section 12.
1993 c. 21.	The Osteopaths Act 1993.	Section 38.
1994 c. 17.	The Chiropractors Act 1994.	Section 38.
1994 c. 19.	The Local Government (Wales) Act 1994.	In Schedule 13, paragraph 30.
1994 c. 33.	The Criminal Justice and Public Order Act 1994.	Section 161.
1994 c. 39.	The Local Government (Scotland) Act 1994.	In Schedule 13, paragraph 154.

PART II
REVOCATIONS

Number	Title	Extent of revocation
S.I. 1991/1142.	The Data Protection Registration Fee Order 1991.	The whole Order.
S.I. 1991/1707 (N.I. 14).	The Access to Personal Files and Medical Reports (Northern Ireland) Order 1991.	Part II. The Schedule.
S.I. 1992/3218.	The Banking Co-ordination (Second Council Directive) Regulations 1992.	In Schedule 10, paragraphs 15 and 40.
S.I. 1993/1250 (N.I. 4).	The Access to Health Records (Northern Ireland) Order 1993.	In Article 2(2), the definitions of 'child' and 'parental responsibility'. In Article 3(1), the words from 'but does not include' to the end. In Article 5, paragraph (1)(a) to (d) and, in paragraph (6)(a), the words 'in the case of an application made otherwise than by the patient'. Article 6(1) and (2). In Article 7(1)(a)(i), the words 'of the patient or' and the word 'other'.
S.I. 1994/429 (N.I. 2).	The Health and Personal Social Services (Northern Ireland) Order 1994.	In Schedule 1, the entries relating to the Access to Personal Files and Medical Reports (Northern Ireland) Order 1991.
S.I. 1994/1696.	The Insurance Companies (Third Insurance Directives) Regulations 1994.	In Schedule 8, paragraph 8.
S.I. 1995/755 (N.I. 2).	The Children (Northern Ireland) Order 1995.	In Schedule 9, paragraphs 177 and 191.

Number	Title	Extent of revocation
S.I. 1995/3275.	The Investment Services Regulations 1995.	In Schedule 10, paragraphs 3 and 15.
S.I. 1996/2827.	The Open-Ended Investment Companies (Investment Companies with Variable Capital) Regulations 1996.	In Schedule 8, paragraphs 3 and 26.

Appendix 3
Statutory Instruments

DATA PROTECTION ACT 1998 (COMMENCEMENT) ORDER 2000
(SI 2000 No. 183)

1.   This Order may be cited as the Data Protection Act 1998 (Commencement) Order 2000.

2.—(1)   The provisions of the Data Protection Act 1998, other than those referred to in section 75(2) (provisions coming into force on the day on which that Act was passed) and section 56 (prohibition of requirement as to production of certain records), shall come into force on 1st March 2000.

(2)   The coming into force of section 62 of the Data Protection Act 1998 shall not affect the application of section 159 (correction of wrong information) or section 160 (alternative procedure for business consumers) of the Consumer Credit Act 1974[1] in any case where a credit reference agency has, in respopnse to a request under section 158(1) of that Act, complied with section 158(1) and (2) or dealt with the request under section 160(3) before 1st March 2000.

Mike O'Brien
Parliamentary Under-Secretary of State
Home Office
31 January 2000

Note
[1]1974 c. 39.

THE DATA PROTECTION (CORPORATE FINANCE EXEMPTION) ORDER 2000
(SI 2000 No. 184)

1.   Citation and commencement
(1)   This Order may be cited as the Data Protection (Corporate Finance Exemption) Order 2000 and shall come into force on 1st March 2000.

(2)   In this Order, 'the Act' means the Data Protection Act 1998.

2.   Matters to be taken into account
(1)   The matter set out in paragraph (2) below is hereby specified for the purposes of paragraph 6(1)(b) of Schedule 7 to the Act (matters to be taken into account in determining whether exemption from the subject information provisions is required for the purpose of safeguarding an important economic or financial interest of the United Kingdom).

(2)   The matter referred to in paragraph (1) above is the inevitable prejudicial effect on—

(a)   the orderly functioning of financial markets, or

(b)   the efficient allocation of capital within the economy,

which will result from the application (whether on an occasional or regular basis) of the subject information provisions to data to which paragraph (3) below applies.

(3)   This paragraph applies to any personal data to which the application of the subject information provisions could, in the reasonable belief of the relevant person within the meaning of paragraph 6 of Schedule 7 to the Act, affect—

(a)   any decision of any person whether or not to—

(i)   deal in,

(ii)   subscribe for, or

(iii)   issue, any instrument which is already in existence or is to be, or may be, created; or

(b)   any decision of any person to act or not to act in a way that is likely to have an effect on any business activity including, in particular, an effect on—

(i)   the industrial strategy of any person (whether the strategy is, or is to be, pursued independently or in association with others),

(ii)   the capital structure of an undertaking, or

(iii)   the legal or beneficial ownership of a business or asset.

Mike O'Brien
Parliamentary Under-Secretary of State
Home Office
31 January 2000

THE DATA PROTECTION (CONDITIONS UNDER PARAGRAPH 3 OF PART II OF SCHEDULE 1) ORDER 2000
(SI 2000 No. 185)

1.   Citation and commencement
This Order may be cited as the Data Protection (Conditions under Paragraph 3 of Part II of Schedule 1) Order 2000 and shall come into force on 1st March 2000.

2.   Interpretation
In this Order, 'Part II' means Part II of Schedule 1 to the Data Protection Act 1998.

3.   General provisions
(1)   In cases where the primary condition referred to in paragraph 3(2)(a) of Part II is met, the provisions of articles 4 and 5 apply.

(2)   In cases where the primary condition referred to in paragraph 3(2)(b) of that Part is met by virtue of the fact that the recording of the information to be contained in the data by, or the disclosure of the data by, the data controller is not a function conferred on him by or under any enactment or an obligation imposed on him by order of a court, but is necessary for compliance with any legal obligation to which the data controller is subject, other than an obligation imposed by contract, the provisions of article 4 apply.

4.   Notices in writing
(1)   One of the further conditions prescribed in paragraph (2) must be met if paragraph 2(1)(b) of Part II is to be disapplied in respect of any particular data subject.

(2)   The conditions referred to in paragraph (1) are that—

(a)   no notice in writing has been received at any time by the data controller from an individual, requiring that data controller to provide the information set out in paragraph 2(3) of that Part before the relevant time (as defined in paragraph 2(2) of that Part) or as soon as practicable after that time; or

(b)   where such notice in writing has been received but the data controller does not have sufficient information about the individual in order readily to determine whether he is processing personal data about that individual, the data controller shall send to the individual a written notice stating that he cannot provide the information set out in paragraph 2(3) of that Part because of his inability to make that determination, and explaining the reasons for that inability.

(3)   The requirement in paragraph (2) that notice should be in writing is satisfied where the text of the notice—

    (a)   is transmitted by electronic means,

    (b)   is received in legible form, and

    (c)   is capable of being used for subsequent reference.

5.   Further condition in cases of disproportionate effort

(1)   The further condition prescribed in paragraph (2) must be met for paragraph 2(1)(b) of Part II to be disapplied in respect of any data.

(2)   The condition referred to in paragraph (1) is that the data controller shall record the reasons for his view that the primary condition referred to in article 3(1) is met in respect of the data.

Mike O'Brien
Parliamentary Under-Secretary of State
Home Office
31 January 2000

THE DATA PROTECTION (FUNCTIONS OF DESIGNATED AUTHORITY) ORDER 2000
(SI 2000 No. 186)

1.   Citation and commencement

This Order may be cited as the Data Protection (Functions of Designated Authority) Order 2000 and shall come into force on 1st March 2000.

2.   Interpretation

(1)   In this Order:

'the Act' means the Data Protection Act 1998;

'foreign designated authority' means an authority designated for the purposes of Article 13 of the Convention by a party (other than the United Kingdom) which is bound by that Convention;

'register' means the register maintained under section 19(1) of the Act;

'request' except in Article 3, means a request for assistance under Article 14 of the Convention which states—

    (a)   the name and address of the person making the request;

    (b)   particulars which identify the personal data to which the request relates;

    (c)   the rights under Article 8 of the Convention to which the request relates;

    (d)   the reasons why the request has been made;

and 'requesting person' means a person making such a request.

(2)   In this Order, references to the Commissioner are to the Commissioner as the designated authority in the United Kingdom for the purposes of Article 13 of the Convention.

3.   Co-operation between the Commissioner and foreign designated authorities

(1)   The Commissioner shall, at the request of a foreign designated authority, furnish to that foreign designated authority such information referred to in Article 13(3)(a) of the Convention, and in particular the data protection legislation in force in the United Kingdom at the time the request is made, as is the subject of the request.

(2)   The Commissioner shall, at the request of a foreign designated authority, take appropriate measures in accordance with Article 13(3)(b) of the Convention, for furnishing to that foreign designated authority infortnation relating to the processing of personal data in the United Kingdom.

(3)   The Commissioner may request a foreign designated authority to furnish to him or, as the case may be, to take appropriate measures for furnishing to him, the information referred to in Article 13(3) of the Convention.

4.   Persons resident outside the United Kingdom

(1)   This article applies where a person resident outside the United Kingdom makes a request to the Commissioner under Article 14 of the Convention, including a request forwarded to the Commissioner through the Secretary of State or a foreign designated authority, seeking assistance in exercising any of the rights under Article 8 of the Convention.

(2)   If the request—
   (a)   seeks assistance in exercising the rights under section 7 of the Act; and
   (b)   does not indicate that the data controller has failed, contrary to section 7 of the Act, to comply with the same request on a previous occasion,
the Commissioner shall notify the requesting person of the data controller's address for the receipt of notices from data subjects exercising their rights under that section and of such other information as the Commissioner considers necessary to enable that person to exercise his rights under that section.

(3)   If the request indicates that a data protection principle has been contravened by a data controller the Commissioner shall either—
   (a)   notify the requesting person of the rights of data subjects and the remedies available to them under Part II of the Act together with such particulars as are contained in the data controller's entry in the register as are necessary to enable the requesting person to avail himself of those remedies; or
   (b)   if the Commissioner considers that notification in accordance with sub-paragraph (a) would not assist the requesting person or would, for any other reason, be inappropriate, treat the request as if it were a request for an assessment which falls to be dealt with under section 42 of the Act.

(4)   The Commissioner shall not be required, in response to any request referred to in paragraphs (2) and (3) above, to supply to the requesting person a duly certified copy in writing of the particulars contained in any entry made in the register other than on payment of such fee as is prescribed for the purposes of section 19(7) of the Act.

5.   Persons resident in the United Kingdom

(1)   Where a request for assistance in exercising any of the rights referred to in Article 8 of the Convention in a country or territory (other than the United Kingdom) specified in the request is made by a person resident in the United Kingdom and submitted through the Commissioner under Article 14(2) of the Convention, the Commissioner shall, if he is satisfied that the request contains all necessary particulars referred to in Article 14(3) of the Convention, send it to the foreign designated authority in the specified country or territory.

(2)   If the Commissioner decides that he is not required by paragraph (1) above to render assistance to the requesting person he shall, where practicable, notify that person of the reasons for his decision.

6. Restrictions on use of information

Where the Commissioner receives information from a foreign designated authority as a result of either—

    (a)   a request made by him under article 3(3) above; or

    (b)   a request received by him under articles 3(2) or 4 above,

the Commissioner shall use that information only for the purposes specified in the request.

Mike O'Brien
Parliamentary Under-Secretary of State
Home Office
31 January 2000

THE DATA PROTECTION (FEES UNDER SECTION 19(7)) REGULATIONS 2000
(SI 2000 No. 187)

    1.   These Regulations may be cited as the Data Protection (Fees under section 19(7)) Regulations 2000 and shall come into force on 1st March 2000.

    2.   The fee payable by a member of the public for the supply by the Data Protection Commissioner under section 19(7) of the Data Protection Act 1998 of the duly certified written copy of the particulars contained in any entry made in the register maintained under section 19(1) of that Act shall be £2.

Mike O'Brien
Parliamentary Under-Secretary of State
Home Office
31 January 2000

THE DATA PROTECTION (NOTIFICATION AND NOTIFICATION FEES) REGULATIONS 2000
(SI 2000 No. 188)

1. Citation and commencement

These Regulations may be cited as the Data Protection (Notification and Notification Fees) Regulations 2000 and shall come into force on 1st March 2000.

2. Interpretation

In these Regulations—

    'the Act' means the Data Protection Act 1998;

    'the register' means the register maintained by the Commissioner under section 19 of the Act.

3. Exemptions from notification

Except where the processing is assessable processing for the purposes of section 22 of the Act, section 17(1) of the Act shall not apply in relation to processing—

    (a)   falling within one or more of the descriptions of processing set out in paragraphs 2 to 5 of the Schedule to these Regulations (being processing appearing to the Secretary of State to be unlikely to prejudice the rights and freedoms of data subjects); or

(b)   which does not fall within one or more of those descriptions solely by virtue of the fact that disclosure of the personal data to a person other than those specified in the descriptions—

(i)   is required by or under any enactment, by any rule of law or by the order of a court, or

(ii)   may be made by virtue of an exemption from the non-disclosure provisions (as defined in section 27(3) of the Act).

4.   Form of giving notification

(1)   Subject to regulations 5 and 6 below, the Commissioner shall determine the form in which the registrable particulars (within the meaning of section 16(1) of the Act) and the description mentioned in section 18(2)(b) of the Act are to be specified, including in particular the detail required for the purposes of that description and section 16(1)(c), (d), (e) and (f) of the Act.

(2)   Subject to regulations 5 and 6 below, the Commissioner shall determine the form in which a notification under regulation 12 (including that regulation as modified by regulation 13) is to be specified.

5.   Notification in respect of partnerships

(1)   In any case in which two or more persons carrying on a business in partnership are the data controllers in respect of any personal data for the purposes of that business, a notification under section 18 of the Act or under regulation 12 below may be given in respect of those persons in the name of the firm.

(2)   Where a notification is given in the name of a firm under paragraph (1) above—

(a)   the name to be specified for the purposes of section 16(1)(a) of the Act is the name of the firm, and

(b)   the address to be specified for the purposes of section 16(1)(a) of the Act is the address of the firm's principal place of business.

6.   Notification in respect of the governing body of, and head teacher at, any school

(1)   In any case in which a governing body of, and a head teacher at, any school are, in those capacities, the data controllers in respect of any personal data, a notification under section 18 of the Act or under regulation 12 below may be given in respect of that governing body and head teacher in the name of the school.

(2)   Where a notification is given in the name of a school under paragraph (1) above, the name and address to be specified for the purposes of section 16(1)(a) of the Act are those of the school.

(3)   In this regulation, 'head teacher' includes in Northern Ireland the principal of a school.

7.   Fees to accompany notification under section 18 of the Act

(1)   This regulation applies to any notification under section 18 of the Act, including a notification which, by virtue of regulation 5 or 6 above, is given in respect of more than one data controller.

(2)   A notification to which this regulation applies must be accompanied by a fee of £35.

8.   Date of entry in the register

(1)   The time from which an entry in respect of a data controller who has given a notification under section 18 of the Act in accordance with these Regulations is to be treated for the purposes of section 17 of the Act as having been made in the register shall be determined as follows.

(2)   In the case of a data controller who has given the notification by sending it by registered post or the recorded delivery service, that time is the day after the day on which it is received for dispatch by the Post Office.

(3)   In the case of a data controller who has given a notification by some other means, that time is the day on which it is received by the Commissioner.

9.   Acknowledgment of receipt of notification in the case of assessable processing

(1)   In any case in which the Commissioner considers under section 22(2)(a) of the Act that any of the processing to which a notification relates is assessable processing within the meaning of that section he shall, within 10 days of receipt of the notification, give a written notice to the data controller who has given the notification, acknowledging its receipt.

(2)   A notice under paragraph (1) above shall indicate—

(a)   the date on which the Commissioner received the notification, and

(b)   the processing which the Commissioner considers to be assessable processing.

10.   Confirmation of register entries

(1)   The Commissioner shall, as soon as practicable and in any event within a period of 28 days after making an entry in the register under section 19(1)(b) of the Act or amending an entry in the register under section 20(4) of the Act, give the data controller to whom the register entry relates notice confirming the register entry.

(2)   A notice under paragraph (1) above shall include a statement of—

(a)   the date on which—

(i)   in the case of an entry made under section 19(1)(b) of the Act, the entry is treated as having been included by virtue of regulation 8 above, or

(ii)   in the case of an entry made under section 20(4) of the Act, the notification was received by the Commissioner;

(b)   the particulars entered in the register, or the amendment made, in pursuance of the notification; and

(c)   in the case of a notification under section 18 of the Act, the date by which the fee payable under regulation 14 below must be paid in order for the entry to be retained in the register as provided by section 19(4) of the Act.

11.   Additional information in register entries

In addition to the matters mentioned in section 19(2)(a) of the Act, the Commissioner may include in a register entry—

(a)   a registration number issued by the Commissioner in respect of that entry;

(b)   the date on which the entry is treated, by virtue of regulation 8 above, as having been included in pursuance of a notification under section 18 of the Act;

(c)   the date on which the entry falls or may fall to be removed by virtue of regulation 14 or 15 below; and (d)　information additional to the registrable particulars for the purpose of assisting persons consulting the register to communicate with any data controller to whom the entry relates concerning matters relating to the processing of personal data.

12.　Duty to notify changes to matters previously notified

(1)　Subject to regulation 13 below, every person in respect of whom an entry is for the time being included in the register is under a duty to give the Commissioner a notification specifying any respect in which—

(a)　that entry becomes inaccurate or incomplete as a statement of his current registrable particulars, or

(b)　the general description of measures notified under section 18(2)(b) of the Act or, as the case may be, that description as amended in pursuance of a notification under this regulation, becomes inaccurate or incomplete,

and setting out the changes which need to be made to that entry or general description in order to make it accurate and complete.

(2)　Such a notification must be given as soon as practicable and in any event within a period of 28 days from the date on which the entry or, as the case may be, the general description, becomes inaccurate or incomplete.

(3)　References in this regulation to an entry being included in the register include any entry being treated under regulation 8 above as being so included.

13.　Duty to notify changes — transitional modifications

(1)　This regulation applies to persons in respect of whom an entry in the register has been made under paragraph 2(6) of Schedule 14 to the Act.

(2)　In the case of a person to whom this regulation applies, the duty imposed by regulation 12 above shall be modified so as to have effect as follows.

(3)　Every person in respect of whom an entry is for the time being included in the register is under a duty to give the Commissioner a notification specifying—

(a)　his name and address, in any case in which a change to his name or address results in the entry in respect of him no longer including his current name and address;

(b)　to the extent to which the entry relates to eligible data—

(i)　a description of any eligible data being or to be processed by him or on his behalf, in any case in which such processing is of personal data of a description not included in that entry;

(ii)　a description of the category or categories of data subject to which eligible data relate, in any case in which such category or categories are of a description not included in that entry;

(iii)　a description of the purpose or purposes for which eligible data are being or are to be processed in any case in which such processing is for a purpose or purposes of a description not included in that entry;

(iv)　a description of the source or sources from which he intends or may wish to obtain eligible data, in any case in which such obtaining is from a source of a description not included in that entry;

(v)　a description of any recipient or recipients to whom he intends or may wish to disclose eligible data, in any case in which such disclosure is to a recipient or recipients of a description not included in that entry; and

(vi)　the names, or a description of, any countries or territories outside the United Kingdom to which he directly or indirectly transfers, or intends or may wish directly or indirectly to transfer, eligible data, in any case in which such transfer would be to a country or territory not named or described in that entry; and

(c) to the extent to which sub-paragraph (b) above does not apply, any respect in which the entry is or becomes inaccurate or incomplete as—

(i) a statement of his current registrable particulars to the extent mentioned in section 16(1)(c), (d) and (e) of the Act;

(ii) a description of the source or sources from which he currently intends or may wish to obtain personal data; and

(iii) the names or a description of any countries or territories outside the United Kingdom to which he currently intends or may wish directly or indirectly to transfer personal data;

and setting out the changes which need to be made to that entry in order to make it accurate and complete in those respects.

(4) Such a notification must be given as soon as practicable and in any event within a period of 28 days from the date on which—

(a) in the case of a notification under paragraph (3)(a) above, the entry no longer includes the current name and address;

(b) in the case of a notification under paragraph (3)(b) above, the specified practice or intentions are in the particulars there mentioned of a description not included in the entry; and

(c) in the case of a notification under paragraph (3)(c) above, the entry becomes inaccurate or incomplete in the particulars there mentioned.

(5) For the purposes of this regulation, personal data are 'eligible data' at any time if, and to the extent that, they are at that time subject to processing which was already under way immediately before 24th October 1998.

14. Retention of register entries

(1) This regulation applies to any entry in respect of a person which is for the time being included, or by virtue of regulation 8 is treated as being included, in the register, other than an entry to which regulation 15 below applies.

(2) In relation to an entry to which this regulation applies, the fee referred to in section 19(4) of the Act is £35.

15. Retention of register entries — transitional provisions

(1) This regulation applies to any entry in respect of a person which is for the time being included in the register under paragraph 2(6) of Schedule 14 to the Act or, as the case may be, such an entry as amended in pursuance of regulation 12 (including that regulation as modified by regulation 13).

(2) Section 19(4) and (5) of the Act applies to entries to which this regulation applies subject to the modifications in paragraph (3) below.

(3) Section 19(4) and (5) of the Act shall be modified so as to have effect as follows—

'(4) No entry shall be retained in the register after—

(a) the end of the registration period, or

(b) 24th October 2001, or

(c) the date on which the data controller gives a notification under section 18 of the Act,

whichever occurs first.

(5) In subsection (4) ''the registration period'' has the same meaning as in paragraph 2(2) of Schedule 14.'

Mike O'Brien
Parliamentary Under-Secretary of State
Home Office
31 January 2000

Regulation 3   SCHEDULE
PROCESSING TO WHICH SECTION 17(1) DOES NOT APPLY

1. Interpretation

In this Schedule—
    'exempt purposes' in paragraphs 2 to 4 shall mean the purposes specified in sub-paragraph (a) of those paragraphs and in paragraph 5 shall mean the purposes specified in sub-paragraph (b) of that paragraph;
    'staff' includes employees or office holders, workers within the meaning given in section 296 of the Trade Union and Labour Relations (Consolidation) Act 1992,[1] persons working under any contract for services, and volunteers.

Note
[1] 1992 c. 52.

2. Staff administration exemption

The processing—
    (a) is for the purposes of appointments or removals, pay, discipline, superannuation, work management or other personnel matters in relation to the staff of the data controller;
    (b) is of personal data in respect of which the data subject is—
        (i) a past, existing or prospective member of staff of the data controller; or
        (ii) any person the processing of whose personal data is necessary for the exempt purposes;
    (c) is of personal data consisting of the name, address and other identifiers of the data subject or information as to—
        (i) qualifications, work experience or pay; or
        (ii) other matters the processing of which is necessary for the exempt purposes;
    (d) does not involve disclosure of the personal data to any third party other than—
        (i) with the consent of the data subject; or
        (ii) where it is necessary to make such disclosure for the exempt purposes; and
    (e) does not involve keeping the personal data after the relationship between the data controller and staff member ends, unless and for so long as it is necessary to do so for the exempt purposes.

3. Advertising, marketing and public relations exemption

The processing—
    (a) is for the purposes of advertising or marketing the data controller's business, activity, goods or services and promoting public relations in connection with that business or activity, or those goods or services;

(b)   is of personal data in respect of which the data subject is—

(i)   a past, existing or prospective customer or supplier; or

(ii)   any person the processing of whose personal data is necessary for the exempt purposes;

(c)   is of personal data consisting of the name, address and other identifiers of the data subject or information as to other matters the processing of which is necessary for the exempt purposes;

(d)   does not involve disclosure of the personal data to any third party other than—

(i)   with the consent of the data subject; or

(ii)   where it is necessary to make such disclosure for the exempt purposes; and

(e)   does not involve keeping the personal data after the relationship between the data controller and customer or supplier ends, unless and for so long as it is necessary to do so for the exempt purposes.

4.   Accounts and records exemption

(1)   The processing—

(a)   is for the purposes of keeping accounts relating to any business or other activity carried on by the data controller, or deciding whether to accept any person as a customer or supplier, or keeping records of purchases, sales or other transactions for the purpose of ensuring that the requisite payments and deliveries are made or services provided by or to the data controller in respect of those transactions, or for the purpose of making financial or management forecasts to assist him in the conduct of any such business or activity;

(b)   is of personal data in respect of which the data subject is—

(i)   a past, existing or prospective customer or supplier; or

(ii)   any person the processing of whose personal data is necessary for the exempt purposes;

(c)   is of personal data consisting of the name, address and other identifiers of the data subject or information as to—

(i)   financial standing; or

(ii)   other matters the processing of which is necessary for the exempt purposes;

(d)   does not involve disclosure of the personal data to any third party other than—

(i)   with the consent of the data subject; or

(ii)   where it is necessary to make such disclosure for the exempt purposes; and

(e)   does not involve keeping the personal data after the relationship between the data controller and customer or supplier ends, unless and for so long as it is necessary to do so for the exempt purposes.

(2)   Sub-paragraph (1)(c) shall not be taken as including personal data processed by or obtained from a credit reference agency.

5.   Non profit-making organisations exemptions

The processing—

(a)   is carried out by a data controller which is a body or association which is not established or conducted for profit;

(b)   is for the purposes of establishing or maintaining membership of or support for the body or association, or providing or administering activities for individuals who are either members of the body or association or have regular contact with it;

(c)   is of personal data in respect of which the data subject is—

(i)   a past, existing or prospective member of the body or organisation;

(ii)   any person who has regular contact with the body or organisation in connection with the exempt purposes; or

(iii)   any person the processing of whose personal data is necessary for the exempt purposes;

(d)   is of personal data consisting of the name, address and other identifiers of the data subject or information as to—

(i)   eligibility for membership of the body or association; or

(ii)   other matters the processing of which is necessary for the exempt purposes;

(e)   does not involve disclosure of the personal data to any third party other than—

(i)   with the consent of the data subject; or

(ii)   where it is necessary to make such disclosure for the exempt purposes; and

(f)   does not involve keeping the personal data after the relationship between the data controller and data subject ends, unless and for so long as it is necessary to do so for the exempt purposes.

THE DATA PROTECTION TRIBUNAL (ENFORCEMENT APPEALS) RULES 2000
(SI 2000 No. 189)

1.   Citation and commencement

These Rules may be cited as the Data Protection Tribunal (Enforcement Appeals) Rules 2000 and shall come into force on 1st March 2000.

2.   Application and interpretation

(1)   These Rules apply to appeals under section 48 of the Act, and the provisions of these Rules are to be construed accordingly.

(2)   In these Rules, unless the context otherwise requires—

'the Act' means the Data Protection Act 1998;

'appeal' means an appeal under section 48 of the Act;

'appellant' means a person who brings or intends to bring an appeal under section 48 of the Act;

'chairman' means the chairman of the Tribunal, and includes a deputy chairman of the Tribunal presiding or sitting alone;

'costs'—

(a)   except in Scotland, includes fees, charges, disbursements, expenses and remuneration;

(b)   in Scotland means expenses, and includes fees, charges, disbursements and remuneration;

'disputed decision' means—

(a)   in relation to an appeal under section 48 of the Act other than an appeal under section 48(3)(b), the decision of the Commissioner, and

(b)   in relation to an appeal under section 48(3)(b) of the Act the effect of a decision of the Commissioner,

against which the appellant appeals or intends to appeal to the Tribunal;

'party' has the meaning given in paragraph (3) below; and

'proper officer' in relation to a rule means an officer or member of staff provided to the Tribunal under paragraph 14 of Schedule 5 to the Act and appointed by the chairman to perform the duties of a proper officer under that rule.

(3)   In these Rules, 'party' means the appellant or the Commissioner, and, except where the context otherwise requires, references in these Rules to a party (including references in rule 12 below) include a person appointed under rule 16 below to represent his interests.

(4)   In relation to proceedings before the Tribunal in Scotland, for the words 'on the trial of an action' in rules 11(4), 12(8) and 23(2) below there is substituted 'in a proof'.

3.   Method of appealing

(1)   An appeal must be brought by a written notice of appeal served on the Tribunal.

(2)   The notice of appeal shall—

(a)   identify the disputed decision and the date on which the notice relating to such decision was served on or given to the appellant; and

(b)   state—

(i)   the name and address of the appellant;

(ii)   the grounds of the appeal;

(iii)   whether the appellant considers that he is likely to wish a hearing to be held or not;

(iv)   where applicable, the special circumstances which the appellant considers justify the Tribunal's accepting jurisdiction under rule 4(2) below; and

(v)   an address for service of notices and other documents on the appellant.

(3)   Where an appeal is brought under section 48(1) of the Act in relation to an information notice, the notice of appeal shall also contain a statement of any representations the appellant wishes to make as to why it might be necessary in the interests of justice for the appeal to be heard and determined otherwise than by the chairman sitting alone as provided by rule 18(2) below.

(4)   A notice of appeal may include a request for an early hearing of the appeal and the reasons for that request.

4.   Time limit for appealing

(1)   Subject to paragraph (2) below, a notice of appeal must be served on the Tribunal within 28 days of the date on which the notice relating to the disputed decision was served on or given to the appellant.

(2)   The Tribunal may accept a notice of appeal served after the expiry of the period permitted by paragraph (1) above if it is of the opinion that, by reason of special circumstances, it is just and right to do so.

(3)   A notice of appeal shall if sent by post in accordance with rule 27(1) below be treated as having been served on the date on which it is received for dispatch by the Post Office.

5. Acknowledgement of notice of appeal and notification to the Commissioner

(1)   Upon receipt of a notice of appeal, the proper officer shall send—

(a)   an acknowledgement of the service of a notice of appeal to the appellant, and

(b)   subject to paragraph (3) below, a copy of the notice of appeal to the Commissioner.

(2)   An acknowledgement of service under paragraph (1)(a) above shall be accompanied by a statement of the Tribunal's powers to award costs against the appellant under rule 25 below.

(3)   Paragraph (1)(b) above does not apply to a notice of appeal relating to an appeal under section 48(3) of the Act, but in such a case—

(a)   the proper officer shall send a copy of the notice of appeal to the Commissioner if the Tribunal is of the opinion that the interests of justice require the Commissioner to assist it by giving evidence or being heard on any matter relating to the appeal, and

(b)   where a copy is sent to the Commissioner under subparagraph (a) above, the jurisdiction referred to in paragraph 6(2) of Schedule 6 to the Act shall not be exercised ex parte.

6. Reply by Commissioner

(1)   The Commissioner shall take the steps specified in paragraph (2) below—

(a)   where he receives a copy of a notice of appeal under rule 5(1)(b) above, within 21 days of the date of that receipt, and

(b)   where he receives a copy of a notice of appeal under rule 5(3)(a) above, within such time, not exceeding 21 days from the date of that receipt, as the Tribunal may allow.

(2)   The steps are that the Commissioner must—

(a)   send to the Tribunal a copy of the notice relating to the disputed decision, and

(b)   send to the Tribunal and the appellant a written reply acknowledging service upon him of the notice of appeal, and stating—

(i)   whether or not he intends to oppose the appeal and, if so,

(ii)   the grounds upon which he relies in opposing the appeal.

(3)   Before the expiry of the period referred to in paragraph (1) above which is applicable to the case, the Commissioner may apply to the Tribunal for an extension of that period, showing cause why, by reason of special circumstances, it would be just and right to do so, and the Tribunal may grant such extension as it considers appropriate.

(4)   Where the appellant's notice of appeal has stated that he is not likely to wish a hearing to be held, the Commissioner shall in his reply inform the Tribunal and the appellant whether he considers that a hearing is likely to be desirable.

(5)   Where an appeal is brought under section 48(1) of the Act in relation to an information notice, the Commissioner may include in his reply a statement of representations as to why it might be necessary in the interests of justice for the appeal to be heard and determined otherwise than by the chairman sitting alone as provided by rule 18(2) below.

(6)   A reply under this rule may include a request for an early hearing of the appeal and the reasons for that request.

7. Application for striking out

(1) Subject to paragraph (3) below, where the Commissioner is of the opinion that an appeal does not lie to, or cannot be entertained by, the Tribunal, or that the notice of appeal discloses no reasonable grounds of appeal, he may include in his reply under rule 6(2) above a notice to that effect stating the grounds for such contention and applying for the appeal to be struck out.

(2) An application under this rule may be heard as a preliminary issue or at the beginning of the hearing of the substantive appeal.

(3) This rule does not apply in the case of an appeal under section 48(3) of the Act.

8. Amendment and supplementary grounds

(1) With the leave of the Tribunal, the appellant may amend his notice of appeal or deliver supplementary grounds of appeal.

(2) Paragraphs (1) and (3) of rule 5 above apply to an amended notice of appeal and to supplementary grounds of appeal provided under paragraph (1) above as they do to a notice of appeal.

(3) Upon receipt of a copy of an amended notice of appeal or amended grounds of appeal under rule 5(1)(b) or (3)(a) above, the Commissioner may amend his reply to the notice of appeal, and must send the amended reply to the Tribunal and the appellant—

(a) where he receives a copy of a notice of appeal under rule 5(1)(b) above, within 21 days of the date of that receipt, and

(b) where he receives a copy of a notice of appeal under rule 5(3)(a) above, within such time, not exceeding 21 days from the date of that receipt, as the Tribunal may allow.

(4) Rule 6(3) above applies to the periods referred to in paragraph (3) above.

(5) Without prejudice to paragraph (3) above, the Commissioner may, with the leave of the Tribunal, amend his reply to the notice of appeal, and must send the amended reply to the Tribunal and the appellant.

9. Withdrawal of appeal

(1) The appellant may at any time withdraw his appeal by sending to the Tribunal a notice of withdrawal signed by him or on his behalf, and the proper officer shall send a copy of that notice to the Commissioner.

(2) A notice of withdrawal shall if sent by post in accordance with rule 27(1) below have effect on the date on which it is received for dispatch by the Post Office.

(3) Where an appeal is withdrawn under this rule a fresh appeal may not be brought by the appellant in relation to the same disputed decision except with the leave of the Tribunal.

10. Consolidation of appeals

(1) Subject to paragraph (2) below, where in the case of two or more appeals to which these Rules apply it appears to the Tribunal—

(a) that some common question of law or fact arises in both or all of them, or

(b) that for some other reason it is desirable to proceed with the appeals under this rule,

the Tribunal may order that the appeals be consolidated or heard together.

(2) The Tribunal shall not make an order under this rule without giving the parties an opportunity to show cause why such an order should not be made.

11. Directions

(1)   Subject to paragraphs (4) and (5) below, the Tribunal may at any time of its own motion or on the application of any party give such directions as it thinks proper to enable the parties to prepare for the hearing of the appeal or to assist the Tribunal to determine the issues.

(2)   Such directions may in particular—

(a)   provide for a particular matter to be dealt with as a preliminary issue and for a pre-hearing review to be held;

(b)   provide for—

(i)   the exchange between the parties of lists of documents held by them which are relevant to the appeal,

(ii)   the inspection by the parties of the documents so listed,

(iii)   the exchange between the parties of statements of evidence, and

(iv)   the provision by the parties to the Tribunal of statements or lists of agreed matters;

(c)   require any party to send to the Tribunal and to the other party—

(i)   statements of facts and statements of the evidence which will be adduced, including such statements provided in a modified or edited form;

(ii)   a skeleton argument which summarises the submissions which will be made and cites the authorities which will be relied upon, identifying any particular passages to be relied upon;

(iii)   a chronology of events;

(iv)   any other particulars or supplementary statements which may reasonably be required for the determination of the appeal;

(v)   any document or other material which the Tribunal may require and which it is in the power of that party to deliver.,

(vi)   an estimate of the time which will be needed for any hearing; and

(vii)   a list of the witnesses the party intends to call to give evidence at any hearing;

(d)   limit the length of oral submissions and the time allowed for the examination and cross-examination of witnesses; and

(e)   limit the number of expert witnesses to be heard on either side.

(3)   The Tribunal may, subject to any specific provisions of these Rules, specify time limits for steps to be taken in the proceedings and may extend any time limit.

(4)   Nothing in this rule may require the production of any document or other material which the party could not be compelled to produce on the trial of an action in a court of law in that part of the United Kingdom where the appeal is to be determined.

(5)   It shall be a condition of the supply of any information or material provided under this rule that any recipient of that information or material may use it only for the purposes of the appeal.

(6)   The power to give directions may be exercised in the absence of the parties.

(7)   Notice of any directions given under this rule shall be served on the parties, and the Tribunal may, on the application of any party, set aside or vary such directions.

12. Power to require entry of premises for testing of equipment or material

(1)   Subject to paragraph (8) below, the Tribunal may, for the purpose of determining an appeal, make an order requiring the occupier of any premises ('the

occupier') to permit the Tribunal to enter those premises at a specified time and inspect, examine, operate or test any equipment on those premises used or intended to be used in connection with the processing of personal data, and to inspect, examine or test any documents or other material on those premises connected with the processing of personal data.

(2)   An order under paragraph (1) above shall also require the occupier to permit the Tribunal to be accompanied by—

(a)   the parties, and

(b)   such number of the officers or members of staff provided to the Tribunal under paragraph 14 of Schedule 5 to the Act as it considers necessary.

(3)   The Tribunal shall serve a copy of the order on the occupier and the parties.

(4)   The time specified in the order shall not be earlier than 7 days after the date of service of the copy.

(5)   The Tribunal may upon the application of the occupier set the order aside.

(6)   Subject to paragraph (4) above, the Tribunal may upon the application of any person mentioned in paragraph (3) above alter the time specified in the order without being obliged to serve further copies under that paragraph, but shall notify the other persons so mentioned of the revised time.

(7)   This rule also applies where the occupier is a party to the appeal.

(8)   Documents or other material which the appellant could not be compelled to produce on the trial of an action in that part of the United Kingdom where the appeal is to be determined shall be immune from inspection, examination or testing under this rule.

13.   Power to determine without a hearing

(1)   Where either—

(a)   the parties so agree in writing, or

(b)   it appears to the Tribunal that the issues raised on the appeal have been determined on a previous appeal brought by the appellant on the basis of facts which did not materially differ from those to which the appeal relates and the Tribunal has given the parties an opportunity of making representations to the effect that the appeal ought not to be determined without a hearing,

the Tribunal may determine an appeal, or any particular issue, without a hearing.

(2)   Before determining any matter under this rule, the Tribunal may if it thinks fit direct any party to provide in writing further information about any matter relevant to the appeal within such time as the Tribunal may allow.

14.   Time and place of hearings

(1)   Except where rule 13 above applies, as soon as practicable after notice of appeal has been given, and with due regard to the convenience of the parties and any request made under rule 3(4) or 6(6) above, the Tribunal shall appoint a time and place for a hearing of the appeal.

(2)   The proper officer shall send to each party a notice informing him of the time and place of any hearing.

(3)   The reference to a 'party' in paragraph (2) above does not include the Commissioner in the case of an appeal under section 48(3) of the Act other than a case to which rule 5(3)(a) above applies.

(4)   The time notified under paragraph (1) above shall not be earlier than 14 days after the date on which the notice is sent unless—

(a)   the parties agree otherwise, or

(b)   the appellant agrees otherwise, and the hearing relates to an appeal under section 48(3) of the Act.

(5)   A notice to a party under this rule shall inform him of the effect of rule 17 below.

(6)   The Tribunal may—

(a)   postpone the time appointed for any hearing;

(b)   adjourn a hearing to such time as the Tribunal may determine; or

(c)   alter the place appointed for any hearing;

and, if it exercises any of the above powers, it shall notify each party previously notified of that hearing under this rule, and any person summoned under rule 15 below to attend as a witness at that hearing, of the revised arrangements.

15.   Summoning of witnesses

(1)   Subject to paragraph (2) below, the Tribunal may by summons require any person in the United Kingdom to attend as a witness at a hearing of an appeal at such time and place as may be specified in the summons and, subject to rule 23(2) and (3) below, at the hearing to answer any questions or produce any documents in his custody or under his control which relate to any matter in question in the appeal.

(2)   No person shall be required to attend in obedience to a summons under paragraph (1) above unless he has been given at least 7 days' notice of the hearing or, if less than 7 days, he has informed the Tribunal that he accepts such notice as he has been given.

(3)   The Tribunal may upon the application of a person summoned under this rule set the summons aside.

(4)   A person who has attended a hearing as a witness in obedience to a summons shall be entitled to such sum as the Tribunal considers reasonable in respect of his attendance at, and his travelling to and from, the hearing; and where the summons was issued at the request of a party such sum shall be paid or tendered to him by that party.

(5)   In relation to proceedings before the Tribunal in Scotland, in this rule 'summons' means citation and the provisions of this rule are to be construed accordingly.

16.   Representation at a hearing

(1)   At any hearing by the Tribunal a party may conduct his case himself or may appear and be represented by any person whom he may appoint for the purpose.

(2)   In this rule, references to a 'party' do not include the Commissioner in the case of an appeal under section 48(3) of the Act other than a case to which rule 5(3)(a) above applies.

17.   Default of appearance at hearing

If, without furnishing the Tribunal with sufficient reason for his absence, a party fails to appear at a hearing, having been duly notified of the hearing, the Tribunal may, if that party is the appellant, dismiss the appeal or, in any case, hear and determine the appeal, or any particular issue, in the party's absence and may make such order as to costs as it thinks fit.

18. Hearings and determinations in the case of appeals against an information notice

(1)   This rule applies to any appeal under section 48(1) of the Act in respect of an information notice.

(2)   Subject to paragraph (3) below, any hearing of or relating to an appeal to which this rule applies shall be by the chairman sitting alone, and any appeal or issue relating to an appeal to which this rule applies shall be determined by the chairman sitting alone.

(3)   Paragraph (2) above does not apply where it appears to the chairman that a hearing or determination by the Tribunal constituted in accordance with paragraph 4 of Schedule 6 to the Act is necessary in the interests of justice, taking into account any representations made under rule 3(3) or 6(5) above.

19. Hearings in public or in private

(1)   All hearings by the Tribunal (including preliminary hearings) shall be in public unless, having regard to the desirability of safeguarding—

(a)   the privacy of data subjects, or

(b)   commercially sensitive information,

the Tribunal directs that the hearing or any part of the hearing shall take place in private.

(2)   Without prejudice to paragraph (3) below, the following persons, in addition to the parties, may attend a hearing notwithstanding that it is in private—

(a)   the chairman or any deputy chairman or member of the Tribunal in his capacity as such, notwithstanding that they do not constitute the Tribunal for the purpose of the hearing; and

(b)   any other person with the leave of the Tribunal and the consent of the parties present.

(3)   Whether or not a hearing is held in public, a member of the Council on Tribunals or the Scottish Committee of the Council on Tribunals in his capacity as such may attend the hearing, and may remain present during the deliberations of the Tribunal but must not take part in the deliberations.

20. Conduct of proceedings at hearing

(1)   Subject to rule 17 above, the Tribunal shall at the hearing of an appeal give to each party an opportunity—

(a)   to address the Tribunal and to amplify orally written statements previously furnished under these Rules, to give evidence and to call witnesses, and to put questions to any person giving evidence before the Tribunal, and

(b)   to make representations on the evidence (if any) and on the subject matter of the appeal generally but, where evidence is taken, such opportunity shall not be given before the completion of the taking of evidence.

(2)   Subject to paragraph (3) below, in this rule, references to a 'party' do not include the Commissioner in the case of an appeal under section 48(3) of the Act.

(3)   In a case to which rule 5(3)(a) above applies, the Tribunal shall give the Commissioner the opportunity referred to in paragraph (1) above to the extent that it is of the opinion that the interests of justice require the Commissioner to assist it by giving evidence or being heard on any matter relating to the appeal.

(4)   Except as provided by these Rules, the Tribunal shall conduct the proceedings in such manner as it considers appropriate in the circumstances for discharging its

functions and shall so far as appears to it appropriate seek to avoid formality in its proceedings.

21. Preliminary and incidental matters
As regards matters preliminary or incidental to an appeal the chairman may act for the Tribunal under rules 4(2), 6(1) and (3), 8 to 12, 14(1) and (6)(a) and (c) and 15.

22. Burden of proof
In any proceedings before the Tribunal relating to an appeal to which these Rules apply, other than an appeal under section 48(3) of the Act, it shall be for the Commissioner to satisfy the Tribunal that the disputed decision should be upheld.

23. Evidence
(1) The Tribunal may receive in evidence any document or information notwithstanding that such document or information would be inadmissible in a court of law.

(2) No person shall be compelled to give any evidence or produce any document which he could not be compelled to give or produce on the trial of an action in a court of law in that part of the United Kingdom where the appeal is to be determined.

(3) The Tribunal may require oral evidence of a witness (including a party) to be given on oath or affirmation and for that purpose the chairman or the proper officer shall have power to administer oaths or take affirmations.

24. Determination of appeal
(1) As soon as practicable after the Tribunal has determined an appeal, the chairman shall certify in writing that determination and sign and date the certificate.

(2) The certificate shall include—
  (a) any material finding of fact, and
  (b) the reasons for the decision.

(3) The proper officer shall send a copy of the certificate to the parties.

(4) The Tribunal shall make arrangements for the publication of its determination but in doing so shall have regard to the desirability of safeguarding the privacy of data subjects and commercially sensitive information, and for that purpose may make any necessary amendments to the text of the certificate.

25. Costs
(1) In any appeal before the Tribunal, including one withdrawn under rule 9 above, the Tribunal may make an order awarding costs—
  (a) against the appellant and in favour of the Commissioner where it considers that the appeal was manifestly unreasonable;
  (b) against the Commissioner and in favour of the appellant where it considers that the disputed decision was manifestly unreasonable;
  (c) where it considers that a party has been responsible for frivolous, vexatious, improper or unreasonable action, or for any failure to comply with a direction or any delay which with diligence could have been avoided, against that party and in favour of the other.

(2) The Tribunal shall not make an order under paragraph (1) above awarding costs against a party without first giving that party an opportunity of making representations against the making of the order.

(3) An order under paragraph (1) above may be to the party or parties in question to pay to the other party or parties either a specified sum in respect of the costs incurred by that other party or parties in connection with the proceedings or the whole or part of such costs as taxed (if not otherwise agreed).

(4) Any costs required by an order under this rule to be taxed may be taxed in the county court according to such of the scales prescribed by the county court rules for proceedings in the county court as shall be directed by the order.

(5) In relation to proceedings before the Tribunal in Scotland, for the purposes of the application of paragraph (4) above, for the reference to the county court and the county court rules there shall be substituted references to the sheriff court and the sheriff court rules and for the reference to proceedings there shall be substituted a reference to civil proceedings.

26. Irregularities

(1) Any irregularity resulting from failure to comply with any provision of these Rules or of any direction of the Tribunal before the Tribunal has reached its decision shall not of itself render the proceedings void, but the Tribunal may, and shall if it considers that any person may have been prejudiced by that irregularity, give such directions or take such steps as it thinks fit before reaching its decision to cure or waive the irregularity, whether by amendment of any document, the giving of notice or otherwise.

(2) Clerical mistakes in any document recording or certifying a direction, decision or determination of the Tribunal or chairman, or errors arising in such a document from an accidental slip or omission, may at any time be corrected by the chairman, by certificate signed by him.

27. Notices etc.

(1) Any notice or other document required or authorised by these Rules to be served on or sent to any person or authority may be sent by post in a registered letter or by the recorded delivery service—

    (a)   in the case of the Tribunal, to the proper officer of the Tribunal;

    (b)   in the case of the Commissioner, to him at his office;

    (c)   in the case of an appellant, to him at his address for service under these Rules; and

    (d)   in the case of an occupier within the provisions of rule 12 above, to him at the premises in question.

(2) An appellant may at any time by notice to the Tribunal change his address for service under these Rules.

Mike O'Brien
Parliamentary Under-Secretary of State
Home Office
31 January 2000

THE DATA PROTECTION (INTERNATIONAL CO-OPERATION) ORDER 2000
(SI 2000 No. 190)

1. Citation and commencement

This Order may be cited as the Data Protection (International Co-operation) Order 2000 and shall come into force on 1st March 2000.

2. Interpretation

In this Order:

'the Act' means the Data Protection Act 1998;

'supervisory authority' means a supervisory authority in an EEA State other than the United Kingdom for the purposes of the Data Protection Directive;

'transfer' means a transfer of personal data to a country or territory outside the European Economic Area.

3. Information relating to adequacy

(1) Subject to paragraph (2), this article applies in any case where the Commissioner is satisfied that any transfer or proposed transfer by a data controller has involved or would involve a contravention of the eighth principle.

(2) In cases where an enforcement notice has been served in respect of a contravention of the eighth principle, this article shall not apply unless—

(a) the period within which an appeal can be brought under section 48

(c) of the Act has expired without an appeal being brought; or

(b) where an appeal has been brought under section 48(1), either—

(i) the decision of the Tribunal is to the effect that there has been a breach of that eighth principle, or

(ii) where any decision of the Tribunal is to the effect that there has not been a breach of that eighth principle, the Commissioner has appealed successfully against that finding.

(3) In cases to which this article applies, the Commissioner shall inform the European Commission and the supervisory authorities of the reasons why he is satisfied that any transfer or proposed transfer has involved or would involve a contravention of the eighth principle.

(4) In this article, 'the eighth principle' means the eighth principle set out in paragraph 8 of Part I of Schedule 1 to the Act, having regard to paragraphs 13, 14 and 15 of Part II of that Schedule.

4. Objections to authorisations

(1) This article applies where—

(a) a transfer has been authorised by another Member State in purported compliance with Article 26(2) of the Data Protection Directive, and

(b) the Commissioner is satisfied that such authorisation is not in compliance with that Article.

(2) The Commissioner may inform the European Commission of the particulars of the authorisation together with the reasons for his view that the authorisation is not in compliance with Article 26(2) of the Directive.

5. Requests from supervisory authorities in relation to certain data controllers

(1) This article applies in any case where a data controller is processing data in the United Kingdom—

(a) in circumstances other than those described in section 5(1) of the Act, and

(b) within the scope of the functions of a supervisory authority in another EEA State.

(2) The Commissioner may, at the request of a supervisory authority referred to in paragraph (1)(b), exercise his functions under Part V of the Act in relation to the processing referred to in paragraph (1) as if the data controller were processing those data in the circumstances described in section 5(1)(a) of the Act.

(3)   Where the Commissioner has received a request from a supervisory authority under paragraph (2), he shall—

(a)   in any case where he decides to exercise his functions under Part V of the Act, send to the supervisory authority as soon as reasonably practicable after exercising those functions such statement of the extent of the action that he has taken as he thinks fit; and

(b)   in any case where he decides not to exercise those functions, send to the supervisory authority as soon as reasonably practicable after making the decision the reasons for that decision.

6.   Requests by Commissioner in relation to certain data controllers

(1)   This article applies in any case where a data controller is processing data in another EEA State in circumstances described in section 5(1) of the Act.

(2)   The Commissioner may request the supervisory authority of the EEA State referred to in paragraph (1) to exercise the functions conferred on it by that EEA State pursuant to Article 28(3) of the Data Protection Directive in relation to the processing in question.

(3)   Any request made under paragraph (2) must specify—

(a)   the name and address in the EEA State, in so far as they are known by the Commissioner, of the data controller; and

(b)   such details of the circumstances of the case as the Commissioner thinks fit to enable the supervisory authority to exercise those functions.

7.   General exchange of information

The Commissioner may supply to the European Commission or any supervisory authority information to the extent to which, in the opinion of the Commissioner, the supply of that information is necessary for the performance of the data protection functions of the recipient.

Mike O'Brien
Parliamentary Under-Secretary of State
Home Office
31 January 2000

THE DATA PROTECTION (SUBJECT ACCESS) (FEES AND MISCELLANEOUS PROVISIONS) REGULATIONS 2000 (SI 2000 No. 191)

1.   Citation, commencement and interpretation

(1)   These Regulations may be cited as the Data Protection (Subject Access) (Fees and Miscellaneous Provisions) Regulations 2000 and shall come into force on 1st March 2000.

(2)   In these Regulations 'the Act' means the Data Protection Act 1998.

2.   Extent of subject access requests

(1)   A request for information under any provision of section 7(1)(a), (b) or (c) of the Act is to be treated as extending also to information under all other provisions of section 7(1)(a), (b) and (c).

(2)   A request for information under any provision of section 7(1) of the Act is to be treated as extending to information under the provisions of section 7(1)(d) only where the request shows an express intention to that effect.

(3)   A request for information under the provisions of section 7(1)(d) of the Act is to be treated as extending also to information under any other provision of section 7(1) only where the request shows an express intention to that effect.

3.   Maximum subject access fee
Except as otherwise provided by regulations 4, 5 and 6 below, the maximum fee which may be required by a data controller under section 7(2)(b) of the Act is £10.

4.   Limited requests for subject access where data controller is credit reference agency
(1)   In any case in which a request under section 7 of the Act has been made to a data controller who is a credit reference agency, and has been limited, or by virtue of section 9(2) of the Act is taken to have been limited, to personal data relevant to an individual's financial standing—
(a)   the maximum fee which may be required by a data controller under section 7(2)(b) of the Act is £2, and
(b)   the prescribed period for the purposes of section 7(8) of the Act is seven working days.
(2)   In this regulation 'working day' means any day other than—
(a)   Saturday or Sunday,
(b)   Christmas Day or Good Friday,
(c)   a bank holiday, within the meaning of section 1 of the Banking and Financial Dealings Act 1971,[1] in the part of the United Kingdom in which the data controller's address is situated.
(3)   For the purposes of paragraph (2)(c) above—
(a)   the address of a registered company is that of its registered office, and
(b)   the address of a person (other than a registered company) carrying on a business is that of his principal place of business in the United Kingdom.

Note
[1] 1971 c. 80.

5.   Subject access requests in respect of educational records
(1)   This regulation applies to any case in which a request made under section 7 of the Act relates wholly or partly to personal data forming part of an accessible record which is an educational record within the meaning of Schedule 11 to the Act.
(2)   Except as provided by paragraph (3) below, a data controller may not require a fee under section 7(2)(b) of the Act in any case to which this regulation applies.
(3)   Where, in a case to which this regulation applies, the obligation imposed by section 7(1)(c)(i) of the Act is to be complied with by supplying the data subject with a copy of information in permanent form, the maximum fee which may be required by a data controller under section 7(2)(b) of the Act is that applicable to the case under the Schedule to these Regulations.
(4)   In any case to which this regulation applies, and in which the address of the data controller to whom the request is made is situated in England and Wales, the prescribed period for the purposes of section 7(8) of the Act is fifteen school days within the meaning of section 579(1) of the Education Act 1996.[1]

Note
[1] 1996 c. 56.

6. Certain subject access requests in respect of health records — transitional provisions

(1) This regulation applies only to cases in which a request made under section 7 of the Act—

(a) relates wholly or partly to personal data forming part of an accessible record which is a health record within the meaning of section 68(2) of the Act,

(b) does not relate exclusively to data within paragraphs (a) and (b) of the definition of 'data' in section 1(1) of the Act, and

(c) is made before 24th October 2001.

(2) Where in a case to which this regulation applies, the obligation imposed by section 7(1)(c)(i) of the Act is to be complied with by supplying the data subject with a copy of information in permanent form, the maximum fee which may be required by a data controller under section 7(2)(b) of the Act is £50.

(3) Except in a case to which paragraph (2) above applies, a data controller may not require a fee under section 7(2)(b) of the Act where, in a case to which this regulation applies, the request relates solely to personal data which—

(a) form part of an accessible record—

(i) which is a health record within the meaning of section 68(2) of the Act, and

(ii) at least some of which was made after the beginning of the period of 40 days immediately preceding the date of the request; and

(b) do not fall within paragraph (a) or (b) of the definition of 'data' in section 1(1) of the Act.

(4) For the purposes of paragraph (3) above, an individual making a request in any case to which this regulation applies may specify that his request is limited to personal data of the description set out in that paragraph.

Mike O'Brien
Parliamentary Under-Secretary of State
Home Office
31 January 2000

Regulation 5(3)   SCHEDULE
MAXIMUM SUBJECT ACCESS FEES WHERE A COPY OF
INFORMATION CONTAINED IN AN EDUCATIONAL RECORD
IS SUPPLIED IN PERMANENT FORM

1. In any case in which the copy referred to in regulation 5(3) includes material in any form other than a record in writing on paper, the maximum fee applicable for the purposes of regulation 5(3) is £50.

2. In any case in which the copy referred to in regulation 5(3) consists solely of a record in writing on paper, the maximum fee applicable for the purposes of regulation 5(3) is set out in the table below.

TABLE

Number of pages of information comprising the copy	*Maximum fee*
fewer than 20	£1
20–29	£2
30–39	£3
40–49	£4
50–59	£5
60–69	£6
70–79	£7
80–89	£8
90–99	£9
100–149	£10
150–199	£15
200–249	£20
250–299	£25
300–349	£30
350–399	£35
400–449	£40
450–499	£45
500 or more	£50

THE DATA PROTECTION TRIBUNAL (NATIONAL SECURITY APPEALS) RULES 2000
(SI 2000 No. 206)

1.   Citation and commencement
These Rules may be cited as the Data Protection Tribunal (National Security Appeals) Rules 2000 and shall come into force on 1 March 2000.

2.   Application and interpretation
(1)   These Rules apply to appeals under section 28 of the Act, and the provisions of these Rules are to be construed accordingly.

(2)   In these Rules, unless the context otherwise requires—

'the Act' means the Data Protection Act 1998;

'appeal' means an appeal under section 28 of the Act;

'appellant' means a person who brings or intends to bring an appeal under section 28 of the Act;

'costs'—

(a)   except in Scotland, includes fees, charges, disbursements, expenses and remuneration;

(b)   in Scotland means expenses, and includes fees, charges, disbursements and remuneration;

'disputed certification' means—

(a)   in relation to an appeal under section 28(4) of the Act, the certificate against which the appeal is brought or intended to be brought, and

(b)   in relation to an appeal under section 28(6) of the Act, the claim by the data controller, against which the appeal is brought or intended to be brought, that a certificate applies to any personal data;

'party' has the meaning given in paragraph (3) below;

'president' means the person designated by the Lord Chancellor under paragraph 3 of Schedule 6 to the Act to preside when the Tribunal is constituted under that paragraph;

'proper officer' in relation to a rule means an officer or member of staff provided to the Tribunal under paragraph 14 of Schedule 5 to the Act and appointed by the chairman to perform the duties of a proper officer under that rule;

'relevant Minister' means the Minister of the Crown who is responsible for the signing of the certificate under section 28(2) of the Act to which the appeal relates, and except where the context otherwise requires, references in these Rules to the relevant Minister include a person appointed under rule 21 below to represent his interests; and

'respondent data controller' in relation to an appeal under section 28(6) of the Act means the data controller making the claim which constitutes the disputed certification.

(3)   In these Rules, except where the context otherwise requires, 'party' means the appellant or—

(a)   in relation to an appeal under section 28(4) of the Act, the relevant Minister, and

(b)   in relation to an appeal under section 28(6) of the Act, the respondent data controller,

and, except where the context otherwise requires, references in these Rules to a party or to any such party include a person appointed under rule 21 below to represent his interests.

(4)   In relation to proceedings before the Tribunal in Scotland, for the words 'on the trial of an action' in rules 15(6) and 26(2) below there is substituted 'in a proof'.

3.   Constitution and general duty of the Tribunal

(1)   When exercising its functions under these Rules, the Tribunal shall secure that information is not disclosed contrary to the interests of national security.

(2)   Paragraph 6(1) of Schedule 6 to the Act applies only to the exercise of the jurisdiction of the Tribunal in accordance with rule 11 below.

(3)   For the purposes of paragraph (1) above, but without prejudice to the application of that paragraph, the disclosure of information is to be regarded as contrary to the interests of national security if it would indicate the existence or otherwise of any material.

4.   Method of appealing

(1)   An appeal must be brought by a written notice of appeal served on the Tribunal.

(2)   The notice of appeal shall—

(a)   identify the disputed certification; and

(b)   state—

(i)   the name and address of the appellant;

(ii)   the grounds of the appeal; and

(iii) an address for service of notices and other documents on the appellant.

(3)   In the case of an appeal under section 28(6) of the Act, the notice of appeal shall also state—

(a)   the date on which the respondent data controller made the claim constituting the disputed certification;

(b)   an address for service of notices and other documents on the respondent data controller; and

(c)   where applicable, the special circumstances which the appellant considers justify the Tribunal's accepting jurisdiction under rule 5(3) below.

5.   Time limit for appealing

(1)   In the case of an appeal under section 28(4) of the Act, a notice of appeal may be served on the Tribunal at any time during the currency of the disputed certification to which it relates.

(2)   In the case of an appeal under section 28(6) of the Act, subject to paragraph (3) below, a notice of appeal must be served on the Tribunal within 28 days of the date on which the claim constituting the disputed certification was made.

(3)   The Tribunal may accept a notice of appeal served after the expiry of the period permitted by paragraph (2) above if it is of the opinion that, by reason of special circumstances, it is just and right to do so.

(4)   A notice of appeal shall if sent by post in accordance with rule 30(1) below be treated as having been served on the date on which it is received for dispatch by the Post Office.

6.   Acknowledgment of notice of appeal and notification by the Tribunal

(1)   Upon receipt of a notice of appeal, the proper officer shall send—

(a)   an acknowledgment of the service of a notice of appeal to the appellant, and

(b)   a copy of the notice of appeal to—

(i)   the relevant Minister,

(ii)   the Commissioner, and

(iii)   in the case of an appeal under section 28(6) of the Act, the respondent data controller.

(2)   An acknowledgment of service under paragraph (1)(a) above shall be accompanied by a statement of the Tribunal's powers to award costs against the appellant under rule 28 below.

7.   Relevant Minister's notice in reply

(1)   No later than 42 days after receipt of a copy of a notice of appeal under rule 6(1)(b) above, the relevant Minister shall send to the Tribunal—

(a)   a copy of the certificate to which the appeal relates, and

(b)   a written notice in accordance with paragraph (2) below.

(2)   The notice shall state—

(a)   with regard to an appeal under section 28(4) of the Act, whether or not he intends to oppose the appeal and, if so—

(i)   a summary of the circumstances relating to the issue of the certificate, and the reasons for the issue of the certificate;

(ii)   the grounds upon which he relies in opposing the appeal; and

(iii)   a statement of the evidence upon which he relies in support of those grounds; and

(b)   with regard to an appeal under section 28(6) of the Act, whether or not he wishes to make representations in relation to the appeal and, if so—

(i)   the extent to which he intends to support or oppose the appeal;

(ii)   the grounds upon which he relies in supporting or opposing the appeal; and

(iii) a statement of the evidence upon which he relies in support of those grounds.

(3) Except where the Tribunal proposes to determine the appeal in accordance with rule 11 below, and subject to rule 12 below, the proper officer shall send a copy of the notice to—

(a) the appellant,

(b) the Commissioner, and

(c) in the case of an appeal under section 28(6) of the Act, the respondent data controller.

8. Reply by respondent data controller

(1) A respondent data controller shall, within 42 days of the date on which he receives a copy of a notice of appeal under rule 6(1)(b) above, send to the Tribunal a written reply acknowledging service upon him of the notice of appeal, and stating—

(a) whether or not he intends to oppose the appeal and, if so,

(b) the grounds upon which he relies in opposing the appeal.

(2) Before the expiry of the period of 42 days referred to in paragraph (1) above, the respondent data controller may apply to the Tribunal for an extension of that period, showing cause why, by reason of special circumstances, it would be just and right to do so, and the Tribunal may grant such extension as it considers appropriate.

(3) Except where the Tribunal proposes to determine the appeal in accordance with rule 11 below, the proper officer shall send a copy of the reply to—

(a) the relevant Minister; and

(b) subject to paragraph (4) and rule 12 below, the appellant and the Commissioner.

(4) No copy may be sent under paragraph (3)(b) above before the period of 42 days referred to in 12(2)(b) below has expired, otherwise than in accordance with rule 12, unless the relevant Minister has indicated that he does not object.

9. Amendment and supplementary grounds

(1) With the leave of the Tribunal, the appellant may amend his notice of appeal or deliver supplementary grounds of appeal.

(2) Rule 6(1) above and rule 11(1)(a) below apply to an amended notice of appeal and to supplementary grounds of appeal provided under paragraph (1) above as they do to a notice of appeal.

(3) Upon receipt of a copy of an amended notice of appeal or amended grounds of appeal under rule 6(1) above, the relevant Minister may amend his notice in reply and, in the case of an appeal under section 28(6) of the Act, the respondent data controller may amend his reply to the notice of appeal.

(4) An amended notice or reply under paragraph (3) above must be sent to the Tribunal within 28 days of the date on which the copy referred to in that paragraph is received.

(5) Without prejudice to paragraph (3) above, and with the leave of the Tribunal—

(a) the relevant Minister may amend a notice in reply, and

(b) the respondent data controller may amend a reply to the notice of appeal.

(6) Rule 7(3) above and rules 11(1)(b) and 12(1)(a) below apply to an amended notice in reply by the relevant Minister provided under paragraph (3) or (5) above as they do to a notice in reply.

(7)   Rule 8(3) and (4) above and rules 11(1)(c) and 12(1)(b) below apply to an amended reply by the respondent data controller provided under paragraph (3) or (5) above as they do to a reply.

10.   Application for striking out
(1)   Where the relevant Minister or, in the case of an appeal under section 28(6) of the Act, the respondent data controller is of the opinion that an appeal does not lie to, or cannot be entertained by, the Tribunal, or that the notice of appeal discloses no reasonable grounds of appeal, he may include in his notice under rule 7 or, as the case may be, his reply under rule 8 above a notice to that effect stating the grounds for such contention and applying for the appeal to be struck out.

(2)   An application under this rule may be heard as a preliminary issue or at the beginning of the hearing of the substantive appeal.

11.   Summary disposal of appeals
(1)   Where, having considered—
  (a)   the notice of appeal,
  (b)   the relevant Minister's notice in reply, and
  (c)   in the case of an appeal under section 28(6) of the Act, the respondent data controller's reply,
the Tribunal is of the opinion that the appeal is of such a nature that it can properly be determined by dismissing it forthwith, it may, subject to the provisions of this rule, so determine the appeal.

(2)   Where the Tribunal proposes to determine an appeal under paragraph (1) above, it must first notify the appellant and the relevant Minister of the proposal.

(3)   A notification to the appellant under paragraph (2) above must contain particulars of the appellant's entitlements set out in paragraph (4) below.

(4)   An appellant notified in accordance with paragraph (2) above is entitled, within such time as the Tribunal may reasonably allow—
  (a)   to make written representations, and
  (b)   to request the Tribunal to hear oral representations
against the proposal to determine the appeal under paragraph (1) above.

(5)   Where an appellant requests a hearing under paragraph (4)(b) above, the Tribunal shall, as soon as practicable and with due regard to the convenience of the appellant, appoint a time and place for a hearing accordingly.

(6)   The proper officer shall send to the appellant a notice informing him of—
  (a)   the time and place of any hearing under paragraph (5) above, which, unless the appellant otherwise agrees, shall not be earlier than 14 days after the date on which the notice is sent, and
  (b)   the effect of rule 22 below.

(7)   The Tribunal must as soon as practicable notify the appellant and the relevant Minister if, having given a notification under paragraph (2) above, it ceases to propose to determine the appeal under paragraph (1) above.

12.   Relevant Minister's objection to disclosure
(1)   Where the relevant Minister objects, on grounds of the need to secure that information is not disclosed contrary to the interests of national security, to the disclosure of—

(a)   his notice in reply to the appellant, the Commissioner or, in the case of an appeal under section 28(6) of the Act, the respondent data controller; or

(b)   the reply of a respondent data controller to the appellant or the Commissioner,

he may send a notice of objection to the Tribunal.

(2)   A notice of objection under paragraph (1) above must be sent—

(a)   where paragraph (1)(a) above applies, with the notice in reply; and

(b)   where paragraph (1)(b) above applies, within 42 days of the date on which he receives the copy mentioned in rule 8(3) above.

(3)   A notice of objection under paragraph (1) above shall—

(a)   state the reasons for the objection; and

(b)   where paragraph (1)(a) above applies, if and to the extent it is possible to do so without disclosing information contrary to the interests of national security, be accompanied by a version of the relevant Minister's notice in a form which can be shown to the appellant, the Commissioner or, as the case may be, the respondent data controller.

(4)   Where the relevant Minister sends a notice of objection under paragraph (1) above, the Tribunal must not disclose the material in question otherwise than in accordance with rule 17 below.

13.   Withdrawal of appeal

(1)   The appellant may at any time withdraw his appeal by sending to the Tribunal a notice of withdrawal signed by him or on his behalf, and the proper officer shall send a copy of that notice to—

(a)   the relevant Minister,

(b)   the Commissioner, and

(c)   in the case of an appeal under section 28(6) of the Act, the respondent data controller.

(2)   A notice of withdrawal shall if sent by post in accordance with rule 30(1) below have effect on the date on which it is received for dispatch by the Post Office.

(3)   Where an appeal is withdrawn under this rule a fresh appeal may not be brought by the same appellant in relation to the same disputed certification except with the leave of the Tribunal.

14.   Consolidation of appeals

(1)   Subject to paragraph (2) below, where in the case of two or more appeals to which these Rules apply it appears to the Tribunal—

(a)   that some common question of law or fact arises in both or all of them, or

(b)   that for some other reason it is desirable to proceed with the appeals under this rule,

the Tribunal may order that the appeals be consolidated or heard together.

(2)   The Tribunal shall not make an order under this rule without giving the parties and the relevant Minister an opportunity to show cause why such an order should not be made.

15.   Directions

(1)   This rule is subject to rule 16 below.

(2)   In this rule, references to a 'party' include the relevant Minister notwithstanding that he may not be a party to an appeal under section 28(6) of the Act.

(3)   Subject to paragraphs (6) and (7) below, the Tribunal may at any time of its own motion or on the application of any party give such directions as it thinks proper to enable the parties to prepare for the hearing of the appeal or to assist the Tribunal to determine the issues.

(4)   Such directions may in particular—

(a)   provide for a particular matter to be dealt with as a preliminary issue and for a pre-hearing review to be held;

(b)   provide for—

(i)   the exchange between the parties of lists of documents held by them which are relevant to the appeal,

(ii)   the inspection by the parties of the documents so listed,

(iii)   the exchange between the parties of statements of evidence, and

(iv)   the provision by the parties to the Tribunal of statements or lists of agreed matters;

(c)   require any party to send to the Tribunal and to the other parties—

(i)   statements of facts and statements of the evidence which will be adduced, including such statements provided in a modified or edited form;

(ii)   a skeleton argument which summarises the submissions which will be made and cites the authorities which will be relied upon, identifying any particular passages to be relied upon;

(iii)   a chronology of events;

(iv)   any other particulars or supplementary statements which may reasonably be required for the determination of the appeal;

(v)   any document or other material which the Tribunal may require and which it is in the power of that party to deliver;

(vi)   an estimate of the time which will be needed for any hearing; and

(vii)   a list of the witnesses he intends to call to give evidence at any hearing;

(d)   limit the length of oral submissions and the time allowed for the examination and cross-examination of witnesses; and

(e)   limit the number of expert witnesses to be heard on either side.

(5)   The Tribunal may, subject to any specific provisions of these Rules, specify time limits for steps to be taken in the proceedings and may extend any time limit.

(6)   Nothing in this rule may require the production of any document or other material which the party could not be compelled to produce on the trial of an action in a court of law in that part of the United Kingdom where the appeal is to be determined.

(7)   It shall be a condition of the supply of any information or material provided under this rule that any recipient of that information or material may use it only for the purposes of the appeal.

(8)   The power to give directions may be exercised in the absence of the parties.

(9)   Notice of any directions given under this rule shall be served on all the parties, and the Tribunal may, on the application of any party, set aside or vary such directions.

16.   Applications by relevant Minister

(1)   This rule applies in any case where the Tribunal proposes to—

(a)   give or vary any direction under rule 15 above or rule 18(2) below,

(b)   issue a summons under rule 20 below, or

(c)   certify or publish a determination under rule 27 below.

(2)   Before the Tribunal proceeds as proposed in any case to which this rule applies, it must first notify the relevant Minister of the proposal.

(3)   If the relevant Minister considers that proceeding as proposed by the Tribunal would cause information to be disclosed contrary to the interests of national security, he may make an application to the Tribunal requesting it to reconsider the proposal or reconsider it to any extent.

(4)   An application by the relevant Minister under paragraph (3) above must be made within 14 days of receipt of notification under paragraph (2), and the Tribunal must not proceed as proposed in any case to which this rule applies before that period has expired, otherwise than in accordance with rule 17 below, unless the relevant Minister has indicated that he does not object.

(5)   Where the relevant Minister makes an application under this rule, the Tribunal must not proceed as proposed otherwise than in accordance with rule 17 below.

17.   Determinations on relevant Minister's objections and applications

(1)   Except where rule 11 above applies, the Tribunal shall determine whether to uphold any objection of the relevant Minister under rule 12 above, and any application under rule 16 above, in accordance with this rule.

(2)   Subject to paragraph (3) below, proceedings under this rule shall take place in the absence of the parties.

(3)   The relevant Minister (or a person authorised to act on his behalf) may attend any proceedings under this rule, whether or not he is a party to the appeal in question.

(4)   An objection under rule 12 above must be considered under this rule as a preliminary issue, and an application under rule 16 above may be considered as a preliminary issue or at the hearing of the substantive appeal.

(5)   Where, in the case of an objection under rule 12 above, the Tribunal is minded to overrule the relevant Minister's objection, or to require him to provide a version of his notice in a form other than that in which he provided it under rule 12(3)(b) above, the Tribunal must invite the relevant Minister to make oral representations.

(6)   Where the Tribunal under paragraph (5) above overrules an objection by the relevant Minister under rule 12 above, or requires him to provide a version of his notice in a form other than that in which he provided it under rule 12(3)(b) above, the Tribunal shall not disclose, and the relevant Minister shall not be required to disclose, any material which was the subject of the unsuccessful objection if the relevant Minister chooses not to rely upon it in opposing the appeal.

(7)   Where, in the case of an objection under rule 12 above, the Tribunal upholds the relevant Minister's objection and either—

(a)   approves the version of his notice provided under rule 12(3)(b), or

(b)   requires him to provide a version of his notice in a form other than that in which he provided it under rule 12(3)(b),

rule 7(3) above applies to that version of the notice.

18.   Power to determine without a hearing

(1)   Without prejudice to rule 11 above, where either—

(a)   the parties so agree in writing, or

(b)   it appears to the Tribunal that the issues raised on the appeal have been determined on a previous appeal brought by the appellant on the basis of facts which

did not materially differ from those to which the appeal relates and the Tribunal has given the parties an opportunity of making representations to the effect that the appeal ought not to be determined without a hearing,
the Tribunal may determine an appeal, or any particular issue, without a hearing.

(2)   Before determining any matter under this rule, the Tribunal may, subject to rule 16 above, if it thinks fit direct any party to provide in writing further information about any matter relevant to the appeal within such time as the Tribunal may allow.

19.   Time and place of hearings

(1)   Except where rule 11 or 18 above applies, as soon as practicable after notice of appeal has been given, and with due regard to the convenience of the parties, the Tribunal shall appoint a time and place for a hearing of the appeal.

(2)   Except in relation to a hearing under rule 11(5) above, the proper officer shall send to each party, the Commissioner and the relevant Minister a notice informing him of the time and place of any hearing, which, unless the parties otherwise agree, shall not be earlier than 14 days after the date on which the notice is sent.

(3)   A notice to a party under this rule shall inform him of the effect of rule 22 below.

(4)   The Tribunal may—
   (a)   postpone the time appointed for any hearing;
   (b)   adjourn a hearing to such time as the Tribunal may determine; or
   (c)   alter the place appointed for any hearing;
and, if it exercises any of the above powers, it shall notify each person previously notified of that hearing under this rule or rule 11(6) above, and any person summoned under rule 20 below to attend as a witness at that hearing, of the revised arrangements.

20.   Summoning of witnesses

(1)   This rule is subject to rule 16 above.

(2)   Subject to paragraph (3) below, the Tribunal may by summons require any person in the United Kingdom to attend as a witness at a hearing of an appeal at such time and place as may be specified in the summons and, subject to rule 26(2) and (3) below, at the hearing to answer any questions or produce any documents in his custody or under his control which relate to any matter in question in the appeal.

(3)   No person shall be required to attend in obedience to a summons under paragraph (2) above unless he has been given at least 7 days' notice of the hearing or, if less than 7 days, he has informed the Tribunal that he accepts such notice as he has been given.

(4)   The Tribunal may upon the application of a person summoned under this rule set the summons aside.

(5)   A person who has attended a hearing as a witness in obedience to a summons shall be entitled to such sum as the Tribunal considers reasonable in respect of his attendance at, and his travelling to and from, the hearing; and where the summons was issued at the request of a party such sum shall be paid or tendered to him by that party.

(6)   In relation to proceedings before the Tribunal in Scotland, in this rule 'summons' means citation and the provisions of this rule are to be construed accordingly.

21. Representation at a hearing

(1)   At any hearing by the Tribunal, other than a hearing under rule 11 above—

(a)   a party may, subject to rules 17(2) above and 23(3) below, conduct his case himself or may appear and be represented by any person whom he may appoint for the purpose, and

(b)   the relevant Minister may appear and be represented by any person whom he may appoint for the purpose.

(2)   At any hearing by the Tribunal under rule 11(5) above, the appellant may conduct his case himself or may appear and be represented by any person whom he may appoint for the purpose.

22. Default of appearance at hearing

If, without furnishing the Tribunal with sufficient reason for his absence, a party fails to appear at a hearing, having been duly notified of the hearing, the Tribunal may, if that party is the appellant, dismiss the appeal or, in any case hear and determine the appeal, or any particular issue, in the party's absence and may make such order as to costs as it thinks fit.

23. Hearings to be in private

(1)   All hearings by the Tribunal (including preliminary hearings) shall be in private unless the Tribunal, with the consent of the parties and the relevant Minister, directs that the hearing or any part of the hearing shall take place in public.

(2)   Where the Tribunal sits in private it may, with the consent of the parties and the relevant Minister, admit to a hearing such persons on such terms and conditions as it considers appropriate.

(3)   Where the Tribunal considers it necessary for any party other than the relevant Minister to be excluded from proceedings or any part of them in order to secure that information is not disclosed contrary to the interests of national security, it must—

(a)   direct accordingly,

(b)   inform the person excluded of its reasons, to the extent that it is possible to do so without disclosing information contrary to the interests of national security, and record those reasons in writing, and

(c)   inform the relevant Minister.

(4)   The relevant Minister, or a person authorised to act on his behalf, may attend any hearing, other than a hearing under rule 11 above, notwithstanding that it is in private.

24. Conduct of proceedings at hearing

(1)   Subject to rules 22 and 23(3) above, the Tribunal shall at the hearing of an appeal give to each party and the relevant Minister an opportunity—

(a)   to address the Tribunal and to amplify orally written statements previously furnished under these Rules, to give evidence and to call witnesses, and to put questions to any person giving evidence before the Tribunal, and

(b)   to make representations on the evidence (if any) and on the subject matter of the appeal generally but, where evidence is taken, such opportunity shall not be given before the completion of the taking of evidence.

(2)   Except as provided by these Rules, the Tribunal shall conduct the proceedings in such manner as it considers appropriate in the circumstances for discharging its functions and shall so far as appears to it appropriate seek to avoid formality in its proceedings.

25. Preliminary and incidental matters
As regards matters preliminary or incidental to an appeal the president may act for the Tribunal under rules 5(3), 8(2), 9, 13 to 15, 19(1) and (4)(a) and (c) and 20.

26. Evidence
(1) The Tribunal may receive in evidence any document or information notwithstanding that such document or information would be inadmissible in a court of law.

(2) No person shall be compelled to give any evidence or produce any document which he could not be compelled to give or produce on the trial of an action in a court of law in that part of the United Kingdom where the appeal is to be determined.

(3) The Tribunal may require oral evidence of a witness (including a party) to be given on oath or affirmation and for that purpose the president or the proper officer shall have power to administer oaths or take affirmations.

27. Determination of appeal
(1) As soon as practicable after the Tribunal has determined an appeal, the president shall certify in writing that determination and sign and date the certificate.

(2) If and to the extent that it is possible to do so without disclosing information contrary to the interests of national security, and subject to rule 16 above, the certificate shall include—

    (a) any material finding of fact, and

    (b) the reasons for the decision.

(3) The proper officer shall send a copy of the certificate to—

    (a) the parties,

    (b) the relevant Minister, and

    (c) the Commissioner.

(4) Subject to rule 16 above, the Tribunal shall make arrangements for the publication of its determination but in doing so shall have regard to—

    (a) the desirability of safeguarding the privacy of data, subjects and commercially sensitive information, and

    (b) the need to secure that information is not disclosed contrary to the interests of national security,

and for those purposes may make any necessary amendments to the text of the certificate.

(5) For the purposes of this rule (but without prejudice to its generality), the disclosure of information is to be regarded as contrary to the interests of national security if it would indicate the existence or otherwise of any material.

28. Costs
(1) In any appeal before the Tribunal, including one withdrawn under rule 13 above, the Tribunal may make an order awarding costs—

    (a) in the case of an appeal under section 28(4) of the Act—

        (i) against the appellant and in favour of the relevant Minister where it considers that the appeal was manifestly unreasonable;

        (ii) against the relevant Minister and in favour of the appellant where it allows the appeal and quashes the disputed certification, or does so to any extent;

    (b) in the case of an appeal under section 28(6) of the Act—

        (i) against the appellant and in favour of any other party where it dismisses the appeal or dismisses it to any extent;

(ii)   in favour of the appellant and against any other party where it allows the appeal or allows it to any extent; and

(c)   where it considers that a party has been responsible for frivolous, vexatious, improper or unreasonable action, or for any failure to comply with a direction or any delay which with diligence could have been avoided, against that party and in favour of the other.

(2)   The Tribunal shall not make an order under paragraph (1) above awarding costs against a party without first giving that party an opportunity of making representations against the making of the order.

(3)   An order under paragraph (1) above may be to the party or parties in question to pay to the other party or parties either a specified sum in respect of the costs incurred by that other party or parties in connection with the proceedings or the whole or part of such costs as taxed (if not otherwise agreed).

(4)   Any costs required by an order under this rule to be taxed may be taxed in the county court according to such of the scales prescribed by the county court rules for proceedings in the county court as shall be directed by the order.

(5)   In relation to proceedings before the Tribunal in Scotland, for the purpose of the application of paragraph (4) above, for the reference to the county court and the county court rules there shall be substituted references to the sheriff court and the sheriff court rules and for the reference to proceedings there shall be substituted a reference to civil proceedings.

29.   Irregularities

(1)   Any irregularity resulting from failure to comply with any provision of these Rules or of any direction of the Tribunal before the Tribunal has reached its decision shall not of itself render the proceedings void, but the Tribunal may, and shall if it considers that any person may have been prejudiced by that irregularity, give such directions or take such steps as it thinks fit before reaching its decision to cure or waive the irregularity, whether by amendment of any document, the giving of notice or otherwise.

(2)   Clerical mistakes in any document recording or certifying a direction, decision or determination of the Tribunal or president, or errors arising in such a document from an accidental slip or omission, may at any time be corrected by the president by certificate signed by him.

30.   Notices etc.

(1)   Any notice or other document required or authorised by these Rules to be served on or sent to any person or authority may be sent by post in a registered letter or by the recorded delivery service—

(a)   in the case of the Tribunal, to the proper officer of the Tribunal;

(b)   in the case of an appellant or a respondent data controller, to him at his address for service under these Rules;

(c)   in the case of the relevant Minister or the Commissioner, to him at his office.

(2)   An appellant or respondent data controller may at any time by notice to the Tribunal change his address for service under these Rules.

Mike O'Brien
Parliamentary Under-Secretary of State
Home Office
2 February 2000

CONSUMER CREDIT (CREDIT REFERENCE AGENCY) REGULATIONS 2000 (SI 2000 No. 290)

1. Title, commencement, revocation and savings

(1)   These Regulations may be cited as the Consumer Credit (Credit Reference Agency) Regulations 2000 and shall come into force on 1st March 2000.

(2)   Subject to paragraph (3) below, the Consumer Credit (Credit Reference Agency) Regulations 1977[1] are revoked.

(3)   The Consumer Credit (Credit Reference Agency) Regulations 1977 shall continue to apply—

(a)   in any case where a credit reference agency has, on or before 29th February 2000, received a request under section 158(1) of the 1974 Act (other than a request made by reference to the 1998 Act) but does not, until after that date, comply with section 158(1) and (2) of that Act or deal with the request under section 160(3); and

(b)   in any case where a credit reference agency has received a request under section 158(1) of the 1974 Act and has complied with section 158(1) and (2) of that Act or dealt with the request under section 160(3) before 1st March 2000.

Note
[1]SI 1977/329.

2. Interpretation

In these Regulations—

'the 1974 Act' means the Consumer Credit Act 1974;

'the 1998 Act' means the Data Protection Act 1998;

'agency' means a credit reference agency; and

'business consumer' means a consumer[1] carrying on a business who has been given information under section 160 of the 1974 Act.

Note
[1]'Consumer' is defined in section 158(1) of the Consumer Credit Act 1974, as amended by section 62 of the Data Protection Act 1998.

3. Prescribed period for the purposes of sections 157(1), 158(1) and 160(3) of the 1974 Act

The period of seven working days is prescribed for the purposes of sections 157(1), 158(1) and 160(3) of the 1974 Act.

4. Statement of rights under sections 159 and 160 of the 1974 Act

(1)   The form in Schedule 1, completed in accordance with the footnotes, is prescribed for the purposes of section 9(3) of the 1998 Act.

(2)   The form in Schedule 2, completed in accordance with the footnotes, is prescribed for the purposes of section 158(2) of the 1974 Act.

(3)   The form in Schedule 3, completed in accordance with the footnotes, is prescribed for the purposes of section 160(3) of the 1974 Act.

5. Applications to the relevant authority under section 159(5) of the 1974 Act

(1)   This regulation prescribes the manner in which applications under section 159(5) of the 1974 Act by—

(a) objectors,[1]
(b) business consumers, and
(c) agencies

shall be made to the relevant authority.[2]

(2) An application by an objector, a business consumer or an agency shall state the name and address of the agency and of the objector or business consumer and shall give an indication of when the notice of correction under section 159(3) of the 1974 Act was served by the objector or business consumer on the agency.

(3) An application by an objector or a business consumer shall give particulars of the entry in the file or, as the case may be, of the information received by him from the agency and shall state why he considers the entry or information to be incorrect and why, if it is not corrected, he considers that he is likely to be prejudiced.

(4) An application by an agency shall be accompanied by—

(a) a copy of the file given by the agency to the objector, or of the information given by the agency to the business consumer under section 160(3) of the 1974 Act;

(b) a copy of the notice of correction; and

(c) a copy of related correspondence and other documents which have passed between the agency and the objector or business consumer;

and shall state the grounds upon which it appears to the agency that it would be improper for it to publish the notice of correction.

Kim Howells,
Parliamentary Under-Secretary of State for Consumers and Corporate Affairs, Department of Trade and Industry
8 February 2000

Notes
[1] 'Objector' is defined in section 159(1) of the Consumer Credit Act 1974, as amended by section 62 of the Data Protection Act 1998.
[2] 'Relevant authority' is defined in section 159(8) of the Consumer Credit Act 1974, as amended by section 62 of the Data Protection Act 1998.

Regulation 4(1)   SCHEDULE 1
CREDIT REFERENCE AGENCY FILES
INDIVIDUALS (INCLUDING SOLE TRADERS)

YOUR RIGHTS UNDER SECTION 159 OF THE CONSUMER CREDIT
ACT 1974, AND UNDER THE DATA PROTECTION ACT 1998, IF YOU
THINK ANY ENTRY IN OUR FILE IS WRONG

This statement of your rights is provided by[1] together with all the information we hold about you on our files. Our postal address is.[2]

Your rights are as follows—

If you think that any of the information we have sent you is wrong and that you are likely to suffer because it is wrong, you can ask us to correct it or remove it from our file.

Notes
[1] Insert the name of the credit reference agency issuing the statement.
[2] Insert the credit reference agency's postal address.

You need to write to us telling us what you want us to do. You should explain why you think the information is wrong.

If you write to us, we have to reply in writing within 28 days.

Our reply will tell you whether we have corrected the information, removed it from our file or done nothing. If we tell you that we have corrected the information, you will get a copy.

If our reply says that we have done nothing, or if we fail to reply within 28 days, or if we correct the information but you are not happy with the correction, you can write your own note of correction and ask for it to be included on our file.

To do this, you will need to write to us within 28 days of receiving our reply. If you did not get a reply from us and you want the information we sent you to be corrected, you will need to write to us within 8 weeks of the letter you wrote to us in which you asked us to correct the information or remove it from our file.

Your letter will need to—

- include the note of correction you have written. It must not be more than 200 words long and should give a clear and accurate explanation of why you think the information is wrong. If the information is factually correct but you think it creates a misleading impression, your note of correction can explain why.
- ask us to add your note of correction to our file and to include a copy of it whenever we give anyone any of the information you think is wrong or any information based on it.

If we accept your note of correction, we have to tell you in writing within 28 days that we are going to add it to our file.

If we think it would be wrong to add your note of correction to our file, we have to apply for a ruling from the Data Protection Commissioner.

We will apply for a ruling if we do not want to include your note of correction because we think it is wrong, or because we think it is defamatory, frivolous or scandalous, or unsuitable for publication for some other reason. We can only refuse to include your note of correction if the Commissioner agrees with us.

If we have not written to you within 28 days of receiving your note of correction, or if we have written telling you that we are not going to add your note of correction to our file, you can appeal to the Data Protection Commissioner.

If you want to do this, you will have to write to the following address[1]—

The Data Protection Commissioner
Wycliffe House
Water Lane
Wilmslow
Cheshire
SK95AF

Telephone no. 01625-545700
Fax no. 01625-524510
e-mail: data@commat;wycliffe.demon.co.uk

Note
[1]If the address, telephone number, fax number or e-mail address of the Data Protection Commissioner have changed, substitute the correct details.

When you write, you must give the following details—
- your full name and address
- our name and address
- details of the information you think is wrong, including—
  — why you think it is wrong,
  — why you think you are likely to suffer because it is wrong, and
  — an indication of when you sent us your note of correction.

It would be helpful to the Commissioner if you could include a copy of your note of correction.

Before deciding what to do, the Commissioner may ask us for our side of the story and send us a copy of your letter. In return, you will be sent any comments we make.

The Commissioner can make any order she thinks fit when she has considered your appeal. For example, she can order us to accept your note of correction and add it to our file.

If at any stage we fail to correct or remove wrong information, you can ask the Data Protection Commissioner to check whether we are meeting the requirements of the Data Protection Act 1998.

The Data Protection Act 1998 requires us to take reasonable steps to check the accuracy of personal information. If you think we have failed to correct or remove wrong information about you, you have the right to ask the Data Protection Commissioner, at the above address, to check whether our dealing with your information has met this requirement.

Important Note: The various time limits referred to in this statement (mostly 28 days) start with the day following receipt and end with the day of delivery. That means (for example) that if you have 28 days to reply to a letter from us, the period starts with the day after you receive our letter, and you then have to make sure that your reply is delivered to us no later than 28 days from that date. In order to avoid the risk of losing your rights you should therefore allow for postal delays.

Regulation 4(2)   SCHEDULE 2
CREDIT REFERENCE AGENCY FILES
PARTNERSHIPS AND OTHER UNINCORPORATED BODIES

YOUR RIGHTS UNDER SECTION 159 OF THE CONSUMER CREDIT ACT
1974 IF YOU THINK ANY ENTRY IN YOUR FILE IS WRONG

This statement of your rights is provided by[1] together with all the information we hold about you on our files. Our postal address is.[2]

Your rights are as follows—

If you think that any of the information we have sent you is wrong and that you are likely to suffer because it is wrong, you can ask us to correct it or remove it from our file.

You need to write to us telling us what you want us to do. You should explain why you think the information is wrong.

Notes
[1]Insert the name of the credit reference agency issuing the statement.
[2]Insert the credit reference agency's postal address.

If you write to us, we have to reply in writing within 28 days.

Our reply will tell you whether we have corrected the information, removed it from our file or done nothing. If we tell you that we have corrected the information, you will get a copy.

If our reply says that we have done nothing, or if we fail to reply within 28 days, or if we correct the information but you are not happy with the correction, you can write your own note of correction and ask for it to be included on our file.

To do this, you will need to write to us within 28 days of receiving our reply. If you did not get a reply from us and you want the information we sent you to be corrected, you will need to write to us within 8 weeks of the letter you wrote to us in which you asked us to correct the information or remove it from our file.

Your letter will need to—

- include the note of correction you have written. It must not be more than 200 words long and should give a clear and accurate explanation of why you think the information is wrong. If the information is factually correct but you think it creates a misleading impression, your note of correction can explain why.
- ask us to add your note of correction to our file and to include a copy of it whenever we give anyone any of the information you think is wrong or any information based on it.

If we accept your note of correction, we have to tell you in writing within 28 days that we are going to add it to our file.

If we think it would be wrong to add your note of correction to our file, we have to apply for a ruling from the Director General of Fair Trading.

We will apply for a ruling if we do not want to include your note of correction because we think it is wrong, or because we think it is defamatory, frivolous or scandalous, or unsuitable for publication for some other reason. We can only refuse to include your note of correction if the Director General agrees with us.

If we have not written to you within 28 days of receiving your note of correction, or if we have written telling you that we are not going to add your note of correction to our file, you can appeal to the Director General of Fair Trading.

If you want to do this, you will have to write to the following address[1]—

The Director General of Fair Trading
Office of Fair Trading
Fleetbank House
2/6 Salisbury Square
London
EC4Y 8JX

Telephone no. 0171-211 8000
Fax no. 0171-211 8800
e-mail: enquiries@commat;oft.gov.uk

When you write, you must give the following details—

- your full name and address
- our name and address
- details of the information you think is wrong, including—

Note
[1]Insert the name of the credit refrence agency issuing the statement.

— why you think it is wrong,

— why you think you are likely to suffer because it is wrong, and

— an indication of when you sent us your note of correction.

It would be helpful to the Director General if you could include a copy of your note of correction.

Before deciding what to do, the Director General may ask us for our side of the story and send us a copy of your letter. In return, you will be sent any comments we make.

The Director General can make any order he thinks fit when he has considered your appeal. For example, he can order us to accept your note of correction and add it to our file.

Important Note: The various time limits referred to in this statement (mostly 28 days) start with the day following receipt and end with the day of delivery. That means (for example) that if you have 28 days to reply to a letter from us, the period starts with the day after you receive our letter; and you then have to make sure that your reply is delivered to us no later than 28 days from that date. In order to avoid the risk of losing your rights you should therefore allow for postal delays.

Regulation 4(3)   SCHEDULE 3

CREDIT REFERENCE AGENCY FILESBUSINESS CONSUMERS
(PARTNERSHIPS AND OTHER UNINCORPORATED BODIES ONLY)

YOUR RIGHTS UNDER SECTIONS 159 AND 160 OF THE CONSUMER
CREDIT ACT 1974

This statement of your rights is provided by.[1] Our postal address is.[2]

You asked us for a copy of all the information we hold about you on our files. Under section 160 of the Consumer Credit Act 1974, we have obtained a ruling from the Director General of Fair Trading which means that we do not have to give you all of that information. We are allowed to withhold some of that information because the Director General of Fair Trading is satisfied that letting you have a copy of it would adversely affect the service we provide to our customers.

We are therefore providing you with some of the information we hold about you on our files or information based on it.

Sections 159 and 160 of the Consumer Credit Act 1974 give you certain rights and this statement tells you what those rights are.

Notes

[1]Insert the credit reference agency's postal address.

[3]If the address, telephone number, fax number or e-mail address of the Director General have changed, substitute the correct details.

RIGHTS UNDER SECTION 159

Your rights under section 159 of the Consumer Credit Act 1974 exist where you think that any of the information we have sent you is wrong and that you are likely to suffer because it is wrong.

These rights are available to you whether or not you have appealed to the Director General under section 160 (see the section headed 'RIGHTS UNDER SECTION 160' below).

If you think that any of the information we have sent you is wrong and that you are likely to suffer because it is wrong, you can ask us to correct it or remove it from our file.

You need to write to us telling us what you want us to do. You should explain why you think the information is wrong.

If you write to us, we have to reply in writing within 28 days.

Our reply will tell you whether we have corrected the information, removed it from our file or done nothing. If we tell you that we have corrected the information, you will get a copy.

If our reply says that we have done nothing, or if we fail to reply within 28 days, or if we correct the information but you are not happy with the correction, you can write your own note of correction and ask for it to be included on our file.

To do this, you will need to write to us within 28 days of receiving our reply. If you did not get a reply from us and you want the information we sent you to be corrected, you will need to write to us within 8 weeks of the letter you wrote to us in which you asked us to correct the information or remove it from our file.

Your letter will need to—

- include the note of correction you have written. It must not be more than 200 words long and should give a clear and accurate explanation of why you think the information is wrong. If the information is factually correct but you think it creates a misleading impression, your note of correction can explain why.
- ask us to add your note of correction to our file and to include a copy of it whenever we give anyone any of the information you think is wrong or any information based on it.

If we accept your note of correction, we have to tell you in writing within 28 days that we are going to add it to our file.

If we think it would be wrong to add your note of correction to our file, we have to apply for a ruling from the Director General of Fair Trading.

We will apply for a ruling if we do not want to include your note of correction because we think it is wrong, or because we think it is defamatory, frivolous or scandalous, or unsuitable for publication for some other reason. We can only refuse to include your note of correction if the Director General agrees with us.

If we have not written to you within 28 days of receiving your note of correction, or if we have written telling you that we are not going to add your note of correction to our file, you can appeal to the Director General of Fair Trading.

If you want to do this, you will have to write to the following address[1]—

The Director General of Fair Trading
Office of Fair Trading
Fleetbank House
2/6 Salisbury Square
London
EC4Y 8JX

Telephone no. 0171-211 8000
Fax no. 0171-211 8800
e-mail: enquiries@commat;oft.gov.uk

When you write, you must give the following details—

Note
[1]If the address, telephone number, fax number or e-mail address of the Director General of Fair Trading have changed, substitute the correct details.

- your full name and address
- our name and address
- details of the information you think is wrong, including—
  — why you think it is wrong,
  — why you think you are likely to suffer because it is wrong, and
  — an indication of when you sent us your note of correction.

It would be helpful to the Director General if you could include a copy of your note of correction.

Before deciding what to do, the Director General may ask us for our side of the story and send us a copy of your letter. In return, you will be sent any comments we make.

The Director General can make any order he thinks fit when he has considered your appeal. For example, he can order us to accept your note of correction and add it to our file.

RIGHTS UNDER SECTION 160

If you are not happy with the information we have sent you because it is incomplete (rather than wrong), you can appeal to the Director General of Fair Trading, but you must first of all get in touch with us, telling us why you are unhappy and asking us to help you.

You may be unhappy with the information because, for example, you cannot work out whether it is accurate without seeing information which we have apparently withheld.

You can appeal by writing to the Director General of Fair Trading at the address set out above.

You will need to—

- give the Director General a copy of the information you have received and tell him the date you received it,
- tell him why you are unhappy with the information, and
- say what steps you have taken to persuade us to help you.

You need to do all this within 28 days of receiving the information from us. If you cannot write within 28 days, do so as soon as you can and explain why you could not write earlier.

If the Director General thinks that you have taken all reasonable steps to get a satisfactory response from us without success, he can tell us to send him a copy of all the information we hold about you on our files. The Director General can then pass all or some of that information on to you.

Your rights under section 160 are available whether or not you have written to us under section 159.

Important Note: The various time limits referred to in this statement (mostly 28 days) start with the day following receipt and end with the day of delivery. That means that (for example) if you have 28 days to reply to a letter from us, the period starts with the day after you receive our letter; and you then have to make sure that your reply is delivered to us no later than 28 days from that date. In order to avoid the risk of losing your rights you should therefore allow for postal delays.

THE DATA PROTECTION (SUBJECT ACCESS MODIFICATION) (HEALTH) ORDER 2000 (SI 2000 No. 413)

1. Citation and commencement

This Order may be cited as the Data Protection (Subject Access Modification) (Health) Order 2000 and shall come into force on 1st March 2000.

2. Interpretation

In this Order—

'the Act' means the Data Protection Act 1998;

'the appropriate health professional' means—

(a)   the health professional who is currently or was most recently responsible for the clinical care of the data subject in connection with the matters to which the information which is the subject of the request relates; or

(b)   where there is more than one such health professional, the health professional who is the most suitable to advise on the matters to which the information which is the subject of the request relates; or

(c)   where—

(i)   there is no health professional available falling within paragraph (a) or (b), or

(ii)   the data controller is the Secretary of State and data to which this Order applies are processed in connection with the exercise of the functions conferred on him by or under the Child Support Act 1991[1] and the Child Support Act 1995[2] or his functions in relation to social security or war pensions,

a health professional who has the necessary experience and qualifications to advise on the matters to which the information which is the subject of the request relates;

'care' includes examination, investigation, diagnosis and treatment;

'request' means a request made under section 7;

'section 7' means section 7 of the Act; and

'war pension' has the same meaning as in section 25 of the Social Security Act 1989[3] (establishment and functions of war pensions committees).

Notes
[1]1991 c. 48.
[2]1995 c. 34.
[3]1989 c. 24.

3. Personal data to which Order applies

(1)   Subject to paragraph (2), this Order applies to personal data consisting of information as to the physical or mental health or condition of the data subject.

(2)   This Order does not apply to any data which are exempted from section 7 by an order made under section 38(1) of the Act.

4. Exemption from the subject information provisions

(1)   Personal data falling within paragraph (2) and to which this Order applies are exempt from the subject information provisions.

(2)   This paragraph applies to personal data processed by a court and consisting of information supplied in a report or other evidence given to the court by a local authority, Health and Social Services Board, Health and Social Services Trust, probation officer or other person in the course of any proceedings to which the Family

Proceedings Courts (Children Act 1989) Rules 1991,[1] the Magistrates' Courts (Children and Young Persons) Rules 1992,[2] the Magistrates' Courts (Criminal Justice (Children)) Rules (Northern Ireland) 1999,[3] the Act of Sederunt (Child Care and Maintenance Rules) 1997[4] or the Children's Hearings (Scotland) Rules 1996[5] apply where, in accordance with a provision of any of those Rules, the information may be withheld by the court in whole or in part from the data subject.

Notes
[1] SI 1991/1395, as amended by SI 1991/1991, SI 1992/2068, SI 1994/2166, SI 1994/3156 and SI 1997/1895.
[2] SI 1992/2071 as amended by SI 1997/2420.
[3] SR 1999 No. 7.
[4] SI 1997/291 (s. 19).
[5] SI 1996/3261 (s. 251).

5. Exemptions from section 7

(1) Personal data to which this Order applies are exempt from section 7 in any case to the extent to which the application of that section would be likely to cause serious harm to the physical or mental health or condition of the data subject or any other person.

(2) Subject to article 7(1), a data controller who is not a health professional shall not withhold information constituting data to which this Order applies on the ground that the exemption in paragraph (1) applies with respect to the information unless the data controller has first consulted the person who appears to the data controller to be the appropriate health professional on the question whether or not the exemption in paragraph (1) applies with respect to the information.

(3) Where any person falling within paragraph (4) is enabled by or under any enactment or rule of law to make a request on behalf of a data subject and has made such a request, personal data to which this Order applies are exempt from section 7 in any case to the extent to which the application of that section would disclose information—

(a) provided by the data subject in the expectation that it would not be disclosed to the person making the request;

(b) obtained as a result of any examination or investigation to which the data subject consented in the expectation that the information would not be so disclosed; or

(c) which the data subject has expressly indicated should not be so disclosed, provided that sub-paragraphs (a) and (b) shall not prevent disclosure where the data subject has expressly indicated that he no longer has the expectation referred to therein.

(4) A person falls within this paragraph if—

(a) except in relation to Scotland, the data subject is a child, and that person has parental responsibility for that data subject;

(b) in relation to Scotland, the data subject is a person under the age of sixteen, and that person has parental responsibilities for that data subject; or

(c) the data subject is incapable of managing his own affairs and that person has been appointed by a court to manage those affairs.

6. Modification of section 7 relating to data controllers who are not health professionals

(1) Subject to paragraph (2) and article 7(3), section 7 of the Act is modified so that a data controller who is not a health professional shall not communicate

information constituting data to which this Order applies in response to a request unless the data controller has first consulted the person who appears to the data controller to be the appropriate health professional on the question whether or not the exemption in article 5(1) applies with respect to the information.

(2)   Paragraph (1) shall not apply to the extent that the request relates to information which the data controller is satisfied has previously been seen by the data subject or is already within the knowledge of the data subject.

7.   Additional provision relating to data controllers who are not health professionals

(1)   Subject to paragraph (2), article 5(2) shall not apply in relation to any request where the data controller has consulted the appropriate health professional prior to receiving the request and obtained in writing from that appropriate health professional an opinion that the exemption in article 5(1) applies with respect to all of the information which is the subject of the request.

(2)   Paragraph (1) does not apply where the opinion either—

(a)   was obtained before the period beginning six months before the relevant day (as defined by section 7(10) of the Act) and ending on that relevant day, or

(b)   was obtained within that period and it is reasonable in all the circumstances to re-consult the appropriate health professional.

(3)   Article 6(1) shall not apply in relation to any request where the data controller has consulted the appropriate health professional prior to receiving the request and obtained in writing from that appropriate health professional an opinion that the exemption in article 5(1) does not apply with respect to all of the information which is the subject of the request.

8.   Further modifications of section 7

In relation to data to which this Order applies—

(a)   section 7(4) of the Act shall have effect as if there were inserted after paragraph (b) of that subsection

'or,

(c)   the information is contained in a health record and the other individual is a health professional who has compiled or contributed to the health record or has been involved in the care of the data subject in his capacity as a health professional';

(b)   section 7(9) shall have effect as if—

(i)   there was substituted—

'(9)   If a court is satisfied on the application of—

(a)   any person who has made a request under the foregoing provisions of this section, or

(b)   any other person to whom serious harm to his physical or mental health or condition would be likely to be caused by compliance with any such request in contravention of those provisions,

that the data controller in question is about to comply with or has failed to comply with the request in contravention of those provisions, the court may order him not to comply or, as the case may be, to comply with the request.'; and

(ii)   the reference therein to a contravention of the foregoing provisions of that section included a reference to a contravention of the provisions contained in this Order.

Mike O'Brien
Parliamentary Under-Secretary of State
Home Office
17 February 2000

THE DATA PROTECTION (SUBJECT ACCESS MODIFICATION) (EDUCATION) ORDER 2000 (SI 2000 No. 414)

1.   Citation and commencement
This Order may be cited as the Data Protection (Subject Access Modification) (Education) Order 2000 and shall come into force on 1st March 2000.

2.   Interpretation
In this Order—
'the Act' means the Data Protection Act 1998;
'education authority' in article 6 has the same meaning as in paragraph 6 of Schedule 11 to the Act;
'Principal Reporter' means the Principal Reporter appointed under section 127 of the Local Government etc. (Scotland) Act 1994[1] or any officer of the Scottish Children's Reporter Administration to whom there is delegated under section 131(1) of that Act any function of the Principal Reporter;
'request' means a request made under section 7; and
'section 7' means section 7 of the Act.

Note
[1]1994 c. 39.

3.   Personal data to which the Order applies
(1)   Subject to paragraph (2), this Order applies to personal data consisting of information constituting an educational record as defined in paragraph 1 of Schedule 11 to the Act.

(2)   This Order does not apply—

(a)   to any data consisting of information as to the physical or mental health or condition of the data subject to which the Data Protection (Subject Access Modification) (Health) Order 2000[1] applies; or

(b)   to any data which are exempted from section 7 by an order made under section 38(1) of the Act.

Note
[1]SI 2000/413.

4.   Exemption from the subject information provisions
(1)   Personal data falling within paragraph (2) and to which this Order applies are exempt from the subject information provisions.

(2)   This paragraph applies to personal data processed by a court and consisting of information supplied in a report or other evidence given to the court in the course of proceedings to which the Magistrates' Courts (Children and Young Persons) Rules

1992,[1] the Magistrates' Courts (Criminal Justice (Children)) Rules (Northern Ireland) 1999,[2] the Act of Sederunt (Child Care and Maintenance Rules) 1997[3] or the Children's Hearings (Scotland) Rules 1996[4] apply where, in accordance with a provision of any of those Rules, the information may be withheld by the court in whole or in part from the data subject.

Notes
[1]SI 1992/2071 as amended by SI 1997/2420.
[2]SR 1999 No. 7.
[3]SI 1997/291 (s. 19).
[4]SI 1996/3261 (s. 251).

5. Exemptions from section 7

(1)   Personal data to which this Order applies are exempt from section 7 in any case to the extent to which the application of that section would be likely to cause serious harm to the physical or mental health or condition of the data subject or any other person.

(2)   In circumstances where the exemption in paragraph (1) does not apply, where any person falling within paragraph (3) is enabled by or under any enactment or rule of law to make a request on behalf of a data subject and has made such a request, personal data consisting of information as to whether the data subject is or has been the subject of or may be at risk of child abuse are exempt from section 7 in any case to the extent to which the application of that section would not be in the best interests of that data subject.

(3)   A person falls within this paragraph if—
  (a)   the data subject is a child, and that person has parental responsibility for that data subject; or
  (b)   the data subject is incapable of managing his own affairs and that person has been appointed by a court to manage those affairs.

(4)   For the purposes of paragraph (2), 'child abuse' includes physical injury (other than accidental injury) to, and physical and emotional neglect, ill-treatment and sexual abuse of, a child.

(5)   Paragraph (2) shall not apply in Scotland.

6. Modification of section 7 relating to Principal Reporter

Where in Scotland a data controller who is an education authority receives a request relating to information constituting data to which this Order applies and which the education authority believes to have originated from or to have been supplied by or on behalf of the Principal Reporter acting in pursuance of his statutory duties, other than information which the data subject is entitled to receive from the Principal Reporter, section 7 shall be modified so that—
  (a)   the data controller shall, within fourteen days of the relevant day (as defined by section 7(10) of the Act), inform the Principal Reporter that a request has been made; and
  (b)   the data controller shall not communicate information to the data subject pursuant to that section unless the Principal Reporter has informed that data controller that, in his opinion, the exemption specified in article 5(1) does not apply with respect to the information.

7. Further modifications of section 7

(1)   In relation to data to which this Order applies—

(a)   section 7(4) of the Act shall have effect as if there were inserted after paragraph (b) of that subsection

'or

(c)   the other individual is a relevant person';

(b)   section 7(9) shall have effect as if—

(i)   there was substituted—

'(9)   If a court is satisfied on the application of—

(a)   any person who has made a request under the foregoing provisions of this section, or

(b)   any person to whom serious harm to his physical or mental health or condition would be likely to be caused by compliance with any such request in contravention of those provisions,

that the data controller in question is about to comply with or has failed to comply with the request in contravention of those provisions, the court may order him not to comply or, as the case may be, to comply with the request.'; and

(ii)   the reference to a contravention of the foregoing provisions of that section included a reference to a contravention of the provisions contained in this Order.

(2)   After section 7(ii) of the Act insert—

'(12)   A person is a relevant person for the purposes of subsection (4)(c) if he—

(a)   is a person referred to in paragraph 4(a) or (b) or paragraph 8(a) or (b) of Schedule 11;

(b)   is employed by an education authority (within the meaning of paragraph 6 of Schedule 11) in pursuance of its functions relating to education and the information relates to him, or he supplied the information in his capacity as such an employee; or

(c)   is the person making the request.'

Mike O'Brien
Parliamentary Under-Secretary of State
Home Office
17 February 2000

THE DATA PROTECTION (SUBJECT ACCESS MODIFICATION) (SOCIAL WORK) ORDER 2000 (SI 2000 No. 415)

1.   Citation and commencement

This Order may be cited as the Data Protection (Subject Access Modification) (Social Work) Order 2000 and shall come into force on 1st March 2000.

2.   Interpretation

(1)   In this Order—

'the Act' means the Data Protection Act 1998;

'compulsory school age' in paragraph 1(f) of the Schedule has the same meaning as in section 8 of the Education Act 1996,[1] and in paragraph 1(g) of the Schedule has the same meaning as in Article 46 of the Education and Libraries (Northern Ireland) Order 1986;[2]

Notes
[1] 1996 c. 56, as amended by section 52(1) to (3) of the Education Act 1997 (c. 44).
[2] SI 1986/594 (NI 3). Article 46 was substituted by Article 156 of SI 1989/2406 (NI 20).

'Health and Social Services Board' means a Health and Social Services Board established under Article 16 of the Health and Personal Social Services (Northern Ireland) Order 1972;[1]
'Health and Social Services Trust' means a Health and Social Services Trust established under the Health and Personal Social Services (Northern Ireland) Order 1991;[2]
'Principal Reporter' means the Principal Reporter appointed under section 127 of the Local Government etc. (Scotland) Act 1994[3] or any officer of the Scottish Children's Reporter Administration to whom there is delegated under section 131(1) of that Act any function of the Principal Reporter;
'request' means a request made under section 7;
'school age' in paragraph 1(h) of the Schedule has the same meaning as in section 31 of the Education (Scotland) Act 1980;[4]
'section 7' means section 7 of the Act; and
'social work authority' in article 6 means a local authority for the purposes of the Social Work (Scotland) Act 1968.[5]

(2)   Any reference in this Order to a local authority in relation to data processed or formerly processed by it includes a reference to the Council of the Isles of Scilly in relation to data processed or formerly processed by the Council in connection with any functions mentioned in paragraph 1(a)(ii) of the Schedule which are or have been conferred upon the Council by or under any enactment.

Notes
[1]SI 1972/1265 (NI 14).
[2]SI 1991/194 (NI 1).
[3]1994 c. 39.
[4]1980 c. 44.
[5]1968 c. 49.

3.   Personal data to which Order applies
(1)   Subject to paragraph (2), this Order applies to personal data falling within any of the descriptions set out in paragraphs 1 and 2 of the Schedule.
(2)   This Order does not apply—
(a)   to any data consisting of information as to the physical or mental health or condition of the data subject to which the Data Protection (Subject Access Modification) (Health) Order 2000[1] or the Data Protection (Subject Access Modification) (Education) Order 2000[2] applies; or
(b)   to any data which are exempted from section 7 by an order made under section 38(1) of the Act.

Notes
[1]SI 2000/413.
[2]SI 2000/414.

4.   Exemption from subject information provisions
Personal data to which this Order applies by virtue of paragraph 2 of the Schedule are exempt from the subject information provisions.

5.   Exemption from section 7
(1)   Personal data to which this Order applies by virtue of paragraph 1 of the Schedule are exempt from the obligations in section 7(1)(b) to (d) of the Act in any case to the extent to which the application of those provisions would be likely to

prejudice the carrying out of social work by reason of the fact that serious harm to the physical or mental health or condition of the data subject or any other person would be likely to be caused.

(2)   In paragraph (1) the 'carrying out of social work' shall be construed as including—

(a)   the exercise of any functions mentioned in paragraph 1(a)(i), (d), (f) to (j), (m) or (o) of the Schedule;

(b)   the provision of any service mentioned in paragraph 1(b), (c) or (k) of the Schedule; and

(c)   the exercise of the functions of any body mentioned in paragraph 1(e) of the Schedule or any person mentioned in paragraph 1(p) or (q) of the Schedule.

(3)   Where any person falling within paragraph (4) is enabled by or under any enactment or rule of law to make a request on behalf of a data subject and has made such a request, personal data to which this Order applies are exempt from section 7 in any case to the extent to which the application of that section would disclose information—

(a)   provided by the data subject in the expectation that it would not be disclosed to the person making the request;

(b)   obtained as a result of any examination or investigation to which the data subject consented in the expectation that the information would not be so disclosed; or

(c)   which the data subject has expressly indicated should not be so disclosed, provided that sub-paragraphs (a) and (b) shall not prevent disclosure where the data subject has expressly indicated that he no longer has the expectation referred to therein.

(4)   A person falls within this paragraph if—

(a)   except in relation to Scotland, the data subject is a child, and that person has parental responsibility for that data subject;

(b)   in relation to Scotland, the data subject is a person under the age of sixteen, and that person has parental responsibilities for that data subject; or

(c)   the data subject is incapable of managing his own affairs and that person has been appointed by a court to manage those affairs.

6.   Modification of section 7 relating to Principal Reporter

Where in Scotland a data controller who is a social work authority receives a request relating to information constituting data to which this Order applies and which originated from or was supplied by the Principal Reporter acting in pursuance of his statutory duties, other than information which the data subject is entitled to receive from the Principal Reporter, section 7 shall be modified so that—

(a)   the data controller shall, within fourteen days of the relevant day (within the meaning of section 7(10) of the Act), inform the Principal Reporter that a request has been made; and

(b)   the data controller shall not communicate information to the data subject pursuant to that section unless the Principal Reporter has informed that data controller that, in his opinion, the exemption specified in article 5(1) does not apply with respect to the information.

7.   Further modifications of section 7

(1)   In relation to data to which this Order applies by virtue of paragraph 1 of the Schedule—

(a)   section 7(4) shall have effect as if there were inserted after paragraph (b) of that subsection

'or,

(c)   the other individual is a relevant person';

(b)   section 7(9) shall have effect as if—

(i)   there was substituted—

'(9)   If a court is satisfied on the application of—

(a)   any person who has made a request under the foregoing provisions of this section, or

(b)   any person to whom serious harm to his physical or mental health or condition would be likely to be caused by compliance with any such request in contravention of those provisions,

that the data controller in question is about to comply with or has failed to comply with the request in contravention of those provisions, the court may order him not to comply or, as the case may be, to comply with the request.'; and

(ii)   the reference to a contravention of the foregoing provisions of that section included a reference to a contravention of the provisions contained in this Order.

(2)   After section 7(11) of the Act insert—

'(12)   A person is a relevant person for the purposes of subsection (4)(c) if he—

(a)   is a person referred to in paragraph 1 (p) or (q) of the Schedule to the Data Protection (Subject Access Modification) (Social Work) Order 2000; or

(b)   is or has been employed by any person or body referred to in paragraph 1 of that Schedule in connection with functions which are or have been exercised in relation to the data consisting of the information; or

(c)   has provided for reward a service similar to a service provided in the exercise of any functions specified in paragraph 1(a)(i), (b), (c) or (d) of that Schedule,

and the information relates to him or he supplied the information in his official capacity or, as the case may be, in connection with the provision of that service.'

Mike O'Brien
Parliamentary Under-Secretary of State
Home Office
17 February 2000

Article 3   SCHEDULE
PERSONAL DATA TO WHICH THIS ORDER APPLIES

1.   This paragraph applies to personal data falling within any of the following descriptions—

(a)   data processed by a local authority—

(i)   in connection with its social services functions within the meaning of the Local Authority Social Services Act 1970[1] or any functions exercised by local authorities under the Social Work (Scotland) Act 1968 or referred to in section 5(1B) of that Act,[2] or

Notes
[1] 1970 c. 42.
[2] Section 5(1B) was inserted by paragraph 76(3) of Schedule 13 to the Local Government etc. (Scotland) Act 1994 (c. 39), as amended by paragraph 15(4) of Schedule 4 and Schedule 5 to the Children (Scotland) Act 1995 (c. 36).

(ii) in the exercise of other functions but obtained or consisting of information obtained in connection with any of those functions;

(b) data processed by a Health and Social Services Board in connection with the provision of personal social services within the meaning of the Health and Personal Social Services (Northern Ireland) Order 1972 or processed by the Health and Social Services Board in the exercise of other functions but obtained or consisting of information obtained in connection with the provision of those services;

(c) data processed by a Health and Social Services Trust in connection with the provision of personal social services within the meaning of the Health and Personal Social Services (Northern Ireland) Order 1972 on behalf of a Health and Social Services Board by virtue of an authorisation made under Article 3(1) of the Health and Personal Social Services (Northern Ireland) Order 1994[3] or processed by the Health and Social Services Trust in the exercise of other functions but obtained or consisting of information obtained in connection with the provision of those services;

(d) data processed by a council in the exercise of its functions under Part II of Schedule 9 to the Health and Social Services and Social Security Adjudications Act 1983;[4]

(e) data processed by a probation committee established by section 3 of the Probation Service Act 1993[5] or the Probation Board for Northern Ireland established by the Probation Board (Northern Ireland) Order 1982;[6]

(f) data processed by a local education authority in the exercise of its functions under section 36 of the Children Act 1989[7] or Chapter II of Part VI of the Education Act 1996 so far as those functions relate to ensuring that children of compulsory school age receive suitable education whether by attendance at school or otherwise;

(g) data processed by an education and library board in the exercise of its functions under article 55 of the Children (Northern Ireland) Order 1995[8] or article 45 of, and Schedule 13 to, the Education and Libraries (Northern Ireland) Order 1986[9] so far as those functions relate to ensuring that children of compulsory school age receive efficient full-time education suitable to their age, ability and aptitude and to any special educational needs they may have, either by regular attendance at school or otherwise;

(h) data processed by an education authority in the exercise of its functions under sections 35 to 42 of the Education (Scotland) Act 1980 so far as those functions relate to ensuring that children of school age receive efficient education suitable to their age, ability and aptitude, whether by attendance at school or otherwise;

(i) data relating to persons detained in a special hospital provided under section 4 of the National Health Service Act 1977[10] and processed by a special health authority established under section 11 of that Act[11] in the exercise of any functions similar to any social services functions of a local authority;

Notes

[3] SI 1994/429 (NI 2).
[4] 1983 c. 41.
[5] 1993 c. 47.
[6] SI 1982/172 (NI 10).
[7] 1989 c. 41.
[8] SI 1995/775 (NI 2).
[9] SI 1986/594 (NI 3), as amended by article 27 of SI 1996/274 (NI 1).
[10] 1977 c. 49, as amended by paragraph 2 of Schedule 1 to the Health Authorities Act 1995 (c. 17).
[11] Section 11 was amended by paragraph 6 of Schedule 4 to the Health Act 1999 (c. 8).

(j)   data relating to persons detained in special accommodation provided under article 110 of the Mental Health (Northern Ireland) Order 1986[12] and processed by a Health and Social Services Trust in the exercise of any functions similar to any social services functions of a local authority;

(k)   data processed by the National Society for the Prevention of Cruelty to Children or by any other voluntary organisation or other body designated under this sub-paragraph by the Secretary of State or the Department of Health, Social Services and Public Safety and appearing to the Secretary of State or the Department, as the case may be, to be processed for the purposes of the provision of any service similar to a service provided in the exercise of any functions specified in sub-paragraphs (a)(i), (b), (c) or (d) above;

(l)   data processed by—

(i)   a Health Authority established under section 8 of the National Health Service Act 1977;[13]

(ii)   an NHS Trust established under section 5 of the National Health Service and Community Care Act 1990;[14] or

(iii)   a Health Board established under section 2 of the National Health Service (Scotland) Act 1978,[15]

which were obtained or consisted of information which was obtained from any authority or body mentioned above or government department and which, whilst processed by that authority or body or government department, fell within any sub-paragraph of this paragraph;

(m)   data processed by an NHS Trust as referred to in sub-paragraph (1)(ii) above in the exercise of any functions similar to any social services functions of a local authority;

(n)   data processed by a government department and obtained or consisting of information obtained from any authority or body mentioned above and which, whilst processed by that authority or body, fell within any of the preceding sub-paragraphs of this paragraph;

(o)   data processed for the purposes of the functions of the Secretary of State pursuant to section 82(5) of the Children Act 1989;

(p)   data processed by any guardian ad litem appointed under section 41 of the Children Act 1989, Article 60 of the Children (Northern Ireland) Order 1995[16] or Article 66 of the Adoption (Northern Ireland) Order 1987[17] or by a safeguarder appointed under section 41 of the Children (Scotland) Act 1995;[18]

(q)   data processed by the Principal Reporter.

2.   This paragraph applies to personal data processed by a court and consisting of information supplied in a report or other evidence given to the court by a local authority, Health and Social Services Board, Health and Social Services Trust,

Notes

[12]SI 1986/595 (NI 4).

[13]1977 c.49, as amended by section 1 of theHealth Authorities Act 1995 (c. 17) and paragraph 5 of Schedule 4 to the Health Act 1999 (c. 8).

[14]1990 c. 19, as amended by paragreaph 65 of Schedule 1 to the Health Authorities Act 1995 (c. 17) and sections 13 and 14 of the Health Act 1999 (c. 8).

[15]1978 c. 29.

[16]SI 1995/755 (NI 2).

[17]SI 1987/2203 (NI 22), as amended by paragraph 166 of Schedule 9 to SI 1995/755 (NI 2).

[18]1995 c. 36.

probation officer or other person in the course of any proceedings to which the Family Proceedings Courts (Children Act 1989) Rules 1991,[19] the Magistrates' Courts (Children and Young Persons) Rules 1992,[20] the Magistrates' Courts (Criminal Justice (Children)) Rules (Northern Ireland) 1999,[21] the Act of Sederunt (Child Care and Maintenance Rules) 1997[22] or the Children's Hearings (Scotland) Rules 1996[23] apply where, in accordance with a provision of any of those Rules, the information may be withheld by the court in whole or in part from the data subject.

Notes

[19] SI 1991/1395 as amended by SI 1991/1991, SI 1992/2068, SI 1994/2166, SI 1994/3156 and SI 1997/1895.

[30] SI 1992/2071 as amended by SI 1997/2420.

[31] SR 1999 No. 7.

[32] SI 1997/291 (s. 19).

[33] SI 1996/3261 (s. 251).

THE DATA PROTECTION (CROWN APPOINTMENTS) ORDER 2000
(SI 2000 No. 416)

1.   This Order may be cited as the Data Protection (Crown Appointments) Order 2000 and shall come into force on 1st March 2000.

2.   There shall be exempted from the subject information provisions of the Data Protection Act 1998 (as defined by section 27(2) of that Act) personal data processed for the purposes of assessing any person's suitability for any of the offices listed in the Schedule to this Order.

Mike O'Brien
Parliamentary Under-Secretary of State
Home Office
17 February 2000

Article 2   **SCHEDULE**
EXEMPTIONS FROM SUBJECT INFORMATION PROVISIONS

Offices to which appointments are made by Her Majesty:—

  (a)   Archbishops, diocesan and suffragan bishops in the Church of England
  (b)   Deans of cathedrals of the Church of England
  (c)   Deans and Canons of the two Royal Peculiars
  (d)   The First and Second Church Estates Commissioners
  (e)   Lord-Lieutenants
  (f)   Masters of Trinity College and Churchill College, Cambridge
  (g)   The Provost of Eton
  (h)   The Poet Laureate
  (i)   The Astronomer Royal

THE DATA PROTECTION (PROCESSING OF SENSITIVE PERSONAL DATA) ORDER 2000
(SI 2000 No. 417)

1.—(1)   This Order may be cited as the Data Protection (Processing of Sensitive Personal Data) Order 2000 and shall come into force on 1st March 2000.

(2)   In this Order, 'the Act' means the Data Protection Act 1998.

2.   For the purposes of paragraph 10 of Schedule 3 to the Act, the circumstances specified in any of the paragraphs in the Schedule to this Order are circumstances in which sensitive personal data may be processed.

Mike O'Brien
Parliamentary Under-Secretary of State
Home Office
17 February 2000

Article 2   SCHEDULE
CIRCUMSTANCES IN WHICH SENSITIVE PERSONAL DATA MAY BE
PROCESSED

1.—(1)   The processing—
   (a)   is in the substantial public interest;
   (b)   is necessary for the purposes of the prevention or detection of any unlawful act; and
   (c)   must necessarily be carried out without the explicit consent of the data subject being sought so as not to prejudice those purposes.
(2)   In this paragraph, 'act' includes a failure to act.
2.   The processing—
   (a)   is in the substantial public interest;
   (b)   is necessary for the discharge of any function which is designed for protecting members of the public against—
     (i)   dishonesty, malpractice, or other seriously improper conduct by, or the unfitness or incompetence of, any person, or
     (ii)   mismanagement in the administration of, or failures in services provided by, any body or association; and
   (c)   must necessarily be carried out without the explicit consent of the data subject being sought so as not to prejudice the discharge of that function.
3.—(1)   The disclosure of personal data—
   (a)   is in the substantial public interest;
   (b)   is in connection with—
     (i)   the commission by any person of any unlawful act (whether alleged or established),
     (ii)   dishonesty, malpractice, or other seriously improper conduct by, or the unfitness or incompetence of, any person (whether alleged or established), or
     (iii)   mismanagement in the administration of, or failures in services provided by, any body or association (whether alleged or established);
   (c)   is for the special purposes as defined in section 3 of the Act; and
   (d)   is made with a view to the publication of those data by any person and the data controller reasonably believes that such publication would be in the public interest.
(2)   In this paragraph, 'act' includes a failure to act.
4.   The processing—
   (a)   is in the substantial public interest;

(b)   is necessary for the discharge of any function which is designed for the provision of confidential counselling, advice, support or any other service; and

(c)   is carried out without the explicit consent of the data subject because the processing—

(i)   is necessary in a case where consent cannot be given by the data subject,

(ii)   is necessary in a case where the data controller cannot reasonably be expected to obtain the explicit consent of the data subject, or

(iii)   must necessarily be carried out without the explicit consent of the data subject being sought so as not to prejudice the provision of that counselling, advice, support or other service.

5.—(1)   The processing—

(a)   is necessary for the purpose of—

(i)   carrying on insurance business, or

(ii)   making determinations in connection with eligibility for, and benefits payable under, an occupational pension scheme as defined in section 1 of the Pension Schemes Act 1993;[1]

(b)   is of sensitive personal data consisting of information falling within section 2(e) of the Act relating to a data subject who is the parent, grandparent, great grandparent or sibling of—

(i)   in the case of paragraph (a)(i), the insured person, or

(ii)   in the case of paragraph (a)(ii), the member of the scheme;

(c)   is necessary in a case where the data controller cannot reasonably be expected to obtain the explicit consent of that data subject and the data controller is not aware of the data subject withholding his consent; and

(d)   does not support measures or decisions with respect to that data subject.

(2)   In this paragraph—

(a)   'insurance business' means insurance business, as defined in section 95 of the Insurance Companies Act 1982,[2] falling within Classes I, III or IV of Schedule 1 (classes of long term business) or Classes 1 or 2 of Schedule 2 (classes of general business) to that Act, and

(b)   'insured' and 'member' includes an individual who is seeking to become an insured person or member of the scheme respectively.

Notes
[1] 1993 c. 48.
[2] 1982 c. 50.

6.   The processing—

(a)   is of sensitive personal data in relation to any particular data subject that are subject to processing which was already under way immediately before the coming into force of this Order;

(b)   is necessary for the purpose of—

(i)   carrying on insurance business, as defined in section 95 of the Insurance Companies Act 1982, falling within Classes I, III or IV of Schedule 1 to that Act; or

(ii)   establishing or administering an occupational pension scheme as defined in section 1 of the Pension Schemes Act 1993; and

(c)   either—

(i)   is necessary in a case where the data controller cannot reasonably be expected to obtain the explicit consent of the data subject and that data subject has not informed the data controller that he does not so consent, or

  (ii) must necessarily be carried out even without the explicit consent of the data subject so as not to prejudice those purposes.

  7.—(1) Subject to the provisions of sub-paragraph (2), the processing—

   (a) is of sensitive personal data consisting of information falling within section 2(c) or (e) of the Act;

   (b) is necessary for the purpose of identifying or keeping under review the existence or absence of equality of opportunity or treatment between persons—

    (i) holding different beliefs as described in section 2(c) of the Act, or

    (ii) of different states of physical or mental health or different physical or mental conditions as described in section 2(e) of the Act,

with a view to enabling such equality to be promoted or maintained;

   (c) does not support measures or decisions with respect to any particular data subject otherwise than with the explicit consent of that data subject; and

   (d) does not cause, nor is likely to cause, substantial damage or substantial distress to the data subject or any other person.

  (2) Where any individual has given notice in writing to any data controller who is processing personal data under the provisions of sub-paragraph (1) requiring that data controller to cease processing personal data in respect of which that individual is the data subject at the end of such period as is reasonable in the circumstances, that data controller must have ceased processing those personal data at the end of that period.

  8.—(1) Subject to the provisions of sub-paragraph (2), the processing—

   (a) is of sensitive personal data consisting of information falling within section 2(b) of the Act;

   (b) is carried out by any person or organisation included in the register maintained pursuant to section 1 of the Registration of Political Parties Act 1998[1] in the course of his or its legitimate political activities; and

   (c) does not cause, nor is likely to cause, substantial damage or substantial distress to the data subject or any other person.

  (2) Where any individual has given notice in writing to any data controller who is processing personal data under the provisions of sub-paragraph (1) requiring that data controller to cease processing personal data in respect of which that individual is the data subject at the end of such period as is reasonable in the circumstances, that data controller must have ceased processing those personal data at the end of that period.

Note
[1]1998 c. 48.

  9. The processing—

   (a) is in the substantial public interest;

   (b) is necessary for research purposes (which expression shall have the same meaning as in section 33 of the Act);

   (c) does not support measures or decisions with respect to any particular data subject otherwise than with the explicit consent of that data subject; and

   (d) does not cause, nor is likely to cause, substantial damage or substantial distress to the data subject or any other person.

  10. The processing is necessary for the exercise of any functions conferred on a constable by any rule of law.

THE DATA PROTECTION (DESIGNATED CODES OF PRACTICE) ORDER 2000
(SI 2000 No. 418)

1.   This Order may be cited as the Data Protection (Designated Codes of Practice Order 2000 and shall come into force on 1st March 2000.

2.   The codes of practice listed in the Schedule to this Order shall be designated for the purposes of section 32(3) of the Data Protection Act 1998.

Mike O'Brien
Parliamentary Under-Secretary of State
Home Office
17 February 2000

Article 2   SCHEDULE
DESIGNATED CODES OF PRACTICE

1.   The Code on Fairness and Privacy issued by the Broadcasting Standards Commission in June 1998 pursuant to sections 107 and 108 of the Broadcasting Act 1996.[1]

2.   The ITC Programme Code issued by the Independent Television Commission in Autumn 1998 pursuant to section 7 of the Broadcasting Act 1990.[2]

3.   The Code of Practice published by the Press Complaints Commission in December 1997.

4.   The Producers' Guidelines issued by the British Broadcasting Corporation in November 1996.

5.   The Programme Code issued by the Radio Authority in March 1998 pursuant to section 91 of the Broadcasting Act 1990.

Notes
[1] 1996 c. 55.
[2] 1990 c. 42.

THE DATA PROTECTION (MISCELLANEOUS SUBJECT ACCESS EXEMPTIONS)
(SI 2000 No. 419)

1.   This Order may be cited as the Data Protection (Miscellaneous Subject Access Exemptions) Order 2000 and shall come into force on 1st March 2000.

2.   Personal data consisting of information the disclosure of which is prohibited or restricted by the enactments and instruments listed in the Schedule to this Order are exempt from section 7 of the Data Protection Act 1998.

Mike O'Brien
Parliamentary Under-Secretary of State
Home Office
17 February 2000

Article 2   SCHEDULE
                       EXEMPTIONS FROM SECTION 7
                               PART I
         Enactments and Instruments Extending to the United Kingdom

Human fertilisation and embryology: information about the provision of treatment services, the keeping or use of gametes or embryos and whether identifiable individuals were born in consequence of treatment services. Sections 31 and 33 of the Human Fertilisation and Embryology Act 1990.[1]

Note
[1]1990 c. 37. Section 33 was amended by section 1 of the Human Fertilisation nd Embryology (Disclosure of Information) Act 1992 (c. 54).

                              PART II
         Enactments and Instruments Extending to England and Wales

   (a)   *Adoption records and reports*
Sections 50 and 51 of the Adoption Act 1976.[1]
   Regulations 6 and 14 of the Adoption Agencies Regulations 1983,[2] so far as they relate to records and other information in the possession of local authorities.
   Rules 5, 6, 9, 17, 18, 21, 22 and 53 of the Adoption Rules 1984.[3]
   Rules 5, 6, 9, 17, 18, 21, 22 and 32 of the Magistrates' Courts (Adoption) Rules 1984.[4]
   (b)   *Statement of child's special educational needs*
Regulation 19 of the Education (Special Educational Needs) Regulations 1994.[5]
   (c)   *Parental order records and reports*
Sections 50 and 51 of the Adoption Act 1976[6] as modified by paragraphs 4(a) and (b) of Schedule 1 to the Parental Orders (Human Fertilisation and Embryology) Regulations 1994[7] in relation to parental orders made under section 30 of the Human Fertilisation and Embryology Act 1990.
   Rules 4A.5 and 4A.9 of the Family Proceedings Rules 1991.[8]
   Rules 21E and 21I of the Family Proceedings Courts (Children Act 1989) Rules 1991.[9]

Notes
[1]1976 c. 36. Section 51 was amended by paragraph 20 of Schedule 10 to the Children Act 1989 (c. 41).
[2]SI 1983/1964, as amended by regulation 2 of SI 1997/2308 and regulation 2 of SI 1997/649.
[3]SI 1984/265, as amended by SI 1991/1880.
[4]SI 1984/611, as amended by SI 1989/384 (L. 7) and paragraph 4 of Schedule 2 to SI 1991/1991.
[5]SI 1994/1047.
[6]1976 c. 36.
[7]SI 1994/2767.
[8]SI 1991/1247 as amended by SI 1994/2165.
[9]SI 1991/1395 as amended by SI 1994/2166.

                             PART III
         Enactments and Instruments Extending to Scotland

   (a)   *Adoption records and reports*
Section 45 of the Adoption (Scotland) Act 1978.[1]

Note
[1]1978 c. 28. Section 45 was amended by paragraph 41 of Schedule 10 to the Children Act 1989 (c. 41) and paragraph 22 of Schedule 2 to the Children (Scotland) Act 1995 (c. 36).

Regulation 23 of the Adoption Agencies (Scotland) Regulations 1996,[2] so far as it relates to records and other information in the possession of local authorities.

Rule 67.3 of the Act of Sederunt (Rules of the Court of Session 1994) 1994.[3]

Rules 2.12, 2.14, 2.30 and 2.33 of the Act of Sederunt (Child Care and Maintenance Rules) 1997.[4]

Regulation 8 of the Adoption Allowance (Scotland) Regulations 1996.[5]

(b) *Information provided by principal reporter for children's hearing*

Rules 5 and 21 of the Children's Hearings (Scotland) Rules 1996.[6]

(c) *Record of child or young person's special educational needs*

Section 60(4) of the Education (Scotland) Act 1980.[7]

Proviso (bb) to regulation 7(2) of the Education (Record of Needs) (Scotland) Regulations 1982.[8]

(d) *Parental order records and reports*

Section 45 of the Adoption (Scotland) Act 1978 as modified by paragraph 10 of Schedule 1 to the Parental Orders (Human Fertilisation and Embryology) (Scotland) Regulations 1994[9] in relation to parental orders made under section 30 of the Human Fertilisation and Embryology Act 1990.

Rules 2.47 and 2.59 of the Act of Sederunt (Child Care and Maintenance Rules) 1997.

Rules 81.3 and 81.18 of the Act of Sederunt (Rules of the Court of Session 1994) 1994.[10]

Notes
[2]SI 1996/3266 (s. 254).
[3]SI 1994/1443.
[4]SI 1997/291 (s. 19).
[5]SI 1996/3257.
[6]SI 1996/3261.
[7]1980 c. 44. Section 60 was amended by section 4 of the Education (Scotland) Act 1981 (c. 58).
[8]SI 1982/1222.
[9]SI 1994/1443, as amended by SI 1994/2804 (s. 141).
[10]SI 1994/2806 (s. 143).

PART IV
Enactments and Instruments Extending to Northern Ireland

(a) *Adoption records and reports*

Articles 50 and 54 of the Adoption (Northern Ireland) Act 1987.[1]

Rule 53 of Order 84 of the Rules of the Supreme Court (Northern Ireland) 1980.[2]

Rule 22 of the County Court (Adoption) Rules (Northern Ireland) 1980.[3]

Rule 32 of Order 50 of the County Court Rules (Northern Ireland) 1981.[4]

(b) *Statement of child's special educational needs*

Regulation 17 of the Education (Special Educational Needs) Regulations (Northern Ireland) 1997.[5]

Notes
[1]SI 1987/2203 NI 22. Article 54 was amended by paragraph 158 of Schedule 9 to SI 1995/755 (NI 2).
[2]SR (NI) 1980 No. 346 as amended by SR (NI) 1989 No. 343.
[3]SR (NI) 1981 No. 227.
[4]SR (NI) 1981 No. 225 as amended by SR (NI) 1989 No. 308.
[5]SR (NI) 1997 No. 327.

(c) *Parental order records and reports*

Articles 50 and 54 of the Adoption (Northern Ireland) Order 1987 as modified by paragraph 5(a) and (e) of Schedule 2 to the Parental Orders (Human Fertilisation and Embryology) Regulations 1994 in respect of parental orders made under section 30 of the Human Fertilisation and Embryology Act 1990.

Rules 4, 5 and 16 of Order 84A of the Rules of the Supreme Court (Northern Ireland) 1980.[6]

Rules 3, 4 and 15 of Order 50A of the County Court Rules (Northern Ireland) 1981.[7]

Notes
[6] SR (NI) 1980 No. 346, as amended by SR (NI) 1995 No. 2.
[7] SR (NI) 1981 No. 225, as amended by SR (NI) 1995 No. 48.

NEW DATA PROTECTION TRIBUNAL (NATIONAL SECURITY APPEALS) (TELECOMMUNICATIONS) RULES 2000
(SI 2000 No. 731)

1. Citation and commencement
These Rules may be cited as the Data Protection Tribunal (National Security Appeals) (Telecommunications) Rules 2000 and shall come into force on 5th April 2000.

2. Application and interpretation
(1) These Rules apply to appeals under regulation 32(4) and (6) of the Regulations, and the provisions of these Rules are to be construed accordingly.

(2) In these Rules—
'the Act' means the Data Protection Act 1998;
'appeal' means an appeal under regulation 32 of the Regulations;
'appellant' means a person who brings or intends to bring an appeal under regulation 32 of the Regulations;
'costs,'—
    (a) except in Scotland, includes fees, charges, disbursements, expenses and remuneration;
    (b) in Scotland means expenses, and includes fees, charges, disbursements and remuneration;
'disputed certification' means—
    (a) in relation to an appeal under regulation 32(4) of the Regulations, the certificate against which the appeal is brought or intended to be brought, and
    (b) in relation to an appeal under regulation 32(6) of the Regulations, the claim by the telecommunications provider, against which the appeal is brought or intended to be brought, that a certificate applies to the circumstance in question;
'party' has the meaning given in paragraph (3) below;
'president' means the person designated by the Lord Chancellor under paragraph 3 of Schedule 6 to the Act to preside when the Tribunal is constituted under that paragraph;
'proper officer' in relation to a rule means an officer or member of staff provided to the Tribunal under paragraph 14 of Schedule 5 to the Act and appointed by the chairman to perform the duties of a proper officer under that rule;
'the Regulations' means the Telecommunications (Data Protection and Privacy) Regulations 1999;

'relevant Minister' means the Minister of the Crown who is responsible for the signing of the certificate under regulation 32(2) of the Regulations to which the appeal relates, and except where the context otherwise requires, references in these Rules to the relevant Minister include a person appointed under rule 21 below to represent his interests;

'respondent telecommunications provider' in relation to an appeal under regulation 32(6) of the Regulations means the telecommunications provider making the claim which constitutes the disputed certification; and

'telecommunications provider' means a telecommunications service or network provider as defined in the Regulations.

(3)   In these Rules, except where the context otherwise requires, 'party' means the appellant or—

   (a)   in relation to an appeal under section 32(4) of the Regulations, the relevant Minister, and

   (b)   in relation to an appeal under section 32(6) of the Regulations, the respondent telecommunications provider, and except where the context otherwise requires, references in these Rules to a party include a person appointed under rule 21 below to represent his interests.

(4)   In relation to proceedings before the Tribunal in Scotland, for the words 'on the trial of an action' in rules 15(6) and 26(2) below there is substituted 'in a proof'.

3.   Constitution and general duty of the Tribunal

(1)   When exercising its functions under these Rules, the Tribunal shall secure that information is not disclosed contrary to the interests of national security.

(2)   Paragraph 6(1) of Schedule 6 to the Act applies only to the exercise of the jurisdiction of the Tribunal in accordance with rule 11 below.

(3)   For the purposes of paragraph (1) above, but without prejudice to the application of that paragraph, the disclosure of information is to be regarded as contrary to the interests of national security if it would indicate the existence or otherwise of any material.

4.   Method of appealing

(1)   An appeal must be brought by a written notice of appeal served on the Tribunal.

(2)   The notice of appeal shall—

   (a)   identify the disputed certification; and

   (b)   state—

      (i)   the name and address of the appellant;

      (ii)   the grounds of the appeal; and

      (iii)   an address for service of notices and other documents on the appellant.

(3)   In the case of an appeal under regulation 32(6) of the Regulations, the notice of appeal shall also state—

   (a)   the date on which the respondent telecommunications provider made the claim constituting the disputed certification;

   (b)   an address for service of notices and other documents on the respondent telecommunications provider; and

   (c)   where applicable, the special circumstances which the appellant considers justify the Tribunal's accepting jurisdiction under rule 5(3) below.

5. Time limit for appealing

(1)   In the case of an appeal under regulation 32(4) of the Regulations, a notice of appeal may be served on the Tribunal at any time during the currency of the disputed certification to which it relates.

(2)   In the case of an appeal under regulation 32(6) of the Regulations, subject to paragraph (3) below, a notice of appeal must be served on the Tribunal within 28 days of the date on which the claim constituting the disputed certification was made.

(3)   The Tribunal may accept a notice of appeal served after the expiry of the period permitted by paragraph (2) above if it is of the opinion that, by reason of special circumstances, it is just and right to do so.

(4)   A notice of appeal shall if sent by post in accordance with rule 30(1) below be treated as having been served on the date on which it is received for dispatch by the Post office.

6. Acknowledgment of notice of appeal and notification by the Tribunal

(1)   Upon receipt of a notice of appeal, the proper officer shall send—

   (a)   an acknowledgment of the service of a notice of appeal to the appellant, and

   (b)   a copy of the notice of appeal to—

      (i)   the relevant Minister,

      (ii)   the commissioner, and

      (iii) in the case of an appeal under regulation 32(6) of the Regulations, the respondent telecommunications provider.

(2)   An acknowledgment of service under paragraph (1)(a) above shall be accompanied by a statement of the Tribunal's powers to award costs against the appellant under rule 28 below.

7. Relevant Minister's notice in reply

(1)   No later than 42 days after receipt of a copy of a notice of appeal under rule 6(1)(b) above, the relevant Minister shall send to the Tribunal—

   (a)   a copy of the certificate to which the appeal relates, and

   (b)   a written notice in accordance with paragraph (2) below.

(2)   The notice shall state—

   (a)   with regard to an appeal under regulation 32(4) of the Regulations, whether or not he intends to oppose the appeal and, if so—

      (i)   a summary of the circumstances relating to the issue of the certificate, and the reasons for the issue of the certificate;

      (ii)   the grounds upon which he relies in opposing the appeal; and

      (iii) a statement of the evidence upon which he relies in support of those grounds; and

   (b)   with regard to an appeal under regulation 32(6) of the Regulations, whether or not he wishes to make representations in relation to the appeal and, if so—

      (i)   the extent to which he intends to support or oppose the appeal;

      (ii)   the grounds upon which he relies in supporting or opposing the appeal; and

      (iii) a statement of the evidence upon which he relies in support of those grounds.

(3)   Except where the Tribunal proposes to determine the appeal in accordance with rule 11 below, and subject to rule 12 below, the proper officer shall send a copy of the notice to—

    (a) the appellant,

    (b) the Commissioner, and

    (c) in the case of an appeal under regulation 32(6) of the Regulations, the respondent telecommunications provider.

8.　Reply by respondent telecommunications provider

(1) A respondent telecommunications provider shall, within 42 days of the date on which he receives a copy of a notice of appeal under rule 6(1)(b) above, send to the Tribunal a written reply acknowledging service upon him of the notice of appeal, and stating—

    (a) whether or not he intends to oppose the appeal and, if so,

    (b) the grounds upon which he relies in opposing the appeal.

(2) Before the expiry of the period of 42 days referred to in paragraph (1) above, the respondent telecommunications provider may apply to the Tribunal for an extension of that period, showing cause why, by reason of special circumstances, it would be just and right to do so, and the Tribunal may grant such extension as it considers appropriate.

(3) Except where the Tribunal proposes to determine the appeal in accordance with rule 11 below, the proper officer shall send a copy of the reply to—

    (a) the relevant Minister; and

    (b) subject to paragraph (4) and rule 12 below, the appellant and the Commissioner.

(4) No copy may be sent under paragraph (3)(b) above before the period of 42 days referred to in rule 12(2)(b) below has expired, otherwise than in accordance with rule 12, unless the relevant Minister has indicated that he does not object.

9.　Amendment and supplementary grounds

(1) With the leave of the Tribunal, the appellant may amend his notice of appeal or deliver supplementary grounds of appeal.

(2) Rule 6(1) above and rule 11(1)(a) below apply to an amended notice of appeal and to supplementary grounds of appeal provided under paragraph (1) above as they do to a notice of appeal.

(3) Upon receipt of a copy of an amended notice of appeal or amended grounds of appeal under rule 6(1) above, the relevant Minister may amend his notice in reply and, in the case of an appeal under regulation 32(6) of the Regulations, the respondent telecommunications provider, may amend his reply to the notice of appeal.

(4) An amended notice or reply under paragraph (3) above must be sent to the Tribunal within 28 days of the date on which the copy referred to in that paragraph is received.

(5) Without prejudice to paragraph (3) above, and with the leave of the Tribunal—

    (a) the relevant Minister may amend a notice in reply, and

    (b) the respondent telecommunications provider may amend a reply to the notice of appeal.

(6) Rule 7(3) above and rules 11(1)(b) and 12(1)(a) below apply to an amended notice in reply by the relevant Minister provided under paragraph (3) or (5) above as they do to a notice in reply.

(7) Rule 8(3) and (4) above and rules 11(1)(c) and 12(1)(b) below apply to an amended reply by the respondent telecommunications provider provided under paragraph (3) or (5) above as they do to a reply.

10. Application for striking out

(1)   Where the relevant Minister or, in the case of an appeal under regulation 32(6) of the Regulations, the respondent telecommunications provider is of the opinion that an appeal does not lie to, or cannot be entertained by, the Tribunal, or that the notice of appeal discloses no reasonable grounds of appeal, he may include in his notice under rule 7 or, as the case may be, his reply under rule 8 above a notice to that effect stating the grounds for such contention and applying for the appeal to be struck out.

(2)   An application under this rule may be heard as a preliminary issue or at the beginning of the hearing of the substantive appeal.

11. Summary disposal of appeals

(1)   Where, having considered—
   (a)   the notice of appeal,
   (b)   the relevant Minister's notice under rule 7 above, and
   (c)   in the case of an appeal under regulation 32(6) of the Regulations, the respondent telecommunication provider's reply,
the Tribunal is of the opinion that the appeal is of such a nature that it can properly be determined by dismissing it forthwith, it may, subject to the provisions of this rule, so determine the appeal.

(2)   Where the Tribunal proposes to determine an appeal under paragraph (1) above, it must first notify the appellant and the relevant Minister of the proposal.

(3)   A notification to the appellant under paragraph (2) above must contain particulars of the appellant's entitlements set out in paragraph (4) below.

(4)   An appellant notified in accordance with paragraph (2) above is entitled, within such time as the Tribunal may reasonably allow—
   (a)   to make written representations, and
   (b)   to request the Tribunal to hear oral representations
against the proposal to determine the appeal under paragraph (1) above.

(5)   Where an appellant requests a hearing under paragraph (4)(b) above, the Tribunal shall, as soon as practicable and with due regard to the convenience of the appellant, appoint a time and place for a hearing accordingly.

(6)   The proper officer shall send to the appellant a notice informing him of—
   (a)   the time and place of any hearing under paragraph (5) above, which, unless the appellant otherwise agrees, shall not be earlier than 14 days after the date on which the notice is sent, and
   (b)   the effect of rule 22 below.

(7)   The Tribunal must as soon as practicable notify the appellant and the relevant Minister if, having given a notification under paragraph (2) above, it ceases to propose to determine the appeal under paragraph (1) above.

12. Relevant Minister's objection to disclosure

(1)   Where the relevant Minister objects, on grounds of the need to secure that information is not disclosed contrary to the interests of national security, to the disclosure of—
   (a)   his notice in reply to the appellant, the Commissioner or, in the case of an appeal under regulation 32(6) of the Regulations, the respondent telecommunications provider; or

(b) the reply of a respondent telecommunications provider to the appellant or the Commissioner,

he may send a notice of objection to the Tribunal.

(2) A notice of objection under paragraph (1) above must be sent—

(a) where paragraph (1)(a) above applies, with the notice in reply; and

(b) where paragraph (1)(b) above applies, within 42 days of the date on which he receives the copy mentioned in rule 8(3) above.

(3) A notice of objection under paragraph (1) above shall—

(a) state the reasons for the objection; and

(b) where paragraph (1)(a) above applies, if and to the extent it is possible to do so without disclosing information contrary to the interests of national security, be accompanied by a version of the relevant Minister's notice in a form which can be shown to the appellant, the Commissioner or, as the case may be, the respondent telecommunications provider.

(4) Where the relevant Minister sends a notice of objection under paragraph (1) above, the Tribunal must not disclose the material in question otherwise than in accordance with rule 17 below.

13. Withdrawal of appeal

(1) The appellant may at any time withdraw his appeal by sending to the Tribunal a notice of withdrawal signed by him or on his behalf, and the proper officer shall send a copy of that notice to—

(a) the relevant Minister,

(b) the Commissioner, and

(c) in the case of an appeal under regulation 32(6) of the Regulations, the respondent telecommunications provider.

(2) A notice of withdrawal shall if sent by post in accordance with rule 30 (1) below have effect on the date on which it is received for dispatch by the Post Office.

(3) Where an appeal is withdrawn under this rule a fresh appeal may not be brought by the same appellant in relation to the same disputed certification except with the leave of the Tribunal.

14. Consolidation of appeals

(1) Subject to paragraph (2) below, where in the case of two or more appeals to which these Rules apply it appears to the Tribunal—

(a) that some common question of law or fact arises in both or all of them, or

(b) that for some other reason it is desirable to proceed with the appeals under this rule,

the Tribunal may order that the appeals be consolidated or heard together.

(2) The Tribunal shall not make an order under this rule without giving the parties and the relevant Minister an opportunity to show cause why such an order should not be made.

15. Directions

(1) This rule is subject to rule 16 below.

(2) In this rule, references to a 'party' include the relevant Minister notwithstanding that he may not be a party to an appeal under regulation 32(6) of the Regulations.

(3) Subject to paragraphs (6) and (7) below, the Tribunal may at any time of its own motion or on the application of any party give such directions as it thinks proper

to enable the parties to prepare for the hearing of the appeal or to assist the Tribunal to determine the issues.

(4)   Such directions may in particular—

(a)   provide for a particular matter to be dealt with as a preliminary issue and for a pre-hearing review to be held;

(b)   provide for—

(i)   the exchange between the parties of lists of documents held by them which are relevant to the appeal,

(ii)   the inspection by the parties of the documents so listed,

(iii)   the exchange between the parties of statements of evidence, and

(iv)   the provision by the parties to the Tribunal of statements or lists of agreed matters;

(c)   require any party to send to the Tribunal and to the other parties—

(i)   statements of facts and statements of the evidence which will be adduced, including such statements provided in a modified or edited form;

(ii)   a skeleton argument which summarises the submissions which will be made and cites the authorities which will be relied upon, identifying any particular passages to be relied upon;

(iii)   a chronology of events;

(iv)   any other particulars or supplementary statements which may reasonably be required for the determination of the appeal;

(v)   any document or other material which the Tribunal may require and which it is in the power of that party to deliver;

(vi)   an estimate of the time which will be needed for any hearing; and

(vii)   a list of the witnesses he intends to call to give evidence at any hearing;

(d)   limit the length of oral submissions and the time allowed for the examination and cross-examination of witnesses; and

(e)   limit the number of expert witnesses to be heard on either side.

(5)   The Tribunal may, subject to any specific provisions of these Rules, specify time limits for steps to be taken in the proceedings and may extend any time limit.

(6)   Nothing in this rule may require the production of any document or other material which the party could not be compelled to produce on the trial of an action in a court of law in that part of the United Kingdom where the appeal is to be determined.

(7)   It shall be a condition of the supply of any information or material provided under this rule that any recipient of that information or material may use it only for the purposes of the appeal.

(8)   The power to give directions may be exercised in the absence of the parties.

(9)   Notice of any directions given under this rule shall be served on all the parties, and the Tribunal may, on the application of any party, set aside or vary such directions.

16.   Applications by relevant Minister

(1)   This rule applies in any case where the Tribunal proposes to—

(a)   give or vary any direction under rule 15 above or rule 18(2) below,

(b)   issue a summons under rule 20 below, or

(c)   certify or publish a determination under rule 27 below.

(2)   Before the Tribunal proceeds as proposed in any case to which this rule applies, it must first notify the relevant Minister of the proposal.

(3)   If the relevant Minister considers that proceeding as proposed by the Tribunal would cause information to be disclosed contrary to the interests of national security, he may make an application to the Tribunal requesting it to reconsider the proposal or reconsider it to any extent.

(4)   An application by the relevant Minister under paragraph (3) above must be made within 14 days of receipt of notification under paragraph (2), and the Tribunal must not proceed as proposed in any case to which this rule applies before that period has expired, otherwise than in accordance with rule 17 below, unless the relevant Minister has indicated that he does not object.

(5)   Where the relevant Minister makes an application under this rule, the Tribunal must not proceed as proposed otherwise than in accordance with rule 17 below.

17.   Determinations on relevant Minister's objections and applications

(1)   Except where rule 11 above applies, the Tribunal shall determine whether to uphold any objection of the relevant Minister under rule 12 above, and any application under rule 16 above, in accordance with this rule.

(2)   Subject to paragraph (3) below, proceedings under this rule shall take place in the absence of the parties.

(3)   The relevant Minister (or a person authorised to act on his behalf), may attend any proceedings under this rule, whether or not he is a party to the appeal in question.

(4)   An objection under rule 12 above must be considered under this rule as a preliminary issue, and an application under rule 16 above may be considered as a preliminary issue or at the hearing of the substantive appeal.

(5)   Where, in the case of an objection under rule 12 above, the Tribunal is minded to overrule the relevant Minister's objection, or to require him to provide a version of his notice in a form other than that in which he provided it under rule 12(3)(b) above, the Tribunal must invite the relevant Minister to make oral representations.

(6)   Where the Tribunal under paragraph (5) above overrules an objection by the relevant Minister under rule 12 above, or requires him to provide a version of his notice in a form other than that in which he provided it under rule 12(3) (b) above, the Tribunal shall not disclose, and the relevant Minister shall not be required to disclose, any material which was the subject of the unsuccessful objection if the relevant Minister chooses not to rely upon it in opposing the appeal.

(7)   Where, in the case of an objection under rule 12 above, the Tribunal upholds the relevant Minister's objection and either—

(a)   approves the version of his notice provided under rule 12(3)(b); or

(b)   requires him to provide a version of his notice in a form other than that in which he provided it under rule 12(3)(b),

rule 7(3) above applies to that version of the notice.

18.   Power to determine without a hearing

(1)   Without prejudice to rule 11 above, where either—

(a)   the parties so agree in writing, or

(b)   it appears to the Tribunal that the issues raised on the appeal have been determined on a previous appeal brought by the appellant on the basis of facts which did not materially differ from those to which the appeal relates and the Tribunal has given the parties an opportunity of making representations to the effect that the appeal ought not to be determined without a hearing, the Tribunal may determine an appeal, or any particular issue, without a hearing.

(2)   Before determining any matter under this rule, the Tribunal may, subject to rule 16 above, if it thinks fit direct any party to provide in writing further information about any matter relevant to the appeal within such time as the Tribunal may allow.

19.   Time and place of hearings

(1)   Except where rule 11 or 18 above applies, as soon as practicable after notice of appeal has been given, and with due regard to the convenience of the parties, the Tribunal shall appoint a time and place for a hearing of the appeal.

(2)   Except in relation to a hearing under rule 11(5) above, the proper officer shall send to each party, the Commissioner and the relevant Minister a notice informing him of the time and place of any hearing, which, unless the parties otherwise agree, shall not be earlier than 14 days after the date on which the notice is sent.

(3)   A notice to a party under this rule shall inform him of the effect of rule 22 below.

(4)   The Tribunal may—
    (a)   postpone the time appointed for any hearing;
    (b)   adjourn a hearing to such time as the Tribunal may determine; or
    (c)   alter the place appointed for any hearing;
and, if it exercises any of the above powers, it shall notify each person previously notified of that hearing under this rule or rule 11(6) above, and any person summoned under rule 20 below to attend as a witness at that hearing, of the revised arrangements.

20.   Summoning of witnesses

(1)   This rule is subject to rule 16 above.

(2)   Subject to paragraph (3) below, the Tribunal may by summons require any person in the United Kingdom to attend as a witness at a hearing of an appeal at such time and place as may be specified in the summons and, subject to rule 26(2) and (3) below, at the hearing to answer any questions or produce any documents in his custody or under his control which relate to any matter in question in the appeal.

(3)   No person shall be required to attend in obedience to a summons under paragraph (2) above unless he has been given at least 7 days' notice of the hearing or, if less than 7 days, he has informed the Tribunal that he accepts such notice as he has been given.

(4)   The Tribunal may upon the application of a person summoned under this rule set the summons aside.

(5)   A person who has attended a hearing as a witness in obedience to a summons shall be entitled to such sum as the Tribunal considers reasonable in respect of his attendance at, and his travelling to and from, the hearing; and where the summons was issued at the request of a party such sum shall be paid or tendered to him by that party.

(6)   In relation to proceedings before the Tribunal in Scotland, in this rule 'summons' means citation and the provisions of this rule are to be construed accordingly.

21.   Representation at a hearing

(1)   At any hearing by the Tribunal, other than a hearing under rule 11 above—
    (a)   a party may, subject to rules 17(2) above and 23(3) below, conduct his case himself or may appear and be represented by any person whom he may appoint for the purpose, and

(b)   the relevant Minister may appear and be represented by any person whom he may appoint for the purpose.

(2)   At any hearing by the Tribunal under rule 11 (5) above, the appellant may conduct his case himself or may appear and be represented by any person whom he may appoint for the purpose.

22.   Default of appearance at hearing

If, without furnishing the Tribunal with sufficient reason for his absence, a party fails to appear at a hearing, having been duly notified of the hearing, the Tribunal may, if that party is the appellant, dismiss the appeal or, in any case, hear and determine the appeal, or any particular issue, in the party's absence and may make such order as to costs as it thinks fit.

23.   Hearings to be in private

(1)   All hearings by the Tribunal (including preliminary hearings) shall be in private unless the Tribunal, with the consent of the parties and the relevant Minister, directs that the hearing or any part of the hearing shall take place in public.

(2)   Where the Tribunal sits in private it may, with the consent of the parties and the relevant Minister, admit to a hearing such persons on such terms and conditions as it considers appropriate.

(3)   Where the Tribunal considers it necessary for any party other than the relevant Minister to be excluded from proceedings or any part of them in order to secure that information is not disclosed contrary to the interests of national security, it must—

(a)   direct accordingly,

(b)   inform the person excluded of its reasons, to the extent that it is possible to do so without disclosing information contrary to the interests of national security, and record those reasons in writing, and

(c)   inform the relevant Minister.

(4)   The relevant Minister, or a person authorised to act on his behalf, may attend any hearing, other than a hearing under rule 11 above, notwithstanding that it is in private.

24.   Conduct of proceedings at hearing

(1)   Subject to rules 22 and 23(3) above, the Tribunal shall at the hearing of an appeal give to each party and the relevant Minister an opportunity—

(a)   to address the Tribunal and to amplify orally written statements previously furnished under these Rules, to give evidence and to call witnesses, and to put questions to any person giving evidence before the Tribunal, and

(b)   to make representations on the evidence (if any) and on the subject matter of the appeal generally but, where evidence is taken, such opportunity shall not be given before the completion of the taking of evidence.

(2)   Except as provided by these Rules, the Tribunal shall conduct the proceedings in such manner as it considers appropriate in the circumstances for discharging its functions and shall so far as appears to it appropriate seek to avoid formality in its proceedings.

25.   Preliminary and incidental matters

As regards matters preliminary or incidental to an appeal the president may act for the Tribunal under rules 5(3), 8(2), 9, 13 to 15, 19(1) and (4)(a) and (c) and 20.

26. Evidence

(1) The Tribunal may receive in evidence any document or information notwithstanding that such document or information would be inadmissible in a court of law.

(2) No person shall be compelled to give any evidence or produce any document which he could not be compelled to give or produce on the trial of an action in a court of law in that part of the United Kingdom where the appeal is to be determined.

(3) The Tribunal may require oral evidence of a witness (including a party) to be given on oath or affirmation and for that purpose the president or the proper officer shall have power to administer oaths or take affirmations.

27. Determination of appeal

(1) As soon as practicable after the Tribunal has determined an appeal, the president shall certify in writing that determination and sign and date the certificate.

(2) If and to the extent that it is possible to do so without disclosing information contrary to the interests of national security, and subject to rule 16 above, the certificate shall include—

    (a) any material finding of fact, and

    (b) the reasons for the decision.

(3) The proper officer shall send a copy of the certificate to—

    (a) the parties,

    (b) the relevant Minister, and

    (c) the Commissioner.

(4) Subject to rule 16 above, the Tribunal shall make arrangements for the publication of its determination but in doing so shall have regard to—

    (a) the desirability of safeguarding the privacy of data subjects and commercially sensitive information, and

    (b) the need to secure that information is not disclosed contrary to the interests of national security,

and for those purposes may make any necessary amendments to the text of the certificate.

(5) For the purposes of this rule (but without prejudice to it generally), the disclosure of information is to be regarded as contrary to the interests of national security if it would indicate the existence or otherwise of any material.

28. Costs

(1) In any appeal before the Tribunal, including one withdrawn under rule 13 above, the Tribunal may make an order awarding costs—

    (a) in the case of an appeal under regulation 32(4) of the Regulations—

        (i) against the appellant and in favour of the relevant Minister where it considers that the appeal was manifestly unreasonable;

        (ii) against the relevant Minister and in favour of the appellant where it allows the appeal and quashes the disputed certification, or does so to any extent;

    (b) in the case of an appeal under regulation 32(6) of the Regulations—

        (i) against the appellant and in favour of any other party where it dismisses the appeal or dismisses it to any extent,

        (ii) in favour of the appellant and against any other party where it allows the appeal or allows it to any extent; and

(c) where it considers that a party has been responsible for frivolous, vexatious, improper or unreasonable action, or for any failure to comply with a direction or any delay which with diligence could have been avoided, against that party and in favour of the other.

(2) The Tribunal shall not make an order under paragraph (1) above awarding costs against a party without first giving that party an opportunity of making representations against the making of the order.

(3) An order under paragraph (1) above may be to the party or parties in question to pay to the other party or parties either a specified sum in respect of the costs incurred by that other party or parties in connection with the proceedings or the whole or part of such costs as taxed (if not otherwise agreed).

(4) Any costs required by an order under this rule to be taxed may be taxed in the county court according to such of the scales prescribed by the county court rules for proceedings in the county court as shall be directed by the order.

(5) In relation to proceedings before the Tribunal in Scotland, for the purposes of the application of paragraph (4) above, for the reference to the county court and the county court rules there shall be substituted references to the sheriff court and the sheriff court rules and for the reference to proceedings there shall be substituted a reference to civil proceedings.

29. Irregularities

(1) Any irregularity resulting from failure to comply with any provision of these Rules or of any direction of the Tribunal before the Tribunal has reached its decision shall not of itself render the proceedings void, but the Tribunal may, and shall if it considers that any person may have been prejudiced by that irregularity, give such directions or take such steps as it thinks fit before reaching its decision to cure or waive the irregularity, whether by amendment of any document, the giving of notice or otherwise.

(2) Clerical mistakes in any document recording or certifying a direction, decision or determination of the Tribunal or president, or errors arising in such a document from an accidental slip or omission, may at any time be corrected by the president by certificate signed by him.

30. Notices etc.

(1) Any notice or other document required or authorised by these Rules to be served on or sent to any person'or authority may be sent by post in a registered letter or by the recorded delivery service—

(a) in the case of the Tribunal, to the proper officer of the Tribunal;

(b) in the case of an appellant or a respondent telecommunications provider, to him at his address for service under these Rules;

(c) in the case of the relevant Minister or the Commissioner, to him at his office.

(2) An appellant or respondent telecommunications provider may at any time by notice to the Tribunal change his address for service under these Rules.

Appendix 4
The Telecommunications (Data Protection and Privacy) Regulations 1999

THE TELECOMMUNICATIONS (DATA PROTECTION AND PRIVACY)
REGULATIONS 1999
(SI 1999 No. 2093)

PART I
GENERAL

PART II
TRAFFIC AND BILLING DATA

PART III
CALLING OR CONNECTED LINE IDENTIFICATION

PART IV
DIRECTORIES OF SUBSCRIBERS

PART I
GENERAL

1.   Citation and commencement

(1)   These Regulations may be cited as the Telecommunications (Data Protection and Privacy) Regulations 1999.

(2)   These Regulations shall come into force—
   (a)   for the purposes of regulation 3(2), on 16th August 1999;
   (b)   for all other purposes, on 1st March 2000.

2. Interpretation

(1)   In these Regulations—

'the Act of 1984' means the Telecommunications Act 1984;[1]

'bill' includes an invoice, account, statement or other instrument of the like character and 'billing' shall be construed accordingly;

'corporate subscriber' means a subscriber who is not an individual, that is to say a subscriber who is—

   (a)   a company within the meaning of section 735(1) of the Companies Act 1985;[2]

   (b)   a company incorporated in pursuance of a royal charter or letters patent;

   (c)   a partnership in Scotland;

   (d)   a corporation sole; or

   (e)   any other body corporate or other entity which is a legal person distinct from the persons (if any) of which it is composed;

'the Data Protection Commissioner' and 'the Commissioner' both mean the Commissioner appointed under section 6 of the Data Protection Act 1998;[3]

'the Directive' means Directive 97/66/EC of the European Parliament and of the Council of the European Union;[4]

'the Director' means the Director General of Telecommunications appointed under section 1 of the Act of 1984;

'individual' means a living individual and includes an unincorporated body of such individuals;

'public telecommunications network' means any transmission system, and any associated switching equipment and other resources, which (in either case)—

   (a)   permit the conveyance of signals between defined termination points by wire, by radio, by optical or by other electro-magnetic means, and

   (b)   are used, in whole or in part, for the provision of publicly available telecommunications services;

'relevant telecommunications network', in relation to a telecommunications service provider, means a public telecommunications network which is used by that service provider for the provision of publicly available telecommunications services;

'relevant telecommunications service provider' means—

   (a)   in relation to a user, the provider of the services he uses, and

   (b)   in relation to a subscriber, the provider who provides him with services;

'subscriber' means a person who is a party to a contract with a telecommunications service provider for the supply of publicly available telecommunications services;

Notes
[1] 1984 c. 12.
[2] 1985 c. 6.
[3] 1998 c. 29.
[4] OJ No. L24, 30.1.98, p. 1.

'telecommunications network provider' means a person who provides a public telecommunications network (whether or not he is also a telecommunications service provider);

'telecommunications service provider' means a person who provides publicly available telecommunications services (whether or not he is also a telecommunications network provider);

'telecommunications services' means services the provision of which consists, in whole or in part, of the transmission and routing of signals on telecommunications networks, not being services by way of radio or television broadcasting;

'user' means an individual using a publicly available telecommunications service (whether or not he is a subscriber).

(2)   Section 1 of the Data Protection Act 1998 (basic interpretative provisions) shall have effect for the purposes of these Regulations as it has effect for the purposes of that Act.

(3)   Subject to paragraphs (1) and (2) and except where the context otherwise requires, expressions used in these Regulations which are also used in the Directive have the same meanings in these Regulations as they have in the Directive.

(4)   In a case in which signals are conveyed to telecommunications equipment used by a subscriber wholly or partly otherwise than by line, any reference in these Regulations to a line shall be construed as including a reference to what, in that case, functionally corresponds to a line and 'connected', in relation to a line, shall be construed accordingly.

3.   Revocation and amendment of provisions and modification of contracts

(1)   The Telecommunications (Data Protection and Privacy) (Direct Marketing) Regulations 1998[1] are hereby revoked.

(2)   Until the coming into force of paragraph (1) on 1st March 2000 and the revocation thereby of the said Regulations of 1998, those Regulations shall have effect subject to the amendment set out in Part I of Schedule 1.

(3)   The amendments set out in Part II of Schedule 1 shall have effect.

(4)   To the extent that any term in a contract between—

(a)   a subscriber to, and the provider of, publicly available telecommunications services, or

(b)   such a provider and a telecommunications network provider,

would be inconsistent with a requirement of these Regulations, that term shall be void.

Note
[1] SI 1998/3170.

4.   Requirements of Regulations

Notwithstanding that the requirements of these Regulations are requirements imposed by law, where a person is required to provide, or ensure the provision of, a facility he may make a reasonable charge in respect thereof save insofar as is otherwise provided in regulations 11(2) and (3), 12(2) and (3), 18(1), 19(1) and 31.

5.   Consents, notices, notifications and requests for purposes of Regulations

(1)   Except where the context otherwise requires, a consent, notice or notification for the purposes of these Regulations may be in general or more limited terms and may be subject to conditions.

(2)   A consent, notice, notification or request for the purposes of these Regulations may (without prejudice to any other method of transmission) be sent by post.

PART II
TRAFFIC AND BILLING DATA

6.   Limitation on processing certain traffic data

(1)   This regulation relates to data which—

(a)   are in respect of traffic handled by a telecommunications network provider or a telecommunications service provider;

(b)   are processed to secure the connection of a call and held by the provider concerned; and

(c)   constitute personal data whereof the data subject is a subscriber to, or user of, any publicly available telecommunications service or, in the case of a corporate subscriber, would constitute such personal data if that subscriber were an individual.

(2)   Upon the termination of the call in question, save as provided in regulations 7(2) and 8(2), such data as are mentioned in paragraph (1) shall be erased or shall be so dealt with that they cease to be such data as are mentioned in paragraph (1)(c).

7.   Limitation on processing certain billing data

(1)   This regulation relates to the processing of any such data as are mentioned in Schedule 2 and are held by a telecommunications network provider or a telecommunications service provider for purposes connected with the payment of sums falling to be paid—

(a)   by a subscriber, or

(b)   by way of interconnection charges.

(2)   Such data as are mentioned in paragraph (1) of that regulation, such data as are mentioned in paragraph (1) of this regulation may, and may only, be processed for the purposes there mentioned until the expiry of the period during which legal proceedings may be brought in respect of the payments due, or alleged to be due, or where such proceedings are brought within that period, until those proceedings are finally determined and, for the purposes hereof, the proceedings shall not be taken to be finally determined—

(a)   until the end of the ordinary time for an appeal by either party, if no appeal proceedings are brought within that time, or

(b)   if any such proceedings are so brought, until the conclusion of the appeal proceedings.

(3)   References in paragraph (2) to appeal proceedings include references to an application for leave to appeal.

8.   Processing of billing data for certain marketing purposes by a telecommunications service provider

(1)   This regulation relates to the processing of such data as are mentioned in Schedule 2 which—

(a)   are held by a telecommunications service provider, and

(b)   constitute personal data whereof the data subject is a subscriber to that service or, in the case of a corporate subscriber, would constitute such data if that subscriber were an individual.

(2)   Such data as are mentioned in paragraph (1) of that regulation, such data as are mentioned in paragraph (1) of this regulation may be processed by the telecommunications service provider concerned for the purposes of marketing telecommunications services which he provides if, but only if, the subscriber concerned has given his consent.

9.   Further provisions relating to the processing of traffic and billing data

(1)   This regulation relates to the processing by either a telecommunications network provider or a telecommunications service provider ('the relevant person') of data to which regulation 6, 7 or 8 relates.

(2)   The processing of such data as are mentioned in paragraph (1) shall, without prejudice to any other restriction contained in this Part, be restricted to what is necessary for the purposes of such an activity as is mentioned in paragraph (3) or for the purposes of regulation 6(2) and (unless the relevant person is an individual and the processing is carried out by him personally) processing for such purposes shall only be carried out by a person—

(a)   acting under the authority of the relevant person, and

(b)   whose activities under that authority include such an activity as is mentioned in paragraph (3).

(3)   The activities referred to in paragraph (2) are activities relating to—

(a)   the management of billing or traffic;

(b)   customer enquiries;

(c)   the prevention or detection of fraud, and

(d)   the marketing of any telecommunications services provided by the relevant person.

10.   Savings relating to the settling of disputes

Nothing in this Part shall preclude the furnishing of billing or traffic data to a person who is a competent authority for the purposes of any provision relating to the settling of disputes (by way of legal proceedings or otherwise) which is contained in, or made by virtue of, any enactment.

PART III
CALLING OR CONNECTED LINE IDENTIFICATION

11.   Prevention of calling line identification — outgoing calls

(1)   This regulation relates to outgoing calls on a line.

(2)   The relevant telecommunications service provider shall ensure that a user originating a call has, subject to regulations 13 and 14, as respects that call, a simple means to prevent, without charge, presentation of the identity of the calling line on the connected line.

(3)   The relevant telecommunications service provider shall ensure that a subscriber has, subject to regulations 13 and 14, as respects his line and all calls originating therefrom, a simple means to prevent, without charge, presentation of the identity of his line on any connected line.

12.   Prevention of calling or connected line identification — incoming calls

(1)   This regulation relates to incoming calls on a line.

(2)   Where presentation on the connected line of the identity of the calling line is available, the relevant telecommunications service provider shall ensure that the

called subscriber has a simple means to prevent, without charge for reasonable use of the facility, presentation of the identity of a calling line on the connected line.

(3)   Where presentation on the calling line of the identity of the connected line is available, the relevant telecommunications service provider shall ensure that a called subscriber has a simple means to prevent, without charge, presentation of the identity of the connected line on any calling line.

(4)   Where presentation on the connected line of the identity of the calling line, before the establishment of a call, is available, the relevant telecommunications service provider shall ensure that the called subscriber has, as respects all or particular calls in the case of which such presentation has been prevented as mentioned in regulation 11(2) or (3), a simple means to reject the calls in question.

(5)   In this regulation 'called subscriber' means the subscriber whose line is the called line (whether or not it is also the connected line).

13.   999 or 112 calls

(1)   This regulation relates to calls to the emergency services made using either the national emergency call number 999 or the single European emergency call number 112 ('999 or 112 calls').

(2)   In order to facilitate responses to such calls—

(a)   all 999 or 112 calls shall be excluded from the calls referred to in regulation 11, and

(b)   in relation to 999 or 112 calls, no person shall be entitled to prevent the presentation on the connected line of the identity of the calling line.

14.   Tracing of malicious or nuisance calls

(1)   This regulation shall apply where the relevant telecommunications service provider has been notified by a subscriber that he requests the tracing of malicious or nuisance calls received on his line.

(2)   Until such time as action in pursuance of such a request has ceased, the relevant telecommunications service provider or the provider of a relevant telecommunications network, where the subscriber has made application in that behalf, may—

(a)   in relation to calls in relation to which the subscriber's line is the called line, and

(b)   so far as it appears to the provider in question necessary or expedient for the purposes of such action,

override anything done to prevent the presentation of the identity of the calling line.

(3)   Any term of a contract for the provision of telecommunications services which relates to such prevention shall have effect subject to the provisions of paragraph (2).

(4)   In relation to such calls as are mentioned in paragraph (2)(a), nothing in these Regulations shall preclude the relevant telecommunications service provider, or a provider of a relevant telecommunications network, from holding and making available to a person with a legitimate interest therein, data containing the identification of a calling subscriber which were obtained while paragraph (2) applied.

15.   Facilities for calling or connected line identification to be publicised

A telecommunications service provider who offers facilities for calling or connected line identification shall take all reasonable steps to publicise that he does so and of the effect of this Part in relation thereto.

16.   Supplementary provisions

(1)   Any other telecommunications service provider and any telecommunications network provider shall comply with any reasonable requests made by a relevant telecommunications service provider for the purposes of regulation 11, 12 or 14.

(2)   Where a subscriber has two or more lines, regulations 11 and 12 shall, in his case, have effect separately as respects each line as if that line were his only line.

PART IV
DIRECTORIES OF SUBSCRIBERS

17.   Application and interpretation of Part IV

(1)   This Part shall apply in relation to a directory of subscribers to publicly available telecommunications services, whether in printed form or in electronic form—

(a)   which is made available to the public or a section of the public, or

(b)   information from which is provided by a directory enquiry service.

(2)   In this Part any reference to a directory is a reference to such a directory as is mentioned in paragraph (1), 'production' in relation to a directory means its publication or preparation and cognate expressions shall be construed accordingly.

(3)   Such a request as is mentioned in paragraph (3) of regulation 18 or paragraph (2) of regulation 19 shall be treated for the purposes of the regulation in question as having no application in relation to an edition of a directory which was first produced before the request was received by the producer of the directory; and, for the purposes hereof, an edition of a directory which is revised after it was first produced shall be treated as a new edition.

18.   Entries relating to individuals

(1)   This regulation applies in relation to a directory which includes entries which relate to subscribers who are individuals, and any person who produces such a directory shall, without charge to any such subscriber, ensure that it complies with this regulation.

(2)   Except to the extent, if any, to which the subscriber in question has consented otherwise, such a directory shall not contain any personal data whereof the data subject is a subscriber who is an individual other than data which are necessary to identify him and the number allocated to him.

(3)   Without prejudice to paragraph (2), where a subscriber who is an individual has so requested the producer of such a directory then, in his case—

(a)   no entry relating to a number specified in the request shall be included in that directory;

(b)   no entry therein shall contain a reference which reveals his sex; and

(c)   no such entry shall contain such part of his address as is so specified.

(4)   Where, in connection with the production of a directory, information relating to a particular subscriber is supplied to the producer thereof by some other person—

(a)   where the other person has in his possession such a request by that subscriber as is mentioned in paragraph (3) (to whomsoever made) or a copy or record of such a request, he shall, without undue delay, transmit a copy of that request or a copy of that record to the producer of the directory, and

(b) subject to receipt by the producer of the directory of a copy of a request or of a record thereof so transmitted, the request in question shall be treated for the purposes of paragraph (3) as if it had been made to that producer.

19. Entries relating to corporate subscribers

(1) This regulation applies in relation to a directory which includes entries which relate to corporate subscribers and any person who produces such a directory shall, without charge to any such subscriber, ensure that it complies with this regulation.

(2) Where a corporate subscriber has so requested the producer of such a directory, then, in its case, no entry relating to a number specified in the request shall be included in that directory.

(3) Paragraph (4) of regulation 18 shall have effect for the purposes of this regulation as if any reference therein to paragraph (3) of that regulation were a reference to paragraph (2) of this regulation.

20. Supplementary provisions relating to directory enquiry services

Where a person directs an enquiry relating to a particular subscriber to a directory enquiry service but there is either no entry relating to that subscriber, or no entry relating to his number, in a directory used by that service, nothing in this Part shall be taken to preclude the person in question being told the reason, or possible reason, why there is no such entry, in particular, that, in pursuance of a request made by the subscriber for the purposes of regulation 18(3), regulation 18(3)(a) applies or, in the case of a corporate subscriber, in pursuance of a request made by it for the purposes of regulation 19(2), that provision applies.

PART V
USE OF TELECOMMUNICATIONS SERVICES FOR DIRECT MARKETING PURPOSES

21. Application and interpretation of Part V

(1) This Part shall apply in relation to the use of publicly available telecommunications services for direct marketing purposes.

(2) Any reference in this Part to direct marketing is a reference to the communication of any advertising or marketing material on a particular line.

(3) In this Part, 'caller' means a person using publicly available telecommunications services for direct marketing purposes, except that where such services are so used at the instigation of some other person 'caller' means that other person.

(4) In regulations 26(3) and 27(5) and (6), 'directory of subscribers' means a directory of subscribers to publicly available telecommunications services, whether in printed form or in electronic form, which is made available to the public or a section of the public and, in relation to such a directory, 'producer' means the person by whom the directory is published or prepared.

22. Use of automated calling systems for direct marketing purposes — communications on lines of individual or corporate subscribers

(1) This regulation applies in relation to the use of publicly available telecommunications services by means of an automated calling system (that is to say, a system which, when activated, operates to make calls without human intervention)

for the communication of material for direct marketing purposes, whether the called line is that of a subscriber who is an individual or that of a corporate subscriber.

(2)   A person shall not use, or instigate the use of, publicly available telecommunications services, and a subscriber to such services shall not permit his line to be used, as mentioned in paragraph (1), except where the called line is that of a subscriber who has previously notified the caller that for the time being he consents to such communications as are there mentioned being sent by, or at the instigation of, the caller in question on that line.

23.   Use of fax for direct marketing purposes — unsolicited communications on lines of individual or corporate subscribers

(1)   This regulation applies in relation to the use of publicly available telecommunications services for the unsolicited communication of material, for direct marketing purposes, by means of facsimile transmission, whether the called line is that of a subscriber who is an individual or that of a corporate subscriber; and, in a case in which an automated calling system within the meaning of regulation 22(1) is used, the provisions of this regulation and those of regulation 22 are without prejudice to each other.

(2)   A person shall not use, or instigate the use of, publicly available telecommunications services, and a subscriber to such services shall not permit his line to be used, as mentioned in paragraph (1) where—

(a)   the called line is that of a subscriber who has previously notified the caller (notwithstanding, in the case of a subscriber who is an individual, that he enjoys the benefit of regulation 24) that such unsolicited communications as are so mentioned should not be sent on that line, or

(b)   the number allocated to a subscriber in respect of the called line is one listed in the record kept under paragraph (4).

(3)   For the purposes of paragraphs (1) and (2), the communication of material as mentioned in paragraph (1) shall not be treated as unsolicited where the called line is that of a subscriber who has notified the caller that he does not for the time being object to such communications as are so mentioned being sent by, or at the instigation of, the caller in question on that line.

(4)   For the purposes of this regulation—

(a)   the Director shall maintain and keep up-to-date, in printed form or in electronic form, a record of the numbers allocated to subscribers, in respect of particular lines, who have notified him (notwithstanding, in the case of individuals, that they enjoy the benefit of regulation 24) that they do not for the time being wish to receive such communications as are mentioned in paragraph (1) on the lines in question, and he shall remove a number from the record where he has reason to believe that it has ceased to be allocated to the subscriber by whom he was so notified, and

(b)   on the request of—

(i)   a person wishing to send, or instigate the sending of, such communications, or

(ii)   a subscriber wishing to permit the use of his line for the sending of such communications,

for information derived from that record, the Director shall, unless it is not reasonably practicable so to do, on the payment to him of such fee as is applicable and is, subject to paragraph (5), required by him, make the information requested available to that person or that subscriber.

(5)   For the purposes of paragraph (4)(b) the Director may require different fees—

(a)   for making available information derived from the record in different forms or manners, or

(b)   for making available information derived from the whole or from different parts of the record,

but the fees required by him shall be ones in relation to which the Secretary of State has notified the Director that he is satisfied that they are designed to secure, as nearly as may be and taking one year with another, that the aggregate fees received, or reasonably expected to be received, equal the costs incurred, or reasonably expected to be incurred, by the Director, in discharging his duties under paragraph (4).

(6)   The functions of the Director under paragraph (4), other than the function of determining the fees to be required for the purposes of sub-paragraph (b) thereof, may be discharged on his behalf by some other person in pursuance of arrangements in that behalf made by the Director with that other person.

24.   Use of fax for direct marketing purposes — communications on lines of subscribers who are individuals

(1)   This regulation applies in relation to the use of publicly available telecommunications services for the communication of material, for direct marketing purposes, by means of facsimile transmission where the called line is that of a subscriber who is an individual; and—

(a)   the provisions of this regulation and those of regulation 23 are without prejudice to each other, and

(b)   in a case in which an automated calling system within the meaning of regulation 22(1) is used, the provisions of this regulation and those of regulation 22 are without prejudice to each other.

(2)   A person shall not use, or instigate the use of, publicly available telecommunications services, and a subscriber to such services shall not permit his line to be used, as mentioned in paragraph (1), except where the called line is that of a subscriber who has previously notified the caller that he consents for the time being to such communications as are there mentioned being sent by, or at the instigation of, the caller in question on that line.

25.   Unsolicited calls for direct marketing purposes on lines of subscribers who are individuals

(1)   This regulation applies in relation to the use of publicly available telecommunications services for the purposes of making unsolicited calls, for direct marketing purposes, otherwise than in a case in which the material communicated is communicated by means of facsimile transmission, where the called line is that of a subscriber who is an individual; and, in a case in which an automated calling system within the meaning of regulation 22(1) is used, the provisions of this regulation and those of regulation 22 are without prejudice to each other.

(2)   A person shall not use, or instigate the use of, publicly available telecommunications services, and a subscriber to such services shall not permit his line to be used, as mentioned in paragraph (1) where—

(a)   the called line is that of a subscriber who has previously notified the caller that such unsolicited calls as are there mentioned should not for the time being be made on that line, or

(b)   the number allocated to a subscriber in respect of the called line is one listed in the record kept under paragraph (4).

(3)   For the purposes of paragraphs (1) and (2), a call on a subscriber's line shall not be treated as an unsolicited call if that subscriber has notified the caller that he does not object to calls being made by, or at the instigation of, the caller in question for direct marketing purposes on that line.

(4)   For the purposes of this regulation—

(a)   the Director shall maintain and keep up-to-date, in printed form or in electronic form, a record of the numbers allocated to subscribers who are individuals, in respect of particular lines, who have notified him that they do not for the time being wish to receive unsolicited calls made for direct marketing purposes on the lines in question, and he shall remove a number from the record where he has reason to believe that it has ceased to be allocated to the subscriber by whom he was so notified, and

(b)   on the request of—

(i)   a person wishing to make, or instigate the making of, such calls, or

(ii)   a subscriber wishing to permit the use of his line for the making of such calls,

for information derived from that record, the Director shall, unless it is not reasonably practicable so to do, on the payment to him of such fee as is applicable and is, subject to paragraph (5), required by him, make the information requested available to that person or that subscriber.

(5)   For the purposes of paragraph (4)(b) the Director may require different fees—

(a)   for making available information derived from the record in different forms or manners, or

(b)   for making available information derived from the whole or from different parts of the record,

but the fees required by him shall be ones in relation to which the Secretary of State has notified the Director that he is satisfied that they are designed to secure, as nearly as may be and taking one year with another, that the aggregate fees received, or reasonably expected to be received, equal the costs incurred, or reasonably expected to be incurred, by the Director in discharging his duties under paragraph (4).

(6)   The functions of the Director under paragraph (4), other than the function of determining the fees to be required for the purposes of sub-paragraph (b) thereof, may be discharged on his behalf by some other person in pursuance of arrangements in that behalf made by the Director with that other person.

26.   Notifications for the purposes of regulation 23(4)(a) or 25(4)(a)

(1)   Where any such person as is mentioned in paragraph (3) has in his possession such a notification as is mentioned in regulation 23(4)(a) or regulation 25(4)(a) (to whomsoever it is addressed) or a copy or record of such a notification—

(a)   he shall, without undue delay, transmit a copy of that notification or a copy of that record to the Director, and

(b)   subject to receipt by the Director of a copy of a notification or of a record thereof so transmitted, the notification in question shall be treated for the purposes of regulation 23(4)(a) or, as the case may be, regulation 25(4)(a) as if it had been given to the Director.

(2)   Where the Director has made arrangements in pursuance of paragraph (6) of regulation 23 or, as the case may be, paragraph (6) of regulation 25 for the discharge of functions under paragraph (4) of the regulation in question by some other person on his behalf, paragraph (1) of this regulation shall have effect, in relation to such a notification as is mentioned in paragraph (4)(a) of the regulation in question, as if for the reference to the Director in sub-paragraph (a) and the first reference to him in sub-paragraph (b) there were substituted references to that other person.

(3)   The persons referred to in paragraph (1) are—

    (a)   a telecommunications service provider;

    (b)   the producer of a directory of subscribers; and

    (c)   where, in connection with the production of such a directory, information relating to a particular subscriber is supplied to the producer thereof by some other person, that other person.

27.   Supplementary provisions

(1)   Where publicly available telecommunications services are used for the communication of material for direct marketing purposes—

    (a)   in a case in which an automated calling system within the meaning of regulation 22(1) is used or the material is communicated by means of facsimile transmission, the caller shall ensure that the material communicated includes the particulars mentioned in paragraph (2)(a) and (b) below;

    (b)   otherwise than as mentioned in sub-paragraph (a), the caller shall ensure that the material communicated includes the particulars mentioned in paragraph (2)(a) below and, if the recipient of the call so requests, those mentioned in paragraph (2)(b) below.

(2)   The particulars referred to in paragraph (1) are—

    (a)   the name of the caller;

    (b)   either the address of the caller or a freephone telephone number on which he can be reached.

(3)   Where a person by whom numbers are allocated to subscribers is requested by or on behalf of the Director, for the purposes of his functions under regulation 23(4) or 25(4), to furnish information as to when a particular number ceases to be allocated to a particular subscriber, that person shall comply with the request.

(4)   A caller shall not be held to have contravened regulation 23 or regulation 25 by reason of the making, or instigating the making, of a call and a subscriber shall not be held to have contravened regulation 23 or regulation 25 by permitting his line to be used for the making of a call, by reason only that the number of the called line is one listed in the record kept under paragraph (4) of the regulation in question, if that number was not so listed at any time within the 28 days preceding that on which the call is made.

(5)   Subject to paragraph (6), the producer of a directory of subscribers shall ensure that it contains a statement drawing attention to the provisions of regulations 22, 23, 24, and 25.

(6)   Nothing in paragraph (5) shall apply in relation to a directory of subscribers which is comprised in an edition first published before the coming into force of these Regulations; and, for the purposes hereof, an edition of a directory which is revised after it was first published shall be treated as a new edition.

PART VI
MISCELLANEOUS PROVISIONS

28. Security of telecommunications services

(1) Subject to paragraph (2), a telecommunications service provider shall take technical and organisational measures which are appropriate to secure the security of the service he provides.

(2) If necessary, the measures required by paragraph (1) shall be taken by a telecommunications service provider in conjunction with the provider of the relevant telecommunications network who shall comply with any reasonable requests made by the service provider for the purposes hereof.

(3) Where, notwithstanding the taking of measures required hereby, there is a significant risk to the security of the relevant telecommunications network, the telecommunications service provider shall inform the subscribers concerned of—

(a) that risk;

(b) any measures appropriate to afford safeguards against that risk which they themselves might take, and

(c) the costs involved in the taking of such measures.

(4) For the purposes of this regulation, measures shall only be taken to be appropriate if, having regard to—

(a) the state of technological development, and

(b) the cost of implementing the measures,

they are proportionate to the risks against which they would afford safeguards.

(5) For the purposes of this regulation the security of a public telecommunications service or network shall not be taken to be at risk by reason of the intentional disclosure, or possibility of such disclosure, of any matter falling within subsection (1)(a) or (b) of section 45 of the Act of 1984[1] by a telecommunications service or network provider in a case or circumstances in which he would not be guilty of an offence under that section which, for the purposes of this paragraph, shall have effect as if—

(a) the reference in subsection (1) thereof to a person engaged in the running of a public telecommunications system were a reference to such a provider;

(b) for the words 'that system', in both places where they occur in subsection (1)(a) and (b) thereof, there were substituted the words 'a public telecommunications system'; and

(c) the reference in subsection (1)(a) thereof to a message were a reference to a communication.

Note
[1] Section 45 was amended by section 11(1) of the Interception of Communications Act 1985 (c. 56).

29. Right to bills which are not itemised

At the request of the subscriber concerned, a telecommunications service provider shall only submit to him bills which are not itemised.

30. Itemised billing and privacy

(1) The Secretary of State and the Director shall each have a duty, when exercising any function assigned to him by a provision of the Act of 1984 specified in paragraph (2), to have regard to the need to reconcile the rights of subscribers

receiving itemised bills with the rights to privacy of calling users and called subscribers, for example by ensuring that sufficient alternative means for the making of calls or methods of paying therefor are available to such users and subscribers.

(2)   For the purposes of paragraph (1), the specified provisions of the Act of 1984 are sections 7, 8, 12, 13, 15, 16, 17, 18, 47, 48, 49, and 50.

31.   Termination of unwanted automatic call forwarding

Where calls originally directed to another line are being automatically forwarded to a subscriber's line as a result of action taken by a third party and the subscriber so requests the relevant telecommunications service provider ('the subscriber's provider'), that provider shall ensure, without charge, that such forwarding ceases without any avoidable delay, and any other telecommunications service provider and any telecommunications network provider shall comply with any reasonable requests made by the subscriber's provider for the purposes of this regulation.

32.   National security

(1)   Nothing in any of the provisions of these Regulations shall require a telecommunications service or network provider to do, or refrain from doing, anything (including the processing of data) if exemption from the requirement in question is required for the purpose of safeguarding national security.

(2)   Subject to paragraph (4), a certificate signed by a Minister of the Crown certifying that exemption from any requirement of these Regulations is or at any time was required for the purpose of safeguarding national security shall be conclusive evidence of that fact.

(3)   A certificate under paragraph (2) may identify the circumstances in which it applies by means of a general description and may be expressed to have prospective effect.

(4)   Any person directly affected by the issuing of a certificate under paragraph (2) may appeal to the Tribunal against the certificate.

(5)   If on an appeal under paragraph (4), the Tribunal finds that, applying the principles applied by a court on an application for judicial review, the Minister did not have reasonable grounds for issuing the certificate, the Tribunal may allow the appeal and quash the certificate.

(6)   Where in any proceedings under or by virtue of these Regulations it is claimed by a telecommunications service or network provider that a certificate under paragraph (2) which identifies the circumstances in which it applies by means of a general description applies in the circumstances in question, any other party to the proceedings may appeal to the Tribunal on the ground that the certificate does not apply in those circumstances and, subject to any determination under paragraph (7), the certificate shall be conclusively presumed so to apply.

(7)   On any appeal under paragraph (6), the Tribunal may determine that the certificate does not so apply.

(8)   In this regulation 'the Tribunal' means the Data Protection Tribunal referred to in section 6 of the Data Protection Act 1998 and—

(a)   subsections (8), (9), (10) and (12) of section 28 of that Act and Schedule 6 thereto shall apply for the purposes of, and in connection with, this regulation as if any references therein to subsection (2), (4) or (6) of the said section 28 were, respectively, references to paragraph (2), (4) or (6) of this regulation and

(b)   section 58 of that Act shall so apply as if the reference therein to the functions of the Tribunal under that Act included a reference to the functions of the Tribunal under paragraphs (4) to (7) of this regulation.

33.   Legal requirements, law enforcement etc.

Nothing in any of the provisions of these Regulations shall require a telecommunications service or network provider to do, or refrain from doing, anything (including the processing of data)—

(a)   if compliance with the requirement in question—

(i)   would be inconsistent with any requirement imposed by or under any enactment, by any rule of law or by the order of a court, or

(ii)   would be likely to prejudice the prevention or detection of crime or the apprehension or prosecution of offenders; or

(b)   if exemption from the requirement in question—

(i)   is required for the purposes of, or in connection with, any legal proceedings (including prospective legal proceedings),

(ii)   is necessary for the purposes of obtaining legal advice, or

(iii)   is otherwise necessary for the purposes of establishing, exercising or defending legal rights.

34.   Transitory and transitional provisions

The provisions in Schedule 3 shall have effect.

PART VII
COMPENSATION AND ENFORCEMENT

35.   Compensation for failure to comply with requirements of Regulations

(1)   A person who suffers damage by reason of any contravention of any of the requirements of these Regulations by any other person shall be entitled to compensation from the other person for that damage.

(2)   In proceedings brought against a person by virtue of this regulation it shall be a defence to prove that he had taken such care as in all the circumstances was reasonably required to comply with the requirement concerned.

36.   Enforcement — extension of Part V of the Data Protection Act 1998

(1)   The provisions of Part V of the Data Protection Act 1998 and of Schedules 6 and 9 thereto are hereby extended for the purposes of these Regulations and, for those purposes, shall have effect subject to the omissions and other modifications set out in Schedule 4.

(2)   In regulations 37 and 38, 'enforcement functions' means the functions of the Data Protection Commissioner under the provisions referred to in paragraph (1) as extended thereby.

(3)   The provisions of this regulation and those of regulation 35 are without prejudice to each other.

37.   Request that Commissioner exercise his enforcement functions

Where it is alleged that there has been contravention of any of the requirements of these Regulations either the Director or a person aggrieved by the alleged contravention may request the Commissioner to exercise his enforcement functions in respect of that contravention, but those functions shall be exercisable by him whether or not he has been so requested.

38. Technical advice to Commissioner

The Director shall comply with any reasonable request made by the Commissioner, in connection with his enforcement functions, for advice on technical and similar matters relating to telecommunications.

Parliamentary Under Secretary of State for Small Firms, Trade and Industry, Department of Trade and Industry
1999

Regulation 3(2) and (3)   SCHEDULE 1
                                      AMENDMENTS

PART I

AMENDMENT OF THE TELECOMMUNICATIONS (DATA PROTECTION AND PRIVACY) (DIRECT MARKETING) REGULATIONS 1998

At the end of regulation 10 of the Telecommunications (Data Protection and Privacy) (Direct Marketing) Regulations 1998[1] (notifications for purposes of regulation 7(4)(a) or 9(4)(a) thereof) there shall be added the two following paragraphs:—

'(5)   Where the number, in respect of a particular line, allocated to a subscriber who is an individual was, immediately before 1st May 1999, included in the list of numbers mentioned in paragraph (6), then, for the purposes of regulation 9(4)(a), that subscriber shall, as respects that line, be deemed to have notified the Director as mentioned therein, and that notification may be withdrawn by him as though it were a notification actually given.

(6)   The list referred to in paragraph (5) is the list kept before 1 May 1999 by the Direct Marketing Association (UK) Ltd for the purposes of the extra-statutory scheme then operated by it which was known as "the Telephone Preference Scheme".'

Note
[1] SI 1998/3170.

PART II

INCIDENTAL AND CONSEQUENTIAL AMENDMENTS

The Telecommunications Act 1984

1.   In section 1(6) of the Act of 1984[1] (payment out of money provided by Parliament) for the words following 'by any of his staff' there shall be substituted the following words—
'in consequence of the provisions of—
      (a)   this Act;
      (b)   the Telecommunications (Open Network Provision) (Voice Telephony) Regulations 1998; or
      (c)   the Telecommunications (Data Protection and Privacy) Regulations 1999.
2.   At the end of section 7(5)(a) of the Act of 1984 (power to license systems) there shall be added the words 'or by regulation 30 of the Telecommunications (Data Protection and Privacy) Regulations 1999.'.

The Data Protection Act 1998

3.   In section 11 of the Data Protection Act 1998 (right to prevent processing for purposes of direct marketing), after subsection (2) there shall be inserted the following subsection—

'(2A)   This section shall not apply in relation to the processing of such data as are mentioned in paragraph (1) of regulation 8 of the Telecommunications (Data Protection and Privacy) Regulations 1999 (processing of telecommunications billing data for certain marketing purposes) for the purposes mentioned in paragraph (2) of that regulation.'.

The Telecommunications (Open Network Provision) (Voice Telephony) Regulations 1998

4.   In regulation 2(1) of the Telecommunications (Open Network Provision) (Voice Telephony) Regulations 1998[2] (interpretation), for the definitions of 'Data Protection Registrar' and of 'relevant data protection legislation' there shall be substituted respectively, the following definitions—

'"Data Protection Commissioner" means the Commissioner appointed under section 6 of the Data Protection Act 1998';

'"relevant data protection legislation" means the Data Protection Act 1998, the instruments from time to time in force thereunder and the Telecommunications (Data Protection and Privacy) Regulations 1999;'

5.   In regulation 10 of the said Regulations (directory services — systemless providers), both in paragraph (8)(a) and in paragraph (9), for the words 'Data Protection Registrar' there shall be substituted the words 'Data Protection Commissioner' and at the end of the said regulation there shall be added the following paragraph—

'(10)   For the purposes of paragraphs (8)(a) and (9) above, anything done before the commencement of section 6(1) of the Data Protection Act 1998 by the Data Protection Registrar appointed under section 3 of the Data Protection Act 1984 shall be treated as if it had been done by the Data Protection Commissioner.'.

6.   In regulation 21(6)(b)(iii) of the said Regulations (conditions of access and use and essential requirements), for the words 'imposed only in accordance' there shall be substituted the word 'compatible'.

Notes
[1] Section 1(6) was amended by paragraph 1 of Schedule 1 to the Telecommunications (Data Protection and Privacy) (Direct Marketing) Regulations 1998 (SI 1998/3170).
[2] SI 1998/1580.

Regulations 7(1) and 8(1)   SCHEDULE 2
DATA REFERRED TO IN REGULATIONS 7 AND 8

1.   The data referred to in regulations 7(1) and 8(1) are data which constitute personal data whereof the data subject is a subscriber to, or user of, any publicly available telecommunications service or, in the case of a corporate subscriber, would constitute such data if that subscriber were an individual, and which comprise information in respect of all or any of the following matters, namely—

(a)   the number or other identification of the subscriber's station;
(b)   the subscriber's address and the type of the station;

reference therein to a relevant requirement included a reference to a requirement of the said Regulations of 1998.

(3)   Schedule 9 to the said Act of 1998, as extended as aforesaid, shall have effect as if any reference therein to these Regulations (including a reference to 'the 1999 Regulations') included a reference to the Telecommunications (Data Protection and Privacy) (Direct Marketing) Regulations 1998.

Regulation 36(1)   SCHEDULE 4
MODIFICATIONS TO PART V OF THE DATA PROTECTION ACT 1998 AND SCHEDULES 6 AND 9 THERETO AS EXTENDED BY REGULATION 36

1.   In section 40—
   (a)   in subsection (1), for the words 'data controller' there shall be substituted the word 'person', for the words 'data protection principles' there shall be substituted the words 'requirements of the Telecommunications (Data Protection and Privacy) Regulations 1999 (in this Part referred to as "the relevant requirements")' and for the words 'principle or principles' there shall be substituted the words 'requirement or requirements';
   (b)   in subsection (2), the words 'or distress' shall be omitted;
   (c)   subsections (3), (4), (5), (9) and (10) shall be omitted; and
   (d)   in subsection (6)(a), for the words 'data protection principle or principles' there shall be substituted the words 'relevant requirement or requirements'.
2.   In section 41, for the words 'data protection principle or principles', in both places where they occur, there shall be substituted the words 'relevant requirement or requirements'.
3.   Section 42 shall be omitted.
4.   In section 43—
   (a)   for subsections (1) and (2) there shall be substituted the following provisions—
      '(1)   If the Commissioner reasonably requires any information for the purpose of determining whether a person has complied or is complying with the relevant requirements, he may serve that person with a notice (in this Act referred to as "an information notice") requiring him, within such time as is specified in the notice, to furnish the Commissioner, in such form as may be so specified, with such information relating to compliance with the relevant requirements as is so specified.
      (2)   An information notice must contain a statement that the Commissioner regards the specified information as relevant for the purpose of determining whether the person has complied, or is complying, with the relevant requirements and his reason for regarding it as relevant for that purpose.'.
   (b)   in subsection (6)(a), after the word 'under' there shall be inserted the words 'the Telecommunications (Data Protection and Privacy) Regulations 1999 or';
   (c)   in subsection (6)(b), after the words 'arising out of' there shall be inserted the words 'the said Regulations or'; and
   (d)   subsection (10) shall be omitted.
5.   Sections 44, 45 and 46 shall be omitted.
6.   In section 47(1) and (2), for the words 'an information notice or a special information notice', in both places where they occur, there shall be substituted the words 'or an information notice'.

7.   In section 48—

(a)   in subsections (1) and (3), for the words 'an information notice or a special information notice', in both places where they occur, there shall be substituted the words 'or an information notice';

(b)   in subsection (3) for the words '43(5) or 44(6)' there shall be substituted the words 'or 43(5)'; and

(c)   subsection (4) shall be omitted.

8.   In section 49, subsection (5) shall be omitted.

9.   In paragraph 4(1) of Schedule 6, for the words '(2) or (4)' there shall be substituted the words 'or (2)'.

10.   In paragraph 1 of Schedule 9—

(a)   for sub-paragraph (1)(a) there shall be substituted the following provision—

'(a)   that a person has contravened or is contravening any of the requirements of the Telecommunications (Data Protection and Privacy) Regulations 1999 (in this Schedule referred to as ''the 1999 Regulations''), or', and

(b)   sub-paragraph (2) shall be omitted.

11.   In paragraph 9 of Schedule 9—

(a)   in sub-paragraph (1)(a), after the words 'rights under' there shall be inserted the words 'the 1999 Regulations or', and

(b)   in sub-paragraph (1)(b), after the words 'arising out of' there shall be inserted the words 'the 1999 Regulations or'.

Appendix 5

Sections 158–160, Consumer Credit Act 1974, as amended by the Data Protection Act 1998

158   Duty of Agency to disclose filed information

(1)   A credit reference agency, within the prescribed period after receiving:

(a)   a request in writing to that effect from any partnership or other unincorporated body of persons not consisting entirely of bodies corporate (the 'consumer') and

(b)   such particulars as the agency may reasonably require to enable them to identify the file, and

(c)   a fee of [£1],

shall give the consumer a copy of the file relating to him kept by the agency.

(2)   When giving a copy of the file under subsection (1), the agency shall also give the consumer a statement in the prescribed form of the consumer's rights under section 159.

(3)   If the agency does not keep a file relating to the consumer it shall give the consumer notice of that fact, but need not return any money paid.

(4)   If the agency contravenes any provision of this section it commits an offence.

(5)   In this Act 'file', in relation to an individual, means all the information about him kept by a credit reference agency, regardless of how the information is stored and 'copy of the file', as respects information not in plain English, means a transcript reduced into plain English.

159   Correction of wrong information

(1)   Any individual (the 'objector') given—

(a)   information under section 7 of the Data Protection Act 1998 by a credit reference agency, or

(b)   information under section 158,

who considers that an entry in his file is incorrect, and that if it is not corrected he is likely to be prejudiced, may give notice to the agency requiring it either to remove the entry from the file or amend it.

(2)   Within 28 days after receiving a notice under subsection (1), the agency shall by notice inform the objector that it has—

(a)   removed the entry from the file, or

(b)   amended the entry, or

(c)   taken no action,
and if the notice states that the agency has amended the entry it shall include a copy of the file so far as it comprises the amended entry.

(3)   Within 28 days after receiving a notice under subsection (2) or, where no such notice was given, within 28 days after the expiry of the period mentioned in subsection (2), the objector may, unless he has been informed by the agency that it has removed the entry from his file, serve a further notice from the agency requiring it to add to the file the accompanying notice of correction (not exceeding 200 words) drawn up by the objector and include a copy of it when furnishing information included in or based on that entry.

(4)   Within 28 days after receiving a notice under subsection (3), the agency, unless it intends to apply to the relevant authority under subsection (5), shall by notice inform the objector that it has received the notice under subsection (3) and intends to comply with it.

(5)   If—

(a)   the objector has not received a notice under subsection (4) within the time required, or

(b)   it appears to the agency that it would be improper for it to publish a notice of correction because it is incorrect, or unjustly defames any person, or is frivolous or scandalous, or is for any other reason unsuitable,
the objector or, as the case may be, the agency may, in the prescribed manner and on payment of the specified fee, apply to the relevant authority, who make such order on the application as he thinks fit.

(6)   If a person to whom an order under this section is directed fails to comply with it within the period specified in the order he commits an offence.

(7)   The Data Protection Commissioner may vary or revoke any order made by him under this section.

(8)   In this section 'the relevant authority' means—

(a)   where the objector is a partnership or other unincorporated body of persons, the Director, and

(b)   in any other case the Data Protection Commissioner.

160   Alternative procedure for business consumers

(1)   The Director, on an application made by a credit reference agency, may direct that this section shall apply to the agency if he is satisfied—

(a)   that compliance with section 158 in the case of consumers who carry on a business would adversly affect the service provided to its customers by the agency, and

(b)   that, having regard to the methods employed by the agency and to any other relevant factors, it is probable that consumers carrying on a business would not be prejudiced by the making of the direction.

(2)   Where an agency to which this section applies receives a request, particulars and a fee under section 158(1) from a consumer who carries on a business, and section 158(3) does not apply, the agency, instead of complying with section 158, may elect to deal with the matter under the following subsections.

(3)   Instead of giving the consumer a copy of the file, the agency shall within the prescribed period give notice to the consumer that it is proceeding under this section, and by notice give the consumer such information included in or based on entries in

the file as the Director may direct, together with a statement in the prescribed form of the consumer's rights under subsection (4) and (5).

(4)   If within 28 days after receiving the information given to the consumer under subsection (3), or such longer period as the Director may allow, the consumer—

(a)   gives notice to the Director that the consumer is dissatisfied with the information, and

(b)   satisfies the Director that the consumer has taken such steps in relation to the agency as may be reasonable with a view to removing the cause of the consumer's dissatisfaction, and

(c)   pays the Director the specified fee,

the Director may direct the agency to give the Director a copy of the file, and the Director may disclose to the consumer such of the information on the file as the Dirctor thinks fit.

(5)   Section 159 applies with any necessary modifications to information given to the consumer under this section as it applies to information given under section 158.

(6)   If an agency making an election under subsection (2) fails to comply with subsection (3) or (4) it commits an offence.

(7)   In this section 'consumer' has the same meaning as in section 158.

Appendix 6
Useful Addresses and Websites

To obtain the BSC Code:
Broadcasting Standards Commission
7 The Sanctuary
LONDON
SW1P 3JS

Tel: 020 7233 0544
Fax: 020 7233 0397
www.bsc.org.uk

For legal advice on data protection:
Charles Russell
8–10 New Fetter Lane
LONDON
EC4A 1RS

Tel: 020 7203 5000
Fax: 020 7203 5300
www.charlesrussell.co.uk

For sales and enquiries relating to other British, European and International Standards:
Customer Services British Standards Institution
389 Chiswick High Road
LONDON
W4 4AL
UK

Tel: 020 8996 9001
Fax: 020 8996 7001
E-mail: info@bsi.org
www.bsi.org.uk

For Data Protection Guidelines:
Data Protection Registrar
Wycliffe House
Water Lane
Wilmslow
Cheshire
SK9 5AF
UK

Tel: 01625 545 700
Fax: 01625 524 510
www.dataprotection.gov.uk

For courses and seminars on data protection:
Data Protection Training
44 Tregarvan Road
London
SW11 5QE

Tel: 07949 168245
Fax: 0870 137 7871
E-mail: info@legaleducation.co.uk
www.legaleducation.co.uk

For enquiries on government initiatives in Information Security Management:
Department of Trade and Industry
Information Security Policy Group
Department of Trade and Industry
2.112 Red Core
151 Buckingham Palace Road
LONDON
SW1W 9SS
UK

Tel: 020 7215 1962 [enquiries]
Tel: 020 7215 1399 [publications]
Fax: 020 7931 7194
www.isi.gov.uk

For all BS 7799 and c:cure enquiries:
DISC British Standards Institution
389 Chiswick High Road
LONDON
W4 4AL
UK

Tel: 020 8995 7799
Fax: 020 8995 6411
E-mail: c_cure@bis.org.uk

To obtain the ITC Code:
Independent Television Commission
33 Foley Street
LONDON
W1P 7LB

Tel: 020 7255 3000
Fax: 020 7306 7800
www.itc.org.uk

To obtain the PCC Code:
Press Complaints Commission
1 Salisbury Square
LONDON
EC4Y 8JB

Tel: 020 7353 1248
Fax: 020 7353 8355
www.pcc.org.uk

Relevant legislation:
The Stationery Office
Publications Centre
PO Box 276
LONDON
SW8 5DT
UK

Tel: 020 7873 9090
Fax: 020 7873 8200
www.hmso.gov.uk

Information on becoming a certification body for BS 7799:
United Kingdom Accreditation Service (UKAS)
UK Accredited Certification Service
21–47 High Street
Feltham
Middlesex
TW13 4UN
UK

Tel: 020 8917 8400
Fax: 020 8917 8500
www.ukas.com

Index